FROMMER'S

COMPREHENSIVE TRAVEL GUIDE

PARIS '93-'94

by Darwin Porter
Assisted by Danforth Prince

PRENTICE HALL TRAVEL

NEW YORK • LONDON • TORONTO • SYDNEY • TOKYO • SINGAPORE

FROMMER BOOKS

Published by Prentice Hall General Reference
A division of Simon & Schuster Inc.
15 Columbus Circle
New York, NY 10023

ISBN 0-13-333741-3
ISSN 0899-3203

Design by Robert Bull Design
Maps by Geografix Inc.

FROMMER'S PARIS '93-'94
Editor-in-Chief: Marilyn Wood
Senior Editors: Judith de Rubini, Alice Fellows
Editors: Thomas F. Hirsch, Paige Hughes, Sara Hinsey Raveret, Lisa
    Renaud, Theodore Stavrou
Assistant Editors: Margaret Bowen, Peter Katucki, Ian Wilker
Managing Editor: Leanne Coupe

Special Sales
Bulk purchases of Frommer's Travel Guides are available at special discounts. The publishers are happy to custom-make publications for corporate clients who wish to use them as premiums or sales promotions. We
can excerpt the contents, provide covers with corporate imprints, or create
books to meet specific needs. For more information write to Special Sales,
Prentice Hall Travel, Paramount Communications Building, 15 Columbus
Circle, New York, NY 10023.

Manufactured in the United States of America

CONTENTS

10 EASY EXCURSIONS FROM PARIS 253

LIST OF MAPS

INVITATION TO THE READERS

In researching this book, I have come across many wonderful establishments, the best of which I have included here. I am sure that many of you will also come across wonderful hotels, inns, restaurants, guesthouses, shops, and attractions. Please don't keep them to yourself. Share your experiences, especially if you want to comment on places that I have included in this edition that have changed for the worse. You can address your letters to me:

Darwin Porter
Frommer's Paris
c/o Prentice Hall Travel
15 Columbus Circle
New York, NY 10023

A DISCLAIMER

Readers are advised that prices fluctuate in the course of time and travel information changes under the impact of the varied and volatile factors that affect the travel industry. The author and the publisher cannot be held responsible for the experiences of readers while traveling. Readers are invited to write to the publisher with ideas, comments, and suggestions for future editions.

SAFETY ADVISORY

Whenever you're traveling in an unfamiliar city or country, stay alert. Be aware of your immediate surroundings. Wear a moneybelt and keep a close eye on your possessions. Be particularly careful with cameras, purses, and wallets, all favorite targets of thieves and pickpockets.

CHAPTER 1

INTRODUCING PARIS

Paris has been celebrated in so many songs, poems, stories, books, paintings, and movies that for millions of people it is an abstraction rather than a city. To French people living in the provinces, Paris is the center of the universe, the place where laws and careers are made and broken. To North American tourists, it is still "Gay Paree" inviting you for a fling, the hub of everything "European," and the epitome of that nebulous attribute known as "chic." Say "Paris" and you produce an instant image of sidewalk cafés and strolling lovers beneath the Eiffel Tower.

To Hemingway, Paris was "a moveable feast" and the city to which "there is never any ending." To me, Paris is by day a stone mosaic of delicate gray and green, by night a stunning, unforgettable sea of lights—white, red, and orange. Broad, tree-lined boulevards open before you, mansions loom tall, ornate, and graceful. Everywhere you look are trees, squares, and monuments. Whether you see it for the first or fiftieth time, the discovery of the city, and making it your own, is and always has been the most compelling reason for coming to Paris.

1. GEOGRAPHY & PEOPLE

GEOGRAPHY Paris reigns without challenge as the most important commercial, artistic, and financial community in France.

The nation's capital lies on both banks of the Seine, near the center of a low-lying region known as the Paris Basin. Rich in history and cultural implications, the river undulates in a gentle S-shaped curve through the city, sheltering amid its currents the pair of islands upon which Paris was born. The river's many bridges (32 in all) gracefully unite Paris into a coherent and unusually beautiful whole.

Centuries of city planning have developed some of the most deliberately splendid panoramas in the world, vistas whose perspectives are one of the city's most memorable features. The river's northern part is called the Right Bank (*Rive Droite*), and the southern part (site of a university since the 12th century) the *Rive*

☑ WHAT'S SPECIAL ABOUT PARIS

Great Neighborhoods
☐ The Latin Quarter, precinct of the Sorbonne on the Left Bank, where students meet and fall in love.

☐ The Marais, center of fashion and aristocratic Paris in the 17th century.

Monuments
☐ Eiffel Tower, with a fabulously dizzying view over a 40-mile radius on a clear day.

☐ Arc de Triomphe, the gateway to the Champs-Elysées and a tribute to the glory of France, built to pay homage to the Napoleonic campaigns.

Buildings
☐ Notre-Dame, a cathedral for the ages, through which everyone from Napoléon and Josephine to Quasimodo and his beloved Esmeralda has passed.

☐ Conciergerie, the infamous prison of the Revolution that housed Marie-Antoinette and others.

Museums
☐ The Louvre, the largest single museum in the West, the largest palace in Europe, and repository of some of the masterworks of Western civilization.

☐ Musée d'Orsay, a "bridge" between the works in the Louvre and the modern art of Pompidou Center.

☐ Pompidou Center, controversial in design, is a modern building dedicated to 20th-century art.

☐ Musée Picasso, housing most of this prolific painter's vast works and his favorite art by other masters.

Parks/Gardens
☐ Tuileries Gardens, elegantly mapped out by Andre Le Nôtre, "the king's gardener," in the heart of the Right Bank.

☐ Luxembourg Gardens, a 60-acre playground in the center of the Left Bank, saved from Baron Haussmann's greedy wreckers.

☐ Bois de Boulogne, beloved by Parisians, is a former royal hunting ground now acclaimed for grand restaurants, such racetracks as Longchamp, and flower gardens.

Events/Festivals
☐ The Festival Estival (summertime), with live performances of 700 years of musical tradition in the churches and auditoriums throughout Paris.

☐ Paris Auto Show, with all the hype, glamor, and excitement to draw thousands "from everywhere."

For the Kids
☐ Montmartre, a walking carnival where kids can visit the waxworks of the Butte, sit for a charcoal sketch at place du Tertre, and take a funicular up the hill.

☐ Cité des Sciences et de l'Industrie, where everything's like a giant 3-D cinema, with several special exhibitions for the little ones.

Gauche. These designations make sense when you stand on a bridge facing downstream and watch the waters flow out toward Normandy and the sea—to your right is the north bank; the south is on your left.

PEOPLE If there is one characteristic the Parisians share, it is their big-city spirit, the somewhat-aggressive, novelty-addicted, extremely cynical metropolitanism that makes "provincial" the worst insult in their dictionary.

Tolerance, gentleness, and patience are not their strongest points. They don't suffer fools gladly (although they adore eccentrics), and the gravest crime a public figure can commit in their eyes is to make himself ridiculous.

The Parisians' behavior is a result of their environment. Paris, for all its matchless splendor, is a difficult place in which to scramble for a living. Working hours are long, competition murderous, traffic nerve-grinding, accommodations crowded and difficult to get; the pace is hectic and the cost of everything is the highest in France.

But a hard shell often protects a soft center. There is a startling contrast between the face Parisians show to passing strangers and their manner toward anyone with whom they share even the slightest personal rapport.

Compliment a surly bistro owner on his or her cuisine and—9 times out of 10—he or she will melt before your eyes. Admire a Parisian's car or dog and you'll find you have a loquaciously knowledgeable companion for the next five minutes. Ask about the correct pronunciation of a French word (before you mispronounce it), and you'll instantly have a language teacher.

Paris is so packed with minority groups that the true natives ironically refer to themselves as the "Parisians of Paris." There are Russians (descendants of the flood of White Russian refugees who poured into Paris after the Bolshevik Revolution), Poles, English, Belgians, Italians, and Spaniards. Here, too, are vast colonies of Vietnamese, Algerians, Moroccans, Lebanese, and West Africans, all mingling with less friction than anyone who's ever heard a UN debate would believe possible.

2. HISTORY & POLITICS

HISTORY

THE ROMANS & THE MEROVINGI-ANS Paris originally developed at the crossroads of three major traffic arteries on the muddy island that today is known as the Ile de la Cité.

By around 2000 B.C., the island served as the fortified headquarters of the Parisii tribe, who referred to it as Lutetia. The pair of crude wooden bridges that connected the island to the left and right banks of the river were considered of vital strategic importance. Julius Caesar, in his *Commentaries,* mentioned how these bridges were burned

DATELINE

- **2000 B.C.** Paris (ancient Lutetia) thrives along a strategic crossing of the Seine, the fortified headquarters of the Parisii tribe.
- **52 B.C.** Julius Caesar conquers Paris during the Gallic Wars.
- **A.D. 150** Lutetia
(continues)

DATELINE

flourishes as a Roman colony, expanding to Paris's Left Bank.

- **200** Barbarian Gauls force Romans to retreat to the fortifications on Ile de la Cité.

- **300** "Paris" officially named as such. Roman power weakens in northern France.

- **350** Beginnings of Paris's Christianization.

- **400s** Frankish invasions of Paris, with social transformation from Roman to Gallo-Roman culture.

- **466** Birth of Clovis, founder of the Merovingian dynasty, first non-Roman ruler of Paris since the Parisii.

- **800** Coronation of Charlemagne, founder of the Carolingian dynasty and first Holy Roman Emperor, who rules from Aachen in modern Germany.

- **987** Hugh Capet, founder of France's foremost early medieval dynasty, rises to power. He and his heirs rule from Paris.

- **1066** Viking descendents (traditional pillagers of northern France and Paris) invade England at the Battle of Hastings, forever linking the histories of France and England.

(continues)

during the Gallic War of 52 B.C., and how the town on the island was pillaged, sacked, and transformed into a Roman-controlled stronghold.

Within a century, Lutetia had developed into a full-fledged Roman town whose inhabitants had partially abandoned the frequently flooded island in favor of the higher ground on what today is called the Left Bank. Within its boundaries the Romans laid out their streets and monuments in a standardized format that matched hundreds of other Roman-built towns throughout the Empire. By the year A.D. 200, barbarian invasions increasingly threatened the stability of Roman Gaul, and the populace retreated from the surrounding hills to the fortified safety of the island. A wall almost 8 feet thick was built around the perimeter of the island, its marshes were filled in, and the population grew denser. An excavated milestone carved during the early 300s indicates the name of the city as "Paris" (not Lutetia) for the first time.

Within about 50 years, a Christian community gained a tenuous foothold on the island of Paris. Although according to legend, St. Denis served as the city's first bishop (beginning around 250), it required the tenures of an additional eight bishops before St. Marcel was able to erect a crude wooden church within the Ile de la Cité. Although the political power of the Roman Empire had begun to wane within the Paris region by this time, the cultural and religious attachment of the community to the Christian bishops of Rome grew even stronger.

During the 400s, with the Roman armies in great decline, Germanic tribes from the east (the Salian Franks) invaded Paris and fell under the Latin cultural sway, becoming more civilized during the process. The first of these Frankish kings, Clovis (466–511), founder of the Merovingian dynasty, embraced Christianity as his tribe's official religion. Recognizing the easy defensibility and convenience of the Ile de la Cité, he made his capital at Paris, establishing a precedent that many (but not all) other rulers would follow.

CHARLEMAGNE & THE CAROLINGIANS

The Merovingian dynasty was replaced by the Carolingians, whose heyday began with the coronation of Charlemagne in 800. Neither Charlemagne nor any member of his dynasty ever considered Paris as the capital of an empire that sprawled over western Germany and eastern France. Responding to immediate political needs, they moved their capital to more easterly cities, which included Metz, Reims, Cologne, and—most important—Aachen (Aix-la-Chapelle). Despite its loss of political stature, Paris remained a commercial and religious center, sacred to the memory of St. Genevieve, who had supposedly protected it during the attempted sacks of the city by the Huns during the final days of the Roman Empire.

The Carolingian dynasty died out in 987. Regional loyalties were activated that signaled for the first time the political and linguistic divisions between what would eventually become modern France and modern Germany. Within a few generations, Hugh Capet (ruling from 987 to 996), count of Paris and duke of France, became the first of a new dynasty, the Capetians, whose kings would rule from Paris throughout the Middle Ages.

THE MIDDLE AGES Beginning around 1100, Paris became a great city, with a university established on what is today known as the city's Left Bank. It drew scholars from throughout Europe. Medieval sculpture flourished, while kings and bishops began building the great Gothic cathedrals of France. The earliest of these, St Denis and Chartres, lay within an easy day's journey of Paris. Their stone and stained-glass grandeur was soon challenged by Paris's Notre Dame, a soaring ecclesiastical monument rising from the very heart of the city. The population of Paris increased greatly, augmenting the city's mercantile zest. During the 1200s, a virtual explosion of building transformed the skyline with convents and churches (including the jewellike Sainte-Chapelle, completed within an astonishingly short two years beginning in 1247). Within another century, the increasingly powerful French kings added dozens of monuments of their own.

As time progressed, the fortunes of Paris were closely linked to the luck and skill of the French monarchs at gathering power from the disparate and highly competitive feudal entities of the outlying provinces. Civil unrest, a series of plagues (of which the famous Black Death was one), the takeovers

DATELINE

- **1100** The Université de Paris attracts scholars from throughout Europe.

- **1200s** Construction of cathedrals at St-Denis, Chartres, and Paris. Numerous churches, convents, and royal buildings also built in Paris. Paris's population and power grow, although frequently unsettled by plagues and feudal battles.

- **1422** Paris invaded by England during the Hundred Years' War.

- **1429** Joan of Arc tries unsuccessfully to regain Paris for the French. The Burgundians later capture and sell her to the English, who burn her at the stake in Rouen.

- **1500s** François I, considered first of the French Renaissance kings, embellishes Paris but chooses to maintain court in the Loire Valley.

- **1549** Henri II rules France from Paris. Construction of public and private residences begins, many of them in the Marais neighborhood.

- **1564** Construction of Catherine de Médicis's Tuileries Palace. Building façades in Paris transform from half-timbered to more *(continues)*

DATELINE

durable chiseled
stonework.

- **1574** The Wars of
Religion reach their
climax with the mas-
sacre of Protestants
on St. Bartho-
lomew's Day.
- **1598** Henri IV,
most eccentric and
enlightened monarch
of his era, endorses
the Edict of Nantes,
granting tolerance to
Protestants, for
which a crazed monk
fatally stabs him 12
years later.
- **1615** Construc-
tion of the Luxem-
bourg Palace by
Henri IV's widow,
Marie de Médicis.
- **1636** Construc-
tion of the Palais-
Royal by Richelieu.
Soon thereafter, two
marshy islands in the
Seine are intercon-
nected and filled in
to create the Ile St-
Louis.
- **1643** Rise to
power of Louis XIV,
"the Sun King," the
most powerful ruler
since the Caesars.
He moves his court
to newly constructed
Versailles.
- **1776** American
Declaration of Inde-
pendence from Brit-
ain, sparking a
revolutionary chord
in France.
- **1789** Outbreak of
the French Revolu-
tion.
- **1793** Louis XVI
and his Austrian-
born queen, Marie
(continues)

of Paris by one warring faction after another, and a dangerous alliance of the English with the powerful rulers of Burgundy during the Hundred Years' War all contributed to the city's problems. To the everlasting humiliation of the French monarchs, the city was invaded by the English army in 1422. Joan of Arc (ca. 1412–31) tried unsuccessfully to reconquer Paris in 1429, two years before being burned at the stake in Rouen (Normandy) by the English. Paris was reduced to poverty and economic stagnation and its embittered and greatly reduced population turned to banditry and street crime.

THE RENAISSANCE & THE REFORMATION The first of the Renaissance monarchs, François I, began extensive enlargements of Paris's Louvre in attempts to make it suitable as a royal residence. Despite the building's embellishment, and the continued designation of Paris as the French capital, he spent much of his time at other châteaux amid the fertile hunting grounds of the Loire Valley. Intermittently, future monarchs would share his opinion that the narrow streets and teeming commercialism of Paris were unhealthy and upsetting.

The supremacy of Paris within France had been frequently eclipsed by the wishes of earlier monarchs to live elsewhere. Only the triumphant arrival in Paris in 1549 of Henri II, who successfully ruled France from within the city's borders, cemented Paris as the nation's undisputed capital. Responding to their ruler's initiative, fashionable aristocrats quickly began an architectural orgy, building private residences on the right bank, within a marshy low-lying neighborhood known at the time and ever since as *Le Marais* (The Swamp).

Paris as the world knows it today came into existence during this period. The expansion of the Louvre continued, and Catherine de Médicis began building her Tuileries palace in 1564. From the shelter of dozens of elegant urban residences, the aristocracy of France imbued Paris with their sense of architectural and social style, and the mores and manners of the Renaissance. Stone quays were added to the banks of the Seine, defining their limits and preventing future flood damage, and royal decrees were passed defining a series of building codes. To an increasing degree,

Paris adopted the planned perspectives and visual grace of the preferred residence of an absolute monarchy.

During the late 1500s and 1600s, Protestantism was persecuted brutally by the French monarchs. The bloodletting reached a high point when Henri III, plotting with his tirelessly scheming Florentine mother, Catherine de Médicis, murdered hundreds of Protestants during the St. Bartholomew massacre in 1572.

Henri III's tragic and eccentric successor, Henri IV, ended the wars of religion by endorsing the Edict of Nantes (1598), which offered religious freedom to the Protestants of France, and laid out the lines for one of the most memorable of the plazas of Paris, the place des Vosges. His reward for his political leniency was death by stabbing from a deranged monk infuriated by his religious tolerance.

After his death, his second wife, Marie de Médicis (acting as regent), laid out the Luxembourg Palace (1615), whose gardens have functioned ever since as a rendezvous for Parisians. In 1636, Cardinal Richelieu (who virtually ruled France during the minority of Louis III) built the sprawling premises of the Palais-Royale.

Under Louis XIII (1601–43) two uninhabited islands in the Seine were joined together with landfill, connected to the Ile de la Cité and also to the mainland with bridges, and renamed the Ile St Louis. Also laid out were the Jardin des Plantes, whose flowers and medicinal herbs corresponded to the fashion at the time of scientifically and medically categorizing plants.

LOUIS XIV & THE FRENCH REVOLUTION

Louis was crowned king of France when he was only nine years old. The government in Paris was almost completely dominated during Louis's minority by his Sicilian-born chief minister, Mazarin (1602–61).

This era marked the emergence of the French kings as absolute monarchs with unquestioned power. As if to symbolize their power, the face of Paris was embellished with many of the monuments that still serve as symbols of the city. These included new alterations in the endless process of building the Louvre, and construction of the Pont-Royal, the quai Peletier, the place des

DATELINE

Antoinette, are publicly guillotined.

- **1799** Napoléon Bonaparte crowns himself Master of France. Paris is further embellished with neoclassical splendor.

- **1803** Napoléon abandons French overseas expansion and sells Louisiana to America.

- **1812** Defeat of Napoléon in the Russian Winter campaign.

- **1814** Aided by a military coalition of France's enemies, especially England, the Bourbon monarchy, under Louis XVIII, is restored.

- **1821** Death of Napoléon Bonaparte.

- **1824** Death of Louis XVIII; Charles X accedes.

- **1830** Charles X is deposed, the more liberal Louis-Philippe is elected king. Paris prospers as it industrializes.

- **1848** Violent working-class revolution deposes Louis-Philippe, who is replaced by autocratic Napoléon III. Forced redesigning of Paris's landscapes by Baron Haussmann.

- **1863** Birth of Impressionism.

- **1870** Franco-Prussian War ends

(continues)

DATELINE

in the defeat of
France; Paris is
threatened with
bombardment by
Prussian cannons
placed on the out-
skirts of the city. A
revolution in the af-
termath of this de-
feat destroys the
Tuileries Palace and
overthrows the gov-
ernment. Rise of the
Third Republic and
its elected president,
Marshal MacMahon.

• **1878–1937** A
series of internation-
al expositions adds
many enduring mon-
uments to the Paris
skyline, including the
Eiffel Tower.

• **1914–18** World
War I

• **1940** German
troops invade Paris.
The official French
government, under
Pétain, evacuates to
Vichy, while the
French Resistance
under de Gaulle
maintains symbolic
headquarters in Lon-
don.

• **1944** Paris liber-
ated by U.S. troops.
De Gaulle returns
from London in tri-
umph.

• **1948** Revolt in
French colony of
Madagascar costs
80,000 French lives.
France's empire con-
tinues to collapse in
Southeast Asia and
Equatorial Africa.

• **1954–62** War in
and eventual loss of
Algeria. Paris is
(continues)

Victoires, the place Vendôme, the Champs-Elysées, and the Hôtel des Invalides. Despite these improvements to his capital, Louis XIV preferred to absent himself from the city center, constructing—at staggering expense—the palace at Versailles, 13 miles southwest of Paris. Today, its echoing and sometimes tiresome splendor is the single most visible monument to the most flamboyantly ostentatious era of French history.

Meanwhile, however, the rising power of England, particularly its navy, represented a serious threat to a France that otherwise ruled as the most powerful nation in the world. One of the many theaters of the Anglo-French conflict was the War for American Independence, during which the French kings had supported the American revolutionaries in their war against the crown. Ironically, within 15 years the same revolutionary fervor would cross the Atlantic and destroy the French monarchy.

None of this occurred within a philosophical vacuum. For years before the outbreak of hostilities between the American revolutionaries and the British, the Enlightenment and its philosophers, usually formulating their views within the sophisticated salons of Paris, had been fostering a new generation of thinkers that encouraged the struggle against absolutism, religious fanaticism, and superstition. Revolution had been brewing for almost 50 years, and after the French Revolution's explosive and world-shaking events, Europe was completely changed, never to be the same again.

Beginning in 1789 with moderate aims, the revolutionary events soon became dominated by the radical Jacobins, led by Robespierre.

On August 10, 1792, troops from Marseilles, aided by a Parisian mob, threw Louis XVI and his Austrian-born queen, Marie Antoinette, into prison. Several months later, after countless humiliations and a bogus trial, they were guillotined at the place de la Revolution (later renamed the place de la Concorde) on January 21, 1793. The Reign of Terror continued for another 18 months, with Parisians of all political persuasions fearing for their lives.

THE RISE OF NAPOLEON It required the militaristic fervor of Napoléon to unite France once again. Considered then and today a genius with almost limitless ambition, he restored to Paris and to France a national pride that had been diminished during the horror of the Revolution. In 1799 at the age of 30, after many impressive political and military victories, he entered Paris and crowned himself First Consul and Master of France.

A brilliant politician, Napoléon moderated the atheistic ridigity of the early adherents of the Revolution by coming to peace with The Vatican. Soon thereafter, the legendary love of Parisians for their amusements began to revive; the boulevard des Italiens became the rendezvous point of the fashionable, while the boulevard du Temple, which housed many of the capital's vaudeville and cabaret theaters, became the favorite watering hole of the working class. In his self-appointed role as a French Caesar, Napoléon continued to alter the face of Paris with the construction of the neoclassical arcades of the rue de Rivoli (1801), the triumphal arches of the Arc du Carrousel and the place de l'Etoile, and the neoclassical grandeur of the Church of the Madeleine. On a less grandiose scale, the city's slaughterhouses and cemeteries were sanitized and moved away from the center of town, and new industries began to crowd workers from the countryside into the cramped slums of a newly industrialized Paris.

Napoléon's victories had made him the envy of Europe, but his famous retreat from Moscow during the winter of 1812 reduced his formerly invincible army to tatters as 400,000 Frenchmen lost their lives. After a complicated series of events that included his return from exile, Napoléon was defeated at Waterloo by the combined armies of the English, the Dutch, and the Prussians. Exiled to the British-held island of St. Helena in the remote reaches of the South Atlantic, he died in 1821, probably the victim of an unknown poisoner. Some time later, his body was interred within a massive porphyry sarcophagus within Louis XIV's monument to the ailing and fallen warriors of France, Les Invalides in Paris.

In the power vacuum that followed the expulsion and death of Napoléon, Paris became the scene of intense lobbying concerning the future fate of France. The Bourbon monarchy was soon reestablished, but with reduced powers. In 1830, the regime was thrown out. Louis-Philippe, duke of Orléans and the son of a duke who had voted in 1793 for the death of Louis XVI, was elected king under a liberalized constitution. His calm, prosperous reign lasted for 18 years, during which England and France more or less collaborated on matters of foreign policy.

Paris reveled in its new prosperity, grateful for the funds and

DATELINE

flooded with refugees, the nation bitterly divided over its North African policies.

• **1958** France's Fourth Republic collapses. General de Gaulle is called out of retirement to head the Fifth Republic.

• **1968** General revolt by Paris's students and factory workers. The French government is overhauled in the aftermath.

• **1981** François Mitterand is elected France's first socialist president since the 1940s. Reelected in 1988.

• **1989** Paris celebrates the Bicentennial of the French Revolution.

• **1990–91** France joins the U.S., Britain, and other Allies in a successful war against Iraq's invasion of Kuwait.

• **1992** Euro Disney opens on Paris's outskirts.

glamour that had elevated it to one of the premier cultural and commercial magnets of the planet. As a fringe benefit of France's campaigns in the Egyptian desert, Paris received the Luxor Obelisk as a gift from the Caliphs of Egypt. The transport across the Mediterranean and re-erection on a granite plinth within the place de la Concorde was considered a major triumph of engineering in 1836. Paris received its first railway line in 1837 (running from the center of town to a suburb near St-Germain), and shortly thereafter the first gas-fed streetlights.

THE SECOND EMPIRE This was a time of wealth, grace, and the expansion of the arts for most French people, although the industrialization of certain working-class districts of Paris produced some of the most horrible poverty of the 19th century. The era also witnessed the development of French cuisine to the high art form as which it exists today, while a newly empowered *bourgeoisie* revelled in its attempts to create for itself the good life.

In 1848, a series of revolutions spread catalytically from one European capital to the next. The violent upheaval in Paris brought to light the increasingly organized dissatisfaction of many members of the working class. Fueled by a financial crash and scandals within the government, the revolt forced Louis-Philippe out of office. That year, on the dawn of the Second Republic, the Emperor Napoléon's nephew, Napoléon III, was elected president by moderate and conservative elements. Appealing to the property-owning instinct of a nation that hadn't forgotten the violent revolution of less than a century before, he established a right-wing government and eventually assumed complete power—as emperor—in 1851.

In 1853, Napoléon III undertook the largest urban redevelopment project in the history of Europe. He commissioned Baron Haussmann (1809–91) to redesign the city of Paris. Haussmann created a vast network of boulevards interconnected with a series of squares (*places*) that cut across old neighborhoods. While this redesigning greatly enhanced the capital and gave it the look for which it is famous today, the screams of outrage over demolished buildings and medieval neighborhoods could be heard over most of France.

By 1866, the entrepreneurs of an increasingly industrialized Paris began to regard the Second Empire as a hindrance to its development, rather than an encouragement. In 1870, during the Franco-Prussian War, the Prussians defeated Napoléon III at Sedan and held him prisoner along with 100,000 of his soldiers. Paris was threatened with bombardments from German cannon—by far the most advanced of their age—that were set up on the city's eastern periphery.

Agitated diplomacy encouraged a Prussian withdrawal, although the event's legacy of international humiliation and perceived military incompetence sparked a revolt in Paris. The revolt's immediate effect was the burning to a cinder of one of Paris's most historic palaces, the Tuileries. Today, only the sprawling gardens of this once-great palace remain. The after effects of the events of 1870 ushered in the Third Republic and its elected president, Marshal MacMahon, in 1873.

Peace and prosperity gradually returned; Paris regained its glamour. A series of Universal Expositions held in 1878, 1889, 1900, and 1937 was the catalyst for the construction of such enduring Paris monuments as the Trocadéro, the Palais de Chaillot, the Eiffel Tower, both the Grand and the Petit Palais des Champs-Elysées, and the

Neo-Byzantine church of Sacré-Coeur in Montmartre. Simultaneously, the *réseau métropolitain* (the Métro, or Paris subway) was
constructed, providing a model for subsequent subway systems
throughout Europe.

WORLD WARS I & II International rivalries and conflicting
alliances led to World War I, which, after decisive German victories
for two years, degenerated into the mud-slogged horror of trench
warfare. Industrialization during and after the war transformed Paris
and its outlying boroughs into one vast interconnected whole, by
now one of the largest metropolitan areas in Europe and undisputed
ever since as the center of France's intellectual and commercial life.

Immediately after the Allied victory, grave economic problems,
coupled with a populace demoralized from years of fighting, encouraged the rise of socialism and the formation of a Communist party.
The headquarters for both of these reigned undisputed within Paris.
Also from Paris, the French government, led by the almost obsessively
vindictive Clemenceau, occupied Germany's Ruhr Valley, then and
now one of the most profitable and industrialized regions of
Germany, and demanded every centime of reparations it could wring
from its humiliated neighbor, a policy that contributed to the
outbreak of World War II.

Thanks to an array of alliances, France had no choice but to
declare war on Germany in 1939 when Germany invaded France's
ally, Poland. Within only a few months, on June 14, 1940, Nazi
armies marched arrogantly down the Champs-Elysées. Newsreel
cameras recorded the French openly weeping at the sight of the
destruction of their world. The city suffered little from the war
materially, and was never the seat of particularly severe street-
fighting, but for four years it survived in a kind of half-life, cold, dull,
and drab, fostering scattered pockets of fighters who resisted sometimes passively, sometimes actively, often with sabotage of Nazi
plans.

During the Nazi occupation of Paris, the French government,
under Marshal Petain (1856–1951), moved to the quiet and isolated
resort of Vichy and cooperated (or actually collaborated, depending
on your point of view) with the Nazis. Tremendous internal dissen-
sion, the memory of which still simmers today, pitted many factions
against one another. The Free French Resistance fled for its own
safety to London, where it was headed by Charles de Gaulle
(1880–1970).

POSTWAR PARIS Despite its gains in both prestige and prosperity after the end of World War II, Paris was rocked many times by
internal dissent as domestic and international events embroiled the
French government in dozens of controversies. In 1951, Paris forgot
its cares by celebrating the 2,000th anniversary of the founding of the
city, and poured much of its energy into rebuilding its image as a
center of fashion, lifestyle, and glamor. Paris became internationally
recognized as both a touristic staple in the travel diets of many North
Americans, and as a beacon for art and artists. The War of Algerian
Independence (1954–58) was an anguishing event, more devastating
than the earlier loss of France's colonies. Algeria had been previously
considered a *département* (an integral extension of the French
nation). The population of France (and Paris in particular) ballooned
immediately as French citizens, fleeing with few possessions and
much bitterness, escaped from Algeria. In 1958, as a result of the

enormous loss of lives, money, and prestige in the Algerian affair, France's Fourth Republic collapsed, and de Gaulle was called out of retirement at his farm in northern France to form a new government. The Fifth Republic was launched. In 1962, the Algerian war of liberation ended with victory for Algeria, as France's colonies in Central and Equatorial Africa became independent one by one. The sun had finally set on an empire that had transformed Paris, during the period of its most spectacular construction, into a mighty city.

In 1968, a general revolt by students in Paris transformed the capital into an armed camp, causing a near-collapse of the national government and the very real possibility of total civil war.

Paris today struggles with additional social unrest in Corsica and from Muslim fundamentalists residing both in and outside of France. In 1981, François Mitterand (with a very close vote of 51%) was elected as the first socialist president of France since World War II. The flight of massive amounts of capital held by French millionaires slowed somewhat after some initial jitters, although many wealthy Parisians still choose to secretly expatriate their investments into more fiscally cooperative climates. Although much feared by the rich, Mitterand was elected again in 1988, and (according to many of his critics) soon thereafter adopted a kind of imperial demeanor better suited to a French monarch than to a duly elected president.

In 1989, Paris celebrated the Bicentennial of the French Revolution with much fanfare. In the winter of 1990–91, France joined with the United States, Great Britain, and other Allies in a successful war against Iraq, in response to that country's invasion of Kuwait. On the architectural front, new and daring designs (including Pei's iconoclastic addition of a glass pyramid within the courtyard of the Louvre, and the construction of a series of new museums and urban attractions) continued to give Paris the controversial zest for which it has traditionally been famous.

The postwar passion for exhibition of the French culture's art objects has included the opening or redesigning of such museums as the Musée d'Orsay, the Centre Pompidou at the place Beaubourg, the Musée Picasso, the newly renovated Orangerie of the Tuileries, the newly gentrified Marais district, the Forum des Halles, the Cité des Sciences et de l'Industrie at La Villette, and the much-publicized opening of the largest theme park in Europe, Euro Disney.

POLITICS

France is a republic. Its Parliament, chosen through free elections, consists of the National Assembly and the Senate. The National Assembly makes the laws. The president of the Republic is elected by a simple majority and serves a term of seven years. After that, he or she can be elected once more. The president represents France in international negotiations and is considered the representative of the most "permanent and immutable interests of the state." Political parties are not always well organized in France on a national level. Their political opinions range from the far right to socialist to the extreme left, these last exemplified by the most militant of the Communists. Sometimes loose and temporary coalitions among some of the political parties are formed, but these alliances tend to be weak and can easily fracture over one issue.

3. FAMOUS PARISIANS

Josephine Baker (1906–75) Although born in an African-American ghetto in St. Louis, this singer and cabaret entertainer became the toast of *tout Paris*. The French called her "La Baker."

Honoré de Balzac (1799–1850) This French novelist dropped out of law school and became the greatest portrayer of the mores and values of 19th-century French society. Always in debt, he produced more than 350 lengthy works. Among his most famous works—collectively called *La comédie humaine*—are *Eugénie Grandet, La Cousine Bette,* and *Père Goriot.*

Charles Baudelaire (1821–67) The work of this French impressionist poet was condemned by mainstream critics as obscene and decadent. Considered one of the world's first modern poets, he ended his life in abject poverty, hopelessly addicted to opiates. His most famous work is *Les Fleurs du mal (Flowers of Evil,* 1857).

Simone de Beauvoir (1908–86) A French essayist and novelist, she was the leading female writer of the existentialist movement and the on-again, off-again lover of Jean-Paul Sartre. Awarded the Prix Goncourt in 1945 for her novel *The Mandarins,* she was also one of the most articulate spokespersons for the postwar feminist movement. Her most influential feminist books are *All Men Are Mortal* and *The Second Sex. Memoirs of a Dutiful Daughter* amounts to an autobiography.

Louis Braille (1809–52) French musician and educator of the blind, he invented the reading and writing system for the blind using a system of embossed dots. Himself blind from the age of three, Braille became a noted organist and cellist and was far more famous as a musician during his lifetime than as the inventor of braille. Braille died impoverished and alone.

Gabrielle ("Coco") Chanel (1883–1971) This French image-maker and designer created chic, simple women's clothing, the classic lines of which have endured longer than those of any other designer in the world. Establishing her career from a shop on the boardwalk of Deauville, she promoted small and pert hats to replace the garlands of fruit, swaths of veils, and masses of straw or linen that were fashionable during the Edwardian age. In the 1950s she introduced her famous "little black dress."

Jean Cocteau (1889–1963) A multimedia French artist, Cocteau was a style-setter and *enfant terrible.* After experimenting in the surrealistic and avant-garde movements of the 1910s and 1920s, Cocteau wrote novels, poems, film scripts, essays, and scenarios for plays; painted church murals; designed restaurant menus; invented costumes; choreographed parties; and directed films. *Blood of a Poet, Beauty and the Beast,* and *Orphée* are three of his best-known films. His important writings include *Les enfants terribles, Journal d'un inconnu,* and *La difficulté d'être.* He was buried with full honors from the Academie Française.

Marie Curie (1867–1934) A French physicist and chemist, born Marie Slodowska in Poland, she and her French-born husband,

Pierre Curie, discovered radium and determined its radioactive properties in 1898. Winner of two Nobel prizes for her experimentation with the curative effects of radiation, she died in 1934, worn out and exhausted, from radium poisoning.

Georges Jacques Danton (1759–94) A revolutionary and political philosopher, his policies of relative moderation evoked the rage of more radical factions, who had him guillotined. At his most powerful he served as minister of justice and president of the Committee of Public Safety shortly after the fall of Louis XVI.

Honoré Daumier (1808–79) Cartoonist, caricaturist, and painter, Daumier was the most acerbic and accurate cartoonist of the 19th century, exposing in his more than 4,000 cartoons the smugness, corruption, arrogance, and silliness of the 19th-century French bourgoisie.

Christian Dior (1905–57) This fashion designer helped revolutionize the French fashion industry with the "New Look" after establishing his own couture business in 1947. The recognition, prestige, and money his work brought to a France ravaged by the traumas of World War II eventually earned him membership in the French Legion of Honor.

Jean-Honoré Fragonard (1732–1806) His paintings, more than anyone else's, capture the illusionary sweetness of upper-class life during the ancien régime. His best-known work, *The Swing,* is an unabashedly rococo portrayal full of ribbons, flowers, and blue satin, of fey and perhaps fickle young lovers joyously appreciating the airborne rhythms of a swing in a highly idealized garden.

Yves Montand (1921–91) The last of the great French entertainers, Montand symbolized every American's idea of a debonair Frenchman, even though he was born in Italy. He had great success in such films as *The Wages of Fear* in the 1950s and later there was Costa-Gavras's *Z*. His scandalous love affair with Marilyn Monroe during the filming of *Let's Make Love* attracted international publicity, as he was married to actress Simone Signoret. Signoret died of cancer in 1985. In 1991, Montand was buried next to her at Père-Lachaise Cemetery.

Edith Piaf (1915–63) The quintessential Parisian singer, who could move listeners to tears, was born Edith Gassion, the daughter of a circus acrobat. She was raised by her grandmother, who owned and operated a brothel. Piaf began singing in the streets at age 15 and later began appearing in cafés. Beautiful only when her plain features were illuminated while singing, Piaf was nicknamed "The Little Sparrow" by her ardent admirers. Companion of pimps, thieves, prostitutes, and drug addicts, she led a life filled with tragedy, illness, despair, and lost love. Her best-loved songs include "Milord," "A quoi ça sert, l'amour," "La Foule," and "La Vie en Rose."

Cardinal Richelieu (Armand Jean du Plessis, duc de Richelieu; 1585–1642) A French financier and prelate, Richelieu effectively controlled France after the death of Louis XIII's mother, Catherine de Médicis. Merciless in his hatred and persecution of Protestants, Richelieu starved and destroyed the Huguenot strongholds of France, most notably La Rochelle. He founded the Academie Française to impose linguistic and grammatical rules on the then loosely defined language that we now know as French.

Marquis de Sade (Donatien Alphonse Françoise, comte de Sade; 1740–1814) A French soldier and libertine, his sexually explicit novels, *Justine* and *Juliette,* so outraged the religious and political authorities of his era that he was thrown into prison and mental asylums for most of his life. He was, in modern times, the first to advocate formally inflicting pain on others for the enhancement of self-pleasure. The psychological tendencies and the sexual acts that he encouraged were called *sadism* after him.

Madame de Staël (Anne-Louise-Germaine Necker, baronne de Staël-Holstein; 1766–1817) This French writer maintained the most sought-after salon in Paris prior to, during, and after the French Revolution. She popularized and praised German romanticism in her most widely read book, *De l'Allemagne,* which, although at first suppressed by Napoléon, later encouraged the Romantic movement in France.

---

4. ART & ARCHITECTURE

ART Paris's true artistic flowering began around 1150, when the city's active trade, growing population, and struggles for political and ecclesiastic power added dozens of new buildings to the city's skyline. Between 1200 and 1400, the city flowered into the Gothic explosion whose legacy includes the city's architectural symbol—the Cathedral of Notre-Dame—as well as the Cathedral of St-Denis on the city's eastern outskirts. In these and other Gothic buildings, the medieval sculptures on the facades and inside the buildings became less incidental to the structures they adorned and more fully developed as artistic expressions in their own right. Secondary crafts, such as the manufacture and installation of stained glass (as represented by the windows in Paris's Sainte-Chapelle), became an art form in their own right, French glass of this age attaining an intensity of blues and reds that has never been duplicated.

Gothic painters became adept at the miniaturization of religious and secular scenes that art lovers (in an era without corrective lenses for myopia) could richly appreciate close at hand. The most famous of these, Pol de Limbourg's *Les très riches heures du duc de Berri* and Fouquet's *Heures d'Etienne Chevalier,* showed occasional scenes of medieval Paris in a charmingly idealized celebration of the changing of the seasons. Around 1360, Paris provided the setting for the painting of what is usually credited by art historians as the first (known) portrait, that of Jean le Bon (artist unknown), and the

---

IMPRESSIONS

Paris (in each shape and gesture and avenue and cranny of her being) was continuously expressing the humanness of humanity. Everywhere I sensed a miraculous presence, not of mere children and women and men, but of living human beings.
—E. E. CUMMINGS

Paris is a sphinx. I will drag her secret from her.
—MIRABEAU

weaving of one of the most famous tapestries in history, the *Angers Apocalypse.*

The evolution of French art slowed almost to a standstill during much of the 1400s. By the 1500s, however, Paris was marked by a great rebirth in the arts, thanks to a military campaign into Italy and the subsequent fascination with all things Italian. Two of that era's main sculptors, who embellished the facades and fountains of Paris, were Jean Goujon (1510–85), whose inspiration came mainly from the ancient Greeks as reinterpreted by Renaissance themes, and Germain Pilon (1535–90), whose carvings at Saint-Denis of the French kings followed mostly religious, rather than neoclassical, themes. By the late 1500s, under the auspices of the Renaissance king François I, the royal château at Fontainebleau, 37 miles south of Paris, became a cauldron of the arts, eventually producing a style of painting known later as the school of Fontainebleau.

The arts in and around Paris during the 1600s so permeated French culture that the century has been known ever since as "Le Grand Siècle" (the grand century). France's monarchy by now was so powerfully entrenched, and the society so stable and centralized, that the arts flowered as Paris was embellished with hundreds of aristocratic mansions within *Le Marais* district. Important painters included Philippe de Champaigne (1602–47), famous for his severe portraits, Charles le Brun (1619–90), who painted the Galerie d'Apollon at the Louvre, and his rival Pierre Mignard (1610–95), painter of the interior of the cupola in the church of Val-de-Grace. Simultaneously, the art of tapestry weaving was given a tremendous boost thanks to the establishment and royal patronage of the *Manufacture Royale des Gobelins.*

During the early 1700s, the taste for the grandiose in France was profoundly influenced by the personality of the Sun King, Louis XIV. His construction and furnishing of Versailles called for mind-boggling quantities of art and decoration, giving lavish commissions to sculptors and craftsmen of every kind. In furnishing the thousands of salons and apartments within the palace, the techniques of fine cabinetry reached their apogée under such cabinetmakers as André-Charles Boulle (1642–1732). Boulle's writing tables, secretaries, and *bombé*-fronted chests, either ebonized or inlaid with tortoise shell, mother-of-pearl, and gilded bronze ornaments (*ormolu*), are today considered among the finest pieces of cabinetry in European history, and command appropriately stratospheric prices. Boulle was supplanted by Crescent and Oeben, under Louis XV, who were themselves replaced by such neoclassic-inspired masters as Weisweiler and Kiesner during the reign of Louis XVI.

Painters from the era of Louis XIV and XV include Largillière and Rigaud and the skilled portraitists La Tour (1704–66) and Perronneau (1715–88), whose coloring techniques have been likened to those used by the impressionists more than a century later. Also noteworthy, both as an artist and a sociological phenomenon, was the female artist Vigée-Lebrun (1755–1842), whose lavish but natural style won her a position as Marie Antoinette's preferred painter. Especially famous paintings from this era are the works of Fragonard (1732–1806) and Boucher (1703–70), whose canvasses captured better than anyone else's the sweetness and whimsy of aristocratic life during the ancien régime.

In sculpture, painting, and furniture, the 18th century in Paris began with an allegiance to the baroque curve and a robustly sensual kind of voluptuousness, and ended with a return to the straight line and the more rigid motifs of the classical age. Especially indicative of this return to sobriety was Houdon (1741–1828), who is especially remembered for his extraordinarily lifelike portrait busts such as that of Voltaire.

The French Revolution, whose first violence had erupted in 1789, brought a new politicization to the arts. Noteworthy was David (1748–1825), whose painting *Oath of the Horatii* has been credited as one of the most revolution-inducing catalysts in the history of Europe. To reward his zeal, David was appointed as director of the Arts of the Revolution, an incentive that helped produce such richly idealized paintings as *The Murder of Marat*. Always in control of his own political destiny, David was later appointed as court painter to Napoléon.

Meanwhile, as France grew wealthy from the fruits of the industrial revolution and the expansion of the colonial empire, Paris blossomed with the paintings of Ingrès (1780–1867) and his bitter rival, Delacroix (1798–1863). Primary among their academic disputes were allegiances to the beauty of line (Ingrès) and the subleties of color (Delacroix).

Between 1855 and 1869, the partial demolition of medieval Paris and its reconstruction into the series of panoramic plazas and monuments that the world today knows as the City of Light was engineered by Napoléon III's chief architect, Baron Haussmann.

The birth of impressionism is generally credited with the presentation, in Paris in 1863, of the *Salon des Refusés*. There, the works of such painters as Manet—rejected by the mainline art establishment—were presented in an event that marks the birth of modern art in general and impressionist art in particular. One of the most memorable paintings at that exposition was Manet's then-scandalous and still-riveting *Déjeuner sur les Herbes*. Prior to that, the subtle colorings of the landscape artist Corot (1796–1875) had presaged impressionism by several years. Soon after, such artists as Sisley, Pissaro, Degas, Renoir, and the immortal Monet painted in the open air, often evoking the everyday life and cityscapes of Paris and its surroundings.

Later, the best scenes ever painted of Paris would be credited to Utrillo (1883–1955) and, to a lesser degree, Marquet (1875–1947). Utrillo in particular concentrated on the unpretentious, often working-class neighborhoods (especially Montmartre) rather than the city's more famous monumental zones. Marquet, whose work helped to establish the definition of the fauve school of painting, often executed his stylized and brightly colored works from the balcony of his Paris apartment.

Though many of them never made a career out of painting Paris itself, other 20th-century painters who for the most part made Paris their home included Vlaminck, Derain, Vuillard, Bonnard, Braque, Picasso, Dufy, and Matisse.

IMPRESSIONS

He gazed at me with lowered lids, his eyes blazing, and then, with the same expression that he had before his works, he came toward me. He ran his hands over my neck, breast, stroked my arms and ran his hands over my hips, my bare legs and feet. He began to knead my whole body as if it were clay.
—ISADORA DUNCAN, ON MEETING RODIN

Among sculptors, Paris's greatest contribution to the art of the late 19th century was Auguste Rodin (1840–1917), whose figures added new dimensions to the human form. Especially famous was the raw power emanating from his rough-surfaced sculptures *The Thinker* and *The Kiss*.

ARCHITECTURE Despite its role as an outpost of ancient Rome, the development of Paris into a bustling community of traders, merchants, and clerics didn't really evolve until the 1100s, relatively late in the history of France. Historians cite the abandonment of Romanesque building techniques within the Ile de France at some-time around 1150. Because of that, the city has surprisingly few Romanesque buildings, good examples of which are more common in such French provinces as Burgundy. Identified by their thick walls, barrel vaults and groined vaults, small windows, and minimal carvings, the city's most important Romanesque buildings include the churches of St-Germain-des-Près, St-Pierre-de-Montmartre, St-Martin des Champs, and—in the suburbs—the Church of Morienval.

The genius of Paris's architects, however, flowered abundantly during the Gothic age, the beginning of which was signalled early in the 1200s with the construction of the cathedrals of St-Denis, in Paris's eastern suburbs; Chartres, 60 miles to the city's southwest; and Notre-Dame of Paris, situated prominently on the Ile de la Cité itself. Before around 1450, Gothic architecture would transform the skyline of Paris as dozens of new churches, chapels, and secular buildings outdid their neighbors in lavishness, beauty, and intricacy of design.

Although Gothic architecture was firmly rooted in the principles of the Romanesque, it differs from its ancestor in its complicated patterns of vaulting and columns, and walls that became increasingly thinner as the weight of ceilings and roofs were transferred onto newly developed systems of abutment piers (flying buttresses). Because of the thinner walls, larger openings became architecturally feasible. Churches became filled with light filtered through stained glass, and enormous rose windows awed their observers with the delicate tracery of their stonework.

During the Renaissance, beginning around 1500, influences from Italy rendered the Gothic style obsolete. In its place arose the yearning for a return to the aesthetics of ancient Greece and Rome. Massive arcades, often decorated with bas-relief sculpture of symbols of triumph, as well as Corinthian, Doric, and Ionic pediments, added grandeur to the Paris of the Renaissance kings. All links of royal residences to feudal fortresses vanished as the aristocrats of Paris competed with one another in the construction of elegant town houses and villas filled with sunlight, tapestries, paintings, music, and fine furniture.

During the early 17th century, many of Paris's distinctive Italian-ate baroque domes were created. Louis XIV employed such Italian-inspired architects as Le Vau, Perrault, both Mansarts, and Bruand for his buildings and Le Nôtre for the rigidly intelligent layouts of his gardens at Versailles. Paris and the region around it flourished with the construction of the lavishly expensive château of Vaux-le-Vicomte and the even more lavish royal residence of Versailles. Meanwhile, wealthy entrepreneurs, some of royal blood, others not, spurred on the development of new expressions of artistic and architectural beauty from the intellectual ferment of the many literary and artistic salons sprouting up throughout the city.

By the early 19th century, a newly militaristic Paris, flushed with the titanic changes of the Revolution and the subsequent victories of Napoléon, returned to a restrained and dignified form of classicism. Modeling their urban landscape on an idealized interpretation of imperial Rome, buildings such as the Church of the Madeleine evoked the militaristic rigidity and grandeur of the classical age.

By 1850, enjoying a cosmopolitan kind of prosperity, Paris grew bored with things Greek and Roman. Despite a brief flirtation with Egyptology (based on Napoléon's campaign in the Egyptian desert and the unravelling of the secrets of the Rosetta stone) a new school of eclecticism added controversial and often extremely elegant influences of the Paris landscape. Among them were the voluptuous lines of the art nouveau movement, whose aesthetic was inspired by the surging curves of the botanical world. Stone, cast iron, glass, and wood were carved or molded into forms resembling orchids, vines, laurel branches, and tree trunks, each richly lyrical and based on new building techniques made possible by the Industrial Age. Youthful and creative architects began to specialize in the use of iron as the structural support of bridges, viaducts, and buildings—such as the National Library (1860). These techniques opened the way for Gustav Eiffel to design and erect the most frequently slurred building of its day, the Eiffel Tower, for the Paris exposition of 1889.

During the 1920s and 1930s, a newly simplified aesthetic was highly refined and greatly appreciated within Paris. Art deco, a style reflecting the newly developed materials and decorative techniques of the machine age, captured sophisticated sensibilities around the world. After Braque defined cubism, the angular simplicity of the new artistic movement influenced architectural styles as well. Le Corbusier, a Swiss-born architect who settled definitively in Paris in 1917, eventually developed his jutting, gently curved planes of concrete, opening the doors for a new, but often less talented, school of modern French architects.

In recent years, critics have not been kind to the exposed, rapidly rusting structural elements of Paris's Centre Beaubourg, and the new Opera House has also stirred controversy. The most recent controversial structure to evoke rage in a city where everyone presumably has an architectural opinion is without a doubt I. M. Pei's glass pyramid jutting upward from the courtyard of the Louvre.

Despite the dozens of often captivating architectural influences that have converged upon Paris, all but a handful of buildings constructed in the center within the past 150 years have been designed at roughly the same height, giving the city an evenly spaced skyline and helping to justify its claim to be the most beautiful city in the world.

5. FOOD & DRINK

Volumes have been written about French gastronomy—my comments are meant to be a brief introduction only. First, as any French person will tell you, French food is the best in the world. That's as true today as it was in the days of the great Escoffier. More than ever, young *chefs du cuisine* are making creative statements in the kitchen, and never in the history of the country has there been such an emphasis on super-fresh ingredients One chef I know in Paris has been known to shut down his restaurant for the day if he doesn't find exactly what he wants in the marketplace that morning.

Of course, you may want to ask, "What will it cost?" Paris has gained a reputation as being a damnably expensive place in the food department. True, its star-studded, internationally famous establishments—such as Tour d'Argent—are very expensive indeed. In such culinary cathedrals, you pay not only for superb decor and regal service but also for the art of celebrated chefs on ministerial salaries.

There is also a vast array of expensive restaurants in Paris that exist almost exclusively for the tourist trade. Their food may be indifferent or downright bad, but they'll also have ice water and ketchup to anesthetize your tastebuds, trilingual waiters, and quadrilingual menus. Luckily, there are others—hundreds of others. Paris, which is said to have more restaurants than any other city on earth, has many good, reasonably priced ones. And they aren't hard to find. I've counted 18 of them on a single, narrow Left Bank street.

MEALS & DINING CUSTOMS French restaurants by law add a service charge of 12% to 15% to your bill: Your bill will say *service compris,* which means that the tip is included. However, it's customary to leave a little something extra.

In many of the less expensive places described in this guide, the menu will be handwritten, in French only. Don't let that intimidate you. Nor should you be timid about ordering dishes without knowing precisely what they are. You'll get some delightful surprises. I know a woman who wouldn't have dreamed of asking for escargots if she'd realized they were snails cooked in garlic sauce. As it was, she ate this appetizer in a spirit of thrift rather than adventure—and has been addicted to it ever since. As for vegetables, the French regard them as a separate course and eat them apart from the meat or poultry dishes. But I wouldn't advise you to order them specially unless you're an exceptionally hearty eater. Most main courses come with a small helping, or *garni,* of vegetables anyway.

You'll find a large number of specific dishes explained in the glossary of menu terms in the appendix as well as in the restaurant descriptions themselves. No one, however, can explain the subtle nuances of flavor that distinguish them. Those you have to taste for yourself.

As a rule, it's better to order an apéritif—often the house will have a specialty—rather than a heavy drink such as a martini before a classic French dinner. Vodka or scotch can assault your palate, destroying your tastebuds for the festive repast to come.

Allow plenty of time for a gourmet dinner. Orders are often prepared individually, and it takes time to absorb the wine and the flavors. Sometimes sorbet (a sherbet) is served midway in your meal to cleanse the palate.

Making reservations is important, and please try to show up on time. Too many Americans make reservations and then become a "no-show," which creates ill will, especially since many nine-table

---

IMPRESSIONS

I am the man who accompanied Jacqueline Kennedy to Paris, and I have enjoyed it.
—JOHN F. KENNEDY

restaurants must be filled completely every night in order to make a profit. If you're window-shopping for a restaurant, you'll find the menu most often displayed outside. Parisians read it like a book. It's there for you to study and ponder—so read it in anticipation. Most French people have their main meal during the day; you, too, may want to follow that custom, dining more lightly in the evening.

Most meals consist of several small courses. You can begin, for example, with hors d'oeuvres or a light potage (soup). The classic restaurant used to serve a small order of fish after the appetizer, then the meat or poultry course, but nowadays it's likely to be either fish or meat. A salad follows the main course, then a selection of cheese (there are 365 registered French cheeses) and dessert (often a fruit concoction or a sorbet). In this book, prices are given for fixed-price or à la carte meals. The price for an à la carte meal is based on a three-course meal.

If you find the food "too rich, with too many sauces," that may be because you've been overdoing it. Elaborately prepared gourmet banquets should not be consumed for both lunch and dinner, or even every day. Sometimes an omelet or a roast chicken can make a delightful light meal, and you can "save up" for your big dining experience.

THE CUISINE The revolution against Escoffier has been raging for so long that many of the early rebels are now returning to the old style of cookery, as exemplified by the boeuf bourguignon, the blanquette de veau, and the pot-au-feu.

The battle between haute cuisine and nouvelle cuisine didn't begin in Paris. One would like to imagine that it started when Michel Guérard's beautiful Christine murmured in his ear, "Vous savez, Michel, if you would lose some weight, you'd look great."

For a man who loved food as much as Guérard, this was a formidable challenge. But he set to work and, ultimately, invented the "cuisine minceur," which is a way to cook good French food without the calories. The world now makes its way to Guérard's restaurant, at Eugénie-les-Bains in the Landes, just east of the Basque country. His *Cuisine minceur* became a bestseller in North America, and food critic Gael Greene hailed Guérard as "the brilliant man who is France's most creative chef." Cuisine minceur is more a diet cuisine than nouvelle cuisine, which, despite the fact that it is no longer *nouvelle,* remains a viable part of the Paris dining scene.

The "new cuisine," like cuisine minceur, represents a major break with haute cuisine, while still being based on the classic principles of French cookery. Rich sauces, for example, are eliminated. Cooking times that can destroy the best of fresh ingredients are considerably shortened. The aim is to release the natural flavor of food without covering it with heavy layers of butter and cream. New flavor combinations in this widely expanding repertoire are often inspired.

Many chefs, including some of the finest in Paris, dislike the word "nouvelle" when applied to cuisine. They call theirs "moderne" instead—a blend of the finest dishes of the classic repertoire with those of the nouvelle kitchen. Broadly defined, moderne means paying homage to the integrity of ingredients—certainly fresh ones—and working in the kitchen to bring out natural flavors and aromas.

There is really no such thing as Parisian cuisine. The capital of France borrows from all the other provinces, all of which have distinctive cuisines. Even if you don't venture outside the city limits, you can get a good sampling of the diversified regional cooking of France, because all French kitchens are represented in Paris. Some restaurants specialize in one cuisine—such as that of Normandy—while others offer various dishes that might range from Brittany to Provence.

WINE French cookery achieves palate perfection only when lubricated by wine, which is not considered a luxury or even an addition, but rather an integral part of every meal. Certain rules about wine drinking have been long established in France, but no one except traditionalists seems to follow them anymore. "Rules" would dictate that if you're having a roast, steak, or game, a good burgundy should be your choice. If it's chicken, lamb, or veal, you would choose a red from the Bordeaux country, certainly a full-bodied red with cheese such as camembert, and a blanc-de-blanc with oysters. A light rosé can go with almost anything, especially if enjoyed on a summer terrace overlooking the Seine.

Let your own good taste—and sometimes almost as important, your pocketbook—determine your choice of wine. Most wine stewards, called sommeliers, are there to help you in your choice, and only in the most dishonest of restaurants will they push you toward the most expensive selections. Of course, if you prefer only bottled water or perhaps a beer, then be firm and order either without embarrassment. In fact, bottled water might be a good idea at lunch if you're planning to drive later. Some restaurants include a beverage in their menu rates (*boisson compris*), but that's only in the cheaper places. Nevertheless, some of the most satisfying wines I've drunk in Paris came from unlabeled house bottles or carafes, called a *vin de la maison*. In general, unless you're a real connoisseur, don't worry about labels and vintages.

When in doubt, you can rarely go wrong with a good burgundy or bordeaux, but you may want to be more adventurous than that. That's when the sommelier can help you, particularly if you tell him or her your taste in wine (semidry or very dry, for example). State frankly how much you're willing to pay and what you plan to order for your meal. If you're dining with others, you may want to order two or three bottles with an entire dinner, selecting a wine to suit each course. However, Parisians at informal meals—and especially if there are only two persons dining—select only one wine to go with all their platters, from hors d'oeuvres to cheese. As a rule of thumb, expect to spend about one-third of the restaurant tab for wine.

Wine Labels Since the latter part of the 19th century, French wines sold in France (and sometimes elsewhere) have been labeled. The general label is known as *appellations contrôlées*. These controls, for the most part, are by regions such as Bordeaux and the Loire. These are the simple, honest wines of the district. They can be blended from grapes grown at any place in the region. Some are composed of the vintages of different years.

In most cases, the more specific the label, the better the wine. For example, instead of a bordeaux, the wine might be labeled "Médoc" (pronounced *may*-doc), which is the name of a triangle of land extending some 50 miles north from Bordeaux. Wine labels can be narrowed down to a particular vine-growing property, such as a Château Haut-Brion, one of the most famous and greatest of red wines of Bordeaux (this château produces only about 10,000 cases a year).

On some burgundies, you are likely to see the word *clos* (pronounced cloe). Originally, that meant a walled or otherwise enclosed vineyard, as in Clos-de-Bèze, which is a celebrated Burgundian vineyard producing a superb red wine. *Cru* (pronounced "croo," and meaning "growth") suggests a wine of superior quality when it appears on a label as a *vin-de-cru*. Wines and vineyards are often divided into crus. A grand cru or premier cru should, by implication, be an even superior wine.

Labels are only part of the story. It's the vintage that counts. Essentially vintage is the annual grape harvest and the wine made from those grapes. Therefore, any wine can be a vintage wine unless it is a blend. But there are good vintages and bad vintages. The variation between wine produced in a "good year" and wine produced in a "bad year" can be great, and even noted by the neophyte.

Finally, champagne is the only wine that can be correctly served through all courses of a meal—but only to those who can afford its astronomical cost.

6. RECOMMENDED BOOKS & FILMS

BOOKS

Becoming more familiar with France before you go can greatly enhance your trip. There are numerous books on all aspects of French history and society—ranging from the very general, such as the section on France in the *Encyclopedia Americana*, International Edition (Grolier, 1989), which presents an excellent, illustrated overview of the French people and their way of life, to the very specific, such as Judi Culbertson and Tom Randall's *Permanent Parisians: An Illustrated Guide to the Cemeteries of Paris* (Chelsea Green, 1986), which vividly depicts the lives of many famous French and foreign people who are buried in Paris. The books I have selected below are grouped into four categories: history, biography, the arts, and fiction.

HISTORY In addition to the encyclopedia reference above, a broad overview of French history can be found in other encyclopedias and general history books. One very good one is *History of France* by Guillaume de Bertier de Savigny and David H. Pinkney (Forum Press, 1983), a comprehensive history with illustrations and plenty of obscure but interesting facts.

Two books that present French life and society in the 17th century are Warren Lewis's *The Splendid Century* (William Morrow, 1978) and Madame de Sévigné's *Selected Letters*, edited by Leonard W. Tancock (Penguin, 1982), which contains imaginative and witty letters written to her daughter during the reign of Louis XIV.

Simon Schama's *Citizens* (Alfred A. Knopf, 1989) is "a magnificent and electrifyingly new history of the French Revolution"—long, but very enjoyable.

Moving into the 20th century, *Pleasure of the Belle Epoque: Entertainment and Festivity in Turn-of-the-Century France,* by

Charles Rearick (Yale University Press, 1985), depicts public diversions in the changing and troubled times of the Third Republic. *Paris Was Yesterday, 1925–1939* (Harcourt Brace Jovanovich, 1988) is a fascinating collection of excerpts from Janet Flanner's "Letters from Paris" column of the *New Yorker*. Larry Collins and Dominique Lapierre have written a popular history of the liberation of Paris in 1944 called *Is Paris Burning?* (Warner Books, 1991).

Finally, two unusual approaches to French history are Rudolph Chleminski's *The French at Table* (William Morrow, 1985), a funny and honest history of why the French know how to eat better than anyone and how they go about it, and *Paris: A Century of Change, 1878–1978*, by Normal Evenson (Yale University Press, 1979), a notable study of the urban development of Paris.

BIOGRAPHY You can get a different look at history by reading biographies of historical figures. Hugh Ross Williamson brings to life Catherine de Médicis in his *Catherine de Medici* (Viking Press, 1973) by combining text and magnificent illustrations from the art of the 16th century. This queen of France was the dominant personality during her nation's religious wars and mother of three kings of France, a queen of Spain, and a queen of Navarre.

Representing a very different era are *A Moveable Feast* (Collier Books, 1987), Ernest Hemingway's recollections of Paris during the 1920s, and Morley Callaghan's *That Summer in Paris: Memories of Tangled Friendships with Hemingway, Fitzgerald and Some Others* (1963), an anecdotal account of the same period. Another interesting read is *The Autobiography of Alice B. Toklas,* by Gertrude Stein (Vintage Books, 1990). It's not only the account of 30 years in Paris, but also the biography of Gertrude Stein.

Simone de Beauvoir, by Deirdre Bair (Summit Books, 1990), was described by one critic as a biography "*à l'Americaine*—that is to say, long, with all the warts of its subject unsparingly described." The story of the great feminist intellectual was based in part on tape-recorded conversations and unpublished letters. *Colette: A Life,* by Herbert R. Lottman (Little, Brown, 1991), is a painstakingly researched biography of the celebrated French writer and her fascinating life—which included not only writing novels and appearing in cabarets but also dabbling in lesbianism and, on the darker side, perhaps even collaborating with the enemy during the Nazi occupation.

THE ARTS Much of France's beauty can be found in its art. Three excellent books that approach France from this perspective are *The History of Impressionism,* by John Rewald (Museum of Modern Art, 1973), which is a collection of documents, both writings and quotations of the artists, clearly illuminating this valuable period in the history of art; *The French Through Their Films,* by Robin Buss (Ungar, 1988), an exploration of the history and themes of more than 100 widely circulated films; and *The Studios of Paris: The Capital of Art in the Late Nineteenth Century,* by John Milner (Yale University Press, 1988). In the last, Milner presents the dynamic forces that made Paris one of the most complex centers of the art world in the early modern era.

Nightlife of Paris: The Art of Toulouse-Lautrec, by Patrick O'Connor (Universe, 1992), is an enchanting 80-page book with lively anecdotes about the hedonistic luminaries of belle époque Paris, with paintings, sketches, and lithographs by the artist.

Olympia: Paris in the Age of Manet, by Otto Friedrich (Harper-

Collins, 1992), takes its inspiration from the celebrated art work in the Musée d'Orsay in Paris. From here the book takes off on an anecdote-rich gossipy chain of historical associations, tracing the rise of the impressionist school of modern painting, but incorporating social commentary too, such as the pattern of prostitution and venereal disease in 19th-century France.

FICTION The *Chanson de Roland,* edited by F. Whitehead (2nd ed.; Basil Blackwell, 1942), written between the 11th and 14th centuries, is the earliest and most celebrated of the "songs of heroic exploits." *The Misanthrope* and *Tartuffe* (Harcourt, Brace and World, 1965) are two masterful satires on the frivolity of the 17th century by the great comic dramatist Molière. François-Marie Arouet Voltaire's *Candide* (Bantam Classics, 1981) is a classic satire attacking both the philosophy of optimism and the abuses of the ancien régime.

A few of the masterpieces of the 19th century are *Madame Bovary,* by Gustave Flaubert (Random House, 1982), in which the carefully wrought characters, setting, and plot attest to the genius of Flaubert in presenting the tragedy of Emma Bovary; Victor Hugo's *Les Misérables* (Modern Library, 1983), a classic tale of social oppression and human courage set in the era of Napoléon I; and the collection *Selected Stories* by the master of short stories, Guy de Maupassant (New American Library, 1984).

Honoré de Balzac's *La comédie humaine* depicts life in France from the fall of Napoléon to 1848. Henry James's *The Ambassadors* and *The American* both take place in Paris. *The Vagabond,* by Colette, evokes the life of a French music-hall performer.

Tropic of Cancer is the semiautobiographical story of Henry Miller's early years in Paris. One of France's leading thinkers, Jean-Paul Sartre, shows individuals struggling against their freedom in *No Exit and Three Other Plays* (Random House, 1955). Finally, writer Georges Simenon and illustrator Frederick Franck combined to create *Simenon's Paris* (1970), a beautifully illustrated book of Simenon's Paris stories.

FILMS

Although Americans understood—and very quickly, too—the commercial wealth to be made from films, the French are credited with the scientific and technical inventions that made them possible. French physicists had laid the groundwork for a movie camera as early as the mid-1880s, and the world's first movie was shown in Paris on December 28, 1895. Its makers were the Lumière brothers, who considered filmmaking a scientific oddity and stubbornly confined its use to the production of international newsreels. Later, a vaudevillian actor and illusionist, Georges Méliés, used film to convey plot and drama.

Charles Pathé and Léon Gaumont were the first to exploit filmmaking on a grand scale. Beginning in 1896, they produced and distributed their own films, building their company into a giant before World War I. When Gaumont made his first film, he enlisted his secretary, Alice Guy-Blanché, to create the plot, design the scenery, and direct it. She proved so successful that she was eventually promoted to the head of Paris's largest studio and became the world's first female director.

Before World War I the many talented actors arriving *en scène* included Max Linder, a popular French comic, whose style influenced Charlie Chaplin and helped him develop his keen sense of timing. After World War I a flood of film imports from the United States and an economic depression slowed down the growth of French filmmaking.

By the 1920s the French began to view filmmaking as an art form, and infused it with surreal and dada themes. These were eventually named avant-garde and included experiments viewed (sometimes skeptically, sometimes encouragingly) in Hollywood and around the world. Examples include Man Ray's *Le retour à la raison* (1923), Fernand Léger's *Le ballet mécanique* (1924), and Jean Cocteau's *Le sang d'un poète* (1930).

The golden age of the French silent screen on both sides of the Atlantic was 1927–29. Actors were directed with more sophistication, and technical abilities reached an all-time high. One of my favorite films—despite its mind-numbing length—is Abel Gance's sweepingly evocative masterpiece *Napoléon* (1927); its grisly battle scenes are easily as chilling as any war film made today. Other highlights from this era included René Clair's *Un chapeau de paille d'Italie* (*An Italian Straw Hat;* 1927), Carl Dreyer's *La passion de Jeanne d'Arc* (1928), and an adaptation of Emile Zola's *Thérèse Raguin* (1928) by Jacques Feyder.

Experiments with the early productions of "talkies" were less successful. One popular film director, Pagnol, declared outright that the role of films was to publicize to the masses the benefits of the theatrical stage. During this period, many of the counter culture's most gifted directors either left France altogether (as did René Clair, who emigrated to England in 1934) or died (Jean Vigo, *Zéro de Conduite*).

In 1936 the Cinémathèque Française was established to find and preserve old (usually silent) French films. By that time, French cinematographers had divorced themselves completely from the value systems of the stage and had found a style of their own. An average of 130 films a year were made in France, by (among others) Jean Renoir, Charles Spaak, and Marcel Carne. This was also the era that brought such French luminaries as Claudette Colbert and Maurice Chevalier to Hollywood.

During World War II, the best known (to Americans) of the French directors fled to Hollywood. Those who remained were heavily censored by the Vichy government. Despite that, more than 350 French films, many relating to long past (and therefore uncontroversial) events were produced. Exceptions were Carne's *Les enfants du paradis* (*Children of Paradise;* 1945).

In 1946 France slapped a heavy quota system onto the importation of foreign (especially American) films. A semigovernmental film authority (Le Centre National du Cinéma Français) financed independent French film companies and encouraged liasions between the French and Italian film industries. Many directors who had supported the Vichy government's Nazi collaboration were soon accepted back into the cinematic community.

Two strong traditions—film noir and a return to literary traditions—grew strong. Film noir included such existentially inspired nihilistic themes as André Cayatte's *Nous sommes tous des assassins* (*We Are All Assassins;* 1952) and Yves Allegret's *Dedée d'Anvers* (1948). Examples of the literary tradition include Bresson's *Journal d'un curé de campagne* (*Diary of a Country Priest;* 1951) and a film rendition of Stendahl's *Le rouge et le noir* (*The Red and the Black;* 1954) by Autant-Lara. By the 1950s comedy adopted a new kind of genre with Jacques Tati's *Les vacances de Monsieur Hulot (Mr. Hulot's Holiday)*. By the mid-1950s French filmmaking ushered in the era of enormous budgets, à la Hollywood, and the creation of such frothy potboilers as *And God Created Woman*, which helped make Brigitte Bardot a penthouse name around the world, contributing greatly to the image in America of France as a kingdom of sexual liberation.

By the late 1950s François Truffaut, widely publicizing his *auteur* theories, rebelled with a series of short films (the most famous of which was *The 400 Blows, 1959*), which was partly financed by government funds, partly by wealthy benefactors. With Jean-Luc Godard (*A bout de soufflé*, or *Breathless*) and Claude Chabrol (*Le beau Serge; 1959*), they pioneered one of the most publicized movements in 20th-century French art, *la nouvelle vogue*. In the early 1960s dozens of new directors joined the movement, furiously making films, some of which are considered classics, others of which have been thrown into the dustbin of forgotten artistic endeavors. Enthusiastically endorsed by the counterculture on both sides of the Atlantic, these directors included Resnais (*Muriel*), Roger Vadim, Agnès Varda (*Le Bonheur*), Jacques Demy (*Les parapluies de Cherbourg*), Godard (*Pierrot-le-Fou*), Louis Malle, Chris Marker, and Marguerite Duras (*Detruire, dit-elle*).

After a switch to political themes (Costa Gavras's *Z*) during the 1968 rebellions (and a politically motivated abandonment of the film festival at Cannes by at least a dozen prominent French directors), French cinema turned to comedy in the early 1970s. Examples include Buñuel's *Le charme discret de la bourgeoisie* (1972) and Yanne's *Tout le monde il est beau, tout le monde il est gentil* (1972).

Many American films—still shown rather frequently on TV— were filmed in Paris (or else used sets to simulate Paris). Notable ones have included the classic *An American in Paris*, starring Gene Kelly, and *Moulin Rouge*, starring José Ferrer as Toulouse-Lautrec. Truffaut's *The Last Metro* and Clément's *Is Paris Burning?* gained worldwide audiences, as did *The Sun Also Rises*, an adaptation of Hemingway's celebrated novel, with Ava Gardner and Tyrone Power. *Last Tango in Paris*, with Marlon Brando, was one of the most controversial films set in Paris, and the always controversial Roman Polanski used Paris as a setting for his *Frantic*.

La Belle Noiseuse, in French, with English subtitles, is a four-hour film that opened in New York in 1991. Director Jacques Rivette tells the story of a once-celebrated painter, Edouard Frenhofer, who attempts to transform a beautiful young woman into his crowning masterpiece.

In 1992, Michael Bene directed *Le ciel de Paris*, about emotional isolation. The film, which opened in New York, starred Sandrine Bonnaire and Marc Fourastier. It was Mr. Bene's first and last feature film, as he died of AIDS before its release.

Betty Blue, the stylish Jean-Jacques Beineix film about a torrid summertime love affair, was released in English in 1992. It was first shown in France in 1986 when it was that country's nominee for the Oscar as best foreign film.

Today the transatlantic movie deal is a relatively common occurrence, and movie executives from California, New York, and Paris regularly collaborate and compete on films suitable for both cultures.

PLANNING A TRIP TO PARIS

This chapter is devoted to the where, when, and how of your trip—the advance-planning issues required to get it together and take it on the road.

After deciding where to go, most people have two fundamental questions: "What will it cost?" and "How do I get there?" This chapter will answer both those questions and also resolve important issues such as when to go, what insurance coverage is necessary, and where to obtain more information about the destination.

The chapter also covers various alternative and specialty travel options, and includes tips for special travelers such as the disabled or senior citizens.

1. INFORMATION, ENTRY REQUIREMENTS & MONEY

SOURCES OF INFORMATION

Your best source of information before you go—besides this guide— is the **French Government Tourist Office,** which can be reached at the following addresses.

In the U.S.: 628 Fifth Ave., New York, NY 10020; 645 N. Michigan Ave., Suite 630, Chicago, IL 60611; 2305 Cedar Springs Blvd., Dallas, TX 75201; 9454 Wilshire Blvd., Beverly Hills, CA 90212-2967. To request information, call the **France on Call** hotline (tel. 900/990-0040); each call costs 50¢ per minute.

In Canada, write to Maison de la France/French Government Tourist Office at either 1981 av. McGill College, Tour Esso, Suite 490, Montréal, PQ H3A 2W9 (tel. 514/288-4264); or 1 Dundas St. W., Box 8, Toronto, ON M5G 1ZE (tel. 416/593-4723).

In Great Britain, write to Maison de la France/French Government Tourist Office at 178 Piccadilly, London, W1V 0AL (tel. 071/629-9376).

In Australia, write to the French Tourist Office at Kindersley House, 33 Bligh St., Sydney, N.S.W. 2000 (tel. 612/233-3277).

In Ireland, write to the Maison de la France/French Government Tourist Office at 35 Lower Abbey St., Dublin 2, Ireland (tel. 01/771-871).

Currently there is no representative in New Zealand, so New Zealanders should write to the representative in Australia.

IN PARIS You need never be totally alone in Paris. There's always someone who speaks your language standing ready to dispense aid, give you information, and help you solve problems. **Welcome Offices** in the center of the city will give you free maps, informative booklets, and "Paris Monthly Information," an English-language listing of all current shows, concerts, and theater. At 127 Champs-Elysées, 8e (tel. 47-23-61-72), you can get information regarding both Paris and the provinces. The office is open daily from 9am to 8pm. Métro: Charles-de-Gaulle–Etoile.

ENTRY REQUIREMENTS

DOCUMENTS In recent years Americans and Canadians traveling to France were required to obtain a visa in advance. However, since July 1989 only special groups, such as journalists on assignment and students enrolling in French schools, must still obtain visas. For tourism or business visits of less than 90 days, all you need now is a valid passport.

With today's ever-changing political climate, it's always a good idea to confirm the situation. Contact the French Embassy (4101 Reservoir Road NW, Washington, DC 20007; tel. 202/944-6000), or the French Consulate (935 Fifth Avenue, New York, NY 10021; tel. 212/606-3653).

Canadian, Swiss, and Japanese citizens and citizens of E.C. countries, such as Britain and Ireland, are exempt from any visa requirement, but check with your nearest French consulate, as the situation can change overnight. Citizens of Australia need a visa to enter France, but citizens of New Zealand must produce only a valid passport.

U.S. and Canadian **driver's licenses** are valid in France, but if you're touring Europe by car, you may want to invest in an International Driver's License just to be on the safe side. Apply at a branch of the American Automobile Association (AAA). You must be 18 years old and include two 2-by-2-inch photographs, a $10 fee, and your valid U.S. driver's license with your application. If AAA doesn't have a branch in your hometown, send a photograph of your driver's license (both the front and the back) with the fee and photos to AAA, 1000 AAA Dr., Heathrow, FL 32746-5063 (tel. 407/444-8000 or 800/556-1166 in the U.S.). You should always carry your original license with you to Europe, however.

In Canada, you pay $10 Canadian and apply to CAA, the Canadian Automobile Association, 2 Carlton St., Toronto, ON M5B 1K4 (tel. 416/964-3170).

You must also have an **international insurance certificate,** called a green card (*carte verte* in French), to drive. The car-rental agency will provide one if you're renting.

CUSTOMS Customs restrictions differ for citizens of the European Community and for citizens of non–E.C. countries. Non–E.C. nationals can bring in duty free 200 cigarettes or 100 cigarillos or 50 cigars or 250 grams of smoking tobacco. This amount is doubled if you live outside Europe. You can, as well, bring in 2 liters of wine and

1 liter of alcohol over 38.80 proof and 2 liters of wine under 38.80 proof. In addition, you can bring in 50 grams of perfume, a quarter liter of toilet water, 500 grams of coffee, and 200 grams of tea. Passengers 15 years of age and over may also bring in other goods totaling 4,200F ($777). Those 14 and under can bring in other goods totaling 1,100F. ($203.50).

Visitors from E.C. countries can bring in 300 cigarettes or 150 cigarillos or 75 cigars or 400 grams of smoking tobacco. The limit for "spirits" is five liters of table wine, 1½ liters of alcohol over 38.80 proof, and three liters of alcohol under 38.80 proof. In addition, visitors can bring in 75 grams of perfume, ⅜ of a liter of toilet water, 400 grams of coffee, and 80 grams of tea. Visitors over 14 can bring in other goods totaling 2,800F ($518); for those under 25 the limit is 700F ($129.50).

Items destined for personal use, including bicycles and sports equipment, already in use, whether or not contained in personal luggage, are admitted without formality providing the quantity or the type of goods imported does not indicate the owner's intention to carry out a commercial transaction. They cannot be sold or given away in France and must be reexported.

MONEY

CASH/CURRENCY   French currency is based on the **franc (F)**, which consists of 100 **centimes** (c). Coins come in units of 5, 10, 20, and 50 centimes; and 1, 2, 5, and 10 francs. Notes come in denominations of 10, 20, 50, 100, 200, and 500 francs.

All banks are equipped for foreign exchange, and you will find exchange offices at the airports and airline terminals. Banks are open from 9am to noon and 2 to 4pm Monday through Friday. Major bank branches also open their exchange departments on Saturday between 9am and noon.

When converting your home currency into French francs, know that rates vary. Your hotel will offer the worst rate of exchange. In general, banks offer the best rate, but even banks charge a commission for the service, often $2 or $3, depending on the transaction. Whenever you can, stick to the big banks of Paris, like Credit Lyonnais, which offer the best exchange rates and charge the least commission for exchanging money or traveler's checks. Always make sure you have enough francs for the weekend.

At this writing $1=approximately 5.4F (or 1F=18¢), and this was the rate of exchange used to calculate the dollar values given in this book (rounded to the nearest nickel). This rate fluctuates from time to time and may not be the same when you travel to France.

Prices quoted in francs throughout these pages are accurate at press time, but, inflation being what it is worldwide, they cannot be guaranteed. The wise traveler will allow for increases in the prices. Therefore the following table should be used only as a guide:

CONVERSION TABLE

French Francs	U.S. Dollars	French Francs	U.S. Dollars
1	.18	30	5.55
2	.37	35	6.48
3	.55	40	7.40
4	.74	45	8.33

French Francs	U.S. Dollars	French Francs	U.S. Dollars
5	.93	50	9.25
6	1.10	75	13.88
7	1.30	100	18.50
8	1.48	110	20.35
9	1.67	120	22.20
10	1.85	130	24.05
11	2.04	140	25.90
12	2.22	150	27.75
13	2.40	175	32.38
14	2.59	200	37.00
15	2.78	250	46.25

TRAVELER'S CHECKS Before leaving home, purchase traveler's checks and change $50 or so into French francs, obtainable from major banks, so that you can avoid waiting in long lines at the currency-exchange offices upon arrival in France.

American Express (tel. 800/221-7282 in the U.S. and Canada) is the most widely recognized traveler's check abroad; the agency imposes a 1% commission. Checks are free to members of the American Automobile Association.

Bank of America (tel. 800/227-3460 in the U.S., or 415/624-5400, collect, in Canada) also issues checks in U.S. dollars for a 1% commission everywhere but California.

Citicorp (tel. 800/645-6556 in the U.S., or 813/623-1709, collect, in Canada) issues checks in U.S. dollars, pounds, or German marks.

MasterCard International (tel. 800/223-9920 in the U.S., or 212/974-5696, collect, in Canada) issues checks in about a dozen currencies.

Barclays Bank (tel. 800/221-2426 in the U.S. and Canada) issues checks in both U.S. and Canadian dollars and British pounds.

Thomas Cook (tel. 800/223-7373 in the U.S., or 212/974-5696, collect, in Canada) issues checks in U.S. or Canadian dollars or British pounds. It's affiliated with MasterCard.

Each of these agencies will refund your checks if they are lost or stolen, provided you can produce sufficient documentation. Of course, your documentation should be carried in a safe place—never along with your checks. When purchasing checks from one of the banks listed, ask about refund hotlines; American Express and Bank of America have the most offices around the world. Purchase checks in a variety of denominations—$20, $50, and $100.

Sometimes you can purchase traveler's checks in the currency of the country you're planning to visit, thereby avoiding a conversion fee, sometimes as much as $5. American Express, for example, issues checks in French francs. Note, also, that you always get a better rate if you cash traveler's checks at the institutions issuing them: VISA at Barclays, American Express at American Express, and so forth.

CREDIT CARDS Credit cards are useful in France. Both **American Express** and **Diners Club** are widely recognized. The French equivalent for VISA is Carte Bleue. If you see the **Eurocard** sign on an establishment, it means it accepts MasterCard.

You may make a purchase with a credit card thinking it will be at a certain rate, only to find that the dollar has declined by the time your bill arrives, and you're actually paying more for an item than you bargained for. But those are the rules of the game. It also can work in your favor if the dollar should unexpectedly rise after you make a purchase.

Some **automatic-teller machines** in Paris accept U.S. bank cards such as VISA or MasterCard. Exchange rates are often good, and the convenience of obtaining cash on the road is without equal. Check with your credit-card company or bank before leaving home.

WHAT THINGS COST IN PARIS	U.S. $
Taxi from Charles de Gaulle Airport to the city center	28.00
Taxi from Orly Airport to the city center	20.00
Public transportation for an average trip within the city from a Métro *carnet* (packet) of 10	.65
Local telephone call	.20
Double room at the Ritz (very expensive)	500.00
Double room at Lord Byron (moderate)	148.00
Double room at Family (budget)	100.00
Lunch for one, without wine, at Chez Georges (moderate)	25.00
Lunch for one, without wine, at Le Drouot (budget)	16.00
Dinner for one, without wine, at Le Grand Véfour (very expensive)	100.00
Dinner for one, without wine, at Chez André (moderate)	40.00
Dinner for one, without wine, at Aux Charpentiers (budget)	25.00
Glass of wine	3.00
Coca-Cola	3.50
Cup of coffee	3.00
Roll of ASA 100 film, 36 exposures	7.00
Admission to the Louvre	6.00
Movie ticket	7.50
Theater ticket (at the Comédie-Française)	20.00

2. WHEN TO GO — CLIMATE, HOLIDAYS & EVENTS

In August, Parisians traditionally evacuate for their annual holiday and put the city on a skeleton staff to serve visitors. Now, too, July has become a popular vacation month, with many a restaurateur shuttering up for a month-long respite.

From May through September, the city is swamped with tourists, and you must write well in advance for hotel reservations. Avoid the first two weeks in October, when the annual motor show draws thousands of boy-at-heart enthusiasts.

The best time to come to Paris is off-season, in the early spring or late autumn, when the tourist trade has trickled to a manageable flow and everything is easier to come by—hotel rooms, Métro seats, even good-tempered waiters.

THE CLIMATE Balmy weather in Paris has probably prompted more popular songs and love ballads than weather conditions in any other city in the world. The main characteristic of the city's weather is its changeability. Rain is much more common than snow throughout the winter, prompting many long-time residents to complain about the occasional bone-chilling dampness.

The average annual number of days experiencing snowfalls in Paris during the past decade is only around 15, and oppressively hot temperatures (that is, over 86° F) occur only during a few days in midsummer. Perhaps the most disturbing aspect of Parisian weather is the blasts of rapidly moving air—perhaps the result of a wind tunnel effect caused by the city's long boulevards being bordered by buildings of uniform height. Other than the occasional winds and rain (which add an undeniable drama to many of the city's panoramas), Paris offers among the most pleasant weather conditions of any capital in Europe, with a highly tolerable average temperature of 53° F.

Paris's Average Daytime Temperature & Rainfall

	Jan	Feb	Mar	Apr	May	June	July	Aug	Sept	Oct	Nov	Dec
Temp °F	38	39	46	51	58	64	66	66	61	53	45	40
Rainfall ″	3.2	2.9	2.4	2.7	3.2	3.5	3.3	3.7	3.3	3.0	3.5	3.1

HOLIDAYS In France, holidays are known as *jours feriés*. Shops and banks are closed, as well as many (but not all) restaurants and museums. Major holidays include January 1, Easter, Ascension Day (40 days after Easter), Pentecost (seventh Sunday after Easter), May 1, May 8 (V-E Day), July 14 (Bastille Day), August 15 (Assumption of the Virgin Mary), November 1 (All Saints' Day), November 11 (Armistice Day), and December 25 (Christmas).

PARIS CALENDAR OF EVENTS

JANUARY

☐ **The Boat Fair,** one of Europe's largest. Mid-December.
☐ **Paris fashion shows** for the upcoming summer collections. Mid-January to mid-February.

FEBRUARY

☐ **Fashion shows.** Through mid-February.

MARCH

☐ **Foire du Trône,** Neuilly Lawn of the Bois de Vincennes, a mammoth amusement park, operates from end of March through May daily from 2pm to midnight.

MAY

☐ **French Open Tennis Championship** at Stade Roland-Garros. May 24–June 6.
☐ **Paris Marathon,** with runners competing from around the world. 2nd weekend.
☐ **Illuminated fountains at Versailles.** May to September.
☐ **Festival de Versailles** (tel. 30-21-20-20) featuring opera, concerts, theater, and ballet. Late May to late June.
☐ **Festival de Musique de St-Denis** (tel. 42-43-72-72), with music in the church. Late May through late June.
☐ **Festival de Paris,** 38 rue des Blancs-Manteaux, 4e (tel. 40-26-45-34), an assemblage of some of the world's leading orchestras and choruses. Mid-May to late June. Tickets: 50F–500F ($9.25–$92.50).

JUNE

☐ **Paris Air Show,** at Le Bourget Airport. Early June in alternate years only.
☐ **Grand Steeplechase de Paris,** in the Bois de Boulogne, Auteuil Racetrack. Mid-June.
☐ **Grand Prix de Paris,** at Longchamp Raceway. Late June.
☐ **Festival du Marais.** Many events—theater, exhibitions, classical and jazz music—are presented in renovated Renaissance buildings and courtyards. For details, contact Festival du Marais, 68 rue François Minon, 4e (tel. 45-23-18-25). Mid-June to mid-July.

JULY

✪ *Bastille Day. The nation's festivities reach their peak in Paris with street fairs, pageants, fireworks, and feasts. The day begins with a parade down the Champs-Elysées and ends with fireworks at Montmartre. Wherever you are, before the end of the day you'll hear Piaf warbling "La Foule" ("The Crowd"), the song that celebrated her passion for the stranger whom she met and later lost in a crowd on Bastille Day.*

When: July 14. Where: Bars, restaurants, streets, and private homes throughout Paris. How: Hum the Marseillaise; outfit yourself with a beret, a pack of Gauloises, and a bottle of cheap wine; leave your hotel; and stamp around the neighborhood.

☐ **Festival Estival (Summertime Festival),** with music at churches and concert halls throughout Paris. For details, write to Festival Estival de Paris, 20 rue Geoffroy l'Asnier, 75004 Paris (tel. 48-04-98-01). Mid-July to late September.

☐ **Le Grand Tour de France.** Europe's most visible bicycle race decides its winner at a finish line drawn across the Champs-Elysées. Late July.

AUGUST

☐ **Festival Estival.** All month.

SEPTEMBER

☐ **Festival Estival.** Through late September.

☐ **Festival d'Automne.** Concentrating mainly on modern music, ballet, theater, and modern art, it's the most eclectic of the festivals. For details, write to the Festival d'Automne, 156 rue de Rivoli, 75001 Paris (tel. 42-96-12-27). Late September until just before Christmas.

OCTOBER

☐ **Festival d'Automne.** All month.

✪ *Paris Auto Show* *Glistening metal, glitzy women, lots of hype, and the latest models from world auto makers, this is the showcase for European car design.*
   Where: Parc des Expositions, near the Porte de Versailles in western Paris. When: 10 days in early October. How: Check Pariscope for details or contact the French Government Tourist Office (see the addresses and telephone numbers in "Information, Entry Requirements & Money," above).

☐ **Prix de l'Arc de Triomphe.** France's answer to the horsey set at Ascot is the country's most prestigious horse race. Early October.

☐ **International Fair of Contemporary Artists,** at the Grand-Palais. Late October to early November.

NOVEMBER

☐ **Festival d'Automne.** All month.

☐ **Armistice Day,** celebrated with a military parade from the Arc de Triomphe to the Hôtel des Invalides. November 11.

DECEMBER

☐ **Festival d'Automne.** Through late December.

☐ **Fête de St-Sylvestre** (New Year's Eve). It's best celebrated in the *quartier Latin* around the Sorbonne. At midnight, the city explodes. Strangers kiss strangers. Boulevard St-Michel becomes a virtual pedestrian mall, as does the Champs-Elysées.

3. HEALTH & INSURANCE

HEALTH You aren't required to have any particular inoculations to enter France (except for yellow fever, and then only if you're arriving from an infected area). Paris should not pose any major health hazards, although many travelers suffer from diarrhea. This is generally caused by the overly rich cuisine—heavy cream sauces, butter, and wine. Take along some antidiarrhea medicine, moderate your eating habits, and, even though the water in Paris is considered safe, consume mineral water only. Sometimes travelers find that a change of diet leads to constipation. If this occurs, eat a high-fiber diet and drink plenty of mineral water. Avoid large lunches and dinners with wine. Consult your pharmacist about taking an over-the-counter drug such as Colace, a stool softener, or Metamucil.

Take along an adequate supply of any prescription drugs that you need and a prescription that uses the generic name of the drug as well—not just the brand name.

If you're subject to motion sickness on a plane or train, remember to bring along motion-sickness medicine as well.

Of course, carry all your vital medicine and drugs (the legal kind) with you in your carry-on luggage, in case your checked luggage is lost.

If you suffer from a chronic illness, talk to your doctor before taking the trip. For such conditions as epilepsy, diabetes, or a heart condition, wear a **Medic Alert Identification Tag,** which will immediately alert any doctor to your condition and provide the number of Medic Alert's 24-hour hotline so that a foreign doctor can obtain medical records for you. For a lifetime membership, the cost is $35, $40, or $50. The cost depends on the metal that goes into the tag. Contact the Medic Alert Foundation, P.O. Box 1009, Turlock, CA 95381-1009 (tel. toll free 800/432-5378).

Before you leave home, you can obtain a list of English-speaking doctors in Paris from the **International Association for Medical Assistance to Travelers (IAMAT)**—in the United States at 417 Center St., Lewiston, NY 14092 (tel. 716/754-4883); in Canada at 40 Regal Rd., Guelph, ON N1K 1B5 (tel. 519/836-0102). In Europe, the address is 57 Voirets, 1212 Grand-Lancy-Geneva, Switzerland.

INSURANCE Insurance needs for the traveler abroad fall into three categories: (1) health and accident, (2) trip cancellation, and (3) lost luggage.

First, review your present policies before traveling internationally—you may already have adequate coverage between them and what is offered by credit-card companies.

Many credit-card companies insure their users in case of a travel accident, providing a ticket was purchased with their card. Sometimes fraternal organizations have policies that protect members in case of sickness or accidents abroad.

Incidentally, don't assume that Medicare is the answer to illness in France. It covers U.S. citizens who travel south of the border to Mexico or north of the border to Canada. Canadians, though, are generally protected with health-insurance plans from their individual provinces.

Many homeowners' insurance policies cover theft of luggage during foreign travel and loss of documents—your Eurailpass, your passport, or your airline ticket, for instance. Coverage is usually limited to about $500 U.S. To submit a claim on your insurance, remember that you'll need police reports or a statement from a medical authority that you did in fact suffer the loss or experience the illness for which you are seeking compensation. Such claims, by their very nature, can be filed only when you return from France.

Some policies (and this is the type you should have) provide cash advances or tranfers of funds so that you won't have to dip into your precious travel funds to settle medical bills.

If you've booked a charter flight, you will probably have to pay a cancellation fee if you cancel a trip suddenly, even if it is because of an unforeseen crisis. It's possible to get insurance against such a possibility from some travel agencies, and often flight insurance against a cancelled trip is written into tickets paid for by credit cards from such companies as VISA and American Express. Many tour operators or insurance agents also provide this type of insurance.

Among the companies offering such policies are the following:

Travel Guard International, 1145 Clark Street, Stevens Point, WI 54481 (tel. toll free 800/826-1300), offers a comprehensive seven-day policy for $52 that covers basically everything, including lost luggage, emergency assistance, accidental death, trip cancellation and interruption, and medical coverage abroad. There are restrictions, however, which you should understand before you buy the policy.

Travel Insurance Pak, Travelers Insurance Co., 1 Tower Square, 10 NB, Hartford, CT 06183-5040 (tel. toll free 800/243-3174 or 203/277-2318), offers illness and accident coverage, costing from $10 for 6 to 10 days. For lost or damaged luggage, $500 worth of coverage costs $20 for 6 to 10 days. You can also get trip-cancellation insurance for $5.50.

Mutual of Omaha (Tele-Trip Company, Inc.), 3201 Farnam Street, Omaha, NE 68131 (tel. toll free 800/228-9792), charges $13 and up for travel insurance packages that feature travel assistance services, trip cancellation and interruption, baggage loss and baggage delay, accident, sickness, death and dismemberment, and medical evacuation coverages. Application for insurance can be taken over the phone for major credit card holders.

HealthCare Abroad (MEDEX), Wallack & Co., 107 W. Federal St., P.O. Box 480, Middleburg, VA 22117-0480 (tel. toll free 800/237-6615), offers a policy, good for 10 to 120 days, costing $3 a day, including accident and sickness coverage to the tune of $100,000. Medical evacuation is also included, along with a $25,000 accidental death and dismemberment compensation. Trip cancellation and lost or stolen luggage can also be written into this policy at a nominal cost.

WorldCare Travel Assistance Association, 1150 S. Olive St., Suite T2233, Los Angeles, CA 90015 (tel. 213/745-5550, or toll free 800/253-1877), features a 9- to 15-day policy, costing $105, including trip cancellation, lost or stolen luggage, legal assistance, and medical coverage and evacuation.

Access America, 6600 W. Broad St., Richmond, VA 23230 (tel. 804/285-3300, or toll free 800/424-3391), has a 24-hour hotline in case of an emergency and offers $10,000 medical coverage for 9 to 15 days, costing $49. If you want medical plus trip cancellation, the charge is $80 for 9 to 15 days. A comprehensive package for $111 grants 9- to 15-day blanket coverage, including $50,000 worth of death benefits.

4. WHAT TO PACK

Parisians are both stylish *and* conservative; city clothes are in order here. Pack what you might wear to visit San Francisco or New York. Unlike the British, the French tend to dress down rather than up, but always with style. Parisian women go to work, restaurants, or the theater wearing beautifully cut and tailored pants suits. While ties for men are advisable in the posh places, they are seldom required in more moderate restaurants. Even churches don't insist that women wear head coverings, although that, of course, is your option.

Always pack as light as possible. Sometimes it's hard to get a porter or a baggage cart in rail and air terminals. Also, airlines are increasingly strict about how much luggage you can bring aboard, not only carry-on items, but checked suitcases as well. This is particularly true when flights are fully booked (or overbooked, as the case may be). Checked baggage should not be measure than 62 inches (width plus length plus height) and shouldn't weigh more than 70 pounds. Carry-on luggage shouldn't measure more than 45 inches (width plus length plus height) and must fit under your seat or in the bin above.

Whatever the season, bring a raincoat and umbrella to Paris, just to be on the safe side.

The general rule of packing is to bring four of everything. For men that means four pairs of socks, four pairs of slacks, four shirts, and four sets of underwear. At least two of these will always be either dirty or in the process of drying. Women could follow the same rule, four of each of the "basics," such as undergarments and stockings.

Take at least one outfit for chilly weather and one outfit for warm weather, especially if you plan to tour the rest of France after visiting Paris. Always take two pairs of shoes for walking Paris streets during the day. You may get your shoes soaked and need that extra pair.

5. TIPS FOR THE DISABLED, SENIORS, SINGLES, FAMILIES & STUDENTS

FOR THE DISABLED Facilities for the disabled are certainly above the world average. The French government every year does more and more to help ease life for the disabled in the public facilities of the country.

If you're contemplating a trip to Paris, contact one of the French Government Tourist Offices abroad (see "Information," in Section 1, above). You'll be sent a publication with an English glossary, called **Touristes Quand Même.** It provides a province-by-province overview of the facilities for the disabled in the French transportation system and at monuments and museums. There is a special emphasis on Paris. The book was last issued in 1984, however, and there have been many improvements since then.

Nearly all modern hotels in Paris now provide rooms especially built with the disabled in mind. Older hotels, unless they've been renovated, may not provide such important features as elevators, special toilet facilities, or ramps for wheelchair access. For a list of hotels in Paris providing facilities for the disabled, contact the **Association des Paralysés de France,** 17 bd. Auguste-Blanqui, 75013 Paris (tel. 45-80-82-40).

Another source of information is **Travel Information Service,** Moss Rehabilitation Hospital, 12th St. and Tabor Rd., Philadelphia, PA 19141 (tel. 215/456-9603). It charges $5 per package for its data, which will contain names and addresses of accessible hotels, restaurants, and attractions, often based on firsthand reports of travelers who have been there.

You can also obtain a copy of *Air Transportation of Handicapped Persons,* published by the U.S. Department of Transportation. It's free if you write to Free Advisory Circular No. AC12032, Distribution Unit, U.S. Department of Transportation, Publications Division, M-4332, Washington, DC 20590.

You may also want to consider joining a tour for disabled travelers. Names and addresses of such tour operators can be obtained by contacting the **Society for the Advancement of Travel for the Handicapped,** 347 Fifth Avenue, New York, NY 10016 (tel. 212/447-7284). Yearly membership dues in this society are $40, $25 for senior citizens and students. Send a stamped self-addressed envelope.

The **Federation of the Handicapped,** 211 West 14th St., New York, NY 10011 (tel. 212/727-4200), also operates summer tours for members, who pay a yearly fee of $4.

For the blind, the best information source is the **American Foundation for the Blind,** 15 West 16th St., New York, NY 10011 (tel. 212/620-2000, or toll free 800/232-5463).

In France, most high-speed trains can deal with wheelchairs. Guidedogs ride free. Older trains have special compartments built for wheelchair boarding. On the Paris Métro, handicapped persons are able to sit in wider seats provided for their comfort. Some stations don't have escalators or elevators, and these obviously present problems.

FOR SENIORS Many discounts are available for seniors—that is, men and women who have reached, as the French say, "the third age." Be advised, however, that you have to be a member of an association to obtain certain discounts. The French domestic airline, **Air Inter,** honors "third agers" by offering them 25% to 50% reductions on its regular, nonexcursion flights, but restrictions do apply. At any railway station in the country, senior citizens (men and women 60 years or older) can obtain a **Carte Vermeil (Vermilion Card)** for a cost of 139F ($25.70). This card is valid for one year and entitles you to a 50% discount on train fares in both first- and second-class compartments, but not during peak periods. Further discounts include a 10% reduction on all rail excursions. Carte Vermeil also offers reduced prices on certain regional bus lines and on about 20 weekly Air France flights to Nice. Finally, reduced-price theater tickets and half-price admission to state-owned museums are yet other discounts offered. For more information, contact a French Government Tourist Office (see "Information, Documents & Money," above).

For information before you go, write to *Travel Tips for Senior Citizens* (publication no. 8970), distributed for $1 by the Superintendent of Documents, U.S. Government Printing Office, Washington, DC 20402 (tel. 202/783-5238). Another booklet—and this one is distributed free—is called *101 Tips for the Mature Traveler,* available from Grand Circle Travel, 347 Congress Street, Suite 3A, Boston, MA 02210 (tel. 617/350-7500 or toll free 800/221-2610).

One of the most dynamic travel organizations for seniors is **Elderhostel,** 75 Federal St., Boston, MA 02110 (tel. 617/426-7788), established in 1975, which operates an array of programs throughout Europe, including France. Most courses, lasting around 3 weeks, represent good value since they include airfare, accommodations in student dormitories or modest inns, all meals, and tuition. Courses involve no homework, are ungraded, and are often liberal arts oriented. They're not luxury vacations, but they are fun and fulfilling. Participants must be 60 years or older. However, if two members go as a couple, only one member needs to be of age. Write or call for their free newsletter and a list of upcoming courses and destinations.

SAGA International Holidays is also well known for its all-inclusive tours for seniors. They prefer that joiners be at least 60 years or older. Insurance is included in the net price of any of their tours, all of which encompass dozens of locations in Europe and last for an average of 17 nights. Contact SAGA International Holidays, 120 Boylston St., Boston, MA 02116 (tel. 800/343-0273).

The **American Association of Retired Persons,** 601 E. Street, NW, Washington, DC 20049 (tel. 202/434-2277), offers members discounts on car rentals, hotels, and airfares. The association's group travel is provided by the AARP Travel Experience from American Express. Tours may be purchased through any American Express office or travel agent or by calling toll-free 800/927-0111. Cruises may be purchased only by telephone through toll-free 800/745-4567. Flights to the various destinations are handled by either of these toll free numbers as part of land arrangements or cruise bookings.

Information is also available from the **National Council of Senior Citizens,** 925 15th Street, NW, Washington, DC 20005 (tel. 202/347-8800).

See also "Grand Circle Travel," below.

FOR SINGLE TRAVELERS   A recent American census showed that 77 million Americans over 15 years of age are single. The travel industry, though, is far better geared for double occupancy of hotel rooms. One company that has made heroic efforts to match single travelers with like-minded companions is now the largest and best-listed company in the United States. **Jens Jurgen,** the German-born founder, charges $36 to $66 for a six-month listing in his well-publicized records. New applicants desiring a travel companion fill out a form stating their preferences and needs. They then receive a minilisting of the kinds of potential partners who might be suitable for travel. Companions of the same or opposite sex can be requested. His listings are extensive, and it's very likely that you'll find a travel companion. For an application and more information, write to Jens Jurgen, Travel Companion, P.O. Box P-833, Amityville, NY 11701 (tel. 516/454-0880).

Singleworld Cruises & Tours, 401 Theodore Fremd Ave., Rye, NY 10580 (tel. 914/967-3334 or toll free 800/223-6490), is a travel agency that operates tours for solo travelers. Some, but not all, are for people under 35. Annual dues are $25.

Another agency to check is **Grand Circle Travel,** 347 Congress St., Boston, MA 02210 (tel. 617/350-7500, or toll free 800/221-

2610), which offers escorted tours and cruises for retired people, including singles.

FOR FAMILIES Advance planning is the key to a successful overseas family vacation. If you have very small children you should discuss your vacation plans with your family doctor and take along such standard supplies as children's aspirin, a thermometer, Band-Aids, and the like.

On airlines, a special menu for children must be requested at least 24 hours in advance, but if baby food is required, bring your own and ask a flight attendant to warm it to the right temperature. Take along a "security blanket" for your child—a pacifier, a favorite toy or book, or, for older children, something to make them feel at home in different surroundings—a baseball cap, a favorite T-shirt, or some good-luck charm.

Make advance arrangements for cribs, bottle warmers, and car seats if you're driving anywhere (in France small children aren't allowed to ride in the front seat).

Ask the hotel if it stocks baby food, and, if not, take some with you and plan to buy the rest in local supermarkets.

Draw up guidelines on bedtime, eating, keeping tidy, being in the sun, even shopping and spending—they'll make the vacation more enjoyable.

Babysitters can be found for you at most hotels, but you should always insist, if possible, that you secure a babysitter with at least a rudimentary knowledge of English.

Family Travel Times is a newsletter on traveling with children. Subscribers can also call in with travel questions, but only from 1am to 1pm Eastern Standard Time (later in the West), on Wednesday only. Contact **TWYCH**, which stands for **Travel With Your Children,** 14 W. 18th St., New York, NY 10011 (tel. 212/206-0688).

Another family-travel organization that might be worth contacting is the **American Institute for Foreign Study,** 102 Greenwich Ave., Greenwich, CT 06830 (tel. 203/863-6087, or toll free 800/727-2437), which offers a family-vacation program in France.

Parents planning to travel by rail in France can purchase a *Carte KIWI* if their child is under 16. Selling for 370F ($68.45), it offers a 50% reduction on trips covering 300 days a year, falling either in the *période bleue* or *période blanche* (blue or white period). Naturally, holiday travel such as at Christmas isn't included. Everybody traveling with the child—up to a limit of four people—can benefit from this 50% reduction. For details, write French National Railroads, 610 Fifth Ave., New York, NY 10020 (tel. 212/582-2110).

FOR STUDENTS The largest travel service for students is **Council Travel,** a subsidiary of the Council on International Educational Exchange (CIEE), 205 East 42nd St., New York, NY 10017 (tel. 212/661-1450), providing details about budget travel, study abroad, working permits, and insurance. It also sells a number of publications, including *Work, Study, Travel Abroad: The Whole World Handbook; Volunteer: The Comprehensive Guide to Voluntary Service in the U.S. and Abroad;* and *The Teenager's Guide to Study, Travel and Adventure Abroad.* It offers the *Student Travel Catalogue,* which is available free. It issues to bonafide students, for $14, an International Student Identity Card. Council Travel offices are located throughout the United States. Call toll free 800/GET-ANID to find out where the closest office is to you. There is also a Council

Travel Office in France at 49 rue Pierre Charron, 75008 Paris (tel. 43-59-23-69).

For real budget travelers it's worth joining **IYHF (International Youth Hostel Federation).** For information write AYH (American Youth Hostels), P.O. Box 37613, Washington, DC 20013-7613 (tel. 202/783-6161). Membership costs $25 annually except for under-18s, who pay $10, or over-54s, who pay $15.

6. ALTERNATIVE/ADVENTURE TRAVEL

EDUCATION/STUDY TRAVEL The **Alliance Française,** 101, bd. Raspail, 75270 Paris CEDEX 06 (tel. 45-44-38-28)—a state-appointed, nonprofit organization that has a network of 1,200 establishments in more than 100 countries—offers French language courses to some 350,000 students. The international school in Paris is open all year, and you can enroll for a minimum of a month-long session. Fees tend to be reasonable, and the school offers numerous activities and services. Write for information and application forms at least one month before your departure for Paris.

The **National Registration Center for Studies Abroad** (NRCSA), 823 N. 2nd St., Milwaukee, WI 53203 (tel. 414/278-0631), has a catalogue ($2) of schools in France, including the Sorbonne, in Paris. They will register you at the school of your choice, arrange for room and board, and make your airline reservations, all for no extra fee. Contact them and ask for a (free) copy of their newsletter.

COOKING SCHOOLS In a nation devoted to the pursuit of gastronomic excellence, you'll find a wide array of chefs (skilled or otherwise) eager to impart for a fee a few of their culinary insights. A knowledge of at least rudimentary French is a good idea before you enroll yourself as a student, although a visual demonstration of any culinary technique is often worth far more than reading or hearing about it. Most of the organizations listed below will mail information in English or French if you write to them in advance, and many might be attended by professional chefs and very serious and competitive connoisseurs. Here follows a listing of some of Paris's more visible cooking schools.

Ecole de Gastronomie Française Ritz-Escoffier, 38 rue Cambon, 75001 Paris (tel. 42-60-38-30). Famed for his titantic rages within the kitchens of the French and English aristocrats who engaged him to prepare their banquets, and his well-publicized culinary codifications, Georges-Auguste Escoffier (1846–1935) taught the Edwardian age how to eat. Today, the Ritz Hotel, site of many of Escoffier's meals, maintains a school that articulates the conservative doctrines of the master's techniques. Courses last from one to six weeks and are taught in French and English.

Paris en Cuisine, 49 rue de Richelieu, 75001 Paris (tel. 42-61-35-23), is a company established by St. Louis–born entrepreneur Robert Noah. A long-term resident of Paris who pays careful attention to the translational needs of his clients, Mr. Noah offers half-day insights into culinary Paris that are especially attractive to amateurs unwilling to devote an entire season to finessing their cuisine. A walking tour of the wholesale food markets at Rungis departs at least once a week (usually Tuesday) from downtown Paris at 5:30am, includes transportation and breakfast, and has visitors back in Paris, depending on the traffic, by around 9:30am. The price is 425F ($78.60). The company also offers half-day walking tours through the kitchens of three top restaurants (which might, depending on their availability, include Drouant, Ledoyen, and Prunier), for a net price of 250F ($46.25). Advance reservations are required, and groups rarely exceed 10. Noah also offers one-week gastronomic tours of Paris loaded with fine food and intelligent discourse on its provenance and preparation.

Le Cordon Bleu, 8 bis rue Léon Delhomme, 75015 Paris (tel. 48-56-06-06 or toll-free 800/457-2433 in the U.S.). Originally established in the 1890s, it is probably the most famous of the French cooking schools, and the one with the most sophisticated marketing techniques (call the toll-free number in the U.S. and the school will mail you its brochures on request). Cordon Bleu's most famous courses last for 11 weeks, at the end of which certificates of competence are issued that are highly sought after within the restaurant world. Many readers of this guidebook, however, are interested in either the four- or five-day programs (usually held during Easter and Christmas), or the two-hour demonstration classes. Attendance at these is available on a first-come, first-serve basis, cost around 150F ($27.75) each, and offer sometimes unexpected insights into the culinary subculture of Paris.

SAILING UP THE SEINE   The river that winds through the heart of Paris, the Seine, is the third-longest of the four great rivers of France, yet its role within French history is probably greater than that of the other three waterways combined. Sailing between its banks, with the architecture of what is probably the most beautiful city in the world passing on either side of you, is probably one of the most rewarding experiences in France.

For a description of the glass-sided *bateaux-mouches* that offer short-term river excursions through the monumental zone of Paris, refer to Chapter 6. Some visitors, however, prefer longer excursions along the river that birthed the French nation. **Paris Canal** (tel. 42-40-96-97) requires advance reservations for 3½-hour waterborne tours that begin either at the quays in front of the Musée d'Orsay (Métro: Solferino) or in front of the Musée de Science et Industrie at Parc de la Villette (Métro: Porte de Pantin). Excursions negotiate the waterways and canals of Paris, which include the Seine, an underground tunnel below the place de la Bastille, and the Canal St-Martin.

HOME STAYS   The **Friendship Force,** 575 South Tower, 1 CNN Center, Atlanta, GA 30303 (tel. 404/522-9490), is a nonprofit organization existing for the sole purpose of fostering and encouraging friendship among people worldwide. Dozens of branch offices throughout North America arrange en masse–visits, usually once a year. Because of group bookings, the airfare to the host country is usually less than you'd pay if you bought an individual APEX ticket. Each participant is required to spend two weeks in the host country, one full week as a guest in the home of a family. Most volunteers spend the second week traveling in the host country.

Servas, 11 John St., New York, NY 10038 (tel. 212/267-0252), is a nonprofit, nongovernmental, international, interfaith network of travelers and hosts whose goal is to help build world peace, goodwill, and understanding. Servas (translated from the Esperanto, it means "to serve") travelers are invited to share living space within a community, normally staying without charge for visits lasting a maximum of two days. Day visits as well as a single shared meal can also be arranged. Visitors pay a $55 annual fee, fill out an application, and are interviewed for suitability. They then receive a Servas directory listing the names and addresses of Servas hosts on six continents who welcome visitors into their homes.

For $6 **International Visitors Information Service,** 1623 Belmont St., NW, Washington, DC 20009 (tel. 202/939-5566), will mail anyone a booklet listing opportunities for contact with residents in foreign countries. France is heavily featured. Checks should be made out to Meridian House/IVIS.

After World War I, a work-camp program for youth was set up to promote "peace and understanding." Participants arrange their own travel and sometimes—depending on the camp—pay for bed and board. Registration fees range from $25 to $70. For information contact **Volunteers for Peace,** 43 Tiffany Rd., Belmont, VT 05730 (tel. 802/259-2759), which issues a work-camp directory covering 36 countries and costing $10.

People to People International, 501 East Armour Blvd., Kansas City, MO 64109 (tel. 816/531-4701), defines its purpose as the promotion of international understanding among individuals through educational and cultural exchanges. It was established by Pres. Dwight D. Eisenhower in the late 1950s and organizes two- to three-week adult professional exchanges around the world in many different specialized fields. There is also a summer, four-week high school educational program. A collegiate summer study-abroad program offers courses by American professors for credit. Located throughout the United States and abroad, local chapters help provide homestay possibilities for members. Privileges include access to membership travel opportunities, newsletters, and a magazine. Costs are $25 annually for families, $15 for individuals, and $10 for students.

HOME EXCHANGES For home exchanges, which can be fun and save you money, contact the following:

International Home Exchange Service, Box 190070, San Francisco, CA 94119 (tel. 415/435-3497), charges $35 for three directories annually. The fee includes a listing of your name in one of them. Seniors get 20% off.

Vacation Exchange Club, P.O. Box 820, Haleiwa, HI 96712 (tel. 808/638-8747 or toll free 800/638-3841), although it has fewer listings, offers the same service. For $50, you get four directories a year and you're listed in one.

The **Invented City,** 41 Sutter St., Suite 1090, San Francisco, CA 94104 (tel. 415/673-0347, or toll free 800/788-CITY), is another international home exchange agency. Home exchange listings are published three times a year: February, May, and November. A membership fee of $50 allows you to list your home, and you can also state your preferred time to travel, your occupation, and your hobbies.

OPERA TOURS **Dailey-Thorp,** 315 West 57th St., New York, NY 10019 (tel. 212/307-1555), is probably the best-regarded organizer of music and opera tours in America. Because of its "favored" relationship with European box offices, it's often able to purchase blocks of otherwise unavailable tickets to such events as the Salzburg

Festival, the Vienna, Milan, Paris, and London operas, or the Bayreuth Festival in Germany. Tours range from 7 to 21 days, including first-class or deluxe accommodations and meals in top-rated European restaurants. Dailey-Thorp also offers visits to operas in Eastern Europe and the regional operas of Italy.

---

7. GETTING THERE

BY PLANE

The flying time to Paris from New York is about 7 hours; from Chicago, 9 hours; from Los Angeles, 11 hours; from Atlanta, 8 hours, from Miami, 8½ hours; and from Washington, 7½ hours.

THE MAJOR AIRLINES

Until not very long ago, Paris-bound passengers had to fly from their hometowns to New York, then transfer onto a transatlantic flight to Paris. Changing air routes and regulations, however, as well as the diminishing role of New York as the exclusive gateway to Europe, have encouraged the development of many nonstop flights to Paris (sometimes on airlines you might not have thought of) from such North American hubs as Atlanta, Cincinnati, Houston, Chicago, and Orlando.

One of the best choices for passengers flying to Paris from both the southeastern United States and the Midwest is **Delta Airlines** (tel. 800/241-4141), whose network greatly expanded after its adoption of some of the routes of the now-defunct Pan Am. From such cities as New Orleans, Savannah, Phoenix, Columbia (S.C.), Birmingham, and Nashville, Delta flies to Atlanta, connecting every evening with a nonstop flight to Orly Airport in Paris. Delta also operates a daily nonstop flight to Paris from both Cincinnati and New York's JFK. Both of these leave late enough in the afternoon to permit easy transfers from much of Delta's vast North American network. An additional recent acquisition from Pan Am involves nonstop flights to Orly four times a week from Orlando, Florida.

Another excellent choice for Paris-bound passengers is **United Airlines** (tel. 800/538-2929), with nonstop flights from Chicago, Washington, D.C., Los Angeles, and San Francisco to Paris's Charles de Gaulle Airport. United also offers attractive promotional fares—especially in the low and shoulder seasons—to London's Heathrow from at least seven major North American hubs. From London, it's an easy train and hovercraft connection to Paris, a fact that tempts many passengers to spend a weekend in London either before or after their visit to Paris.

American Airlines (tel. 800/433-7300) offers daily nonstop flights to Paris (Orly) from Dallas/Fort Worth, Raleigh/Durham, Chicago, and New York's JFK.

Continental Airlines (tel. 800/231-0856) offers daily nonstop flights to Paris's Orly from its hubs in Newark (N.J.) and Houston.

TWA (tel. 800/221-2000) operates frequent (usually daily) non-stop service to Paris's Charles de Gaulle from Boston, St. Louis, New York's JFK, and Washington, D.C.'s Dulles. TWA also offers service to Paris (with one touchdown en route in Washington, D.C.) from Los Angeles.

Aircraft belonging to the **Air France Group** (tel. 800/237-2747) fly frequently across the Atlantic. Formed by a merger in the late 1980s that combined three of France's largest nationalized airlines: Air France, UTA (*Union des Transports Aériens*), and France's internal domestic airline, Air Inter. At press time, the conglomerate flew from both Newark (N.J.) and New York's JFK to both Charles de Gaulle and Orly in Paris. The group also flies to Paris from about 10 U.S. cities (including Los Angeles and San Francisco), as well as from Mexico City (via Houston), Montréal, and Toronto.

USAir (tel. 800/622-1015) offers daily nonstop service from Philadelphia International Airport to Paris's Orly. Because Philadelphia is one of USAir's most important hubs, connections are excellent throughout the airline's North American network.

REGULAR AIRFARES   Fares and conditions for the flights of each of the airlines listed above are highly competitive. All of them offer a consistently popular **advance-purchase excursion (APEX)** fare that requires a 30-day advance payment and a minimum stay of between 7 and 21 days. In most cases this ticket, although reasonably priced, is nonrefundable or only partially refundable and requires you to pay a penalty if you change flight dates or destination.

American Airlines offers a "30-day Advance Purchase" fare from New York to Paris costing $844 on weekdays in high season (summer) and $622 on weekdays in low season. (Flights on Friday through Sunday require a supplement of $50 each way.) Delta offers the same type of ticket from Atlanta to Paris, charging, depending on the day of travel, from $764 to $824 round-trip in winter, and about $250 more during the peak summer months. (At Delta, the date of the return portion of many APEX tickets can be changed upon payment of a $100 fee.)

Most airlines divide their year roughly into seasonal slots, with the

---

F **FROMMER'S SMART TRAVELER: AIRFARES**

1. Shop all the airlines that fly to your destination.
2. Always ask for the lowest-priced fare, not just for a discount fare.
3. Keep calling the airline—availability of cheap seats changes daily. Airline managers would rather sell a seat than have it fly empty. As the departure date nears, additional low-cost seats become available.
4. Ask about frequent-flyer programs to gain bonus miles when you book a flight.
5. Check "bucket shops" for last-minute discounts even cheaper than their advertised "slashed" fares.
6. Check about discounted land arrangements. Sometimes these are cheaper when booked with an air ticket.
7. Check "standby" fares, if any.
8. Fly free or at a heavy discount as a "courier."
9. Look for special promotional fares offered by major carriers or airlines struggling to gain a foothold in the market.

least expensive fares offered between November 1 and March 14. Shoulder season, the period between the high and low seasons, is only slightly more expensive and includes all of October, which many veteran tourists consider the ideal time to visit France. Shoulder season also extends from mid-March to mid-June.

A regular **economy-class** ticket on American Airlines, for example, is priced year round at about $1,944 (subject to change, of course), plus tax, for a round-trip journey between New York and Paris. With this ticket you can literally catch any flight, depending on seat availability, without regard to advance-booking requirements and without penalty for last-minute changes in your itinerary.

Business class offers wider seats, more leg room, and sometimes—but not always—the advantages of first class. Currently, Delta's year-round fares from Atlanta to Paris are from $3,470 round-trip in business class and $5,684 round trip in first class. Year-round fares from Cincinnati are $3,462 in business class and $5,928 in first class. These fares carry a $28 surcharge for taxes and security fees.

OTHER GOOD-VALUE CHOICES Proceed with caution through the next grab bag of suggestions. What constitutes "good value" keeps changing in the airline industry. It's hard to keep up, even if you're a travel agent. Fares change all the time, and what was the lowest possible fare one day can change the very next day when a new promotional fare is offered. So be aware of how volatile the situation is.

Bucket Shops The name originated in the 1960s, when mainstream airlines gave the then-pejorative term to resellers of blocks of unsold tickets consigned to them by major transatlantic carriers. "Bucket shop" has stuck as a label, but it might be more polite to refer to them as "consolidators." They exist in many shapes and forms. In its purest sense, a bucket shop acts as a clearinghouse for blocks of tickets that airlines discount and consign during normally slow periods of air travel.

Charter operators (see below) and bucket shops used to perform separate functions, but their offerings in many cases have been blurred recently. Many outfits perform both functions.

Tickets are discounted anywhere from 20% to 35% of the full fare. Terms of payment can vary, anywhere from 45 days before departure to last-minute sales offered in a final attempt by an airline to fill a semiempty craft.

Bucket shops abound from coast to coast, but just to get you started, here are some names. Look also for their small one-column ads in your local newspaper's travel section.

One of the biggest U.S. consolidators is **Travac,** 989 Sixth Ave., New York, NY 10018 (tel. 212/563-3303 or toll free 800/TRAV-800), which offers seats throughout the U.S. to most cities in Europe. **Access International,** 101 West 31st St., Suite 1104, New York, NY 10001 (tel. 212/465-0707 or toll free 800/TAKE-OFF), may be the country's biggest consolidator, specializing in discounted tickets to the capitals of Europe, including Paris.

Out West, you can try **Sunline Express Holidays, Inc.,** 607 Market St., San Francisco, CA 94105 (tel. 415/541-7800 or toll free 800/SUNLINE), or **Euro-Asia, Inc.,** 4203 East Indian School Rd., Suite 210, Phoenix, AZ 85018 (tel. 602/955-2742 or toll free 800/525-3876).

Since dealing with unknown bucket shops might be a little risky, it's wise to call the Better Business Bureau in your area to see if complaints have been filed against the company from which you plan to purchase a ticket.

Charter Flights For reasons of economy—never for convenience—some travelers opt for charter flights to France or to one of the countries bordering it.

Strictly speaking, a charter flight occurs on an aircraft reserved months in advance for fixed-time transit to some predetermined point. Before paying for a charter, check carefully the restrictions on your ticket or contract. You may be asked to purchase a tour package and pay far in advance. You'll pay a stiff penalty (or forfeit the ticket entirely) if you cancel. Also, charters are sometimes cancelled when the plane isn't filled. In some cases, the charter ticket seller will offer you an insurance policy for your own legitimate cancellation (hospital certificate or death in the family, for example).

There is no way to predict if a charter flight or a bucket shop will cost less than an APEX or promotional ticket on a regularly scheduled airline. You have to investigate at the time of your trip.

Some charter companies have proved unreliable in the past, leaving passengers stranded. I prefer to deal with subsidiaries (or at least affiliates) of major international carriers. Some of these include the following.

Jet Vacations, 1775 Broadway, New York, NY 10019 (tel. 212/247-0999 or 800/538-0999), is a wholly owned subsidiary of Air France and an obvious charter-line choice for Paris. Committed to filling as many seats on Air France flights as possible, and operating from many cities including New York's JFK, Newark (N.J.), Boston, Washington, D.C. (Dulles), Chicago, Miami, Houston, Los Angeles, and San Francisco, it has no objections to selling one-way tickets to Paris, space available, up until a few days before takeoff of any given flight. One-way tickets, with many restrictions attached, range in price from $250 to $320, depending on the season. Cancellations prior to eight days before your anticipated takeoff exact a penalty of $100, while cancellations within seven days or fewer of your takeoff involve a complete forfeiture of your ticket. Be warned in advance that the telephones for this company (open Monday through Saturday from 9am to 8pm) are often extremely busy, sometimes requiring very long waits. If you're interested, it's probably best to phone in the morning.

If you're visiting other countries in Europe, there are other options.

For example, you might use **Balair Ltd,** 608 Fifth Ave., Suite 803, New York, NY 10020 (tel. 212/581-3411 or toll free 800/322-5247), the charter-airline subsidiary of Swissair. It runs charter flights to Zürich and Geneva (which lies on the border of France), from New York, San Francisco, and Miami. Flights to either city from New York range from around $510 to $660, round-trip, depending on the season.

DER Tours, Inc., 380 N.W. Highway, Suite 330, Des Plaines, IL 60016 (tel. 800/782-2424), sells seats on flights to Paris at discounted prices, usually from the unsold inventories of United or Northwest Airlines. Connections from a network of North American cities are available, always with connections through Minneapolis, Boston, Detroit, or Chicago, and almost always with the added inconvenience of requiring an additional transfer of aircraft in London.

Another possibility, useful for Canadians, is **Europa Travel**

Service, 911 E. 185th St., Cleveland, OH 44119 (tel. 216/481-3612 or 800/677-1313). Especially tailored to service the needs of clients in Canada and the Midwest, it maintains an inventory of discounted seats on Air Canada's flights from Toronto to Paris, though with many restrictions attached. They also offer, depending on market conditions, discounted tickets on American, United, and Lufthansa Airlines. These include flights from anywhere in North America through Chicago to Paris's Orly, as well as to such other cities as Munich, Frankfurt, Düsseldorf, Amsterdam, and London.

Another company arranging charters is the **Council on International Educational Exchange (Council Travel),** 205 E. 42nd St., New York, NY 10017 (tel. 212/661-1414). It also provides student budget airfares in Europe, as well as discounted rail and ferry tickets.

Rebators To confuse the situation even more, rebators also compete in the low-cost airfare market. These outfits pass along to the passenger part of their commission, although many of them assess a fee for their services. Most rebators offer discounts that range from 10% to 25% (but this could vary from place to place), plus a $20 handling charge. They are not the same as travel agents, although they sometimes offer similar services including discounted land arrangements and car rentals. Their advertisements appear in small one-column ads in local newspapers.

Standbys None of the transatlantic airlines to Paris offers standby tickets any more. Even Virgin Atlantic has discontinued them, charging higher rates for last-minute bookings. In other words, the standby policy has radically changed. If anything, spur-of-the-moment tickets to Paris usually entail a surcharge above and beyond the cost to passengers who had prebooked and prepaid within the required number of days prior to departure. This policy, of course, could change by the time you actually took your trip, so if in doubt, check with the airlines yourself.

Going as a Courier This cost-cutting technique has many restrictions and tickets may be hard to come by, so it's not for everybody. Basically, you go as both an airline passenger and a courier. Couriers are hired by overnight air-freight firms hoping to skirt the often tedious Customs hassles and delays on the other end that regular cargo faces. With a courier, the checked freight sails through Customs just as quickly as your luggage would. Don't worry—the courier service is absolutely legitimate; you won't be asked to haul in illegal drugs, for example. For the service, the courier gets greatly discounted airfares or sometimes even flies free.

You're allowed one piece of carry-on luggage only; your baggage allowance is used by the courier firm to transport its cargo. As a courier, you don't actually handle the merchandise you're transporting to Europe; you just carry a manifest to present to Customs.

Upon arrival, an employee of the courier service will reclaim the company's cargo. Incidentally, you fly alone, so don't plan to travel with anyone. (A friend may be able to arrange a flight as a courier on a consecutive day.) Most courier services operate from Los Angeles or New York, but some operate out of other cities, such as Chicago or Miami. The best flight deals to such cities as Paris are during the winter season.

Courier services are often listed in the *Yellow Pages* or in advertisements in travel sections of newspapers.

To get you going, check with **Halbart Express,** 147-05 176th St., Jamaica, NY 11434 (tel. 718/656-8189 from 10am to 3pm daily).

Another firm to try is **Now Voyager** (named for the old Bette Davis movie), 74 Varick St., Suite 307, New York, NY 10013 (tel. 212/431-1616). Call daily from 11:30am to 6pm; at other times you'll get a recorded message.

The **International Association of Air Travel Couriers,** P.O. Box 1349, Lake Worth, FL 33460 (tel. 407/582-8320), for an annual membership of $35, will send you six issues of its newsletter, *Shoestring Traveler,* and about half a dozen issues of *Air Courier Bulletin,* a directory of air courier bargains around the world.

BY TRAIN

If you're already in Europe, you may want to go to Paris by train, especially if you have a Eurailpass. Even if you don't, the cost is relatively low. For example, a one-way fare from London to Paris by train (with a sea crossing) is $107 in first class and $85 in second class; from Rome to Paris (via Genoa, the shortest route) the fare is $179 in first class and $129 in second class; and from Madrid to Paris the fare is $182 in first class and $120 in second class.

Visitors from London may want to consider a British/French joint rail pass, linking the two most popular vacation spots on the Continent—Britain and France. Called **BritFrance Railpass,** it is available to North Americans, providing unlimited train travel in Britain and France, plus a round-trip ticket for travel across the English Channel via hovercraft. You may choose a total of any 5 days of unlimited rail travel during a 15-day consecutive period or 10 days during a single month—on both British and French rail networks. Adult first-class fares (any 5 days of 15) are $335; adult standard fares are $249. Youth standard fares (ages 12 to 25) are $199 for any 5 days of 15. Children ages 4 to 12 travel for half price, and those younger go free. The pass is activated the first time you use it. Passes are available at any office of FrenchRail, Inc. (tel. 800/848-7245) or at BritRail Travel International (tel. 212/575-2667) in New York City.

BY BUS

Bus travel to Paris is available not only from London but also from most major cities on the Continent. European Railways operates **Europabus** and **Eurolines.** These bus lines link Paris to major cities. In Great Britain, bus tickets are sold at all National Express offices. In Paris, the contact is Eurolines, 5 av. de la Porte de la Villette, 75019 Paris (tel. 1/40-38-93-93). If you're in Germany, contact Europabus at Mannheimerstrasse 4, 6000 Frankfurt (tel. 069/23-07-35). In the United States, contact Europabus, German Rail, 747 Third Ave., New York, NY 10017 (tel. 212/308-6447 or 800/223-6063).

BY SHIP

The days of sailing to Paris in the style of Marilyn Monroe and Jane Russell in *Gentlemen Prefer Blondes* are long gone.

The only ocean liner that makes scheduled transatlantic crossings is the **Queen Elizabeth 2** (QE2), the star and flagship of the British Cunard line. Its most frequent itinerary is between New York and England's Channel port of Southampton. From Southampton, you can go by ferry or hovercraft to France, or take a train to London, perhaps taking in a play, museums, and some shopping before flying over to Paris. Cunard offers 27 transatlantic crossings, from April to early December, between New York and Southampton.

Fares are extremely complicated, based on cabin standard and location and the season of sailing. In thrift/superthrift season—roughly defined as late autumn—sailings usually cost a minimum of $1,345 in transatlantic class and around $2,465 in first class. Prices go steeply uphill from there, eventually reaching a maximum of $10,315 for a suite in high season. These prices are per person, based on double occupancy. All passengers pay a $150 port tax and handling charges, regardless of the class of cabin. Call a travel agent or a Cunard representative at 800/221-4770. In New York City, call 212/880-7500.

BY FERRY FROM ENGLAND

About a dozen companies run hydrofoils, ferries, and hovercrafts across *La Manche,* as the French call the Channel. Services operate day and night. Most carry cars, but some hydrofoils carry passengers only. Hovercraft or hydrofoils make the trip in just 40 minutes, while slow-moving ferries might take hours, depending on conditions.

The major routes are between Dover and Folkestone and Calais and Boulogne (about 12 trips a day). Depending on weather conditions, prices and timetables can vary. It's always important to make a reservation, because ferries are crowded.

Call **Sealink** (tel. 071/834-2345) or P & O (tel. 071/734-4431) in England. For **Hoverspeed**, call 0304/21-6205. Special fares are offered, but they change frequently. It's better to contact a travel agent—say, in London—to book your ticket for you. A good travel agent will help you sort out the maze of ferry schedules and find a suitable option.

PACKAGE TOURS

Some people prefer that a tour operator take care of all the travel arrangements. There are many companies operating tours to France, each offering transportation to and within France, prearranged hotel space, and such extras as a bilingual tour guide and lectures geared more or less to your general interests.

Some operate special-interest tours, arranging meetings with local aristocracy, "famous" artists, or leaders of the resistance. Many of these celebrities are legitimate and can contribute much to your tour. Others are not, so beware of any undue sales pressure from a tour operator trying to clinch the deal, especially if the list of guest lecturers reads like the "A-list" from a social event in the ancien régime of Pre-Revolutionary France.

The French Experience, 171 Madison Ave., New York, NY 10016 (tel. 212/986-3800), offers several fly-drive programs using different types and price levels of hotels. The packages cover different regions of France and can be altered to suit individual needs.

American Express Vacations, P.O. Box 5014, Atlanta, GA 30302 (tel. toll free 800/241-1700, or 800/637-6200 in Georgia), is perhaps the most instantly recognizable tour operator in the world. Their offerings in France and the rest of Europe are probably more comprehensive than those of any other company. If they don't offer what you want, and if you are clear enough in your vision, they will package a tour for you.

GETTING TO KNOW PARIS

Ernest Hemingway referred to the many splendors of Paris as a "moveable feast" and wrote, "There is never any ending to Paris, and the memory of each person who has lived in it differs from that of any other." It is this personal discovery of the city that has always been the most compelling reason for coming to Paris. And perhaps that's why France has been called *le deuxième pays de tout le monde*—everybody's second country.

The Seine not only divides Paris into a Right Bank (*Rive Droite*) and a Left Bank (*Rive Gauche*), but it also seems to split the city into two vastly different sections and ways of life. Depending on your time, interest, and budget, you may quickly decide which section of Paris interests you the most.

1. ARRIVING

BY PLANE

Paris has two major international airports: **Orly,** 8½ miles from Paris, and **Charles de Gaulle** (also called Roissy), 14¼ miles from the city. A shuttle operates between the two airports about every 30 minutes, taking 50 to 75 minutes to make the journey. At Orly catch this bus at Exit B.

For information about transportation to Charles de Gaulle Airport, call 47-58-20-18; for Orly, call 45-50-32-30. For airport flight information, call Charles de Gaulle at 48-62-12-12 and Orly at 47-67-12-34.

CHARLES DE GAULLE AIRPORT At Charles de Gaulle Airport, foreign carriers use Aérogare 1, and Air France uses Aérogare 2. From Aérogare 1, you take a moving walkway to the passport checkpoint and the Customs area. The two terminals are linked by a shuttle bus (*navette*).

The **shuttle bus** connecting Aérogare 1 with Aérogare 2 also transports passengers to the Roissy rail station, from which fast **RER trains** leave every 15 minutes to such Métro stations as Gare du Nord, Châtelet, Luxembourg, Port-Royal, and Denfert-Rochereau. A typical fare is 30F ($5.55).

You can also take an **Air France shuttle bus**—to the Arc de Triomphe, for example—for 39F ($7.20). That ride, depending on traffic, takes less than 45 minutes. The shuttle departs about every 12 minutes between 5:45am and 11pm.

Taxis into the city will cost 150F ($27.75) to 200F ($37), depending on traffic. At night (from 8pm to 7am), fares more than double.

Buses *to* Charles de Gaulle Airport leave from the terminal in the basement of the Palais des Congrès at Port Maillot every 15 minutes to Aérogare 2 and every 20 minutes to Aérogare 1. The trip takes about 30 minutes, but during rush hours allow another half hour.

ORLY AIRPORT Orly also has two terminals—Orly Sud (south) for international flights and Orly Ouest (west) for domestic flights. They are linked by a shuttle bus.

Air France buses leave Orly Sud every 12 minutes between 5:45am and 11pm from Exit 1, heading for Gare des Invalides. At Exit D, you can board Bus 215 for place Denfert-Rochereau in the south of Paris.

A **shuttle bus** leaves Orly about every 15 minutes for the **RER train** station, Pont-de-Rungis/Aéroport-d'Orly, from which RER trains take 30 minutes into the city center. A trip to Les Invalides, for example, costs 29F ($5.35).

You can also take a **shuttle bus** from Orly Sud to the Orly train station, where high-speed RER trains leaving every 15 minutes will take you to all the central stops along the Seine. En route you can transfer to any Métro line.

A **taxi** from Orly to the center of Paris costs about 130F ($24.05), more at night. Don't take a meterless taxi from Orly Sud—it's much safer to get a metered cab from the line, which is under the scrutiny of a police officer.

Buses *to* Orly Airport leave from the Invalides terminal to either Orly Sud or Orly Ouest every 15 minutes, taking about 30 minutes.

BY TRAIN

There are six major train stations in Paris: **Gare d'Austerlitz,** 55 quai d'Austerlitz, 13e (servicing the southwest with trains to the Loire Valley, the Bordeaux country, and the Pyrénées); **Gare de l'Est,** place du 11 Novembre 1918, 10e (servicing the east, with trains to Strasbourg, Nancy, Reims, and beyond to Zürich, Basel, Luxembourg, and Austria); **Gare de Lyon,** 20 boulevard Diderot, 12e (servicing the southeast with trains to the Côte d'Azur, Provence, and beyond to Geneva, Lausanne, and Italy); **Gare Montparnasse,** 17 boulevard Vaugirard, 15e (servicing the west, with trains to Brittany); **Gare du Nord,** 18 rue de Dunkerque, 15e (servicing the north with trains to Holland, Denmark, Belgium, and the north of Germany); and **Gare St-Lazare,** 13 rue d'Amsterdam, 8e (servicing the northwest, with trains to Normandy).

For **general train information** from any of these stations, call 45-82-50-50 from 7am to 10pm daily. **To make reservations,** call 45-65-60-60 daily from 8am to 8pm. Buses operate between stations.

Note: The stations and the surrounding areas are usually seedy and frequented by pickpockets, hustlers, prostitutes, and drug addicts. Be alert, especially at night.

Each of these stations also has a Métro stop, making the whole city easily accessible. Taxis are also available at every station at designated stands. Look for the sign that says "TETE DE STATION."

BY BUS

Most buses arrive at **Gare Routière International,** 8 place Stalingrad, 19e (tel. 42-05-12-10; Métro: Stalingrad). Call 40-38-93-93 for information about international routes.

BY CAR

Driving a car in Paris is definitely not recommended. Parking is difficult and traffic is dense. If you do drive, remember that Paris is encircled by a ring road called the *périphérique.* Always obtain detailed directions to your destination, including the name of the exit on the périphérique (exits are not numbered). Avoid rush hours.

Few hotels, except the luxury ones, have garages, but the staff will usually be able to direct you to one nearby.

The major highways into Paris are the A1 from the north (Great Britain and Benelux); the A13 from Rouen, Normandy, and other points of northwest France; the A109 from Spain, the Pyrénées, and the southwest; the A7 from the French Alps, the Riviera, and Italy; and the A4 from eastern France.

TOURIST INFORMATION

The main **tourist information office** is at 127 Champs-Elysées, 8e (tel. 47-23-61-72), where you can secure information about both Paris and the provinces. The office is open daily from 9am to 8pm.

Welcome Offices in the city center will also give you free maps, brochures, and *Paris Monthly Information,* an English-language listing of all current events and performances.

CITY LAYOUT

Paris is surprisingly compact. Occupying 432 square miles (six more than San Francisco), it is home to 10 million people. As mentioned, the River Seine divides Paris into the **Right Bank** (Rive Droite) to the north and the **Left Bank** (Rive Gauche) to the south. These designations make sense when you stand on a bridge and face downstream, watching the waters flow out toward the sea—to your right is the north bank to your left the south. Thirty-two bridges link the Right and Left banks, some providing access to the two small islands at the heart of the city, **Ile de la Cité**—the city's birthplace and site of Notre-Dame—and **Ile St-Louis,** a moat-guarded oasis of sober 17th-century mansions. These islands can cause some confusion to walkers who think they've just crossed a bridge from one bank to the other, only to find themselves caught up in an almost medieval maze of narrow streets and old buildings.

MAIN ARTERIES & STREETS Between 1860 and 1870 Baron Haussmann forever changed the look of Paris by creating the legendary **boulevards:** boulevards St-Michel, St-Germain, Haussmann, Malesherbes, Sebastopol, Magenta, Voltaire, and Strasbourg.

The "main street" on the Right Bank is, of course, the **Champs-Elysées,** beginning at the Arc de Triomphe and running to the place de la Concorde. Haussmann also created avenue de l'Opéra (as well as the Opéra), and the 12 avenues that radiate starlike from the Arc de Triomphe giving it its original name, place de l'Etoile (renamed place Charles-de-Gaulle following the general's death). Today it is often referred to as place Charles-de-Gaulle–Etoile.

Haussmann also cleared Ile de la Cité of its medieval buildings, transforming it into a showcase for Notre-Dame. Finally, he laid out the two elegant parks on the western and southeastern fringes of the city: **Bois de Boulogne** and **Bois de Vincennes.**

FINDING AN ADDRESS The city of Paris is divided into 20 municipal wards called "arrondissements," each with its own mayor, city hall, police station, and central post office. Some even have remnants of market squares. Most city maps are divided by arrondissement, and all addresses include the arrondissement number (written in Roman or Arabic numerals and followed by "e" or "er"). Paris also has its own version of a zip code. Thus the proper mailing address for a hotel is written as, say, 75014 Paris. The last two digits, 14, indicate that the address is in the 14th arrondissement, in this case, Montparnasse.

Numbers on buildings running parallel to the River Seine most often follow the course of the river—that is, east to west. On perpendicular streets, numbers on buildings begin low closer to the river.

ARRONDISSEMENTS IN BRIEF

Paris's 20 arrondissements each possess a unique style and flavor. One of your first tasks will be deciding which district appeals most to you and finding accommodations there. Then try and visit as many areas as you can.

1st Arr. Located on the Right Bank, the 1st has the most popular attractions, including the Louvre, the Forum des Halles (now transformed into a modern shopping mall), Sainte Chapelle, Conciergerie, and the Jardin des Tuileries. Two of the most prestigious addresses are place Vendôme (site of the Hôtel Ritz) and Palais Royal, a section of elegant buildings and galleries surrounding the gardens to the north.

2nd Arr. Home to the Bourse, or stock exchange, the 2nd is in fact primarily a working-class district. Highlights include rue de la Paix, a traditional street of goldsmiths and furriers, and the Bibliothèque Nationale. The Right Bank district lies mainly between the Grands Boulevards and the rue Etienne-Marcel.

3rd Arr. This embraces much of Le Marais ("the marsh"), one of the best-loved Right Bank neighborhoods of Paris. Many of the buildings date from the Middle Ages, and much of the old has been saved and restored. Highlights include the Musée Picasso.

4th Arr. This area contains the Hôtel de Ville (city hall) and such major attractions as Notre-Dame (on Ile de la Cité), the Centre Pompidou, and place des Vosges, site of the Musée Victor Hugo. It also includes Ile Saint-Louis with its aristocratic town houses, courtyards, and antiques shops.

5th Arr. Known as the Latin Quarter, its attractions include the Sorbonne, the Panthéon, the Musée de Cluny, and the Jardin des Plantes. When people refer to the Left Bank they usually mean the 5th and 6th arrondissements—an area filled with students, cafés, bistros, and street life.

6th Arr. This is the heartland of Paris publishing and, for some, the most colorful part of the Left Bank. Waves of earnest young artists can be seen emerging from the Ecole des Beaux-Arts. This is one of the best areas for good budget hotels and restaurants. Highlights include the Jardin du Luxembourg and place St-Germain-des-Prés.

7th Arr. The home of the Eiffel Tower is primarily an upscale Right Bank residential and government-diplomatic area. Other highlights on the Left Bank side include Napoléon's Tomb and the Invalides Musée de l'Armée. Next to the Invalides is the city air terminal.

8th Arr. The 8th is the heart of the Right Bank and its prime showcase is the Champs-Elysées, linking the Arc de Triomphe with the delicate Obelisque on place de la Concorde. Here you'll find the fashion houses, the most elegant hotels, expensive restaurants and shops, and the most fashionably attired Parisians. Other landmarks include the Palais de l'Elysée, home of the French president; the Church of the Madeleine; the Faubourg Saint-Honoré; and the Parc de Monceau.

9th Arr. Visited primarily because of its Grands Boulevards, such as boulevard des Capucines and boulevard des Italiens, the 9th also includes the Quartier de l'Opéra and the strip joints of Pigalle (the infamous "pig alley" for the G.I.s of World War II). Other major attractions are the Musée Grevin (the major waxworks of Paris) and the Folies Bergère.

10th Arr. The Gare du Nord and Gare de l'Est are both in this commercial district. Movie theaters and porno houses often dot this area.

11th Arr. Increasingly fashionable, this is the site of place de la Bastille and the new Bastille opera house. For many decades, it has been a working-class district, attracting immigrants from all over the world.

12th Arr. Very few tourists come here, but when a famous French chef opened the restaurant Au Trou Gascon *tout le monde* showed up (see "Paris Dining," Chapter 5). Its major attraction is the Bois de Vincennes, a popular patch of woodland with boating lakes, a racecourse, and a zoo. The Gare de Lyon is located here, too.

13th Arr. This primarily working-class district grew up around the famous Gobelins tapestries works (which can still be visited today—see Chapter 6). The Gare d'Austerlitz is a landmark.

14th Arr. Montparnasse, home of the "lost generation," is well known to tourists. Stein, Toklas, Hemingway, and other American expatriates gathered here in the 1920s. After World War II it ceased to be the center of intellectual life in Paris, but the memory lingers on in its cafés.

15th Arr. Beginning at Gare Montparnasse, the 15th stretches all the way to the Seine. In land mass and population, it's the largest

PARIS BY ARRONDISSEMENT

RIGHT BANK ARRONDISSEMENTS:

1er 12e
2e 16e
3e 17e
4e 18e
8e 19e
9e 20e
10e
11e

LEFT BANK ARRONDISSEMENTS:

5e
6e
7e
13e
14e
15e

quartier of Paris, but it attracts few tourists and has few attractions, except for the Parc des Expositions and the Institut Pasteur. In the early 20th century, many artists—Chagall, Léger, and Modigliani—lived in this arrondissement in "The Beehive."

16th Arr. Originally the village of Passy, where Benjamin Franklin lived most of his years in Paris, this district is still reminiscent of Proust's world. Highlights include the Bois de Boulogne; the Jardin du Trocadéro; the Musée de Balzac, the Musée Guimet (famous for its Asian collections); and the Cimetière de Passy, resting place of Manet, Talleyrand, Giraudoux, and Debussy.

17th Arr. Although partly in the 8th, Parc Monceau flows into the 17th. This is the home of the Palais des Congrès and Porte Maillot Air Terminal.

18th Arr. The 18th is the most famous outer *quartier* of Paris, embracing Montmartre, associated with such legendary names as the Moulin Rouge, the Basilica of Sacré-Coeur, and the place du Tertre. Utrillo was its native son, Renoir lived here, and Toulouse-Lautrec adopted the area as his own. The most famous enclave of artists in Paris, the Bateau-Lavoir, of Picasso fame, gathered here. Max Jacob, Matisse, and Braque all came and went from here. Today, place Blanche is known for its prostitutes, and Montmarte is filled with honky-tonks and terrible restaurants. Go for the attractions and the *memoires*. The most famous flea market, Marché aux Puces de Saint-Ouen, is another landmark.

19th Arr. Today visitors come to what was once the village of La Villette to see the new Cité des Sciences et de l'Industrie, a spectacular science museum and park. The district also includes Les Buttes–Chaumont, a park where kids can enjoy puppet shows and donkey rides.

20th Arr. Its greatest landmark is Père Lachaise Cemetery, resting place of Edith Piaf, Marcel Proust, Oscar Wilde, Isadora Duncan, Sarah Bernhardt, Gertrude Stein, Colette, and many, many others.

MAPS

If you're staying more than two or three days, purchase an inexpensive, pocket-size book that includes the "plan de Paris" by arrondissement available at all major newsstands and bookshops. Most of these guides provide you with a Métro map, a fold-out map of the city, and indexed maps of each arrondissement, with all streets listed and keyed.

2. GETTING AROUND

Paris is a city for strollers whose greatest joy in life is rambling through unexpected alleyways and squares. Given a choice of conveyance, make it your own two feet every time possible. Only when you're dead tired and can't walk another step, or in a roaring hurry to reach an exact destination, should you consider the following swift and prosaic means of urban transport.

BY PUBLIC TRANSPORTATION

DISCOUNT PASSES If you're staying for a week or longer, purchase one of several long-term passes, any of which allows unlimited travel on the city's Métro and buses within Paris city limits. A six-day pass (*coupon jaune*) costs 54F ($10), a monthly pass (*carte*

1ST ARRONDISSEMENT

0 ———— 250 m
275 y

Arc de Triomphe du Carrousel ⑨	Musée du Louvre ⑪
Forum des Halles ⑰	Musée de l'Orangerie ③
Jardin du Carrousel ⑧	Palais du Louvre ⑫
Jardin du Palais Royal ⑯	Palais Royal ⑮
Jardin des Tuileries ④	Place du Carrousel ⑩
Jeu de Paume ②	Place de la Concorde ①
Louvre des Antiquaires ⑬	Place du Palais Royal ⑭
Musée des Arts Décoratifs ⑦	Place Vendôme ⑤
	St-Germain Auxerrois ⑱
	St-Roch ⑥

PARIS

1er
Arrondissement

orange), 190F ($35.15). Bring an ID photograph with you to apply for the card, and ask for one at any Métro ticket counter.

Another possibility is to purchase a *Le Paris-Visite* pass, a tourist pass valid for three or five days on the public transportation system, including the Métro, city buses, even RER (Réseau Express Régional) trains. (The RER contains both first- and second-class compartments, and the pass lets you travel in first class.) As a special bonus, the funicular ride to the top of Montmartre is also included. The cost is 80F ($14.80) for three days or 130F ($24.05) for five days. The card is available at RATP (Régie Autonome des Transports Parisiens), tourist offices, or at the main Métro stations. It can also be purchased at **Marketing Challenges,** 10 East 21st Street, New York, NY 10010 (tel. 212/529-8484).

BY SUBWAY

The **Métro** (tel. 43-46-14-14 for information) is the most efficient means of transportation, and it's easy to use. Each line is numbered and the final destination of each is clearly marked on subway maps, on the trains themselves, and in the underground passageways. Most stations display a map of the system at the entrance. Figure out the route from where you are to your destination, noting the stations where you will have to change. To make sure you catch the right train, find your destination, then visually follow the line it's on to the end of the route and note its name. This is the *direction* you follow in the stations and see on the train. Transfer stations are known as *correspondances.* (Note that some require long walks—Châtelet is the most notorious.)

Most trips will require only one transfer. Many of the larger stations have maps with pushbutton indicators that will help you plot your route more easily by lighting up automatically when you press the button for your destination. A ride on the urban lines costs the same to any point.

On the Sceaux, the Noisy-Saint-Léger, and the Saint-Germain-en-Laye lines serving the suburbs, fares are based on distance. One ticket costs 5.50F ($10.20). A *carnet* (ticket book) is the best buy—5 tickets for 17.50F ($32.40) or 10 tickets for 34.50F ($63.85).

You can also purchase *Formule 1* for 23F ($42.55), allowing unlimited travel on the city's network of subways for one day.

At the turnstile entrances to the station, insert your ticket in the turnstile and pass through. At some exits tickets are checked, so hold on to your ticket. There are occasional ticket checks on the trains, platforms, and passageways, too.

If you are changing trains, get out and determine toward which *direction* (final destination) on the next line you want to head, and follow the bright-orange "CORRESPONDANCE" signs until you reach the proper platform. Don't follow a "SORTIE" sign, which means "Exit," or else you'll have to pay another fare to resume your journey.

The Métro starts running daily at 5:30am and closes around 1:15am. It's reasonably safe at any hour, but beware of pickpockets.

BY BUS

Bus travel is much slower than the subway. Most buses run from 6:30am to 9:15pm (a few operate until 12:30am, and a handful operate during the early-morning hours). Service is limited on Sunday and holidays. Bus and Métro fares are the same and you can use the same *carnet* tickets on both. Most bus rides require one ticket, but there are some destinations requiring two (never more than two within the city limits).

At certain bus stops, signs list the destinations and numbers of the buses serving that point. Destinations are usually listed north to south, and east to west. Most stops along the way are also posted on

PARIS

2e Arrondissement

Basilique Notre Dame des Victoires ❸

Bibliothèque Nationale ❻

Bourse des Valeurs ❷

Hôtel Colbert ❺

Musée Cognacq-Jay ❽

Notre Dame de Bonne Nouvelle ❶

Place de l'Opéra ❼

Place des Victoires ❹

the sides of the buses. To catch a bus, wait in line at the bus stop. Signal the driver to stop the bus and board in order. During rush hours you may have to take a ticket from the dispensing machine, indicating your position in the line.

If you intend to use the buses frequently, pick up a RATP bus map at the office on place de la Madeleine, 8e; at the tourist offices at RATP headquarters, 53 bis, quai des Grands Augustins, 75006 Paris, or write to them ahead of time. For detailed information on bus and Métro routes, call 43-46-14-14.

BY TAXI

It's impossible to secure one at rush hour, so don't even try. Taxi drivers are strongly organized into an effective lobby to keep their number limited to 14,300.

Watch out for the common rip-offs. Always check the meter to make sure you're not paying the previous passenger's fare. Beware of cabs without meters, which often wait for tipsy patrons outside nightclubs—always settle the tab in advance. Regular cabs can be hailed on the street when their signs read "LIBRE." Taxis are easier to find at the many stands near Métro stations.

The flag drops at 9.50F ($1.75), and you pay 2.58F (50¢) per kilometer. If your trip takes you outside the boundaries of the arrondissements, you'll pay 4.02F (75¢) per kilometer. At night, expect to pay 5.30F ($1) per kilometer.

On airport trips you're not required to pay for the driver's empty return ride, but you'll pay 4.20F (80¢) extra to be delivered to railroad stations.

You are allowed several small pieces of luggage free if they're transported inside and do not weigh more than 5 kg. Heavier suitcases carried in the trunk cost 3.50F (65¢ per piece). Tip 12% to 15%—the latter usually elicits a *merci*.

BY CAR

Don't even consider driving a car in Paris. Streets are narrow and parking is next to impossible. Besides, most visitors don't have the nerve, skill, and ruthlessness required.

If you insist on ignoring my advice, here are a few tips: Get an excellent street map and ride with a co-pilot because there's no time to think at intersections. "Zone Bleue" means that weekdays and Saturdays you can't park without a parking disc, obtainable from garages, police stations, and hotels. Parking is unrestricted in these zones Sunday and holidays. Attach the disc to your windshield, setting its clock to show the time of arrival. Between 9am and noon and from 2:30 to 5pm you may park for one hour, from noon to 2:30pm for 2½ hours.

Watch for the gendarmes, who lack patience and consistently countermand the lights. Horn-blowing is absolutely forbidden except in dire emergencies.

RENTALS The major car-rental companies usually match one another's price schedules and rental conditions. Of the major worldwide competitors, the cheapest weekly arrangements, as of this writing and subject to change, are offered by Avis and Budget, followed by Hertz and National. These relative advantages change (sometimes radically) as the categories of car become more luxurious, but in almost every case, the best deal involves a weekly rental with unlimited mileage and an advance reservation *from within North America* at least two business days in advance. Shop around before you commit yourself, knowing that it pays to ask questions.

Warning: All car-rental bills in France are subject to a 22% government tax, among the highest in Europe.

Renting a car in Paris (and France) is easy. You need a valid driver's license and must be at least 21 years old for the cheaper models, and at least 25 for the more expensive vehicles. Renters must also present

PARIS
3ᵉ & 4ᵉ
Arrondissements

Archives Nationales ❾
Carreau du Temple ❹
Centre Georges Pompidou ⑫
Conservatoire National des Arts et Métiers ❶
Hôtel Dieu de Cité ㉑
Hôtel de Rohan ❽
Hôtel de Ville ⑭
Ile de la Cité ㉒
Ile Saint-Louis ⑰
Musée Carnavalet ❺
Musée de l'Histoire de France ❿
Musée Mickiewicz ⑲
Musée de la Musique Mécanique ⑪
Musée de la Serrure ❻
Musée Picasso ❼
Musée Victor Hugo ⑳
Notre Dame ❷
Palais de la Jeunesse ❷
Saint-Gervais et Saint-Protais ⑮
Saint-Louis-en-l'Ile ⑱
Saint-Nicholas-des-Champs ❸
Tour Saint-Jacques ⑬

a valid passport and a valid credit card unless payment is arranged in North America before leaving home. It usually isn't obligatory, but some small companies sometimes require an international driver's license.

A collision-damage waiver (CDW), costing between 65F ($12) and 90F ($16.65) extra per day, depending on the value of the car, will eliminate most (or all, depending on the company) of your financial responsibility in the event of theft or accidental damage to your car. It's a good idea to take it, although certain credit-card issuers will agree—if the imprint of their credit card appears on the original rental contract—to pay for any accident-related liability. (This varies broadly from company to company and must be confirmed individually with your credit-card issuer.) At all four of the contenders, the least expensive car will probably be a two-door Ford Fiesta with manual transmission and few frills. Prices range between 1,000F ($185) and 1,200F ($222) per week, depending on the company and whatever discount might apply. (Membership in AAA sometimes grants a small discount at some of the companies.) Additional discounts are usually granted for rentals of two weeks or more. Automatic transmission is regarded as a luxury in Europe, so if you need it, you'll pay dearly for it.

Avis (tel. 800/331-1084) has offices in Paris at both Orly and Charles de Gaulle airports, as well as an inner-city headquarters at 5 rue Bixio, 7e (tel. 45-50-32-31), near the Eiffel Tower. The best rates are given to drivers who reserve a car at least two business days before leaving North America.

Budget Rent-a-Car (tel. 800/527-0700) has 29 locations inside Paris and dozens of others throughout France. Cars can usually be picked up in one French city and dropped off in another (and often in large cities in Germany, Switzerland, The Netherlands, and Spain as well) for no additional charge if you notify the company in advance. Otherwise, there's an extra charge of 700F ($129.50). Though its rates were competitive and its cars well-maintained, Budget did not permit its French cars to be driven anywhere within Britain. Clients who want to protect themselves against international currency-exchange fluctuations can ask Budget to "lock" the exchange rate in effect at the time of booking. In such cases, a reservation must be made and paid for in North America at least 14 days before the anticipated pickup of the car.

Hertz (tel. 800/654-3001) has about a dozen locations as well as offices at Orly and Charles de Gaulle. The company's main office in Paris is at 27 rue St-Ferdinand, 17e (tel. 45-74-97-39). A discounted weekly rental must be reserved at least two days in advance. Be sure to ask about any promotional discounts the company might be offering.

National Car Rental (tel. 800/227-3876) is represented in Paris by **Europcar,** whose largest office lies at 145 avenue Malakoff, 16e (tel. 45-00-08-06). It also has offices at both of the Paris airports and at another dozen or so locations within the city. Its headquarters can rent you a car on the spot, but to qualify for the cheaper weekly rental you must reserve at least two days in advance by calling the number above.

Gasoline   Gasoline—or *essence,* as it's known in France—is extraordinarily expensive for the visitor accustomed to North American prices. Currently, *essence ordinaire* sells for about 6F ($1.10) per liter, which works out to around 20F ($3.70) per gallon. All but the least expensive cars usually require an octane rating that the French classify as *super,* which costs about $1 more per gallon. Depending on your car, you'll need either leaded (*avec plomb*) or unleaded (*sans plomb*). What this translates into is that filling the tank of a medium-size car can eventually cost between $40 and $60.

Driving Rules   Everyone in the car, in both the front and back seats, must wear seat belts. Children under 12 must ride in the back seat. Drivers are supposed to yield to the car on their right, except

Alliance Française ❽
Hôtel des Monnaies ❷
Institut de France ❶
Jardin des Plantes ⓮
Jardin du Luxembourg ❼
Musée de Cluny ⓬
Musée Delacroix ❸
Musée National d'Histoire Naturelle ⓯
Observatoire ❾
Palais du Luxembourg ❻
Panthéon ❿
Saint-Germain-des-Prés ❿
Saint-Séverin ⓭
Saint-Sulpice ❺
Sorbonne ⓫

Church ✝   Post Office ■   Métro Ⓜ

where signs indicate otherwise, for instance, at traffic circles. If you violate the speed limits, expect a large fine. Speed limits are usually 130 kmph (80 m.p.h.) on expressways, about 100 kmph (60 m.p.h.) on major national highways, and 90 kmph (56 m.p.h.) on small country roads. In towns, don't exceed 60 kmph (37 m.p.h.).

Maps Before setting out from Paris on a tour of that city's environs, pick up a good regional map of the district you plan to explore. If you're visiting a town, ask at the local tourist office for a town plan. They are usually given away free.

For France as a whole, most motorists opt for the Michelin map 989. For regions, Michelin publishes a series of yellow maps that are quite good. Large travel bookstores in North America carry these maps, but they are commonly available in France and at lower prices. One useful feature of the Michelin map (in this age of congested traffic) is its designations of alternative *routes de dégagement,* which let you skirt big cities and avoid traffic-clogged highways.

Breakdowns/Assistance A breakdown is called *une panne* in France, and it is just as frustrating there as anywhere else. Call the police at 17, anywhere in France, and they will put you in touch with the nearest garage. Most local garages have towing services. If your breakdown should occur on an expressway, find the nearest roadside emergency phone box, pick up the phone, and put a call through. You'll be immediately connected to the nearest breakdown service facility.

BY BICYCLE

To ride a bicycle through the streets and parks of Paris, perhaps with a *baguette* tucked under your arm, might have been a fantasy of yours since you saw your first Maurice Chevalier film. If the idea appeals to you, you won't be alone: The city in recent years has added many miles of right-hand lanes specifically designated for cyclists, and hundreds of bike racks scattered throughout the city. (When these aren't available, many Parisians simply chain their bike to the nearest available fence or lamp post.) Cycling is especially popular within Paris's larger parks and gardens.

One of the largest companies in Paris concerned with bicycle rentals is the **Bicy-Club,** 8 place de la Porte-de-Champerret, 17e (tel. 47-66-55-92; Metro: Porte-de-Champerret) which maintains at least a half-dozen rental outlets within the parks and gardens of the Paris region, usually on weekends and holidays between March and November. Two of the company's most popular outlets include a kiosk behind the Relais du Rois, route de Suresnes, in the Bois de Boulogne, and another kiosk in the Bois de Vincennes near the entrance to the Parc Floral, near the Esplanade du Château. Rates are 17F to 30F ($3.15 to $5.55) per hour, depending on the bike, or else from 68F to 120F ($12.60 to $22.20) per day. Deposits ranging from 1,000F to 2,000F ($185 to $370) must be posted. The centers are open from mid-March through November on Saturday, Sunday, and holidays from 9am to 7pm.

FAST FACTS **PARIS**

Airport See "Arriving" in this chapter.

American Express Offices are located at 11 rue Scribe, 9e (tel. 42-66-09-99), which is close to the Opéra (also the Métro stop). Hours are 9am–5:30pm Mon–Fri. The bank window is open Sat 9am–5pm, but you can't pick up mail until Monday. Other offices are at 5 rue de Chaillot, 16e (tel. 47-23-61-20; Métro: Alma-Marceau), 83 bis, rue de Courcelles, 17e (tel. 47-66-03-00; Métro: Courcelles), and 38 av. de Wagram, 8e (tel. 42-27-58-80; Métro: Ternes).

400 m
0
440 y

pont du Carrousel

pont Royal

pont Solférino

pont de la Concorde

pont Alexandre III

pont des Invalides

pont de l'Alma

pont d'Iéna

Seine

square Chaise Récamier
square Boucicaut
place de Saint Thomas d'Aquin
RUE DU BAC
SEVRES BABYLONE
SOLFERINO
bd. Raspail
MUSÉE D'ORSAY
Jardin de Babylone
rue du Bac
CHAMBRE DES DEPUTES
VANEAU
VARENNE
SAINT FRANCOIS XAVIER
DUROC
bd. des Invalides
INVALIDES
Esplanade des Invalides
place des Invalides
place Vauban
av. de Villars
av. de Breteuil
SEGUR
Jardin de l'Intendant
LATOUR MAUBOURG
ECOLE MILITAIRE
place de l'Ecole Militaire
place de Fontenoy
parc du Champ de Mars
place Joffre
place Jacques Rueff

PARIS
7e Arrondissement

Church ✝ Post Office ⊠ Métro Ⓜ

Basilique Sainte Clotilde ⑫	Musée d'Orsay ⑮	
Ecole Militaire ③	Musée Rodin ⑬	
Eglise du Dôme ⑤	Parc du Champ de Mars ②	
Esplanade des Invalides ⑩	Palais Bourbon ⑪	
Hôtel des Invalides ⑧	Saint François Xavier ⑤	
Hôtel Matignon ⑭	Saint Louis ⑥	
Musée de l'Armée ⑨	Saint Thomas d'Aquin ⑯	
Musée de l'Ordre de la Liberation ⑦	Tour Eiffel ①	
	UNESCO ④	

Area Code Paris's telephone area code is 1, followed by the eight-digit number. No other provinces have area codes. However, to dial long distance anywhere within France, you must first dial 16.

Auto Clubs The Automobile Club de L'Ile de France, 14 av. de la Grande-Armée, 75017 Paris (tel. 43-80-68-58, 24 hours), is open Mon–Fri 9am–6pm. The staff will answer all questions about transportation in France and deliver complimentary documents to those who want to travel in France. They also provide road assistance (call the main office), but not for free. It's not an option for most visitors, though, because you must join for at least six months.

Babysitters **Institut Catholique,** 21 rue d'Assas, 6e (tel. 45-48-31-70), offers a service with its students. The price is 28F ($5.20) an hour. The main office is open from 9am–noon and 2–6pm Mon–Sat only. One tip: It is advisable to verify that the sitter and your child speak the same language before you commit yourself.

Banks American Express may be able to meet most of your banking needs. If not, banks in Paris are open 9am–4:30pm Mon–Fri. A few are open on Saturday. Ask at your hotel for the location of the bank nearest to you. Shops and most hotels will cash your traveler's checks, but not at the advantageous rate a bank or foreign exchange office will give you, so make sure you've allowed enough funds for *le weekend*.

Bookstores Paris has several English-language bookstores carrying American and British books and maps and guides to the city and other destinations. Try **Brentano's,** 37 av. de l'Opéra, 2e (tel. 42-61-52-50; Métro: Opéra), open Mon–Sat 10am–7pm; or **Galignani,** 224 rue de Rivoli, 1e (tel. 42-60-76-07); Métro: Tuileries), open Mon–Sat 10am–7pm. Most famous of all is **Shakespeare and Company,** 37 rue de la Bûcherie, 5e (no phone; Métro or RER: St-Michel). It's open daily 11am–midnight.

Business Hours French business hours are erratic, as befits a nation of individualists. Most **museums** close one day a week (often Tues). They are generally closed on national holidays. Usual hours are 9:30am–5pm. Some museums, particularly the smaller and less-staffed ones, close for lunch from noon–2pm. Most French museums are open Sat; many are closed Sun morning but are open Sun afternoon. Again, refer to the individual museum listings. Generally, **offices** are open Mon–Fri 9am–5pm, but don't count on it. Always call first. **Stores** are open from 9 or 9:30am (often 10am) to 6 or 7pm without a break for lunch. Some shops, particularly those operated by foreigners, open at 8am and close at 8 or 9pm. In some small stores the lunch break can last three hours, beginning at 1pm.

Cameras/Film See "Photographic Needs," below.

Car Rentals See "Getting Around" in this chapter.

Cigarettes Bring in as many as Customs will allow if you're addicted to a particular brand, because American cigarettes are very expensive in France. A possible solution is to learn to smoke French cigarettes. Don't expect them to taste anything like your familiar brand, but you may acquire a liking for the exotic. One of the most popular French cigarettes is called Gauloise Bleu.

Climate See "When to Go" in Chapter 2.

Currency See "Information, Entry Requirements & Money" in Chapter 2.

Currency Exchange For the best exchange rate, cash your traveler's checks at banks or foreign-exchange offices, not at shops and hotels. Most post offices will also change traveler's checks or convert currency. Currency exchanges are also found at Paris airports and train stations. One of the most central currency-exchange branches in Paris is at 154 av. des Champs-Elysées, 8e (tel. 42-25-93-33; Métro: George-V). It's open Mon–Fri 9am–5pm and Sat and Sun 10:30am–6pm. A small commission is charged.

Dentists If a toothache strikes you at night or in the early hours of the morning (and doesn't it always?), telephone 43-37-51-00 anytime between 8pm and 8am Mon–Fri. On Saturday, Sunday, and holidays, you can call this number day or night. You also can call or visit the **American Hospital,** 63 bd. Victor-Hugo, Neuilly (tel. 46-41-25-25). A bilingual (English-French) dental clinic is on the premises. **Métro:** Pont de Levallois or Pont de Neuilly. **Bus:** 82.

Doctors   Some large hotels have a doctor attached to their staff. If yours doesn't, I recommend the **American Hospital,** 63 bd. Victor-Hugo, Neuilly (tel. 46-41-25-25). The emergency room is open 24 hours daily with 43 outpatient and inpatient specialists housed under one roof. **Métro:** Pont de Levallois or Pont de Neuilly. **Bus:** 82.

    Documents Required See "Information, Entry Requirements & Money" in Chapter 2.

    Driving Rules See "Getting Around" in this chapter.

    Drug Laws A word of warning: Penalties for illegal drug possession in France are more severe than those in the United States or Canada. You could go to jail or be deported immediately. By law, the police can stop you and search you at will. *Caveat:* Drug pushers often turn in their customers to the police.

Drugstores Go to the nearest *pharmacie*. If you need a prescription during off-hours, have your concierge get in touch with the nearest Commissariat de Police. An agent there will have the address of a nearby pharmacy open 24 hours a day. French law requires that the pharmacies in any given neighborhood designate which one will remain open all night. The address of the one that will stay open for that particular week will be prominently displayed in the windows of all other drugstores. One of the most centrally located all-night pharmacies is **Pharmacy Dhery,** 84 av. des Champs-Elysées, 8e (tel. 45-62-02-41). **Métro:** George-V.

Electricity   In the main, expect 200 volts, 50 cycles, although you'll encounter 110 and 115 volts in some older establishments. Adapters are needed to fit sockets. Many hotels have two-pin (in some cases, three-pin) sockets for electric razors. It's best to ask at your hotel before plugging in any electrical appliance.

Embassies & Consulates   If you lose your passport or have some such emergency, the consulate can usually handle your individual needs. An embassy is more often concerned with matters of state between France and the home country represented. Hours and offices of the various foreign embassies and consulates follow. **United States:** The embassy at 2 av. Gabriel, 75008 Paris (tel. 42-96-12-02), is open Mon–Fri 9am–4pm. Passports are issued at its consulate at 2 rue St-Florentin (tel. 42-96-12-02, ext. 2531), which lies off the northeast section of place de la Concorde (Métro: Concorde). To get a passport replaced costs about $42. In addition to its embassy and consulate in Paris, the United States also maintains the following consulates: 22 cours du Maréchal-Foch, 33080 Bordeaux (tel. 56-52-65-95); 7 quai Général-Sarrail, 69454 Lyon (tel. 78-24-68-49); 12 bd. Paul-Peytral, 13286 Marseille (tel. 91-54-92-00); and 15 av. d'Alsace, 67082 Strasbourg (tel. 88-35-31-04). **Canada:** The embassy is at 35 av. Montaigne, 75008 Paris (tel. 47-23-01-01), open Mon–Fri 9–11:30am and 2–4pm. The Canadian Consulate is around the corner at 16 rue d'Anjou (same phone). New passports are issued at the latter address (Métro: F.D. Roosevelt or Alma-Marceau). **Great Britain:** The embassy is at 35 rue du Faubourg St-Honoré, 75383 Paris (tel. 42-96-12-02), open Mon–Fri 9:30am–1pm and 2:30–6pm (Métro: Concorde or Madeleine). **Australia:** The embassy is at 4 rue Jean-Rey, 75015 Paris (tel. 40-59-33-00), open Mon–Fri 9:15am–12:15pm and 2–4:30pm (Métro: Bir-Hakeim). **New Zealand:** The embassy is at 7 bis, rue Leonard-de-Vinci, 75016 Paris (tel. 45-00-24-11), open Mon–Fri 9am–1pm and 2:30–6pm (Métro: Victor-Hugo).

Emergencies   For the **police,** call 17; to **report a fire,** 18. For an ambulance, call the fire department at 45-78-74-52; a fire vehicle rushes cases to the nearest emergency room. **S.A.M.U.** (tel. 45-67-50-50) is an independently operated, privately owned ambulance company. Or contact **S.O.S. Médecin** (tel. 47-07-77-77) for a mobile doctor with car radio. You can reach the police at 9 bd. du Palais, 4e (tel. 42-60-33-22; Métro: Cité).

Etiquette   If you make a reservation at a restaurant, keep it or call in good time to cancel. Always refer to your waiter as *"monsieur,"* not *"garçon."* When entering a shop or café, nod and greet strangers with a "Monsieur" or "Madame." Be aware of your voice level in public places—the French are. Refrain from smoking between courses in restaurants. Avoid discussing money, salaries, size of houses, and horsepower of U.S. cars compared with French cars. Discussions about World War II, the Algerian revolution, religion, or politics can sometimes spark violent controversy, especially at gatherings of extended families.

Eyeglasses   **Lissac Brothers (Frères Lissac)** is one of the city's largest chains, with at least 18 branches in greater Paris. On the Right Bank, go to 112–114 rue de Rivoli, 1e (tel. 42-33-44-77; Métro: Louvre), and on the Left, to 51 bd. St-Michel, 5e (tel.

14TH ARRONDISSEMENT

300 m
330 y

13e

Cimetière du Montparnasse ③	Porte de Châtillon ⑩
Cimetière de Montrouge ⑨	Porte d'Orléans ⑧
Cité Internationale Universitaire de Paris ⑦	Porte de Vanves ⑪
Galeries Lafayette ①	Saint-Pierre de Montrouge ⑤
Observatoire de Paris ④	Tour Montparnasse ②
Parc Montsouris ⑥	

PARIS

14e Arrondissement

43-54-24-07; Métro: St-Michel). There's a surcharge for same-day service. Always carry an extra pair.

Hairdressers/Barbers In France, they're known as *coiffeurs*. One of the best is **Alexandre de Paris,** 3 av. Matignon, 8e (tel. 42-25-57-90; Métro: F.D. Roosevelt). Everybody from crowned heads to French film stars comes here for that elegant look. Always call for an appointment. **Harlow,** 24 rue St-Denis, 1er (tel. 42-33-61-36; Métro: Châtelet), is also good. As one satisfied customer put it,

"Harlow is with it and yet not too far out." The team specializes in coiffeurs calling for minimum care. An appointment is needed.

Holidays See "When to Go" in Chapter 2.

Hospitals The **American Hospital,** 63 bd. Victor Hugo, Neuilly (tel. 46-41-25-25), operates 24-hour emergency service. **Métro:** Pont de Levallois or Pont de Neuilly. **Bus:** 82.

Hotlines See Section 3, "Networks & Resources," below.

Information See "Information, Entry Requirements & Money" in Chapter 2.

Language In the wake of two World Wars and many shared experiences, not to mention the influence of English movies, TV, and records, the English language has made major inroads and is almost a second language in some parts of Paris. An American trying to speak French might even be understood. The world's best-selling phrase books are published by Berlitz—*French for Travellers* has everything you'll need.

Laundry/Dry Cleaning Ask at your hotel for the nearest laundry or dry-cleaning establishment. Expensive hotels provide this service, but it costs. Instead, consult the *Yellow Pages* under *laveries automatiques*. For dry-cleaning, look under *nettoyage à sec*. If you're staying in the Latin Quarter, take your clothes for cleaning or pressing to **Moderne des Ecoles,** 34 rue des Ecoles, 5e (tel. 46-33-47-13, Métro: Maubert-Mutalité), open Tues–Sun 8am–7:30pm. Another well-located laundry in the same quarter is **St-Germain Lav' Club,** 9 rue Lobineau, 6e (Metro: Mabillon). Don't call—just show up, dirty laundry in hand. It's open daily 7am–10pm.

Libraries There are many. The **American Library,** 10 rue du Général Camou, 7e (tel. 45-51-46-82; Métro: Alma-Marceau), founded in 1920, allows nonmembers to read for 30F ($5.55) per day. **Bibliothèque Publique Information,** Centre Pompidou, place Georges-Pompidou, 3e (tel. 42-77-12-33; Métro: Rambuteau), has books in English. There's also a video and listening room. You can read on the premises, but you can't check out books. It's open Mon–Fri noon–10pm and Sat and Sun 10am–10pm.

Legal Aid This may be hard to come by in Paris. The French government advises foreigners to consult their embassy or consulate (see "Embassies & Consulates," above) in case of a dire emergency, such as an arrest. Even if a consulate or embassy declines to offer financial or legal help, they will generally offer advice as to how you can obtain help locally. For example, they can furnish a list of attorneys who might represent you. Most arrests are for illegal possession of drugs, and the U.S. embassy and consulate officials cannot interfere with the French judicial system in any way on your behalf. A consulate can only advise you of your rights.

Liquor Laws Visitors will find it easier to get a drink—wine, beer, or other spirits—in France than in England or some other countries. Supermarkets, grocery stores, and cafés sell alcoholic beverages. The legal drinking age is 16. Persons under that age can be served an alcoholic drink in a bar or restaurant if accompanied by a parent or legal guardian. Wine and liquor are sold every day of the week all year round.

Hours of cafés vary throughout the country and with local restrictions. Some open at 6am, serving drinks until 3am; others are open 24 hours a day. Bars and nightclubs may stay open as they wish.

The Breathalyzer test is in use in France, and a motorist is considered "legally intoxicated" with 0.8 grams of alcohol per liter of

PARIS

16e
Arrondissement

Arc de Triomphe **2**
Cimitière de Passy **15**
Hippodrome d'Auteuil **22**
Jardin Ranelagh **18**
Jardins du Trocadéro **9**
Maison de
  Radio-France **24**
Musée Armenian &
  Musée d'Ennery **5**
Musée de l'Art Modern **8**
Musée du Cinéma **10**
Musée Clemenceau **16**
Musée de la
  Contrefaçon **4**
Musée Guimet **6**
Musée Henri
  Bouchard **23**
Musée de l'Homme **13**
Musée de la Marine **14**
Musée Marmottan **21**
Musée des
  Monument Français **1**
Musée du Vin **17**
Palais de Chaillot **12**
Palais Galliera **7**
Porte d'Auteuil **25**
Porte Dauphine **3**
Porte Maillot **1**
Porte Molitor **26**
Porte de la Muette **19**
Porte de Passy **20**
Porte de St-Cloud **27**

16TH ARRONDISSEMENT

Church ✝
Post Office ⊠
Métro Ⓜ

blood. (The more liberal U.S. law is 1 gram per liter.) If convicted, a
motorist faces a stiff fine and a possible prison term of two months to
two years. If bodily injury results, the judge might throw the book at
a convicted person.

Lost Property   Frankly, there isn't much chance of retriev-
ing lost property in Paris. Go to (don't call) the **Bureau des Objets Trouvés,** 36 rue des Morillons, 15e (tel. 45-31-14-80;
Métro: Convention). Open Fri–Mon 8am–5pm and Tues–Thurs
8am–8pm.

Luggage Storage/Lockers   Your best bet is your hotel, especially if you plan to return to Paris after a tour of the provinces. Otherwise try the *consignes* at the railroad stations.

Mail   Most post offices in Paris are open Mon–Fri 8am–7pm and Sat 8am–noon. Allow five to eight days to send or receive mail from your home. To send an *aerogramme* to the U.S. or Canada costs 4.20F (80¢). To send a letter weighing 20 or 30 grams (about an ounce) costs 9.60F ($1.80). A postcard to the U.S. or Canada is 3.40F (65¢).

If you don't have a hotel address in Paris, you can receive mail c/o American Express (see above). However, you may be asked to show an American Express card or traveler's check when you go to pick up your mail.

Another option is to send your mail *poste restante* (general delivery) in care of the major post office in whatever town you plan to visit. You'll need to produce a passport to pick up mail, and you may be charged a small fee for the service. You can also exchange money at post offices.

Many hotels sell stamps.

Maps   See "Getting Around," above, in this chapter.

Medical Emergencies   If you are ill and need medicine at night and on Sunday, the local Commissariat de Police will tell you the location of the nearest drugstore that's open or the address of the nearest doctor on duty. The police or fire department will also summon an ambulance if you need to be rushed to a hospital. Seek assistance first at your hotel desk if language is a problem.

Money   See "Information, Entry Requirements & Money" in Chapter 2.

Newspapers/Magazines   English-language newspapers are available at nearly every kiosk (newsstand) in Paris. Published Monday through Saturday, the *International Herald-Tribune* is the most popular paper with visiting Americans and Canadians. Kiosks are generally open daily 8am–9pm.

Passports   See "Information, Entry Requirements & Money" in Chapter 2.

Pets   If you have certificates from a vet and proof of antirabies vaccination, you can bring most house pets into France.

Photographic Needs   All types of film are available in Paris at fairly modest prices. Unless you're going to be in France for an extended period, I don't recommend that you process your film here, for it takes time. Ask at your hotel for the nearest camera shop.

Police   Call 17. The principal Prefecture is at 7 bd. du Palais, 4e (tel. 42-60-33-22; Métro: Cité).

Post Office   The main post office (P.T.T.) for Paris is **Bureau de Poste,** 52 rue du Louvre, 75001 Paris (tel. 40-28-20-00; Métro: Louvre). Your mail can be sent here *poste restante* (general delivery) for a small fee. Take an ID, such as a passport, if you plan to pick up mail. It's open daily 8am–7pm for most services, 24 hours a day for telegrams and phone calls. Stamps can be purchased also at your hotel reception desk (usually) and at *café-tabacs* (tobacconists).

Radio/TV   The major TV channels in France are Antenne 2, TF1, FR3, La Cinq, and M6. All programs are broadcast in French. However, after a day of sightseeing, you might be able to catch a foreign film late at night in English with French subtitles. In the summer months, the domestic radio France-Inter broadcasts daily news and important traffic conditions in English. Broadcast times are

18TH ARRONDISSEMENT

Legend:

- Bal du Moulin Rouge ⑥
- Basilique du Sacré Coeur ⑬
- Cimetière de Montmartre ⑤
- Cimetière Saint-Pierre ⑪
- Cimetière Saint-Vincent ⑧
- Moulin de la Galette ⑦
- Musée d'Art Juif ⑨
- Musée d'Art Naïf Max Fourny ⑭
- Musée de Montmartre ⑩
- Notre Dame du Bon Conseil ③
- Notre Dame de Clignancourt ④
- Saint-Bernard-de-la-Chapelle ⑯
- Sainte-Geneviève-des-Grandes-Carrières ①
- Sainte-Hélène ②
- Saint-Jean-de-Montmartre ⑮
- Saint-Pierre-de-Montmartre ⑫

Church ■ †
Métro Ⓜ

18e Arrondissement — PARIS

(usually) 8am and 1 and 7pm. Short- or medium-wave radios allow you to tune in to BBC programs.

Religious Services France is a predominantly Roman Catholic country, and churches of this faith are found in every city and town. Many churches in Paris conduct services in English: The nondenominational **American Church in Paris,** 65 quai d'Orsay, 7e (tel. 47-05-07-99; Métro: Invalides); the **First Church of Christ Scientist,** 36 bd. St-Jacques, 14e (tel. 47-07-26-60; Métro: Glacière); **Second Church of Christ Scientist,** 58 bd. Flandrin,

16e (tel. 45-04-37-74; Métro: Dauphine); and the **Third Church of Christ Scientist,** 45 rue La Boétie, 8e (tel. 45-62-19-85; Métro: St-Augustin). The **Great Synagogue** is at 44 rue de la Victoire, 9e (tel. 42-85-71-09; Métro: La Peletier). An English-speaking Roman Catholic church is **St. Joseph's,** 50 av. Hoche, 8e (tel. 42-27-28-56; Métro: Charles-de-Gaulle–Etoile).

Rest Rooms If you are in dire need, duck into a café or brasserie to use the lavatory. It's customary to make some small purchase if you do so. Paris Métro stations and underground garages usually contain public lavatories, but the degree of cleanliness varies. France still has many "hole-in-the-ground" toilets, so be forewarned.

Safety Whenever you're traveling in an unfamiliar city or country, stay alert. Be aware of your immediate surroundings. Wear a moneybelt and keep a close eye on your possessions. Be particularly careful with cameras, purses, and wallets, all favorite targets of thieves and pickpockets.

In Paris, be aware of child pickpockets. They roam the French capital, preying on tourists around sights such as the Louvre, Eiffel Tower, and Notre-Dame, and they especially like to pick your pockets in the Métro, sometimes blocking you off from the escalator. A band of these young thieves can clean your pockets even while you try to fend them off. Their method is to get very close to a target, ask for a handout (sometimes), and deftly help themselves to your money or passport.

Shoe Repairs Ask at your hotel for a nearby repair shop or try **Central Crepins,** 48 rue de Turbigo, 3e (tel. 42-72-68-64; Métro: Etienne-Marcel), which performs at least some of its sewing by hand and does very competent repair work. It's open Mon–Fri. Or try **La Cordonnerie Pulin,** 5 rue Chaveau-Lagarde, 8e (tel. 42-65-08-57; Métro: Madeleine), open Mon–Sat; closed Aug.

Taxes Watch it: You could get burned. As a member of the European Community France routinely imposes a "Value Added Tax" (VAT) on many goods and services—currently 6% or 33.3%. You can get a tax refund on purchases over 1,200F ($222). Ask the shopkeepers to make out an export sales invoice (*bordereau*), which you show to the French Customs officer when you leave the country (at the airport, on the train, at the highway border post). In a number of weeks the shop will send you a check for the amount of the refund. Not all shops participate in the program. Ask before you buy.

Taxis See "Getting Around" in this chapter.

Telegrams/Telex/Fax Telegrams may be sent from any Paris post office during the day (see "Post Office," above) and anytime from the 24-hour central post office. In sending telegrams to the United States, the address is counted in the price, there are no special rates for a certain number of words, and night telegrams cost less. If you're in Paris and wish to send a telegram in English, call 42-33-44-11. The 24-hour public Telex office in Paris is at 103 rue de Grenelle, 7e (tel. 45-50-34-34; Métro: rue-du-Bac). By phone, you can dictate a Telex by calling 42-47-12-12. You can also send Telex and Fax messages at the main post office in each arrondissement of Paris.

Telephone Public phone booths are found in cafés, restaurants, Métro stations, post offices, airports, and train stations and occasionally on the streets. Some of these booths work with tokens called *jetons,* which can be purchased at the post office or from the cashier at any café. (It's usually customary to give a small tip if you buy them at a café.) Pay telephones accept coins of ½, 1, 2, and 5F;

the minimum charge is 1F (20¢). Pick up the receiver, insert the *jeton* or coins, and dial when you hear the tone, pushing the button when there is an answer. The French also use a *telecarte*, a telephone debit card, which can be purchased at rail stations, post offices, and other places. Sold in two versions, it allows callers to use 50 or 120 charge units by inserting the card in a phone booth. They cost 40F ($7.40) and 96F ($17.75), respectively.

If possible, avoid making calls from your hotel, which might double or triple the charges.

When you're calling long distance within France, dial 16, wait for the dial tone, and then dial the eight-digit number of the person or place you're calling. To reach Paris from one of the Provinces, dial 16 and 1, then the eight digit number. To call the U.S. or Canada, first dial 19, listen for the tone, then slowly dial 1, the area code, and the seven-digit number. To place a collect call to North America, dial 19-33-11, and an English-speaking operator will assist you. Dial 19-00-11 for an American AT&T operator.

For information, dial 12.

Television See "Radio/TV," above.

Time French summer time lasts from around April to September, and runs one hour ahead of French winter time. Depending on the time of year, France is six or seven hours ahead of Eastern Standard Time in the United States.

Tipping Tipping is practiced with flourish and style in France, and, as a visitor, you're expected to play the game. All bills, as required by law, show *service compris,* which means the tip is included; customary practices of additional gratuities are as follows.

Waiters: In restaurants, cafés, and nightclubs, service is included; however, it is customary to leave something extra, especially in first-class and deluxe establishments, where 10% to 12% extra is often the rule. In inexpensive places, 8% to 10% will suffice.

Porters: Usually a fixed fee is assessed, about 5F (95¢) to 10F ($1.85) per piece of luggage. You're not obligated to give more; however, many French people do, ranging from .50F (10¢) to 2F (35¢).

Theater ushers: Give at least 2F (35¢) for seating up to two persons.

Hairdressers: The service charge is most often included; otherwise, tip at least 15%, more in swankier places.

Guides: In museums, guides expect 5F (95¢) to 10F ($1.85).

Cloakroom attendants: Often the price is posted; if not, give at least 2F (35¢) to 5F (95¢).

Hotels: The service charge is added, but tip the bellboy extra—from 6F ($1.10) to 20F ($3.70) for three bags (more in deluxe and first-class hotels). A lot depends on how much luggage he has carried and the class of the establishment. Tip the concierge based entirely on how many requests you've made of him or her. Give the maid about 20F ($3.70) if you've stayed for three or more days. The doorman who summons a cab expects another 5F (95¢), likewise your room-service waiter, even though you've already been hit for 15% service. Incidentally, most small services around the hotel should be rewarded with a 5F (95¢) tip.

Toilets See "Rest Rooms" above.

Transit Info For information on the city's public transportation, stop in at either of the two offices of the Services Touristiques de la RATP—at 53 bis, quai des Grands-Augustins, 6e (tel. 40-46-42-12; Métro: St-Michel), or at place de la Madeleine, 8e (tel. 43-46-14-14; Métro: Madeleine).

Useful Telephone Numbers Police 17; fire 18; emergency medical assistance 15.

Visas See "Information, Entry Requirements & Money" in Chapter 2.

Water Drinking water is generally safe, although it has been known to cause diarrhea. If you ask for water in a restaurant it will be served bottled (for which you'll pay) unless you specifically request tap water (*l'eau du robinet*).

Weather Call 36-69-00-00.

Yellow Pages As in North America, the *Yellow Pages* are immensely useful. Your hotel will almost certainly have a copy, but you'll need the help of a French-speaking resident before tackling the French Telephone Company's (PTT's) *Yellow Pages*.

Some words aren't too different from the English. *Pharmacie* (pharmacy), *antiquités* (antiques), *théâtres* (theaters), and *objets d' art* may be easy to decipher. But other words, such as *cordonniers* (shoemakers and shoe-repair shops) and *horlogerie* (watch-repair shop), might be less obvious. Ask someone at the reception desk of your hotel for translations if needed.

Don't ever assume that someone on the other end of the phone speaks English. You may have to ask a French-speaking person to make the call for you.

---

3. NETWORKS & RESOURCES

FOR STUDENTS A good base for students while in Paris is the **Maison d'Etudiants J. de Rufz de Lavison,** 18 rue Jean-Jacques-Rousseau, 75001 Paris (tel. 45-08-02-10), which receives both male and female students from May through October, charging them 95F ($17.60) per person daily, including a continental breakfast, taxes, and service, as well as showers. A three-day minimum stay is required. **Métro:** Louvre.

From June through September, temporary housing (60 beds) for students, male and female, ages 18 to 30, is available at the **Association des Etudiants Protestants de Paris,** 46 rue de Vaugirard, 75006 Paris (tel. 43-54-31-49), on the Left Bank. They have a library and various cultural activities. Rates, including a continental breakfast and showers, are 65F ($12.05) daily in a dormitory (four to six beds), or 78F ($14.45) per person in a double. The single rate is 85F ($15.75) per person. In summer, bookings must be for a minimum of four weeks. **Métro:** Luxembourg, St-Germain, or Odéon.

FOR GAY MEN & LESBIANS **SOS Homosexualité,** 3 bis, rue Clairaut, 17e (tel. 46-27-49-36; Métro: La Fourche), has an English-speaking staff willing to offer information about gay life in Paris for both men and women daily 10am–1pm. It usually offers a reception on Friday at 8pm (but you must call to verify that). Every Sunday at noon, the center offers a nondenominational religious service, which is followed by lunch.

Another helpful source is **La Maison des Femmes,** 8 Cité Prost, 11e (tel. 43-48-25-91; Métro: Charonne), offering information about Paris for lesbians. It sponsors Friday dinners. Call for information about them.

Cinq Sur Cinq is a monthly publication, distributed free in gay bars and bookstores, with extensive nightlife listings, most often for men. Women should pick up a copy of *Lesbia,* which is available at **Les Mots à la Bouche,** 6 rue Ste-Croix-de-la-Bretonerie, 4e (Métro: Hôtel-de-Ville). This store carries several publications of interest to both gay men and lesbians.

FOR WOMEN   The leading feminist bookstore of Paris is **La Librairie des Femmes,** 74 rue de Seine, 6e (tel. 43-29-50-75; Métro: Odéon), open daily 10am–7pm. It features a vast collection of women's literature, much of it in English.

The **Organisation Flora Tristan** (tel. 47-36-96-48) is a women's hotline active 24 hours a day. The rape crisis hotline is **SOS Viol** (tel. 05-05-95-95). It offers counseling and both legal and medical advice Mon–Fri 10am–6pm. In August, it is open Wed–Mon 10am–6pm.

PARIS
ACCOMMODATIONS

Paris offers more than 1,400 hotels—of which a handful at the top of the price scale are world-famous. But many modest hotels also provide decent value. Their only drawback is that they are well known among shrewd travelers and are likely to be booked, especially in summer. I suggest reserving rooms a full month in advance at *any* time of the year and as far as six weeks ahead during the tourist-jammed months from early May through mid-October. You may want to send a one-night deposit just to be sure.

The majority of Parisian hotels share a problem—noise. I'd heartily recommend that late sleepers request rooms at the back of their hotel.

If you crave smartness in your surroundings, choose a Right Bank hotel. That puts you central to all the most elegant shops—Dior, Cardin, Saint-Laurent—and within walking distance of such important sights as the Arc de Triomphe, the place de la Concorde, the Tuileries Gardens, and the Louvre. (The Opéra is also in this area, with its attendant attraction, the American Express office.) And for relaxing after sightseeing during the day or for an apéritif at night, you have all the glittering cafés along the Champs-Elysées.

The best Right Bank hotels are in the 8th arrondissement, and many first-class ones are found in the 16th and 17th arrondissements. If you'd like to be near the place Vendôme, then try for a hotel in the 1st arrondissement.

Other Right Bank hotel sections include the increasingly fashionable Marais and Bastille districts, comprising the 3rd and 4th arrondissements, and Les Halles/Beaubourg, mainly in the 3rd arrondissement, which is the site of the Centre Pompidou and Les Halles shopping mall, site of the former marketplace of Paris.

If you'd like to live more informally with more of a flavor of the Latin Quarter, then head for the Left Bank, where prices are traditionally lower. Hotels here lie mainly in the 5th and 6th arrondissements, which is the area of the Sorbonne, café life, and bookstores. Many hotels in this district cater to students. The 7th arrondissement provides a touch of the life of St-Germain.

If they were so inclined, the French could ask a riddle going something like "When is a hotel not a hotel?" The answer is when it's another kind of building. The world *hôtel* in French has several meanings. It means a lodging house for transients, of course, but it also means a large mansion or town house, such as the Hôtel des

Invalides, once a home for disabled soldiers, now the most important military museum in the world. Hôtel de Ville means town hall; Hôtel des Postes refers to the general post office; and Hôtel-Dieu is a hospital. So watch that word.

It is important to remember that the last two letters of the postal code indicate the arrondissement. A postal code of 75008 Paris means that the hotel lies in the 8th arrondissement; 75005 indicates the hotel is in the 5th arrondissement.

In general, the following price categories have been used: "Very Expensive" doubles from 2,500F ($462.50); "Expensive" 1,100F–2,500F ($203.50–$462.50); "Moderate" 700F–1,100F ($129.50–$203.50); "Inexpensive" anything under 700F ($129.50). *Note:* There are many exceptions to this general rule of thumb, however, as Paris hotels—especially the older ones—have a wide selection of different types of rooms, often at very different prices. Service and tax (Value Added Tax) are included in the rates unless otherwise specified.

Hotel breakfasts are fairly uniform and include your choice of coffee, tea, or chocolate, a freshly baked croissant and roll, plus limited quantities of butter and jam or jelly. It can be at your door moments after you call down for it, and can be served at almost any hour requested. When a breakfast charge is given for an individual listing, it is always a continental breakfast. Breakfasts with eggs, bacon, ham, or other items will have to be ordered from the à la carte menu. For a charge, larger hotels serve the full breakfast—called "English breakfast"—but smaller hotels often serve only the continental variety.

1. 8TH ARRONDISSEMENT

VERY EXPENSIVE

LE BRISTOL, 112 Faubourg St-Honoré, 75008 Paris. Tel. 42-66-91-45. Fax 42-66-68-68. 152 rms, 45 suites. A/C MINIBAR TV TEL **Metro:** Champs-Elysées.

$ Rates: Single 2,300F–2,850F ($425.50–$527.25), double 3,400F–4,200F ($629–$777), suite from 7,000F ($1,295). Breakfast 150F ($27.75) extra. AE, DC, MC, V. **Parking:** Free.

The decor is sumptuous, the art is museum caliber, and the service impeccable. This is one of the top two or three hotels in all Europe. Naturally, its clientele is among the international upper crust, and it has particular appeal with diplomats.

Founded in 1924 by Hippolyte Jammet, Le Bristol is a true palace. It's on the famous shopping street of Paris, near many of the capital's most elegant boutiques. Nearby is the Palais de l'Elysée, the official residence of the French president. The hotel is not large enough to be a monument, as is Le Ritz; instead, it's just the right size for a guest to receive individualized Old World attention. The facade is in classic 18th-century Parisian style, characterized by an entrance of glass and wrought iron. The furnishings are of the highest caliber—signed Louis XV and Louis XVI pieces abound. Some salons open onto a formal patio, landscaped with potted plants and shrubbery. The management has seen to it that all bedrooms and suites are furnished opulently and luxuriously. Original oil paintings, Asian carpets, antiques and skillfully made reproductions, and the customary bronze and crystal have been used extensively.

Dining/Entertainment: The Restaurant d'Eté is open from April to the end of October; the Restaurant d'Hiver is open from November to the end of March. Tea and drinks are served in a large, quiet garden in summer.

Services: 24-hour room service, simultaneous Telex translation, audiovisual equipment rental, laundry, valet.

Facilities: Hairdressing salon, massage parlor, sauna, conference

RIGHT BANK ACCOMMODATIONS

Meurice **56**
Neuville (de) **58**
Novotel Paris Les Halles **59**
Paris Inter-Continental **61**
Pavillon Bastille, Le **89**
Pavillon de la Reine **63**
Pierre **64**
Plaza Athénée **65**
Plaza Etoile **66**

Raphael **69**
Régence Etoile **70**
Regent's Garden **72**
Regina **73**
Résidence Foch **78**
Richmond **79**
Ritz **80**
Royal Alma **81**
Royal Monceau **82**

Saint-Louis **84**
San Regis **87**
Tivoli-Etoile **93**
Trois-Couronnes **94**
Vieux Marais **97**
Warwick **100**
Westminster **102**

rooms, lobby cocktail lounge, heated indoor swimming pool, rooftop
solarium with view of Sacré-Coeur (open daily from 7am to 10pm).

**HOTEL DE CRILLON, 10 place de la Concorde, 75008
Paris. Tel. 42-65-24-24.** Fax 47-42-72-10. 117 rms, 46 suites.
A/C MINIBAR TV TEL **Métro:** Concorde.
$ Rates: Single 2,800F ($518), double 4,500F ($832.50), suite
from 6,000F ($1,110). Breakfast 150F ($27.75) extra. AE, DC,
MC, V.

⭐ The Crillon offers the most dramatic setting in Paris, overlooking the place de la Concorde, where the guillotine claimed the lives of such celebrated victims as Louis XVI, Marie Antoinette, Madame du Barry, Madame Roland, and Charlotte Corday. Designed by the famed Gabriel, the building was the former home of the duke of Crillon. Although more than 200 years old, it has been a hotel only since 1909. As such, it sheltered Woodrow Wilson during his stay in Paris following World War I. More recent guests have included Meryl Streep, Tom Cruise, Madonna, and Debra Winger.

LEFT BANK ACCOMMODATIONS

Pas de Calais [62]	Saints-Pères (des) [86]
Pullman St-Jacques [67]	Select [88]
Quai Voltaire [68]	St-André-des-Arts [90]
Regent's [71]	St-Germain-des-Prés [91]
Relais Christine [74]	St-Thomas-d'Aquin [92]
Relais Saint-Germain [75]	Université (de l') [95]
Résidence du Globe [77]	Verneuil St-Germain [96]
Saint-Gregoire [83]	Vieux Paris (du) [98]
Sainte-Beuve [85]	Villa (La) [99]

The colonnaded exterior is so discreet you won't think it is a hotel at first—instead, it seems the headquarters of a minister of government. The hotel encircles a large, formal courtyard, one of the ideal places in Paris for those of refined taste to order afternoon tea. The formal 18th-century courtyard is surrounded by flowers and plants.

Massively restored, the hotel still evokes the 18th century, with parquet floors, crystal chandeliers, sculpture, 17th- and 18th-century tapestries, gilt moldings, antiques, and paneled walls. If you get a room at the front, you'll be treated to a view of one of the most beautiful plazas in the world. Tranquility seekers should ask for a chamber opening onto an inner courtyard. The rooms, for the most part, are generous in size and classically furnished. All the bathrooms are fresh and well maintained, lined with travertine or pink marble.

Dining/Entertainment: Guests can dine in the elegant Les Ambassadeurs, where a fixed-price meal including wine and service costs at least 280F ($51.80), or the more-informal L'Obelisque, where you can dine for 200F ($37) and up.

Services: 24-hour room service, secretarial and translation services.

Facilities: Meeting and conference rooms, garden-style courtyard with restaurant service, elevators, shops.

GEORGE V, 31 av. George-V, 75008 Paris. Tel. 47-23-54-00. Fax 47-20-40-00. 245 rms, 53 suites. A/C MINIBAR TV TEL **Métro:** George-V.

$ Rates: Single 2,230F–2,890F ($412.55–$534.65), double 2,890F–3,310F ($534.65–$612.35), suite from 5,500F ($1,017.50). Breakfast 150F ($27.75) extra. AE, DC, MC, V.

The George V is affectionately called "George Sank" by the bustling expense-accounters who crowd its ornate lobby. Midway between the Champs-Elysées and the Seine, it is luxurious (reportedly, the management keeps a "black file" on the mysterious "whims and preferences" of its habitués) and often is referred to as "the French Waldorf-Astoria." The service is excellent, beginning with registration at the Empire-style reception desk and continuing in your room, where you just press a buzzer and servants attend to your every whim.

The public lounges are adorned with tapestries and 100- and 200-year-old paintings. Inlaid marble walls in the Pompeiian style add a touch of staid dignity. The preferred rooms overlook the courtyard; those with terrace balconies are also the height of perfection. The hotel is a far cry from the way it was in 1944, when General Eisenhower made it his headquarters during the Liberation of Paris.

Dining/Entertainment: In good weather, haute cuisine luncheons are served in the courtyard's garden-style outdoor café/restaurant. The two more formal restaurants of the hotel are Les Princes and Le Grill, both with meals beginning at 150F ($27.75).

Services: Concierge, 24-hour room service, CBS news service, in-room movies, laundry, valet.

Facilities: Beauty salon, seven conference rooms, tearooms, florist, gift shop

MARRIOTT PRINCE DE GALLES, 33 av. George-V, 75008 Paris. Tel. 47-23-55-11, or toll free 800/228-9290 in the U.S. Fax 47-20-61-05. 140 rms, 30 suites. A/C MINIBAR TV TEL **Métro:** George-V.

$ Rates: Single 2,000F–2,250F ($370–$416.25), double 2,250F–2,500F ($416.25–$462.50), suite from 3,000F ($555). Breakfast 130F ($24.05) extra. AE, DC, MC, V. **Parking:** 150F ($27.75).

When it was constructed in 1927, the cognoscenti of the era's social life adopted the Prince de Galles's art deco/neo-Byzantine courtyard as their preferred rendezvous point. In the 1950s diarist and composer Ned Rorem recorded the trysts and trials of the "unapproachable innermost snob-life of Paris" that transpired within the hotel walls. Eras change but the allure of the "Prince of Wales" remains.

The hotel occupies a platinum location only a short stroll from the Champs-Elysées, the Arc de Triomphe, and the glamorous boutiques of the avenue Montaigne. Guests are greeted at the door with a smile by a team of uniformed attendants, who quickly arrange for cars to be parked and baggage sent to one of the plushly upholstered, very spacious accommodations. A cluster of French sofas and armchairs is grouped around bouquets of flowers, complementing the Regency detailing of the six-sided lobby. The paneled bar, with its leather-upholstered copies of 18th-century armchairs, is one of the great hotel bars of Paris. Both the dining room and the quietest bedrooms look out over the famous courtyard, covered with elaborate mosaics.

Each of the high-ceilinged accommodations contains an ultracomfortable bathroom, the surfaces of which repeat the Edwardian/art deco tilework that so successfully adorn the hotel's facade. The elegantly furnished bedrooms have in-room movies, radios, and plenty of sunny space. A well-trained staff seems eager to respond to queries and requests, and to safeguard the complete privacy that many of this hotel's well-heeled guests demand.

Dining/Entertainment: The paneled bar, with its leather replicas of 18th-century armchairs, is one of the great hotel bars of Paris. The paneled dining room overlooks the garden-style courtyard, which has restaurant service.

Services: 24-hour room service, concierge, babysitting.

Facilities: Conference rooms, elevator, in-room movies.

PLAZA ATHENEE, 23–27 av. Montaigne, 75008 Paris. Tel. 47-23-78-33. Fax 47-20-20-70. 215 rms, 41 suites. A/C MINIBAR TV TEL **Métro:** F.D. Roosevelt.

$ **Rates:** Single 3,200F ($592), double 5,200F ($962), suite from 6,000F ($1,110). Breakfast 130F ($24.05) extra. AE, DC, MC, V.

The Plaza Athénée was known to Mata Hari; it's also been known to about half of all the visiting celebrities of Paris. Between the Seine and the Champs-Elysées, it is a veritable palace of gilded luxury set in the midst of embassies (the rich ones) and the temples of haute couture, from which it draws many of its guests. It is said that there are two employees for each guest in this citadel dedicated to the good life. Arched windows and ornate balconies evoke the pre–World War I style. A liveried attendant stands under a glass shelter waiting to help you out of your taxi. When you check in, the reception staff seats you at a Louis XVI marquetry desk that faces an antique Flemish painting.

The style of the hotel is exemplified by the Montaigne Salon, with its mellow wood-grain paneling and marble fireplace. In the courtyard, tables are sheltered by parasols, and climbing vines and borders of flowers add a touch of gaiety. The more preferred bedrooms overlook this courtyard. The well-maintained units each have a private tile bath that is especially large, with double basins and shower. Other amenities such as ample closet space and taffeta draperies make the rooms elegant, comfortable places to stay.

Dining/Entertainment: Meals are an occasion. The preferred choice for dining is La Régence-Plaza, a room of handsome hand-carved oak paneling, its large curvy-topped windows fronting the avenue Montaigne. It is known for its lobster soufflé. With its bright colors and decoration, the Grill Relais Plaza is the meeting place of *tout Paris,* especially at lunch, drawing dress designers and personalities from the world of publishing, cinema, and art. The Bar Anglais is a favorite spot for a late-night drink (it's open until 1:30am).

Services: 24-hour room service, concierge, laundry, Reuters Telex with international stock quotes.

Facilities: Conference rooms, beauty parlor and hairdresser, massage parlor.

EXPENSIVE

HOTEL BALZAC, 6 rue Balzac, 75008 Paris. Tel. 45-61-97-22. Fax 42-25-24-82. 56 rms. A/C MINIBAR TV TEL **Métro:** George-V.

$ Rates: Single 1,500F ($277.50), double 1,830F ($338.55), suite from 3,800F ($703). Breakfast 125F ($23.15) extra. AE, DC, MC, V. **Parking:** 150F ($27.75).

Possibly the most successful renovation in this part of Paris, Hôtel Balzac opened late in 1985 in a neighborhood well acquainted with 19th-century grandeur. The gilding on the wrought-iron balustrades was barely dry before the place was hailed as one of the most refreshing hotels Paris has seen in this price category in a long time.

When they created it, a team of French and Lebanese designers added well-studied touches of the best decors of England, Italy, and France to a sophisticated series of public rooms that include elements of art deco, Palladian revival, and neo-Byzantine. A recessed alcove in the lobby is covered with hand-painted tendrils and vines, which seem to grow into the glistening white marble of a sun-flooded atrium. Kilim carpets, plum-colored upholstery, burnished paneling, and antique oil portraits add to the allure.

Accommodations are accessed through a glass-walled elevator that glides silently past acres of Turkish-patterned carpeting. Each bedroom is outfitted with a glistening marble bathroom, thick upholstery, and tasteful decors of blue-gray or spice.

Dining/Entertainment: The hotel's Italian restaurant, Bice, is recommended separately in Chapter 5. La Bas, a private nightclub in the basement, is accessible to hotel guests.

Services: Laundry, 24-hour room service, babysitting.

HOTEL SAN REGIS, 12 rue Jean-Goujon, 75008 Paris. Tel. 43-59-41-90. Fax 45-62-05-48. 33 rms, 12 suites. MINIBAR TV TEL **Métro:** F.D. Roosevelt.

$ Rates: Single 1,350F–1,500F ($249.75–$277.50), double 1,950F–2,100F ($360.75–$388.50), suite from 3,000F ($555). Breakfast 100F ($18.50) extra. AE, DC, MC, V.

A fashionable town house until 1922, the San Régis stands in a neighborhood of embassies and exclusive boutiques (Christian Dior is across the street), enjoying, in a quiet and modest way, its position as one of the best hotels in Paris in its price bracket. It is right off the Champs-Elysées, only a short walk from the Seine. Guests here find it much like a private club. There is a small and attentive staff that quickly learns your whims and fancies and makes you feel at home. Each room is unique and decorated with discretion and taste. All units have music and a private bath, a few have a separate sitting room, and many overlook a side garden. Thirty-five are air conditioned.

Dining/Entertainment: The hotel has an elegantly decorated restaurant in the classic style, serving formal French cuisine. There is also a winter garden.

Services: 24-hour room service, laundry/valet, babysitting.

Facilities: Car rental desk.

HOTEL LE WARWICK, 5 rue de Berri, 75008 Paris. Tel.

45-63-14-11. Fax 45-63-75-81. 148 rms, 21 suites. A/C
MINIBAR TV TEL **Métro:** George-V.

$ **Rates:** Single 1,620F–1,920F ($299.70–$355.20), double
1,920F–2,370F ($355.20–$438.45), suite from 3,000F ($555).
Breakfast 110F ($20.35) extra. Children under 12 stay free in
parents' room. AE, DC, MC, V. **Parking:** 150F ($27.75).

The Warwick, which opened in 1981, occupies a desirable location
near the upper end of the Champs-Elysées. It is a bastion of comfort
and convenience, with elegant, contemporary decor. Perhaps because
it is owned by investors from Hong Kong, many of the lacquered
accents in the public rooms are of deep Chinese red, alternating with
mirrors and an abundance of plants. Even the young staff is attired, as
is the establishment's facade, in shades of maroon.

About 30% of the bedrooms have evergreen-covered terraces with
views of the Eiffel Tower and the 18th-century buildings across the
street. Business travelers from North and South America, along with
such celebrities as Boy George and Grace Jones, appreciate the
soundproof windows, the opulent marble-covered baths, the bronze
and peach accents, the 24-hour video on the color TVs, and the
attractively concealed minibars.

Dining/Entertainment: The ground floor contains the Swann
Bar, named after the character in a literary work of Marcel Proust,
with live piano music and views into the hotel's elegant restaurant, La
Couronne.

Services: 24-hour room service, laundry and valet, babysitting.

Facilities: Limousine rentals, car rentals, shopping boutiques.

MODERATE

**RESIDENCE LORD BYRON, 5 rue de Chateaubriand,
75008 Paris. Tel. 43-59-89-89.** Fax 42-89-46-04. 31 rms (all
with bath), 6 suites. MINIBAR TV TEL **Métro:** George-V.

$ **Rates:** Single 580F–720F ($107.30–$133.20), double 720F–
820F ($133.20–$151.70), suite from 1,200F ($222). Breakfast
50F ($9.25) extra. MC, V.

Just off the Champs-Elysées on a curving street of handsome
buildings, the Lord Byron sports fine antique reproductions and
framed prints of butterflies and of scenes in France. The bathrooms
are as attractively decorated as they are functional. If you choose to
have breakfast at the hotel, you can order it in the petit salon or in a
shaded inner garden. Six suites with two beds and two baths are
available.

INEXPENSIVE

**MADELEINE-PLAZA, 33 place de la Madeleine, 75008
Paris. Tel. 42-65-20-63.** Fax 42-65-22-30. 54 rms (all with
bath or shower). MINIBAR TV TEL **Métro:** Madeleine.

$ **Rates:** Single or double with shower 420F ($77.70), double with
bath 490F ($90.65), triple with bath 650F ($120.25). Breakfast
35F ($6.50) extra. AE, MC, V.

The Madeleine-Plaza is a delight. It has a prime Right Bank location,
at the center of all the best shopping districts and within equal
walking distance of the Tuileries and the Opéra. There's a striking
view of the Madeleine Church from its front windows. The bedrooms are not overly spacious, but are contemporary enough to
please the most motel-jaded. Headboards and breakfast tables are of
shiny brown Formica. Black leather easy chairs provide comfortable

resting places. For those who don't want their breakfast in bed (at which the manager can only express wonder), there is a sunlit breakfast room overlooking the church.

HOTEL OPAL, 19 rue Tronchet, 75008 Paris. Tel. 42-65-77-97. Fax 49-24-06-58. 36 rms (all with bath or shower). MINIBAR TV TEL **Métro:** Madeleine.

$ Rates: Single 450F–560F ($83.25–$103.60), double 520F–560F ($96.20–$103.60). Breakfast 45F ($8.35) extra. AE, MC, V. **Parking:** 120F ($22.20).

In the heart of Paris, behind the Madeleine Church and within an easy walk of the Opéra, this rejuvenated hotel is a real find. Decorated with style and taste, it offers entirely renovated but small bedrooms. Some readers may want to ask for one of the closet-size bedrooms on the top floor, reached by a narrow staircase. These are really attic rooms, but some have skylights opening onto the rooftops of Paris.

---

2. 16TH & 17TH ARRONDISSEMENTS

VERY EXPENSIVE

RAPHAEL, 17 av. Kléber, 75116 Paris. Tel. 45-02-16-00. Fax 45-01-21-50. 53 rms, 35 suites. MINIBAR TV TEL **Métro:** Kléber.

$ Rates: Single 1,600F–2,700F ($296–$499.50), double 2,300F–3,900F ($425.50–$721.50), suite from 6,000F ($1,110). Breakfast 110F ($20.35) extra. AE, DC, MC, V.

The Raphaël enjoys special patronage from the Italian-American movie world, plus other world celebrities. Near the Arc de Triomphe, it is an oasis of stately dignity. When you pay your bill you can admire an original Turner (the orange-and-gold painting to the right of the cashier). The tone of the hotel is set by the main hallway, with its dark-paneled walnut walls, oil paintings framed in gilt, and lavish bronze torchères. The rich wood paneling continues into the music salon, with its opera-red carpeting and marble fireplace. The bedrooms are impressive, luxuriously furnished with brass-trimmed chests, tables of inlaid wood, armoires, and silk draperies. Some units are air conditioned. Prices depend on the view.

Dining/Entertainment: Be sure to have a meal in the formal dining room, La Salle à Manger, with its gold-and-red carpeting, white paneled walls, and arched windows with rich draperies, or enjoy your favorite drink in the wood-paneled English Bar.

Services: Room service, laundry, babysitting.

Facilities: Car rental desk.

EXPENSIVE

LE MERIDIEN PARIS ETOILE, 81 bd. Gouvion-St-Cyr, 75017 Paris. Tel. 40-68-34-34. Fax 40-68-31-31. 989 rms, 17 suites. A/C MINIBAR TV TEL **Métro:** Porte Maillot.

$ Rates: Single 1,800F ($333), double 2,050F ($379.25), suite from 4,000F ($740). Breakfast 100F ($18.50) extra. AE, DC, MC, V. **Parking:** 100F ($18.50).

The largest hotel in France, under the aegis of Air France, the Méridien is the first of its kind in Paris, catering to groups as well as to individuals. The location is opposite the air terminal at the Porte-Maillot Métro stop on the Neuilly-Vincennes line. The setting of the hotel is contemporary French, and the overscale lobby chandelier is an eye-catcher. Bedrooms are designed to provide convenience and comfort, and often you get a good view as well.

Dining/Entertainment: The four restaurants feature everything from traditional French cuisine (Le Clos Longchamp) to Japanese specialties. There's a musical apéritif hour at 6pm and a 10pm jazz session at the Lionel Hampton Jazz Club.

Services: Laundry, babysitting, room service, express checkout.

Facilities: Foreign currency exchange, business office with English-language secretarial services, photocopiers.

MODERATE

ALEXANDER, 102 av. Victor-Hugo, 75016 Paris. Tel. 45-53-64-65. Fax 45-53-12-51. 59 rms (all with bath), 3 suites. MINIBAR TV TEL **Métro:** Victor-Hugo.

$ Rates: Single 790F–1,040F ($146.15–$192.40), double 990F–1,140F ($183.15–$210.90), suite from 1,870F ($345.95). Breakfast 60F ($11.10) extra. AE, DC, MC, V.

This really is the perfect bourgeois hotel, the kind you might send an elderly relative to on a first trip to Paris. It's correct and conservative with a few elegant touches, such as chandeliers in each room. A wrought-iron stairwell winds around the elevator. Rooms are carpeted and rather frilly, half of them facing a well-planted, quiet courtyard. One-day laundry service is provided, and room service is available daily from 7am to 9pm.

HOTEL PIERRE, 25 rue Théodore-de-Banville, 75017 Paris. Tel. 47-63-76-69. Fax 43-80-63-96. 50 rms (all with bath). MINIBAR TV TEL **Métro:** Ternes.

$ Rates: Single 630F ($116.55), double 900F ($166.50). Breakfast 60F ($11.10) extra. AE, DC, MC, V.

The Pierre was named as a facetious counterpoint to the owner's favorite North American hotel, the Pierre in New York City. To create it, the owners combined a trio of 19th-century buildings into a clean, modern hotel with art deco styling. Opened in 1986, it sits at the end of a residential street a short walk from the Arc de Triomphe. Each stylish accommodation contains a TV with video movies, a safe with a combination lock, and is outfitted in restful shades of blue and gray.

HOTEL REGENT'S GARDEN, 6 rue Pierre-Demours, 75017 Paris. Tel. 45-74-07-30. Fax 40-55-01-42. 40 rms (all with bath). MINIBAR TV TEL **Métro:** Ternes or Charles-de-Gaulle–Etoile.

$ Rates: Single 600F–775F ($111–$143.40), double 640F–880F ($118.40–$162.80). Breakfast 40F ($7.40) extra. AE, DC, MC, V. **Parking:** 45F ($8.35).

The Regent's Garden has a proud heritage: Napoléon III built this stately château for his physician. It's near the convention center and minutes from the Arc de Triomphe. There are two gardens, one with ivy-covered walls and umbrella tables—a perfect place to meet other guests. The interior resembles a country house with classic touches. The entryway has fluted columns, and the lobby has a casual mixture of comfortable furniture. Rooms have French flower prints on the walls and bedspreads; the furniture is mostly traditional French. The tall French windows are soundproof and have light, airy curtains. Hair dryers are thoughtfully provided.

RESIDENCE FOCH, 10 rue Marbeau, 75016 Paris. Tel. 45-00-46-50. Fax 45-01-98-68. 21 rms (all with bath), 4 suites. TV TEL **Métro:** Porte Dauphine or Porte Maillot.
$ Rates: Single 650F ($120.25), double 730F ($135.05), suite from 1,000F ($185). Breakfast 40F ($7.40) extra. AE, DC, MC, V.
Résidence Foch is a gracious, artistic hotel run by Monsieur and Madame Schneider. Located off avenue Foch, it's only a few minutes from the Arc de Triomphe and a short walk from the Bois de Boulogne. Popular with the diplomatic corps, the hotel is well decorated. Guests drop in for afternoon drinks in the front bar/ lounge, enjoying its warm, quiet atmosphere.

TIVOLI-ETOILE, 7 rue Brey, 75017 Paris. Tel. 42-67-12- 68. Fax 47-64-01-21. 30 rms (all with bath). MINIBAR TV TEL **Métro:** Charles-de-Galle–Etoile.
$ Rates (including continental breakfast): Single 530F–730F ($98.05–$135.50), double 575F–835F ($106.40–$154.50). AE, DC, MC, V.
Rue Brey is a sidestreet branching off avenue de Wagram, one of the spoke avenues of the Etoile. This street has a number of moderately priced hotels (all of which seem to be full all year), but the Tivoli-Etoile offers the best value for its mid-city location. The hotel has a contemporary lobby with a mural and a quiet inner patio. The small rooms, all with radios, contain modern furnishings.

INEXPENSIVE

DES DEUX ACACIAS (Hotel of the Two Locust Trees), 28 rue de l'Arc-de-Triomphe, 75017 Paris. Tel. 43-80-01- 85. Fax 40-53-94-62. 31 rms (all with shower or bath). TEL **Métro:** Charles-de-Gaulle–Etoile.
$ Rates (including continental breakfast): Single 340F ($62.90), double 400F ($74). English breakfast 35F ($6.50) extra. MC, V. **Parking:** 80F ($14.80).
I recommend this semimodern hotel for its cleanliness and location—a block from the Arc de Triomphe. It's also a good bargain in this district of budget hotels. Behind the white marble facade are a small public lounge and neat rooms frequented by visitors seeking to avoid the bustling "student" hotels on the Left Bank.

LES TROIS COURONNES, 30 rue de l'Arc de Triomphe, 75017 Paris. Tel. 43-80-46-81. Fax 46-22-53-96. 20 rms (all with bath). MINIBAR TV TEL **Métro:** Charles-de-Gaulle–Etoile.
$ Rates: Single or double 475F–560F ($87.90–$103.60). AE, DC, MC, V. **Parking:** 75F ($13.90).
This older hotel near the Etoile was renovated by Jean-Louis and Paule Lafont in 1983. The decor is a blend of art deco and art

---

Ⓕ FROMMER'S COOL FOR KIDS: HOTELS

Madeleine-Plaza (see p. 91) This is a good safe bet in a prime Right Bank location. Many rooms here are rented as triples.

Novotel Paris Les Halles (see p. 99) Every room is suitable for a family "doubling up," and the location overlooks Les Halles shopping complex. Kids love the carousel there.

---

nouveau and includes personal objects they've collected over the years. A 19th-century carved oak mantelpiece flanked with bearded statues has been turned into a reception desk. There also are a narrow marble fireplace that came from a private house in Versailles and a winding staircase with a light forged-iron balustrade. An up-to-date security system protects the many treasures. Rooms are cheerfully decorated, with elmwood trim. An elevator takes you to a vaulted breakfast room. Laundry service is available.

3. 1ST ARRONDISSEMENT

VERY EXPENSIVE

HOTEL MEURICE, 228 rue de Rivoli, 75001 Paris. Tel. 42-60-38-60. Fax 42-60-23-71. 148 rms (all with bath), 36 suites. A/C MINIBAR TV TEL **Métro:** Tuileries or Concorde.
$ Rates: Single 2,600F ($481), double 4,000F ($740), suite from 6,000F ($1,110). Breakfast 150F ($27.75) extra. AE, DC, MC, V.
The Meurice offers romantic 18th-century surroundings with a French aura. Its gilded salons were copied from those at the château at Versailles, complete with monumental crystal chandeliers, ornate tapestries, and furnishings from the periods of Louis XIV, XV, and XVI. Built in 1907, the hotel is just off rue de Rivoli and the Tuileries Gardens and within walking distance of the Louvre (you can see the Louvre from the upper floors). The lounge has a circular "star"-studded ceiling.

Rooms are soundproof and richly furnished with some period and modern pieces. Fit for a king, they are more likely to house diplomats, industrialists, and successful authors. The self-proclaimed "mad genius" Salvador Dali made the Meurice his headquarters, occupying Suite 108, which was once used by the deposed and exiled king of Spain, Alfonso XIII. Suite 108 also was used as the office of German General von Choltitz, who was in charge of Paris during the Nazi occupation.

Dining/Entertainment: The Meurice Restaurant serves true French haute cuisine. The Pompadour cocktail lounge is ideal for cocktails and tea, and the elegantly renovated Meurice Bar offers drinks in a warm atmosphere.

Services: 24-hour room service, Telex, fax, "solve-everything" concierge, laundry/valet.

Facilities: Six meeting rooms, summer outdoor patio.

PARIS INTER-CONTINENTAL, 3 rue de Castiglione, 75001 Paris. Tel. 44-77-11-11. Fax 44-77-14-60. 424 rms (all with bath), 16 suites. A/C MINIBAR TV TEL **Métro:** Concorde.

$ Rates: Single 2,500F ($462.50), double 3,300F ($610.50), suite from 4,000F ($740). Breakfast 150F ($27.75) extra. AE, DC, MC, V.

The Inter-Continental is a mixture of French tradition, Gallic know-how, and 20th-century modernism. This belle époque hotel is along rue de Rivoli, across from the Tuileries Gardens. Opened in 1878 as "The Continental," it has welcomed many famous guests, including the Empress Eugénie of France and Jean Giraudoux. In 1883 Victor Hugo was the guest of honor at a luncheon. The great inner courtyard known as "La Cour d'Honneur" is paved with white marble, with a splashing circular fountain and an 1864 statue by Cunny.

The main lounge has Persian carpets, period furnishings, bronze sconces, and marble cocktail tables. The colonnaded front entrance has a pair of bronze candelabra from a palace in St. Petersburg. The rooms and suites are among the finest in Paris. The decor is classic French with many antiques, including Louis XVI reproductions. Each chamber has paneled walls, crystal, fine fruitwoods, bronze hardware, desks, and tables. A one-color theme creates a salon effect. A radio and in-room movies also are provided.

Dining/Entertainment: The Terrasse Fleurie is an elegant gourmet restaurant in the interior courtyard. It's landscaped to depict the four seasons. The belle époque Café Tuileries serves breakfasts, snacks, light meals, informal suppers, cocktails, and French pastries (open until midnight). In fair weather, luncheon, tea, and drinks are served in the courtyard under a canopy. There's also a coffee shop. Estrela, a green-and-gold disco with mirrored walls, is open from 10pm to 4am.

Services: 24-hour room service, concierge, secretarial service, Fax, CBS news service.

Facilities: Conference rooms, underground parking, Jacuzzis in some suites.

LE RITZ, 15 place Vendôme, 75001 Paris. Tel. 42-60-38-30. Fax 42-60-23-71. 187 rms (all with bath), 45 suites. A/C MINIBAR TV TEL **Métro:** Opéra.

$ Rates: Single 2,500F–3,400F ($462.50–$629), double 3,000F–4,200F ($555–$777), suite from 6,000F ($1,110). Breakfast 150F ($27.75) extra. AE, DC, MC, V. **Parking:** 150F ($27.75).

The Ritz is the greatest hotel in Europe. This enduring symbol of elegance and chic is located on one of the most beautiful and historic squares in Paris. César Ritz, the "little shepherd boy from Niederwald," converted the Lazun Mansion into a luxury hotel that opened in 1898. With the help of culinary master Escoffier, the Ritz became a miracle of luxury living, attracting some of the great names of the world, including Edward VII of England.

In 1979 the Ritz family sold the hotel to Egyptian businessman Mohamed Al Fayed, who refurbished it and added a cooking school. Two town houses were annexed, joined by a long arcade lined with miniature display cases representing 125 of the leading boutiques of Paris. The hotel's drawing rooms, salons, three gardens, and courtyards were preserved. The salons are furnished with museum-caliber antiques: gilt pieces, ornate mirrors, Louis XV and Louis XVI furniture, hand-woven tapestries, and 10-foot-high bronze candelabra. The decor of the bathrooms is impeccably French, with wood and marble, antique chests, desks with bronze hardware, and crystal lighting. Every convenience imaginable has been installed.

Dining/Entertainment: The Espadon grill room is one of the finest in Paris. The Ritz Club includes a bar, a salon with a fireplace, a restaurant, and a dance floor. Drinks can be ordered in either Bar Vendôme or Bar Hemingway.

Services: Concierge, 24-hour room service, laundry, valet.

Facilities: Luxury health club with swimming pool and massage parlor, florist, shops, three meeting rooms.

EXPENSIVE

HOTEL CAMBON, 3 rue Cambon, 75001 Paris. Tel. 42-60-38-09. Fax 42-60-30-59. 43 rms (all with bath). A/C MINIBAR TV TEL **Métro:** Concorde.
$ Rates: Single 1,080F ($199.80), double 1,380F–1,880F ($255.30–$347.80). AE, MC, V. Breakfast 70F ($13) extra.
Parking: Nearby lot 150F ($27.75) per 24-hour period.

Conveniently located on a stylish street in the heart of Paris's monument zone, this stone-fronted 19th-century building recently was completely renovated with comfortable contemporary decor. The public rooms are richly furnished with 19th- and 20th-century sculptures and paintings, including the cozy street-level bar, where guests can usually converse with the genial owners, the Simeone family. Bedrooms are each individually decorated, usually with fabric wallcoverings, marble-sheathed bathrooms, and much exposed wood. The staff here seems especially helpful; many of them speak English.

HOTEL DE CASTILLE, 37 rue Cambon, 75001 Paris. Tel. 42-61-55-20. Fax 40-15-97-64. 61 rms (all with bath), 15 suites. MINIBAR TV TEL **Métro:** Madeleine.
$ Rates: Single 950F ($175.75), double 1,680F ($310.80), suite from 3,000F ($555). Breakfast 75F ($13.90) extra. AE, DC, MC, V.

Hôtel de Castille is a renovated hotel near the headquarters of Chanel and across the street from the "back door" of the Ritz. For a hotel so close to major shops, museums, and busy boulevards, the Castille is quiet, and only a few minutes' walk from place Vendôme, place de la Concorde, or place de la Madeleine. During fashion shows hotel prices rise and the rooms fill up quickly.

A series of beige marble panels and large mirrors, wall sconces, and a black-trimmed elevator bank grace the lobby area. The sunny rooms are painted in a variety of pastel colors and outfitted in a streamlined art deco style, featuring clean white baths with gray marble sinks.

Dining/Entertainment: On the premises is a restaurant, Le Relais Castille, done in colors of flame and rust. Lunch and dinner are served in the inside garden court.

HOTEL DE FRANCE ET CHOISEUL, 239 rue St-Honoré, 75001 Paris. Tel. 42-61-54-60. Fax 40-20-96-32. 120 rms (all with bath), 16 suites. MINIBAR TV TEL **Métro:** Concorde, Tuileries, Opéra, or Madeleine.

$ Rates: Single 950F ($175.75), double 1,400F–1,800F ($259–$333), suite from 2,200F ($407). Breakfast 100F ($18.50) extra. AE, DC, MC, V. **Parking:** 70F ($12.95).

The France et Choiseul is a remake of a gracious 1720 town house, just off the place Vendôme. Actually, it's been a hotel since the 1870s, and became a fashionable oasis in fin-de-siècle Paris. Now, more than a century later, it has been completely remodeled. The bedrooms—most of which open onto the inner courtyard—were entirely gutted, then turned into bandbox-size accommodations that are, nevertheless, attractively decorated. All sorts of conveniences are offered as compensation for the lost belle époque glamour, including radios, dressing tables, and decorative tile baths with all the latest gadgets. A few minisuites have been installed on the top floor under the mansard roof, with a staircase leading up to twin beds on a balcony.

Dining/Entertainment: There is a charming restaurant, La Lafayette, opening onto the inner courtyard, on the site of the historic salon where Lafayette received the subsidies to participate in the American War of Independence. It serves breakfast only.

Services: Room service, babysitting, laundry/valet.

HOTEL LOTTI, 7–9 rue de Castiglione, 75001 Paris. Tel. 42-60-37-34. Fax 40-20-96-32. 120 rms, 16 suites. MINIBAR TV TEL **Métro:** Odéon.

$ Rates: Single 1,200F ($222), double 1,600F ($296), suite from 2,000F ($370). Breakfast 85F ($15.75) extra. AE, DC, MC, V. **Parking:** 70F ($12.95).

Located just off the historic place Vendôme, the Lotti is known as a "junior Ritz." Inside its doors an elegant French world of marble and gilt, tapestries and crystal, unfolds. The bedrooms' decorators turned to the 19th century for inspiration, using reproductions of furnishings of that era. Rosewood and mahogany, gilt and silk damask, even tambour desks, re-create the ambience of an elegant town house bedroom. Some of the upper-story rooms were probably used at one time by servants of wealthy clients; each room has its own garret-like style.

Dining/Entertainment: The hotel has a distinguished restaurant, serving classic French cuisine.

Services: Laundry, babysitting, room service.

MODERATE

HOTEL BRIGHTON, 218 rue de Rivoli, 75001 Paris. Tel. 42-60-30-03. Fax 42-60-41-78. 70 rms (all with bath or shower), 1 suite. MINIBAR TV TEL **Métro:** Louvre.

$ Rates (including continental breakfast): Single 400F–745F ($74–$137.85), double 500F–785F ($92.50–$145.25), suite from 1,050F ($194.25). AE, DC, MC, V.

Despite its English name, the Brighton is a very French hotel, and a good one at that. You're in the heart of one of the major shopping streets of Paris, right across from the Louvre. In fact, if you're lucky enough to snare a front room, you'll look out on not only this world-famous art museum but the Tuileries as well. A scattering of accommodations open onto tiny balconies; on a clear day, you can see the Seine and the Eiffel Tower in the distance. Each of the clean, comfortable rooms is furnished in a traditional style, often with brass beds.

NOVOTEL PARIS LES HALLES, place Marguerite-de-Navarre, 75001 Paris. Tel. 42-21-31-31. Fax 40-26-05-79. 271 rms, 14 suites. MINIBAR TV TEL **Métro:** Les Halles.

$ Rates: Single 800F ($148), double 870F ($160.95), suite from 1,400F–1,800F ($259–$333). Breakfast 65F ($12.05) extra. AE, DC, MC, V.

Set alongside the edge of the beaux arts lattices of the place des Halles, this is one of the best Novotels in its worldwide network. Its cubist-inspired, mirror-sheathed facade and sloping skylights mimic the most daring of the Beaubourg neighborhood's futuristic architecture. Built in 1986, the hotel contains a sunny lobby and a small-scale copy of the Statue of Liberty, along with an alluring and stylish bar on a dais above the ground floor.

Each room offers a no-nonsense but comfortable and efficient decor, with one double bed and one single (which serves as a couch or a bed), and a streamlined private bath. All units offer the same floor plan and furnishings, but the most sought-after rooms overlook Les Halles, with its fountains, shrubbery, and carousel. The greenhouse restaurant, The Sun Deck Grill, opens onto the ancient church of St-Eustache on the opposite side of the square.

INEXPENSIVE

BRITANNIQUE, 20 av. Victoria, 75001 Paris. Tel. 42-33-74-59. Fax 42-33-82-65. 40 rms (all with bath). MINIBAR TV TEL **Métro:** Châtelet.

$ Rates: Single 520F ($96.20), double 680F ($125.80). Breakfast 50F ($9.25) extra. AE, DC, MC, V. **Parking:** 50F ($9.25).

After a complete renovation, the Britannique has been rated three stars by the government. It's in the heart of Paris, within easy reach of Les Halles, the Georges Pompidou cultural center, and Notre-Dame. Rooms are small but clean, comfortable, and adequately equipped. The TV satellite receiver picks up programs from the U.S. and U.K.

BUDGET

HOTEL HENRI IV, 25 place Dauphine, 75001 Paris. Tel. 43-54-44-53. 22 rms (none with bath). **Métro:** Pont-Neuf.

$ Rates (including continental breakfast): Single 100F–140F ($18.50–$25.90), double 170F–200F ($31.45–$37). No credit cards.

Four hundred years ago the printing presses for the edicts of Henri IV filled this narrow building. Today the orderly rows of trees in the square outside contribute to one of the loveliest locations in Paris. A sojourn here lures a loyal clientele of budget-conscious academicians, journalists, and francophiles. The low-ceilinged lobby, one flight above street level, is cramped and a bit bleak. But that is dispelled by the friendliness of Monsieur and Madame Maurice Balitrand. The bedrooms, reached by a winding stairwell, saw better days under Clemenceau, but many devotees consider them romantically threadbare. None contains its own bath, shower, or toilet, but each has a sink. The real allure of this place, aside from its dramatic location, is the price.

4. 2ND & 9TH ARRONDISSEMENTS

VERY EXPENSIVE

HOTEL WESTMINSTER, 13 rue de la Paix, 75002 Paris. Tel. 42-61-57-46. Fax 42-60-30-66. 102 rms, 18 suites. A/C MINIBAR TV TEL **Métro:** Opéra.

$ Rates: Single 2,200F ($407), double 2,800F ($518), suite from 4,000F ($740). Breakfast 140F ($25.90) extra. AE, DC, MC, V.

The Westminster lies between the Opéra and the place Vendôme and is the sibling of the contemporary Le Warwick. The Westminster is traditional but, following a massive renovation, it has all the modern comforts as well.

The hotel was originally built during Baron Haussmann's redesigning of Paris in 1846 and incorporated an old convent. By 1907 it had been declared a national monument and is today a landmark. At the turn of the century the hotel was purchased by Monsieur Bruchon, who renovated it and installed a famous collection of clocks, which today is one of the attractions of the hotel. In 1981 it was acquired by Warwick International Hotels, which completely renovated it.

Guest rooms are each individually decorated. Pastel colors blend with rich paneling, molded ceilings, and marble-top fireplaces. Many antiques, mainly from the Louis XIV era, are found in both the public and private guest rooms. Each accommodation has its own luxurious private bath, a radio, and a color TV.

Dining/Entertainment: There is an atmospheric bar and gourmet restaurant, Le Celadon.

Services: 24-hour room service, babysitting, laundry/valet.

INEXPENSIVE

HOTEL RICHMOND, 11 rue du Helder, 75009 Paris. Tel. 47-70-53-20. Fax 48-00-02-10. 63 rms (all with bath). MINIBAR TV TEL **Métro:** Opéra.

$ Rates (including continental breakfast): Single 550F ($101.75), double 675F ($124.90). AE, DC, MC, V.

This three-star hotel is a short walk from the Opéra, near American Express, the Café de la Paix, and many fine shops. Behind the attractive facade is a pleasant lounge with sofas, marble columns, and a Roman-style fountain—all contributing to an Old World feel. Rooms are comfortably, traditionally furnished.

5. 12TH ARRONDISSEMENT

MODERATE

LE PAVILLON BASTILLE, 65 rue de Lyon, 75012 Paris. Tel.

43-43-65-65. Fax 43-43-96-52. 24 rms, 1 suite. MINIBAR TV TEL **Métro:** Bastille.
$ Rates (including continental breakfast): Single or double 915F ($169.30), suite from 1,250F ($231.25). AE, DC, V.

One of the city's newest hotels lies within a garden-fronted white-sided building about a block south of place de la Bastille. Despite the 17th-century fountain that graces one wall of the hotel's cobble-covered courtyard, the hotel incorporates a postmodern aesthetic that gracefully mixes baroque elements with modern accessories and lighting. The establishment's theme colors are blue and yellow, which appear along with marble, leather, glass, and both black and beige granite throughout both the public rooms and the bedrooms. Rooms contain twin or double beds, mirrors, and comfortable contemporary built-in furniture. The English-speaking staff offers personalized service.

Dining/Entertainment: Bar; breakfast room set beneath the ceiling vaults of the cellar.

Services: Room service, babysitting, laundry/valet.

6. 5TH ARRONDISSEMENT

MODERATE

HOTEL LE COLBERT, 7 rue de l'Hôtel-Colbert, 75005 Paris. Tel. 43-25-85-65. 38 rms (all with bath), 2 suites. TV TEL **Métro:** Maubert-Mutualité or St-Michel.
$ Rates: Single 640F ($118.40), double 950F ($175.75), suite from 1,600F ($296). Breakfast 45F ($8.35) extra. AE, V.

How can you miss by staying at this little centuries-old inn? Not only is it on the Left Bank, a minute from the Seine, but it provides a fine view of Notre-Dame from many of its rooms as well. There's even a small courtyard, setting the hotel apart from the bustle of Left Bank life.

You enter a tastefully decorated lobby area, with marble floors, red cut-velvet wallpaper, and a view of the wrought-iron fence separating the evergreen trees of the courtyard from the narrow street outside. A sunny bar area is filled with gilt-accented French furniture. The rooms are well designed and tailored. Most of them provide comfortable chairs and a breakfast area. The baths have been recently renovated, the beds are inviting, and units include plenty of towels and efficient maid service.

GRAND HOTEL MODERNE, 33 rue des Ecoles, 75005 Paris. Tel. 43-54-37-78. Fax 43-29-74-42. 45 rms (all with bath). TV TEL **Métro:** Maubert-Mutualité or St-Michel.
$ Rates (including continental breakfast): Single 530F–720F ($98.05–$133.20), double 580F–810F ($107.30–$149.85). AE, DC, MC, V.

Near Notre-Dame and the Panthéon, the Grand Hotel Moderne is a successful blend of the Paris of yesterday and that of today. It was completely renovated in 1992. Located in the heart of the Latin Quarter, this hotel provides a warm welcome by its charming owner, Madame Gibon. She rents comfortably furnished bedrooms that are spotlessly maintained. There are double-glazed aluminum windows in the rooms fronting the rue des Ecoles, which make for a more tranquil atmosphere.

SELECT, 1 place de la Sorbonne, 75005 Paris. Tel. 46-34-14-80. Fax 46-34-51-79. 69 rms (all with bath). TV TEL **Métro:** St-Michel.

$ Rates: Single 520F ($96.20), double 740F ($136.90). Breakfast 40F ($7.40) extra. AE, DC, MC, V.

Built by Le Mercier between 1635 and 1642, this hotel is the only one that stands directly on this square dominated by the Church of the Sorbonne. Try to get a room overlooking the fountain in this plaza. Nearby, there are cafés on the busy "boul Mich." Rooms in the modernized hotel are comfortably furnished.

INEXPENSIVE

HOTEL AGORA ST-GERMAIN, 42 rue des Bernardins, 75005 Paris. Tel. 46-34-13-00. Fax 46-34-75-05. 39 rms (all with bath or shower). MINIBAR TV TEL **Métro:** Maubert-Mutualité.

$ Rates: Single 525F–575F ($97.15–$106.40), double 650F ($120.25). Breakfast 45F ($8.35) extra. AE, DC, MC, V.

The Agora St-Germain is now one of the best of the moderately priced hotels in this artistic and historical section of Paris. It offers soundproof rooms, each well furnished and equipped with an alarm clock, hair dryer, and safety box. Room service is provided daily from 7:30am to 4:30pm.

HOTEL ELYSA-LUXEMBOURG, 6 rue Gay-Lussac, 75005 Paris. Tel. 43-25-31-74. Fax 46-34-56-27. 30 rms (all with bath). MINIBAR TV TEL **Métro:** Luxembourg.

$ Rates: Single 530F–590F ($98.05–$109.15), double 580F–690F ($107.30–$127.65). Breakfast 45F ($8.35) extra. AE, DC, MC, V. **Parking:** 50F ($9.25).

One of the best choices in the heart of the Latin Quarter is near the Luxembourg Gardens. The completely renovated rooms here are charming, spacious, and soundproof. Some accommodations are reserved for nonsmokers. Guests may use the sauna.

7. 6TH ARRONDISSEMENT

EXPENSIVE

L'HOTEL, 23 rue des Beaux-Arts, 75006 Paris. Tel. 43-25-27-22. Fax 43-25-64-81. 24 rms, 3 suites. A/C MINIBAR TV TEL **Métro:** St-Germain-des-Prés.

$ Rates: Small double 1,000F–1,200F ($185–$222), large double 1,800F–2,300F ($333–$425.50), suite from 3,500F ($647.50). Breakfast 100F ($18.50) extra. AE, DC, MC, V.

L'Hôtel was a 19th-century "fleabag" called the Hôtel d'Alsace, and its major distinction was that Oscar Wilde, broke and down and out, died here. In one of the upstairs rooms he wrote to Frank Harris, the author, asking him to send "the money you owe me." However, today's clients aren't exactly on poverty row. Through the lobby of what is known only as L'Hôtel march many show business and fashion personalities.

L'Hôtel is the love-hobby creation of French actor Guy-Louis Duboucheron. He's responsible for establishing this intimate atmosphere of super-sophistication in a hotel that's been called a "jewel box." A Texas architect, Robin Westbrook, was hired to gut the core of the Alsace, making a circular courtyard and an interior evocative of the Tower of Pisa.

You'll feel like a movie star yourself when you take a bath in your tub of rosy-pink imported Italian marble. At the edge of your tub will be a delicate vase holding a single rose. Throughout the building antiques are used with discretion, an eclectic collection that includes pieces from the periods of Louis XV and Louis XVI, as well as Empire and Directoire.

For nostalgia buffs, the ideal rooms are the re-creation of Wilde's original bedchamber and that of Mistinguette, the legendary star of the French stage. In the latter room, the star's original furniture—designed by Jean-Gabriel Domergue—has been installed. Celebrities from Katharine Hepburn to Mick Jagger have enjoyed these rooms.

Dining/Entertainment: Breakfast is served in a stone cellar, which in the evening becomes a tavern for intimate dinners. The Winter Garden is a luxurious piano bar/restaurant.

Services: Concierge, 24-hour room service, babysitting, laundry/valet.

RELAIS CHRISTINE, 3 rue Christine, 75006 Paris. Tel. 43-26-71-80. Fax 43-26-89-38. 51 rms, 13 suites. A/C MINIBAR TV TEL **Métro:** Odéon.

$ Rates: Single or double 1,300F–2,000F ($240.50–$370). Breakfast 75F ($13.90) extra. AE, DC, MC, V. **Parking:** Free.

Relais Christine welcomes a sophisticated international clientele into what used to be a 16th-century Augustinian cloister. This is really one of the most unusual hotels in this part of town. You enter from a narrow cobblestone street, first into a symmetrical courtyard and then an elegant reception area dotted with baroque sculpture, plush upholsteries, and a scattering of Renaissance antiques. The Auvergne-based Bertrand family converted the building from a warehouse of a nearby publishing company into this elegant hotel in 1979.

You will not have experienced the hotel until you go down into the vaulted breakfast room on the lower level, the ancient well of which is spotlit from within and the massive central stone column having witnessed all the activity in what used to be the cloister's kitchen. Each bedroom is individually decorated with antiques or antique reproductions and plenty of flair. Accents might include massively beamed ceilings and plush wall-to-wall carpeting.

Dining/Entertainment: Just off the reception area is a paneled sitting room and bar area ringed with 19th-century portraits and comfortable leather chairs.

Services: Room service, laundry, babysitting.

RELAIS SAINT-GERMAIN, 9 carrefour de l'Odéon, 75006 Paris. Tel. 43-29-12-05. Fax 46-33-45-30. 10 rms. A/C MINIBAR TV TEL **Métro:** Odéon.

$ Rates (including continental breakfast): Single 1,360F ($251.60), double 1,520F ($281.20). AE, DC, MC, V.

The Saint-Germain is an oasis of charm and comfort. But keep it a secret—it rents only 10 bedrooms, with private bath or shower. A tall, slender hotel adapted from a 17th-century building, its decor is a happy medley of traditional and modern. Of course, all the necessary amenities were tucked in under the beams as well, including soundproofing, private safe, and hairdryer.

HOTEL DES SAINTS-PERES, 65 rue des Sts-Péres, 75006 Paris. Tel. 45-44-50-00. Fax 45-44-90-83. 37 rms (all with bath), 3 suites. MINIBAR TV TEL **Métro:** St-Germain-des-Prés or Sèvres-Babylone.

$ Rates: Single 450F ($83.25), double 1,650F ($305.25), suite from 1,700F ($314.50). Breakfast 55F ($10.20) extra. MC, V.

The best recommendation for this old favorite just off boulevard St-Germain is the long list of habitués, including Edna St. Vincent Millay, who enjoyed the camellia-trimmed garden. The hotel, designed by Louis XIV's architect, is decorated in part with antique paintings, tapestries, and mirrors. The most sought room is the *chambre à la fresque*, which has a 17th-century painted ceiling. The modernized bedrooms face the courtyard, where breakfast is served, weather permitting.

HOTEL DU VIEUX PARIS, 9 rue Git-le-Coeur, 75006 Paris. Tel. 43-54-41-66. Fax 43-26-00-15. 15 rms (all with bath or shower), 5 suites. MINIBAR TV TEL **Métro:** St-Michel.

$ Rates (including continental breakfast): Single 1,200F ($222), double 1,400F–1,600F ($259–$296), suite from 1,900F ($351.50). MC, V.

Tucked away in a building dating from 1480, this former getaway for Henri IV and his mistress is one of those great hard-to-find places. Completely restored, it is near the Sorbonne, Sainte Chapelle, and the Seine. Such members of the Beat Generation as Allen Ginsberg, William S. Burroughs, and Jack Kerouac discovered it in the 1950s and 1960s, but they wouldn't recognize the place today. Rooms are elegantly furnished with "massive showers"; there are Jacuzzis in the suites. Other amenities include hair dryers, safes, and trouser presses. Two of the suites have a mezzanine overlooking the rooftops of Paris.

MODERATE

HOTEL D'ANGLETERRE, 44 rue Jacob, 75006 Paris. Tel. 42-60-34-72. Fax 42-60-16-93. 29 rms (all with bath). TV TEL **Métro:** St-Germain-des-Prés.

$ Rates (including continental breakfast): Single 630F–780F ($116.55–$144.30), double 1,100F ($203.50). AE, DC, V.

Situated amid antique shops and art galleries, this quaint building, constructed in 1650, once housed the British Embassy. Despite the antique plumbing, the Angleterre has long been favored by such illustrious guests as Anne Morrow Lindbergh and Ernest Hemingway, who stayed here once while he was ill. Shut off from street traffic, most of its rooms open onto an exposed courtyard and garden, where tables are set for breakfast.

AVIATIC, 105 rue de Vaugirard, 75006 Paris. Tel. 45-44-38-21. Fax 45-49-35-83. 43 rms (all with bath). MINIBAR TV TEL **Métro:** Montparnasse-Bienvenue.

$ Rates (including continental breakfast): Single 560F–640F ($103.60–$118.40), double 640F–720F ($118.40–$133.20). AE, DC, MC, V. **Parking:** 120F ($22.20).

This is a bit of old Paris, with a modest inner courtyard and a vine-covered lattice on the walls. It's been a family-run hotel of character and elegance for a century. The reception lounge, with its marble columns, brass chandeliers, antiques, and petit salon, provides an attractive traditional setting. Completely remodeled, the hotel lies in an interesting center of Montparnasse, with its cafes frequented by artists, writers, and jazz musicians. The staff speaks English.

HOTEL DE FLEURIE, 32 rue Gregoire-de-Tours, 75006 Paris. Tel. 43-29-59-81. Fax 43-29-68-44. 29 rms (all with bath). MINIBAR TV TEL **Métro:** Odéon.

$ Rates: Single 575F ($106.40), double 725F–975F ($134.15–$180.40). Breakfast 45F ($8.35) extra. AE, DC, MC, V.

Just 70 feet off the boulevard St-Germain on a colorful little Left Bank street, the Fleurie is one of the best of the "new" old hotels. Restored to its former glory in 1988, the facade is studded with statuary that is spotlit by night, recapturing its 17th-century elegance. The stone walls have been exposed in the reception salon, with its refectory desk where guests check in. It has latticework, and an exposed beamed ceiling. An elevator takes you to the well-furnished, modern bedrooms; a spiral staircase leads down to a breakfast room.

ODEON-HOTEL, 3 rue de l'Odéon, 75006 Paris. Tel. 43-25-90-67. Fax 43-25-55-98. 34 rms (all with bath). TV TEL **Métro:** Odéon.

$ Rates: Single 630F–680F ($116.55–$125.80), double 680F–890F ($125.80–$164.65). Breakfast 45F ($8.35) extra. AE, DC, MC, V.

Conveniently located near both the Théâtre de l'Odéon and boulevard St-Germain, the hotel stands on what was, in 1779, the first street in Paris to have pavements and gutters. By the turn of the century this area, which housed the bookshop Shakespeare and Company at no. 12, began attracting such writers as André Gide, Paul Valéry, James Joyce, T. S. Eliot, F. Scott Fitzgerald, Ernest Hemingway, and Gertrude Stein. Today, with its exposed beams, rough stone walls, high crooked ceilings, tapestries, oak-and-bookbinder wallpaper mixed in with bright contemporary fabrics, mirrored ceilings, and black leather furnishings, the Odéon-Hotel is reminiscent of a modernized Norman country inn. After modern plumbing was installed, each room was individually redesigned.

HOTEL DU PAS-DE-CALAIS, 59 rue des Saints-Pères, 75006 Paris. Tel. 45-48-78-74. Fax 45-44-94-57. 41 rms (all with bath). TV TEL **Métro:** St-Germain-des-Prés.

$ Rates (including continental breakfast): Single 590F ($109.15), double 720F ($133.20). AE, MC, V.

Pas-du-Calais is in a historic building with literary connections that has been smartly updated. The five-story structure was built in the 17th century by the Lavalette family and inhabited by Chateaubriand from 1811 to 1814. Possibly its most famous guest was Jean-Paul Sartre, who struggled away with the play *Dirty Hands* in room no. 41 during the hotel's prerestoration days.

Today the hotel retains its elegant facade, complete with its massive wooden doors. Its modern rooms have large baths, color TVs, safety boxes, and hairdryers. The inner rooms surround a modest courtyard, with two garden tables and several green trellises. Off the somewhat sterile lobby is a comfortable, carpeted sitting room with TV.

HOTEL LE SAINTE-BEUVE, 9 rue Ste-Beuve, 75006 Paris. Tel. 45-48-20-07. Fax 45-48-67-52. 23 rms (all with bath), 1 suite. MINIBAR TV TEL **Métro:** Vavin.

$ Rates: Single 675F ($124.90), double 925F ($171.15), suite from 1,600F ($296). Breakfast 75F ($13.90) extra. AE, MC, V.

This is the answer to your dreams: a small, tastefully restored hotel in Montparnasse, with its many memories of long gone but still fabled personalities. Situated around the corner from Rodin's famous statue of Balzac, Sainte-Beuve is a charmer. Its decor was conceived by the celebrated decorator David Hicks, and that means a warm, cozy atmosphere, aglow with rose-colored chintz. Breakfast can be served in bed, and you can also enjoy the intimate lobby bar with a fireplace. The hotel is decorated mainly with provincial pieces. Each accommodation has an individual safe.

HOTEL ST-GERMAIN-DES-PRES, 36 rue Bonaparte, 75006 Paris. Tel. 43-26-00-19. Fax 40-46-83-63. 30 rms (all with bath), 2 suites. MINIBAR TV TEL **Métro:** St-Germain-des-Prés.

$ Rates: Single 675F ($124.90), double 725F–825F ($134.15–$152.65), suite from 1,200F ($222). Breakfast 50F ($9.25) extra. V.

Much of this hotel's allure comes from its enviable location in the Latin Quarter—behind a narrow facade on a well-known Left Bank street near many shops. Janet Flanner, the legendary correspondent for the *New Yorker* in the 1920s, lived here for a while. Each of the bedrooms is small and charming, often with exposed old ceiling beams. Some accommodations are air conditioned. Floral patterns abound in the sitting rooms, and the public rooms often have 18th-century-inspired paneling and wall niches.

HOTEL LE SAINT-GREGOIRE, 43 rue de l'Abbe-Grégoire, 75006 Paris. Tel. 45-48-23-23. Fax 45-48-33-95. 20 rms (all with bath or shower), 1 suite. TV TEL **Métro:** St-Placide.

$ Rates: Single or double 675F–820F ($124.90–$151.70), suite from 1,200F ($222). Breakfast 65F ($12.05) extra. AE, DC, MC, V. **Parking:** 50F ($9.25).

The Saint-Grégoire is a sparkler that opened in 1989. A restored town house–style structure, the well-run hotel is rated three stars. All of its bedrooms are handsomely furnished; some have private terraces as well. Lighting is subtle in the vaulted breakfast room (breakfast is the only meal served). In winter, there's a cozy fire in the sitting room.

LA VILLA, 29 rue Jacob, 75006 Paris. Tel. 43-26-60-00. Fax 46-34-63-63. 30 rms (all with bath), 5 suites. A/C MINIBAR TV TEL **Métro:** St-Germain-des-Prés.

$ Rates: Single 780F–1,100F ($144.30–$203.50), double 1,250F ($231.25), suite from 1,600F ($296). Breakfast 80F ($14.80) extra. AE, MC, V.

La Villa is a four-star choice (formerly the Hotel d'Isly) on the corner of a street where Richard Wagner lived from 1841 to 1842. The rooms and suites of La Villa were designed by Marie-Christine Dorner, one of the best decorators in the field. Each bathroom has a hairdryer.

INEXPENSIVE

DEUX-CONTINENTS, 25 rue Jacob, 75006 Paris. Tel. 43-26-72-46. 40 rms (all with bath or shower). TV TEL **Métro:** St-Germain-des-Prés.

$ Rates (including continental breakfast): Single 450F–580F

($83.25–$107.30), double 520F–640F ($96.20–$118.40). MC, V.

⑤ The Deux-Continents is the domain of Madame Chresteil, who inherited these two continents—that is, two adjoining buildings. She runs the place with a rare combination of sense and candor, good humor, and kindliness. She's furnished the rooms in modern and not-so-modern, installed telephones, and ensured that there are reading lights over the beds. Prices include a breakfast tray brought to the room.

GRAND HOTEL DES BALCONS, 3 rue Casimir-Delavigne, 75006 Paris. Tel. 46-34-78-50. 55 rms (all with bath). TV TEL **Métro:** Odéon.

$ Rates: Single 300F ($55.50), double 380F–420F ($70.30–$77.70). Breakfast 45F ($8.35) extra. MC, V.

This is perhaps the best buy on this little street off the Odéon. The lobby is rust-colored and decorated with art nouveau panels. An unpretentious two-star hotel, it once sheltered Endre Ády (1877-1919), Hungary's greatest lyric poet.

The compact rooms, each with background music, have been renovated by the owners. Ask for rooms above the street level for greater comfort and security.

HOTEL LOUIS II, 2 rue St-Sulpice, 75006 Paris. Tel. 46-33-13-80. Fax 46-33-17-29. 22 rms (all with bath). MINIBAR TV TEL **Métro:** Odéon.

$ Rates: Single or double 450F–620F ($83.25–$114.70), triple 750F ($138.75). Breakfast 38F ($7.05) extra. AE, DC, MC, V.

One of the most skillful, charming renovations on the Left Bank transformed the interiors of a run-down pair of 18th-century buildings into a chintz-covered rustic fantasy. Its decorators exposed as many of the hand-hewn beams as they could, so that in each of the cozy bedrooms wide expanses of mellowed patina contrast pleasantly with flowered wall coverings and plush carpeting. Many repeat visitors request one of the romantic rooms beneath the slope of the building's eaves for an upgraded version of *La Bohème*.

Televisions are available in the bedrooms on request. Morning coffee and afternoon drinks are served in an elegant reception salon, where gilt-framed mirrors, bouquets of fresh flowers, and well-oiled antiques add to a refreshingly provincial allure.

MICHELET-ODEON, 6 place de l'Odéon, 75006 Paris. Tel. 46-34-27-80. Fax 46-34-55-35. 42 rms (all with bath). TV TEL **Métro:** Odéon.

$ Rates: Single or double 330F–380F ($61.05–$70.30), triple 740F ($136.90). Breakfast 38F ($7.05) extra. AE, V.

Conveniently located on place de l'Odéon, the Michelet-Odéon owes its theatrical clientele to the nearby Théâtre de l'Europe. The hotel, with classic columns and a cozy lounge, is comfortable and reasonably priced. Guests will find the more modern accommodations on the fourth and fifth floors; the lower floors, although renovated, maintain a classic decor.

ST-ANDRE-DES-ARTS, 66 rue St-André-des-Arts, 75006 Paris. Tel. 43-26-96-16. 34 rms (28 with bath). TEL **Métro:** Odéon.

$ Rates (including continental breakfast): Single without bath 190F ($35.15), single with bath 290F ($53.65), double with bath 320F–380F ($59.20–$70.30). No credit cards.

S This hotel sits amid a warren of narrow streets known for their bustling nightlife and artistic orientation, just off St-Germain-des-Prés. It tends to be casual, attracting young travelers, models, and performing artists. The facade, painted green with gold lettering, is easy to spot. The interior contains 17th-century walls, with exposed stone, massive wood beams, and plenty of clean white plaster. The bedrooms are scattered along a labyrinth of hallways and winding stairs.

8. 7TH & 15TH ARRONDISSEMENTS

EXPENSIVE

LE DUC DE SAINT-SIMON, 14 rue de St-Simon, 75007 Paris. Tel. 45-48-35-66. Fax 45-48-68-25. 34 rms (all with bath), 5 suites. TEL **Métro:** rue-du-Bac.
$ Rates: Single 1,100F–1,350F ($203.50–$249.75), double 1,110F–1,400F ($203.50–$259), suite from 1,600F ($296). Breakfast 70F ($12.95) extra. No credit cards.

Set on a quiet residential street on the Left Bank, this small villa has a tiny front garden and an 1830s decor with *faux-marbre* trompe-l'oeil panels and a frescoed elevator. The vaulted cellar, formerly reserved for coal storage, contains an intimate bar with an adjacent Louis XIII–style breakfast room. Each bedroom is unique, though sure to include at least one antique. The service, perhaps the best reflection of the owner's extensive training, is helpful but reserved.

HILTON INTERNATIONAL PARIS, 18 av. Suffren, 75015 Paris. Tel. 42-73-92-00, or toll free 800/225-9290 in the U.S. Fax 47-83-62-66. 455 rms, 28 suites. A/C MINIBAR TV TEL **RER:** Champs de Mars.
$ Rates: Single 1,650F–2,000F ($305.25–$370), double 1,750F–2,200F ($323.75–$407), suite from 3,300F ($610.50). Breakfast 100F ($18.50) extra. **Parking:** 130F ($24.05).

On a tract of land near the Eiffel Tower in the 15th arrondissement, Hilton built one of the city's most impressive modern hotels, shattering the Right Bank's monopoly on grand hotels. Today, it has become a focal point of social life in this part of the city.

Built in the Hilton style of maximum comfort, with strong doses of Parisian flavor and virtually every convenience and efficiency, this 11-story hotel is designed around window-walls and contemporary gadgets, backed up by a professional staff along with a computer-age security system.

Each of the well-furnished, soundproof bedrooms has a generous bathroom covered with an appealingly tinted series of marble slabs, an oversize sink, and dozens of square yards of towels, terrycloth bathrobes, and plenty of sweetly scented toilet articles. The emphasis throughout the hotel is on personal service and such amenities as readily available ice cubes.

Dining/Entertainment: A breakfast buffet is served on La Terrasse (one of the best in Paris). There are three bars and Le Western, a steakhouse with a cowboy theme and a definite sense of humor.

Services: Babysitting, same-day laundry and dry cleaning, travel services, beauty parlor, 24-hour room service.

Facilities: Nearby underground garage (most valuable in Paris), several chic boutiques.

MODERATE

HOTEL DE L'ACADEMIE, 32 rue des Saints-Péres, 75007 Paris. Tel. 45-48-36-22. Fax 45-44-75-21. 34 rms (all with bath). MINIBAR TV TEL **Métro:** St-Germain-des-Prés.

$ Rates: Single or double 600F–720F ($111–$133.20). Breakfast 50F ($9.25) extra. AE, DC, MC, V.

The exterior walls and the old ceiling beams are all that remain of this 17th-century residence for the private guards of the duc de Rohan. In 1983 it was completely renovated to include an elegant marble-and-oak reception area, Second Empire–style chairs, and an English-speaking staff. The comfortably up-to-date rooms have Directoire beds, an "Ile de France" decor in soft colors, radios, alarm clocks, and views over the 18th- and 19th-century buildings in the immediate neighborhood.

HOTEL DU QUAI VOLTAIRE, 19 quai Voltaire, 75007 Paris. Tel. 42-61-50-91. Fax 42-61-62-25. 33 rms (all with bath or shower). TV TEL **Métro:** rue du Bac.

$ Rates: Single 430F ($79.55), double 780F ($144.30). Breakfast 45F ($8.35) extra. AE, DC, MC, V.

This is an inn with a past and one of the most magnificent views in all Paris. The hotel occupies a prime site on the Left Bank quays of the Seine, halfway between the pont Royal and the gracefully arched pont du Carrousel. Twenty-nine of its rooms—many of them renovated—gaze over the Louvre, directly across the tree-shaded river. Living here through the years have been Charles Baudelaire, Jean Sibelius, Richard Wagner, and Oscar Wilde. Photos of Wagner and Baudelaire are enshrined in the small, plush sitting room inside the main door. The rooms are pleasantly appointed, but the focal point of every front room is that view—seen through floor-to-ceiling double French windows.

HOTEL DE L'UNIVERSITE, 22 rue de l'Université, 75007 Paris. Tel. 42-61-09-39. Fax 42-60-40-84. 28 rms (all with bath). TV TEL **Métro:** St-Germain-des-Prés.

$ Rates: Single 430F–580F ($79.55–$107.30), double 620F–1,300F ($114.70–$240.50). Breakfast 55F ($10.20) extra. No credit cards.

This has rapidly become the favorite little hotel of those who want to stay in a St-Germain-des-Prés atmosphere. Unusually fine antiques furnish this 300-year-old converted town house. It's the love child of Madame Bergmann, who has a flair for restoring old places and a collector's nose for assembling antiques. She's renovated l'Université completely.

A favorite room is no. 54, all in shades of Gainsborough blue, with a rattan bed and period pieces as well as a marble bath. No. 35, opening onto the courtyard, is another charmer—there's a fireplace and a large provincial armoire decorated in shades of orange. A small breakfast room, in the bistro style, opens onto a tiny courtyard with a fountain. Everything is personal—and reservations are imperative. It's not cheap, but it's well worth the money if you desire a glamorous setting.

INEXPENSIVE

HOTEL LENOX, 9 rue de l'Université, 75007 Paris. Tel. 42-96-10-95. Fax 42-61-52-83. 32 rms (all with bath or shower). TV TEL **Métro:** rue du Bac.

$ Rates (including continental breakfast): Single or double 500F–700F ($92.50–$129.50), double with private salon 875F ($161.90). AE, DC, MC, V.

The Lenox has been a long-standing favorite for those seeking a reasonably priced and desirable nest in St-Germain-des-Prés. Once this was a rather basic little pension. In 1910, in those halcyon years before the Great War, T. S. Eliot spent a hot summer here on "the old man's money." Today this much-improved hotel offers comfortably furnished bedrooms, small and snug, some with elaborate ceiling moldings. The lobby, with its helpful staff and marble fireplace, sets the tone, and a convivial bar off the main reception area is open daily from 5pm to 2am. Many returning guests request the attic duplex with its tiny balcony and skylight.

HOTEL LINDBERGH, 5 rue Chomel, 75007 Paris. Tel. 45-48-35-53. Fax 45-49-31-48. 26 rms (all with bath or shower). TV TEL **Métro:** Sèvres-Babylone or St-Sulpice.

$ Rates: Single 400F–520F ($74–$96.20), double 430F–530F ($79.55–$98.05). Breakfast 35F ($6.50) extra. AE, DC, MC, V.

Hôtel Lindbergh honors the late American aviator whose nonstop solo flight across the Atlantic electrified Paris and the world in 1927. Not long ago, this establishment looked as if nothing had changed since that day, but it now has a modern, elegant exterior and is completely renovated inside. On a somewhat hidden-away Left Bank street two minutes' walk from St-Germain-des-Prés, it's next to a good budget restaurant, off boulevard Raspail. Breakfast is the only meal served in the hotel.

SAINT-THOMAS-D'AQUIN, 3 rue du Pré-aux-Clercs, 75007 Paris. Tel. 42-61-01-22. Fax 42-61-41-43. 21 rms (all with bath or shower). TV TEL **Métro:** St-Germain-des-Prés or rue du Bac.

$ Rates (including continental breakfast): Single 475F–525F ($87.90–$97.15), double 580F ($107.30). AE, DC, MC, V.

The Saint-Thomas-d'Aquin has been entirely renovated and redecorated. Behind a cream-colored facade with shutters and balconies, the hotel stands on a relatively traffic-free street between the busy boulevard St-Germain and rue de l'Université. The staff speaks English and gives you a warm welcome. Bedrooms are fresh and modern, with flowery French wallpaper. Rooms have insulated windows and are serviced by an elevator.

9. 14TH ARRONDISSEMENT

EXPENSIVE

HOTEL MERIDIEN MONTPARNASSE, 19 rue du Commandant-Mouchotte, 75014 Paris. Tel. 43-20-15-51. Fax 43-20-61-03. 950 rms, 33 suites. A/C MINIBAR TV TEL **Métro:** Montparnasse-Bienvenue.

$ Rates: Single 1,650F ($305.25), double 1,950F ($360.75), suite from 3,000F ($555). AE, DC, MC, V. **Parking:** 10F ($1.85) per hour.

This is the largest hotel on the Left Bank, its 25-story skyscraper tower dominating Montparnasse. Rooms are soundproof and color-coordinated, all with views of the city, color cable TVs, and alarm clocks.

Dining/Entertainment: Montparnasse '25 serves a high-level French cuisine and takes its look from the 1920s (black lacquered furniture, gold-leaf sculptures, and reproductions of works by Modigliani and Van Dongen). Glass-enclosed Restaurant Justine overlooks the gardens and serves both a buffet and à la carte specialties. Before-dinner drinks are available in the Platinum Bar and Café Atlantic in the lobby.

Services: Babysitting, 24-hour room service, laundry/valet.
Facilities: Shopping boutiques.

PULLMAN ST-JACQUES, 17 bd. St-Jacques, 75014 Paris. Tel. 45-78-79-80, or toll free 800/223-9862 in the U.S. Fax 45-88-43-93. 797 rms, 14 suites. A/C MINIBAR TV TEL **Métro:** St-Jacques.
$ Rates (including continental breakfast): Single 1,170F–1,460F ($216.45–$270.10), double 1,345F–1,600F ($248.85–$296), suite from 2,200F ($407). AE, DC, MC, V. **Parking:** 50F ($9.25).

Affiliated with Pullman International Hotels, Pullman St-Jacques is a 14-story glass-and-steel hotel, refreshingly stylish and very French. The main lobby has been upgraded, with a marble fountain in the middle. Not only are the public rooms attention-getting, but the bedrooms have color-coordinated textures and fabrics. They come complete with refrigerators, radios, and TVs. The tile bathrooms have both showers and tubs, plus a separate toilet area.

Dining/Entertainment: Le Français is a re-creation of a turn-of-the-century brasserie, with bentwood chairs, 1890s posters, potted palms, and belle époque lighting fixtures.
Services: Laundry/valet, babysitting, 24-hour room service.
Facilities: Business center, shopping boutiques.

10. 3RD & 4TH ARRONDISSEMENTS

EXPENSIVE

LE PAVILLON DE LA REINE, 28 place des Vosges, 75003 Paris. Tel. 42-77-96-40. Fax 42-77-63-06. 30 rms (all with bath), 23 suites. A/C MINIBAR TV TEL **Métro:** Bastille.
$ Rates: Single 1,120F ($207.20), double 1,450F ($268.25), suite from 1,650F ($305.25). Breakfast 85F ($15.75) extra. AE, DC, MC, V. **Parking:** 120F ($22.20).

Lovers of Le Marais long lamented the lack of a hotel on this square where Victor Hugo lived, but the inauguration of this hotel in 1986 changed that oversight. The entrance is through a tunnel leading under the northern border of the square. At the end of the tunnel, flanked with vine-covered lattices and a small formal garden, is a cream-colored villa, the simple neoclassical facade of which blends perfectly into the neighborhood. The hotel of the

Bertrand-Chevalier family is relatively new, but it fits into the landscape so well that you can't tell.

Inside, the Louis XIII decor evokes the heyday of place des Vosges. Wing chairs with flame-stitched upholstery, coupled with iron-banded Spanish antiques, create a feeling of relaxed hospitality. Each bedroom is unique; some are duplexes with sleeping lofts set above a cozy salon, and all feature weathered beams, reproductions of famous paintings, and a marble-sheathed bathroom.

MODERATE

HOTEL DES DEUX-ILES, 59 rue St-Louis-en-l'Ile, 75004 Paris. Tel. 43-26-13-35. Fax 43-29-60-25. 17 rms (all with bath). TV TEL **Métro:** Pont-Marie.

$ Rates: Single 620F ($114.70), double 730F ($135.05). Breakfast 40F ($7.40) extra. No credit cards.

Hôtel des Deux-Iles is a restored 17th-century mansion on this most charming of Seine islands. The interior decorator, Roland Buffat, was so successful with his two other hotels on the same street (Hôtel de Lutèce and Hôtel Saint-Louis) that he decided to open his most elaborate establishment to date. The tropical garden of plants and flowers sets the tone, suggesting the charm and taste level provided by this highly recommended spot. Bamboo and reed are used extensively in both the public and private rooms. Monsieur Buffat suggests a touch of whimsy with his cage of white doves. The favorite meeting place is the rustic-style tavern on a lower level, where guests gather in cool weather around the open fireplace.

HOTEL DE LUTECE, 65 rue St-Louis-en-l'Ile, 75004 Paris. Tel. 43-26-23-52. Fax 43-29-60-25. 23 rms (all with bath). TV TEL **Métro:** Pont-Marie.

$ Rates: Single or double 720F ($133.20). Breakfast 42F ($7.75) extra. No credit cards.

This is like a drink of sparkling champagne—a hotel located on the historic Ile St. Louis, where everybody seemingly wants to live, although there just isn't enough room. You pass through glass entrance doors into what appears to be the attractive and inviting living room of a Breton country house. All this is the creation of interior designer Roland Buffat. The all-purpose reception salon and lounge focuses on a stone fireplace surrounded by downy couches and armchairs. Tall plants and modern paintings add the new look, while antique tables and crude tile floors pay homage to the traditional. Each of the bedrooms is uniquely decorated, many with antiques interspersed with tasteful reproductions. The duke and duchess of Bedford have been known to treat the Lutèce as if it were their Paris town house.

INEXPENSIVE

HOTEL BASTILLE SPERIA, 1 rue de la Bastille, 75004 Paris. Tel. 42-72-04-01. Fax 42-72-56-38. 42 rms (all with bath). MINIBAR TV TEL **Métro:** Bastille.

$ Rates: Single 450F–490F ($83.25–$90.65), double 580F ($107.30). Breakfast 40F ($7.40) extra. AE, DC, MC, V.

The Bastille Speria occupies a seven-story cream-colored building on a corner near the Bastille, the Bastille Opéra, and the Marais. Its completely renovated interior is far more modern than its mansard exterior implies, thanks to a complete overhaul of the building in the late 1980s. Each of the bedrooms contains an acoustical ceiling and simple, but comfortable, furniture.

HOTEL SAINT-LOUIS, 75 rue St-Louis-en-l'Ile, 75004 Paris. Tel. 46-34-04-80. Fax 46-34-02-13. 21 rms (all with bath or shower). TEL **Métro:** Pont-Marie.

$ Rates: Single or double 540F–640F ($99.90–$118.40). Breakfast 40F ($7.40) extra. No credit cards.

Hôtel Saint-Louis is a small hotel, fashionably and romantically positioned on the historic Ile Saint-Louis. Guy Record discovered this hotel and did a good job of conversion. Along with his wife, Andrée, he maintains a charming family atmosphere that is becoming harder and harder to find in Paris. Many of the upper-level accommodations reached by elevator offer views over the rooftops of Paris. I prefer the rooms on the fifth floor, which have the most atmosphere and are decorated with old wood and selections of attractive furniture. Pleasant accessories decorate the rooms, and there are antiques in the small reception lounge. The breakfast room lies in the cellar near a tiny residents' lounge beneath stone vaulting dating from the 14th century.

PARIS DINING

Everything you've ever heard about French cooking is true—it's absolutely superb, and Paris is where you'll find French cuisine at its best. Only in Paris can you turn onto the nearest sidestreet, enter the first ramshackle hostelry you see, sit down at the bare and wobbly table, glance at an illegibly hand-scrawled menu—and get a memorable meal.

In the gastronomic capital of the world, with more than 12,000 restaurants to choose from, it's tough to list all the noteworthy ones. I have opted to include many favorites, listed in a wide range of prices. Some of the restaurants are famous throughout the world; others are lesser known but still deserve the visitor's attention.

Brasserie and bistro customers beware: Granted, Lasserre and Taillevent are fine French restaurants that serve haute cuisine, but there are also restaurants that serve very average food under the guise of haute cuisine and get away with it because of the city's culinary reputation. Don't be wooed by fancy atmosphere or intimidated by haughty maître d's. Use your traveler's common sense: If the locals flock to a particular restaurant, it's probably a sound choice.

Paris restaurants by law add a service charge of 12% to 15% to your bill (*service compris*), which means you don't have to leave a tip. But it is customary to leave something extra. Some restaurants include beverage in their menu rates (*boisson compris*).

Coffee, in France, is served after the meal and carries an extra charge. The French consider it absolutely barbaric to drink coffee along with the courses, and, unless you specifically order it with milk (*au lait*), the coffee will be black. In the more conscientious establishments, it is prepared as the traditional *filtre,* a rather slow but rewarding filter style that takes a bit of manipulating.

DINING WITH CHILDREN Meals at the grand restaurants of Paris are rarely suitable for young children. Nevertheless, many parents drag their children to these deluxe citadels, often to the annoyance of other diners. If you want to dine at a fancy restaurant, consider leaving the kids with a babysitter. However, if you prefer to dine with your children, then you may have to make some compromises. Perhaps you'll have to dine earlier than most Parisians. **Hotel dining rooms** can be another good choice for family dining. They usually have children's menus, or at least one or two plats du jour cooked for children, such as spaghetti with meat sauce.

If you take your child to one of the moderately priced or budget restaurants, ask if the restaurant will serve a child's plate. If not, order a *plat du jour* or *plat garni*, which will be suitable for most children, particularly if a dessert is to follow.

Most **cafés** throughout the day and early evening welcome children. At a café, children always seem to like the sandwiches (try a croque monsieur), the omelets, and most definitely their pommes frites (crispy french fries). **La Samaritaine,** 75 rue de Rivoli (tel. 45-08-33-33; Métro: Pont-Neuf), is a café that serves moderately priced food with a view of Paris.

Les Drug Stores also welcome children, especially in the early evening, as do most **tearooms,** and you can tide the kids over with pastries and ice cream if dinner will be late. Try a **picnic** in the park. Also, there are lots of fast-food bars around the Eiffel Tower, where snacking and sightseeing go hand in hand. Of course, if you're looking for fast-food eateries, such as **Pizza Hut** and **McDonald's,** you will see these chains all over the city.

For a rundown of more kid-friendly establishments, see "Frommer's Cool for Kids: Restaurants," in Section 14.

WHAT THE LISTINGS MEAN Restaurants classified as "very expensive" charge from $100 to $125, or even beyond, plus drinks, for dinner. That's per person, too. In "expensive" restaurants, dinner ranges from $75 to $100; "moderate," $50 to $75. Anything under $50 per person is considered "inexpensive," although such a price tag is luxurious dining in most parts of the world. Any meal for less than $25 is considered "budget" by Parisian standards.

In the addresses listed, such designations as "1er" and "12e," which occur before the telephone numbers, refer (in French form) to the arrondissement in which the establishment is located.

1. 8TH ARRONDISSEMENT

VERY EXPENSIVE

ALAIN SENDERENS' LUCAS-CARTON, 9 place de la Madeleine, 8e. Tel. 42-65-22-90.

Cuisine: FRENCH. **Reservations:** Required several days in advance for lunch, several weeks in advance for dinner. **Métro:** Madeleine.

$ Prices: Appetizers 200F–380F ($37–$70.30); main courses 240F–320F ($44.40–$59.20); fixed price lunch 400F ($74); menu dégustation 850F ($157.25). MC, V.

Open: Lunch Mon–Fri noon–2:30pm, dinner Mon–Fri 8–11:30pm. **Closed:** Three weeks in Aug (dates vary).

This Paris landmark from the belle époque is today a blend of the old and the new, having been taken over by one of Paris's top restaurateurs. Senderens has added his own touches to the historic restaurant, which was created during the reign of British King Edward VII by an Englishman named Lucas and a talented French chef, Francis Carton. The two dining rooms are decorated with expanses of mirrors, sprays of spring flowers offsetting the carved wooden panels, pristine white ceilings and napery, and art nouveau lighting. If General Pershing, Marshal Foch, General de Gaulle, Winston Churchill, and other leaders in both World Wars were looking around today for a proper site to discuss world affairs over lunch, they would probably opt again for Lucas-Carton, as they once did.

The food they would be served, however, would be different from that of half a century and more ago. Senderens, who bakes his own bread, creates such tasty dishes as fresh cod with eggplant, caviar, and fried zucchini; ravioli filled with scallops and served with thyme-flavored zucchini; and mild smoked salmon with a sprinkling of salmon eggs; plus other delicacies from his own smoker and from the

Church ⛪ Post Office ⊠ Information ⓘ

Grande Cascade 🛈	Maquis 🛈	Pied de Cochon 🛈
Guy Savoy 🛈	Marc-Annibal de	Pierre 🛈
Hard Rock Café 🛈	Coconnas 🛈	Restaurant Copenhague
Joe Allen 🛈	Maxim's 🛈	& Flora Danica ·🛈·
Julien 🛈	Meridien 🛈	Robuchon ·🛈·
L'Etoile Verte 🛈	Michel Rostang 🛈	Rose de France ·🛈·
Laduree 🛈	Minim's 🛈	Self-Rivoli ·🛈·
Lasserre 🛈	Moisanderie 🛈	Sir Winston Churchill ·🛈·
Lescure 🛈	Moulin du Village 🛈	Taillevent ·🛈·
Lucas-Carton (Alain	Paul 🛈	Taverne du
Senderen's) 🛈	Petit Bedon 🛈	Sergent Recruteur ·🛈·
Maison d'Alsace 🛈	Petit Montmorency 🛈	Vivarois ·🛈·
Maison Rose 🛈	Pharamond 🛈	

rôtisserie. Senderens is constantly searching for new culinary creations, so you will have to choose from what he has developed by the time you visit. For dessert, if it is on the menu then, I suggest the hot pineapple fritters: beignets d'ananas Eventhia (named for his wife).

LASSERRE, 17 av. Franklin D. Roosevelt, 8e. Tel. 43-59-53-43.
Cuisine: FRENCH. **Reservations:** Required. **Métro:** F.D. Roosevelt.

À la Bonne Crêpe ❶	Café le Depart ㉔
Arpège ❻	Cafetière ㉕
Auberge Basque ⓫	Charpentiers ㉙
Auberge des Deux Signes ⑫	Chez les Anges �34
Bistro de la Gare ⑯	Chez René ㊟
Bistrot de Paris ⑰	Closerie des Lilas ㊵
Bourbonnaise ⑲	Crémerie-Restaurant Polidor ㊸
Cabane d'Auvergne ㉒	Divellec Cuisine de Mer ㊻
Café de Cluny ㉓	

$ **Prices:** Appetizers 190F–240F ($35.15–$44.40), main courses 240F–320F ($44.40–$59.20). MC, V.
Open: Lunch Tues–Sat 12:30–2:30pm, dinner Mon–Sat 7:30–10:30pm. **Closed:** Aug.

⭐ This elegant deluxe restaurant was a simple bistro before the war, a "rendezvous for chauffeurs." Then along came René Lasserre, who bought the dilapidated building and set out to create his dream. His dream turned into a culinary paradise, attracting gourmets from around the world.

LEFT BANK DINING

Two white-painted front doors lead to the dining rooms and a reception lounge with Louis XVI–style furnishings and brocaded walls. The main salon is two stories high; on each side is a mezzanine. Draped with silk, tall arched windows open onto the street. At a table set with fine porcelain, crystal glasses edged in gold, a silver candelabrum, even a silver bird and a ceramic dove, you sit on a Louis XV–style salon chair and carefully study the menu.

Overhead, the ceiling is painted with lamb-white clouds and a cerulean sky, but in fair weather the staff slides back the roof to reveal the real sky, either moonlight or sunshine.

The food is a combination of French classicism and originality. The presentation of dishes is one of the most winning and imaginative aspects of Lasserre. Always count on high drama.

To begin, I'd suggest a specialty, blanc de sandre (zander) à la nage d'étrilles. Among the main fish dishes, try a queues de langoustines (lobster) rôties with an herb-flavored sabayon sauce. Especially recommendable of the meat courses is the steak de Charolais au Bourgueil. For dessert, try a parfait aux noisettes (hazelnuts) grillées, with a honey-flavored sabayon. The cellar of some 180,000 bottles is among the more remarkable in Paris; red wines are decanted into silver pitchers or ornate crystal.

MAXIM'S, 3 rue Royale, 8e. Tel. 42-65-27-94.
 Cuisine: FRENCH. **Reservations:** Required. **Métro:** Concorde.
$ Prices: Appetizers 100F–820F ($18.50–$151.70), main courses 210F–620F ($38.85–$114.70). AE, DC, V.
 Open: Lunch daily 12:30–2pm, dinner daily 7:30–11:30pm.
 Closed: Sun July–Aug.

Maxim's is the world's most legendary restaurant. It preserves the era of belle époque, and was a favorite of Edward VII, then the prince of Wales. He enjoyed the slightly decadent atmosphere, far removed in spirit from the rigid London ruled by his stern mother, Victoria.

The restaurant is known to many North American movie-goers who have never been to Paris. It was the setting for *The Merry Widow,* where John Gilbert "dipped and swayed" with Mae Murray. You can always be sure the orchestra will play that tune at least once a night. Much later in film history, Louis Jourdan—at that time called "the handsomest man in the world"—took Leslie Caron to the restaurant "the night they invented champagne" in the musical *Gigi.*

Over the years, Maxim's has carried on, though the big names of yesterday—Callas, Onassis, and the like—are long gone. Today, tourists from around the world are likely to occupy once-fabled tables. Clothing-industry giant Pierre Cardin took over the restaurant in 1981. The kitchen has a staff of some of the finest and most talented young cooks in France. Many of them train at Maxim's before going on to open an operation of their own. One of the finest soups I've had anywhere—and it's a great opener to a repast at Maxim's—is Billi-By soup, made with mussels, white wine, cream (of course), chopped onions, celery, and parsley, as well as coarsely ground pepper. Another favorite, the sole Albert, named after the late famous maître d'hôtel, is flavored with chopped herbs and bread-crumbs, plus a large glass of vermouth. For dessert, try the tarte ta-tin.

Arrive slightly early so you can have a drink in the Imperial Bar upstairs. Formal dress is de rigueur on Friday. It's fashionable to have an after-theater supper here, listening or dancing to the music.

TAILLEVENT, 15 rue Lamennais, 8e. Tel. 45-63-39-94.
 Cuisine: FRENCH. **Reservations:** Required weeks, even months, in advance for both lunch and dinner. **Métro:** George-V.
$ Prices: Appetizers 235F–465F ($43.50–$86.05), main courses 350F–475F ($64.75–$87.90). MC, V.
 Open: Lunch Mon–Fri noon–2:30pm, dinner Mon–Fri 7–10pm.
 Closed: Aug.

⭐ Taillevent dates from 1946, when the restaurant was founded by the father of present owner Jean-Claude Vrinat. It has climbed steadily in the ranks of excellence since then, and today it is recognized as arguably the most outstanding all-around eating place in Paris.

The setting is a grand 13th-century town house off the Champs-Elysées, once inhabited by the duc de Morny, with paneled rooms and crystal chandeliers. The name of the restaurant honors a famous chef of the 14th century who was the author of one of the oldest known books on French cookery. The place is not huge, but that is as the owner wishes, since it permits him to give personal attention to every facet of the operation, seeing to the continuation of the discreet, London-club atmosphere he so carefully maintains.

You might begin with aspic de foie gras (diced liver and veal sweetbreads in aspic jelly with very fine diced carrots and truffles). Main dish specialties (subject to change, of course) include cassolette de langoustines, and agneau aux trois cuissons (three cuts of lamb—feet, breast, and tenderloin—with various sauces). You might follow these with fondant aux deux parfums (an almond toffee Bavarian cream covered with chocolate). Taillevent's wine list is one of the best in the city. Although Monsieur Vrinat likes Americans, it isn't always easy for visitors from the States and other countries to book a table, since the owner prefers to see his clientele comprise about 60% French people.

EXPENSIVE

AU PETIT MONTMORENCY, 5 rue Rabelais, 8e. Tel. 42-25-11-19.

Cuisine: FRENCH. **Reservations:** Required. **Métro:** F.D. Roosevelt.

$ Prices: Appetizers 105F–260F ($19.45–$48.10), main dishes 150F–260F ($27.75–$48.10). MC, V.

Open: Lunch Mon–Fri noon–2:15pm, dinner Mon–Fri 7:30–10:15pm. **Closed:** Aug.

Paintings, engravings, and hanging lanterns give an old-fashioned touch here, with the ambience heightened by candlelight and fresh flowers. Before Daniel Bouché and his wife, Nicole, opened this place, Bouché trained at a number of restaurants, including Maxim's in Chicago. But he seems to have charted his own culinary course and turns out a delicate and subtle cuisine—hot oysters with a Pomerol sauce and wild-mushroom toast; haddock and watercress with fresh salmon toast; canard Lucifer (roast duck with a hot sauce, semolina, vegetables, and chutney); and, in season, such game as hare, venison, partridge, and pheasant.

For dessert, I recommend le grande dessert au chocolate (bitter chocolate) or one of an assortment of different chocolate cakes served with a small, hot pistachio soufflé and a coffee sauce.

The French wines are well selected, including some choice but little publicized ones.

MODERATE

ANDROUET, 41 rue d'Amsterdam, 8e. Tel. 48-74-26-93.

Cuisine: FRENCH. **Reservations:** Required. **Métro:** St-Lazare or Liège.

$ Prices: Appetizers 65F–150F ($12.05–$27.75); main courses

105F–250F ($19.45–$46.25); dégustation des fromages 240F ($44.40). AE, DC, MC, V.

Open: Lunch Mon–Sat noon–3pm, dinner Mon–Sat 7:30–10pm.

Cheese is king here. Time was when to get invited down to taste the cheese in Monsieur Androuët's cellars was a badge of honor. Now half of Paris and three-quarters of all visiting foreigners who love cheese have probably made their way to this unique restaurant up from the railway station of St-Lazare. On the lower level is a luscious shop selling every conceivable variety of cheese from all regions of France.

For a first course, the ravioles de chevre frais (ravioli stuffed with fresh goat cheese) is a fine choice. A good main dish is filet de boeuf cotentin (beef filet with roquefort sauce flambé with Calvados). Cheese-lovers come here to order "la dégustation de fromages affines dans nos caves" (a sampling of cheese from our cellars). There are as many as 120 varieties.

CHEZ ANDRE, 12 rue Marbeuf, 8e. Tel. 47-20-59-57.
Cuisine: FRENCH. **Reservations:** Recommended. **Métro:** F.D. Roosevelt.
$ Prices: Appetizers 40F–135F ($7.40–$25), main courses 120F–310F ($22.20–$57.35). V.
Open: Lunch Wed–Mon noon–3pm, dinner Wed–Mon 7–11:30pm.

On the corner of rue Clement-Marot is one of the most charming bistros in the neighborhood. A discreet red awning stretches over an

---

Ⓕ FROMMER'S SMART TRAVELER: RESTAURANTS

1. Select the prix-fixe (fixed-price) menu. Most restaurants offer both fixed-price and à la carte menus. The latter is more adventurous but at least 30% more expensive.
2. If you have a big appetite but don't want to pay the prices for multicourse dinners in typical Paris restaurants, head for one of those all-you-can-eat places, such as La Taverne du Sergent Recruteur (see p. 147) or L'Espace Cardin (see p. 123).
3. Look for the plats du jour (daily specials) on any à la carte menu. They're invariably fresh and often carry a lower price tag than regular à la carte listings.
4. Drink vin ordinaire (table wine served in a carafe). It costs only a fraction of the price of bottled wine.
5. Remember that anything consumed standing up at a counter in Paris or sitting on a stool at the bar is invariably cheaper than if consumed at a table.
6. To keep costs really low, patronize rue de la Huchette on the Left Bank (Métro: St-Michel). It has some of the cheapest restaurants in Paris, serving mainly Greek cuisine. Or turn onto rue Zavier-Privas, where couscous (the most famous dish of North Africa, made from semolina, stewed vegetables, and stewed meat) is found in many establishments.

array of shellfish on ice; inside, an art nouveau decor includes etched glass and masses of flowers. You'll probably be seated elbow to elbow with someone whose picture you've seen in a magazine. The old-fashioned menu is hand-scrawled and includes a very French collection of such items as pâté of thrush, roquefort in puff pastry, several kinds of omelets, calves' head vinaigrette, a potage du jour, and an array of fresh shellfish, along with several reasonably priced wines. Desserts might be rum baba, chocolate cake, or a daily pastry.

CHEZ EDGARD, 4 rue Marbeuf, 8e. Tel. 47-20-51-15.

Cuisine: FRENCH. **Reservations:** Required. **Métro:** F.D. Roosevelt.

$ Prices: Appetizers 40F–75F ($7.40–$13.90); main dishes 100F–220F ($18.50–$40.70). AE, DC, V.

Open: Lunch Mon–Sat noon–3pm, dinner Mon–Sat 7pm–12:30am.

A chic coterie of neighborhood residents regard this belle époque eating place as their favorite local restaurant, and ebullient owner Paul Benmussa makes it a point to welcome them during their frequent visits as if they were members of his extended family. Customers include such politicians as Giscard d'Estaing, members of the press, and such show-business personalities as Roman Polanski and Sydney Pollack. Conversation in this scarlet-and-black restaurant can be even noisier than in less expensive restaurants.

Specialties include breast of duckling; red mullet with basil in puff pastry; and several terrines, including one made from scallops. There is also a range of well-prepared meat dishes. In winter, seafood and oysters are shipped in from Brittany. The ice-cream sundaes (listed with other desserts on a special menu) are particularly delectable. There's a small outdoor terrace, but most guests prefer to eat inside on one of the semiprivate banquettes.

L'ESPACE, 1–3 av. Gabriel, 8e. Tel. 42-66-11-70.

Cuisine: FRENCH. **Reservations:** Recommended. **Métro:** Champs-Elysées.

$ Prices: Appetizers 85F–130F ($15.75–$24.05); main courses 135F–285F ($25–$52.75); buffet 210F ($38.85). AE, DC, MC, V.

Open: Lunch Sun–Fri noon–3pm, dinner daily 8:30pm–1am.

What's probably the most lavish buffet in Paris is served daily in a picnic-style decor of plastic chairs, oilcloth coverings, and decorative parasols, a setting you might find at a California beachside restaurant. In reality, however, nothing could be more French. The luminary who established this consciously informal place is Pierre Cardin, whose other more formal culinary endeavors have been well documented thanks to his acquisition of Maxim's.

You'll have access to a buffet of more than 70 hors d'oeuvres, a table rich with salads, vegetables, cold roast meats, and the kind of antipasti you'd expect to find in Italy. The main course is served by a waiter who brings you your choice of a plat du jour. This is followed by a selection from a dessert buffet. Service and drinks are extra (champagne is sold by the glass).

LA FERMETTE MARBEUF 1900, 5 rue Marbeuf, 8e. Tel. 47-23-31-31.

Cuisine: FRENCH. **Reservations:** Not accepted. **Métro:** F.D. Roosevelt.

$ Prices: Appetizers 38F–185F ($7.05–$34.25); main courses

95F–140F ($17.60–$25.90); fixed-price menu 160F ($29.60). AE, DC, MC, V.

Open: Lunch daily noon–3pm, dinner daily 7:30–11:30pm.

La Fermette has a turn-of-the-century decor, reasonable prices, fine cuisine, and a location just a short distance from the Champs-Elysées. The hand-painted tiles and stained-glass windows of the twin dining rooms contribute to the establishment's listing as a national historic monument. Guests come here for the fun of it all, as well as for the well-prepared and flavorful cuisine.

Specialties are likely to include sweetbreads with a ragout of wild mushrooms, a basil-flavored filet of sole with fresh noodles, a bavarois of salmon, and several beef dishes. For dessert, try the chocolate cake with a bittersweet icing.

MOULIN DU VILLAGE, 25 rue Royale, in the Cité Berryer, 8e. Tel. 42-65-08-47.
Cuisine: FRENCH. **Reservations:** Recommended. **Métro:** Concorde or Madeleine.

$ **Prices:** Appetizers 65F–125F ($12.05–$23.15); main dishes 120F–150F ($22.20–$27.75); fixed-price meal 190F ($35.15). V.
Open: Lunch Mon–Fri noon–3pm, dinner Mon–Fri 7–11pm.
Closed: Holidays.

The Moulin is an ideal choice if you're strolling along rue Royale toward the Madeleine district at lunch or dinnertime and are not prepared to pay for a meal at Maxim's prices. Although not right on rue Royale with Maxim's, the Moulin is just around the corner, in a little alleyway where a Tuesday and Friday street market is held. This charming little place serves original, creative, and well prepared food at reasonable prices. Next door is the Blue Fox Wine Bar, named after a 19th-century furrier who used to occupy the premises.

Tasty dishes likely to be served include a minestrone with lobster and fresh basil, roast lamb with sea salt, and Challans duckling with a confit of spring turnips. The chef also does an excellent chicken suprême with wine vinegar.

INEXPENSIVE

L'ASSIETTE AU BOEUF, 123 Champs-Elysées, 8e. Tel. 47-20-01-13.
Cuisine: FRENCH. **Reservations:** Not accepted. **Métro:** George-V.

$ **Prices:** Fixed-price meals 60F ($11.10), 80F ($14.80), and 110F ($20.35). AE, V.
Open: Daily 11am–1am.

L'Assiette au Boeuf offers one of the best fine-dining bargains in Paris. You get simple French food in a glamorous reproduction belle époque setting. The Champs-Elysées entry has a sidewalk "box," offering dramatic views of the Arc de Triomphe. Much of the food is called *cuisine du marché*, which means it is based on fresh produce available at the market on any given day, and the menus are fixed. You might be offered a fish casserole or else a tender slice of beef (served rare if you wish), with a sauce on the side, along with a mound of slender pommes frites. There is a wide choice of desserts, including sorbets. Wine can be ordered in four different amounts, including two sizes of carafe.

If you become a L'Assiette-au-Boeuf aficionado, you'll find other branches of this chain at strategic locations throughout Paris.

LA BOUTIQUE A SANDWICHS, 12 rue du Colisée, 8e. Tel. 43-59-56-69.
Cuisine: ALSATIAN/SWISS. **Reservations:** Recommended.
Métro: F.D. Roosevelt.
$ Prices: Appetizers 22F–42F ($4.05–$7.75); main courses 35F–75F ($6.50–$13.90); sandwiches from 15F ($2.80). MC.
Open: Lunch Mon–Sat 11:45am–1am. **Closed:** Aug 1–20.

La Boutique à Sandwichs is run by two brothers from Alsace, Hubert and Claude Schick. If you're in the Champs-Elysées area, it's a good place to drop in for sandwiches in many types and shapes. You can dine downstairs at the counter, or crowd into the tiny upstairs room, which is extremely active at lunch. Here they offer an unusual specialty, raclette valaisanne. To make this fondue dish, a wheel of cheese is used, part of it is melted, and scraped right onto your plate. It is served with pickles and boiled potatoes, the latter resting in a pot with a crocheted hat. The other house specialty is Pickelfleisch garni (Alsatian corned beef). Naturally, the apple strudel is the dessert most diners order.

2. 16TH ARRONDISSEMENT

VERY EXPENSIVE

FAUGERON, 52 rue Longchamp, 16e. Tel. 47-04-24-53.
Cuisine: FRENCH. **Reservations:** Required. **Métro:** Iéna or Trocadéro.
$ Prices: Appetizers 90F–200F ($16.65–$37); main courses 205F–435F ($37.95–$80.50); business lunch 320F ($59.20); menu dégustation 550F–620F ($101.75–$114.70). MC, V.
Open: Lunch Mon–Fri 12:30–2pm, dinner Mon–Fri 7:30–10pm.
Closed: Aug.

Henri Faugeron is an inspired chef who many years ago established this restaurant as an elegant yet unobtrusive backdrop for his superb cuisine, which he calls "revolutionary." He is viewed as a culinary researcher, and his menu always has one or two platters from the classic French table—perhaps a leg of lamb baked seven hours or rack of hare in the traditional French style. Much of his cookery depends on the season and on his shopping, selecting only the freshest ingredients in the market. Game dishes, frogs' legs, oysters, scallops—whatever—Monsieur Faugeron and his chefs prepare food with style. In this he is aided by Jean-Claude Jambon, one of the premier sommeliers of France—indeed, of the world.

JAMIN, 32 rue Longchamp, 16e. Tel. 47-27-12-27.
Cuisine: FRENCH. **Reservations:** Required, six to eight weeks in advance. **Métro:** Trocadéro.
$ Prices: Appetizers 230F–415F ($42.55–$76.80); main courses 360F–535F ($66.60–$99); prix-fixe menu 900F–1,000F ($166.50–$185). MC.
Open: Lunch Mon–Fri 12:30–2:30pm, dinner Mon–Fri 7:30–10:30pm. **Closed:** July.

⭐ This is where Joël Robuchon, chef and proprietor, basks in his reputation as the country's most innovative cook. Some critics say his restaurant is the finest in France. He is a master of the cuisine moderne, sometimes called *cuisine actuelle*. Foods produced here are light and delicate, with outstanding flavors. He even bakes his own bread fresh every day, and he is known to spend long hours in the kitchen testing (or inventing) new recipes. He has fish and shellfish shipped fresh from Brittany so it doesn't have to "linger" at the Rungis wholesale market.

Among the delectable offerings have been such dishes as kidneys and sweetbreads diced and sautéed with mushrooms, canette rosée (duckling that has been roasted and braised, and flavored with spices such as ginger, nutmeg, cinnamon, and other Chinese-influenced touches), shellfish-filled ravioli steamed in cabbage leaves, and chicken for two, poached in a pig's bladder. His mashed potatoes, once labeled "the silliest dish in the world," are hailed here as a masterpiece—and they are. But the chef won't reveal his secret.

MINIM'S, 76 Faubourg St-Honoré, 8e. Tel. 42-66-10-09.
   Cuisine: FRENCH. **Reservations:** Recommended. **Métro:** Concorde.
$ Prices: Appetizers 45F–75F ($8.35–$13.90), main courses 80F–90F ($14.80–$16.65). AE, DC, MC, V.
   Open: Mon–Sat 10am–6:30pm.

This is Pierre Cardin's "alimentary boutique" on this fashionable street near the Elysée Palace. It's really an ideal luncheon restaurant for rich suburbanites spending their day shopping, and a good choice for afternoon tea or a quick, well-prepared snack. The name, of course, is a tongue-in-cheek adaptation of Cardin's acquisition, Maxim's, and like the decor of its counterpart, the tea house is filled with art nouveau lighting fixtures and stained glass.

You dine at small tables near a collection of turn-of-the-century silver maidens that I was told came from the collection of Cardin himself. It's totally appropriate here to order only a plat du jour. These change daily but might include eggplant caviar, carpaccio with salad, and confit de canard (duck). You can also order sandwiches, as well as pastries prepared according to the recipes of Maxim's. A deluxe delicatessen fills an adjoining room, and an arts boutique is upstairs.

EXPENSIVE

LA GRANDE CASCADE, Bois de Boulogne, 16e. Tel. 45-06-33-51.
   Cuisine: FRENCH. **Reservations:** Required. **Transportation:** You must take a taxi or drive; there's no Métro stop nearby.
$ Prices: Appetizers 155F–320F ($28.70–$59.20), main courses 220F–390F ($40.70–$72.15). AE, DC, MC, V.
   Open: Mid-Apr to Oct lunch daily noon–3pm, dinner daily 7:30–10:30pm; Nov to mid-Dec and mid-Jan to mid-Apr lunch daily noon–3pm. **Closed:** Mid-Dec to mid-Jan.

This is a garden house—a belle époque shrine for lunch, afternoon tea, or dinner in the heart of Paris's fashionable park. Originally, this indoor-outdoor restaurant was built by Baron Haussmann and was used as a hunting lodge for Napoléon III. At the turn of the century it was converted into a restaurant and drew the chic of its day, including Colette.

Today's humbler guest can select a table, choosing the more formal interior with its gilt, crystal, and glass roof, or the more popular front terrace. At the latter, under either parasols or portico shelter, you can order a meal, a drink, or an old-fashioned afternoon tea with a generous helping of the chef's favorite cake. Soft lights at night from the tall frosted lamps and the sound of the nearby cascade enhance the romantic feeling of the place.

The restaurant features such à la carte selections as duckling foie gras, fish poached in seaweed and basil, and veal sweetbreads in truffle-flavored butter. A spectacular finish is provided by crêpes soufflées à l'orange.

LE VIVAROIS, 192 av. Victor-Hugo, 16e. Tel. 45-04-04-31.

Cuisine: FRENCH. **Reservations:** Required. **Métro:** Pompe.
$ Prices: Appetizers 90F–200F ($16.65–$37); main courses 215F–445F ($39.80–$82.35); fixed price lunch 355F ($65.70). AE, DC, MC, V.
Open: Lunch Mon–Fri noon–2pm, dinner Mon–Fri 8–10pm.
Closed: Aug.

Le Vivarois has been called a revelation by food critics. This restaurant opened in 1966 with a modern decor (including chairs by Knoll), and it was, from the start, popular with the American crowd. The American magazine *Gourmet* once hailed it as "a restaurant of our time . . . the most exciting, audacious, and important restaurant in Paris today." It still maintains its standards.

Le Vivarois is the personal statement of its supremely talented owner-chef, Claude Peyrot. His menu is constantly changing. One food critic once said, and quite accurately, "the menu changes with the marketing and his genius." He does a most recommendable coquilles St-Jacques (scallops) en crème, and a pourpre de turbot Vivarois. To many his most winning dish is rognons de veau (veal kidneys).

Madame Peyrot is one of the finest maîtres d'hôtel in Paris. She'll guide you beautifully through wine selections so you'll end up with the perfect complement to her husband's superlative cuisine.

MODERATE

LE PETIT BEDON, 38 rue Pergolese, 16e. Tel. 45-00-23-66.

Cuisine: FRENCH. **Reservations:** Required. **Métro:** Argentine.
$ Prices: Appetizers 105F–220F ($19.45–$40.70); main courses 185F–300F ($34.25–$55.50); fixed price lunch 220F ($40.70). AE, DC, MC, V.
Open: Lunch Mon–Fri 12:15–2pm, dinner Mon–Fri 7:15–10:15pm. **Closed:** Aug.

Le Petit Bedon is traditional but also innovative. The dining room is simply decorated and warm and inviting with only 14 tables. The menu frequently changes. For an appetizer, you might try the thinly sliced salmon, which has been cured and smoked. A black pepper from South America brings out the right seasoning in the dish. If you visit in early spring, you can order milk-fed lamb from the Dordogne region of France. The lamb is delicate and tender and prepared to perfection. The kitchen is also known to do marvelous twists with Challons duckling. A masterpiece of desserts is a plate of mixed sorbets; not only is its presentation a work of art, but you are allowed to try to guess the flavors.

3. 17TH ARRONDISSEMENT

EXPENSIVE

GUY SAVOY, 18 rue Troyon, 17e. Tel. 43-80-40-61.

Cuisine: FRENCH. **Reservations:** Required, one week in advance. **Métro:** Charles de Gaulle–Etoile.

$ Prices: Appetizers 100F–210F ($18.50–$38.85); main courses 200F–320F ($37–$59.20); fixed price lunch 390F ($72.15); menu dégustation from 630F ($116.55). AE, MC, V.

Open: Lunch Mon–Fri noon–1:30pm, dinner Mon–Fri 7:30–10:30pm. **Closed:** Last three weeks July.

Guy Savoy serves the kind of food that Monsieur Savoy himself likes to eat, and it is prepared with consummate skill. When the five or six "hottest" chefs in Europe are named today, he most often is mentioned, and deservedly so. Don't eat all day, then come here and order his menu dégustation. Although it runs to nine courses, the portions are small; you won't be satiated before the meal has run its course.

What will you get? Perhaps red mullet with wild asparagus. Maybe a cassolette of snails flavored with tarragon (no garlic, for a change), or chicken quenelles with chicken livers and cream, the rich-tasting dish sprinkled with strips of delectable black truffles. If you visit in the right season, you may have a chance to order such masterfully prepared game as mallard or venison, even game birds. He is fascinated with the *champignon* in all its many varieties, and has been known to serve as many as a dozen different types of mushrooms, especially in the autumn.

MICHEL ROSTANG, 20 rue Rennequin, 17e. Tel. 47-63-40-77.

Cuisine: FRENCH. **Reservations:** Required. **Métro:** Ternes.

$ Prices: Appetizers 149F–305F ($27.55–$56.45); main courses 205F–270F ($37.95–$49.95); fixed price lunch 280F ($51.80); menu dégustation 505F–670F ($93.45–$123.95). AE, MC, V.

Open: Lunch Mon–Fri 12:30–2:30pm, dinner Mon–Sat 8–10:30pm. **Closed:** First two weeks Aug.

Monsieur Rostang is one of the most creative chefs of Paris. He's the fifth generation of one of the most distinguished French "cooking families," who have been connected with the famed Bonne Auberge at Antibes on the French Riviera.

Small and intimate, the restaurant offers a menu of bourgeois cuisine that changes constantly, depending on Rostang's inspiration. His specialties are likely to include ravioli filled with goat cheese and coated with a sprinkling of chervil bought fresh that morning in the market. If the mood strikes him, he might prepare a young Bresse chicken, considered the finest in France, served with a delicate chervil sauce (as you may have guessed, Rostang is much enamored of fresh chervil). Another specialty is duckling cooked in its own blood. From October to March he is likely to offer quail eggs with a coque of sea urchins. He also prepares on occasion a delicate fricassée of sole. Many interesting wines from the Rhône are available, including Châteauneuf du Pape and Hermitage.

MODERATE

GOLDENBERG'S, 69 av. de Wagram, 17e. Tel. 42-27-34-79.
Cuisine: JEWISH/DELI. **Reservations:** Required. **Métro:** Ternes or Charles de Gaulle–Etoile.
$ Prices: Appetizers 35F–45F ($6.50–$8.35), main courses 74F–120F ($13.70–$22.20). V.
Open: Daily 9am–midnight.

This is a Jewish delicatessen-restaurant in the Champs-Elysées area. Its owner, Albert Goldenberg, is known as "the doyen of Jewish restaurateurs in Paris," and rightly so, since he opened his first delicatessen in Montmartre in 1936. The deli, like many of its New York counterparts, has the front half reserved as the specialty take-out section and the back half for in-house dining. The menu features such specialties as carpe farcie (stuffed carp), blini, cabbage borscht, and pastrami, one of the most popular items. Naturally, everything tastes better if accompanied by Jewish rye bread. For those who want to really get in the spirit, the menu offers Israeli as well as French wines.

INEXPENSIVE

L'ETOILE VERTE, 13 rue Brey, 17e. Tel. 43-80-69-34.
Cuisine: FRENCH. **Reservations:** Recommended. **Métro:** Charles de Gaulle–Etoile.
$ Prices: Appetizers 22F–85F ($4.05–$15.75); main courses 48F–95F ($8.90–$17.60); fixed-price menu 65F ($12.05) until 9pm. AE, DC, MC, V.
Open: Daily, lunch 11am–3pm, dinner 6:30–11pm.

 This "Green Star" is a sign for economy diners. The decor is so simple as to be forgettable, but a large array of well-prepared foods emerges from the kitchen in back, and the staff is helpful. The cookery is that of a typical French bistro of long ago: rabbit pâté, veal marengo, fresh oysters, coq au vin in Cahors, sweetbreads with sautéed endive, mussels ravigote, chateaubriand béarnaise, and ris de veau (sweetbreads). Its least expensive menu, with drink included, is served from 11am to 9pm.

---

4. 1ST ARRONDISSEMENT

VERY EXPENSIVE

LE GRAND VEFOUR, 17 rue de Beaujolais, 1er. Tel. 42-96-56-27.
Cuisine: FRENCH. **Reservations:** Required. **Métro:** Louvre.
$ Prices: Appetizers 130F–330F ($24.05–$61.05); main courses 220F–370F ($40.70–$68.45); fixed price lunch 315F ($58.30). AE, DC, MC, V.

Open: Lunch Mon–Fri 12:30–2:15pm, dinner Mon–Fri 7:30–10:15pm.

⭐ Le Grand Véfour has been an eating place since the reign of Louis XV, and it has had its ups and downs. Although the exact date of its opening as the Café de Chartres is not definitely known, it is more than 200 years old and is classified as a historical treasure. It got its present name in 1812, when Jean Véfour, former chef to a member of the royal family, owned it. Since that time it has attracted such notables as Napoleon and Danton and a host of writers and artists, such as Victor Hugo, Colette, and Jean Cocteau (who designed the menu cover in 1953).

Located amid the arcades of the Palais-Royal, the restaurant had lost its earlier glamor by the early 20th century and was simply a little corner café. It had another "up" period after World War II, under Raymond Oliver, one of the most famous modern French chefs, but as he aged, it again fell into decline. Fortunately, Jean Taittinger of the Taittinger Champagne family purchased the restaurant, and it has now reached—perhaps surpassed—its former glories. From Limoges china, you can feast at a table bearing a brass plaque with the name of a famous former occupant.

The chef, Guy Martin, a native of the Savoy region of France, would surely please the gastronome and former patron Brillat-Savarin, if he were alive today. Monsieur Martin brings originality to French classics. Try his foie gras ravioli in a light truffle cream sauce, or perhaps a delicate white-bean soup perfumed with truffles. He also prepares a poached filet of beef with sweet-onion purée. Fresh roasted sole and sea scallops in a velvety pumpkin sauce are other specialties. He also brings in omble chevalier, or char, a troutlike fish from Lake Geneva, which he feels is so delectable that he prepares it simply, merely sautéeing it and serving it meunière.

EXPENSIVE

CARRE DES FEUILLANTS, 14 rue de Castiglione, 1er. Tel. 42-86-82-82.
Cuisine: FRENCH. **Reservations:** Required. **Métro:** Tuileries, Concorde, Opéra, or Madeleine.
$ Prices: Appetizers 130F–208F ($24.05–$38.50); main courses 168F–260F ($31.10–$48.10); bar lunch 230F ($42.55); business lunch 260F ($48.10); six-course seasonal menu 575F ($106.40). AE, DC, MC, V.
Open: Lunch Mon–Fri noon–2pm, dinner Mon–Sat 7:30–10:30pm.

⭐ Alain Dutournier established his reputation as a leading chef de cuisine at Au Trou Gascon, now run by his wife, Nicole. He moved his showcase to this restaurant, a beautifully restored 17th-century convent, and immediately became an overnight success. The interior is like a turn-of-the-century bourgeois house, with several small salons. These open onto an inviting skylit interior courtyard, across from which a glass-enclosed kitchen can be viewed (no secrets here).

Monsieur Dutournier likes to call his food *cuisine du moment.* He has a whole network of little farms that supply him with the fresh produce on which he casts his magic spell. He is especially known for his beef butchered from one of the oldest breeds of cattle in France, the *race bazadaise,* and for lamb raised in Pauillac.

The sommelier, Jean-Guy Loustau, has an exciting selection,

including several little-known wines along with a fabulous collection of armagnacs. A dozen places in the bar await those who casually walk in without a reservation and order a special fixed-price lunch.

MODERATE

ESCARGOT-MONTORGUEIL, 38 rue Montorgueil, 1er. Tel. 42-36-83-51.

Cuisine: FRENCH. **Reservations:** Required. **Métro:** Les Halles.

$ Prices: Appetizers 50F–148F ($9.25–$27.40); main courses 94F–400F ($17.40–$74); fixed price lunch 150F ($27.75); fixed price dinner 280F ($51.80). AE, DC.

Open: Lunch Tues–Sun noon–2:30pm, dinner daily 8–10:30pm.
Closed: Part of Aug.

The "golden snail" of Les Halles is as golden as ever. Even if the famous market has moved elsewhere, the Escargot-Montorgueil is firmly entrenched, the building supposedly dating from the days of Catherine de Médicis. The restaurant opened its doors in the 1830s, and inside it looks it. (The decor has been described as "authentic Louis Philippe.") The greats, such as Sarah Bernhardt, have paraded through here. The food—in the grand bistro tradition—remains consistently good. The restaurant is run by Madame Saladin-Terrail, known as Kouikette, sister of Claude Terrail, the guiding hand behind La Tour d'Argent.

Everybody but the regulars appears to order escargots, although this dish doesn't seem to get much attention from the chef. I recommend the pieds de porcs and the feather turbot soufflé.

JOE ALLEN, 30 rue Pierre-Lescot, 1er. Tel. 42-36-70-13.

Cuisine: AMERICAN. **Reservations:** Recommended for dinner. **Métro:** Les Halles.

$ Prices: Appetizers 35F–65F ($6.50–$12.05), main courses 85F–135F ($15.75–$25). MC, V.

Open: Daily noon–2am.

About the last place in the world you'd expect to find Joe Allen is Les Halles, that once-legendary Paris market. But the New York restaurateur long ago invaded Paris with the American hamburger. It easily wins as the finest burger in the city, as Joe originally set out to match those served at P.J. Clarke's in New York.

Joe Allen's "little bit of New York"—complete with imported red-checked tablecloths, a green awning over the entrance, and waiters who speak English—was made possible by "grants" from such fans as Lauren Bacall, whose poster adorns one of the walls. The decor is in the New York saloon style, complete with brick walls, oak floors, movie stills, and a blackboard menu listing such items as black-bean soup, chili, and apple pie. A spinach salad makes a good beginning. The barbecued ribs are succulent as well.

Joe Allen's also claims that it is the only place in Paris where you can have real New York cheesecake or pecan pie. The pecans are imported from the United States. Thanks to French chocolate, Joe claims, "we make better brownies than those made in the States." Giving the brownies tough competition is the California chocolate mousse pie, along with the strawberry Romanoff and the coconut cream pie.

Thanksgiving dinner at Joe Allen's in Paris is becoming a tradition (but you'll need a reservation way in advance).

PHARAMOND, 24 rue de la Grande-Truanderie, 1er. Tel. 42-33-06-72.

Cuisine: FRENCH. **Reservations:** Required. **Métro:** Les Halles.

$ Prices: Appetizers 85F–125F ($15.75–$23.15), main courses 88F–155F ($16.30–$28.60). AE, DC, MC, V.

Open: Lunch Tues 12:30–2:30pm, dinner Mon–Sat 7:30–10:45pm. **Closed:** Mid-July to mid-Aug.

The restaurant, part of a neo-Norman structure built in 1832, sits on a street in Les Halles that was once frequented by the vagabonds of Paris.

For an appetizer (available between October and April) work your way through half a dozen of the Breton oysters. Next, the main dish to order here is tripes à la mode de Caen, served over a charcoal burner. Tripe is a delicacy, and if you're at all experimental you'll find no better introduction to it anywhere. Try the coquilles St-Jacques au cidre (scallops in cider) if you're not up to tripe. Other main dish specialties include grillade du feu de bois for two diners, as well as filets de sole normande.

LA ROSE DE FRANCE, 24 place Dauphine, 1er. Tel. 43-54-10-12.

Cuisine: FRENCH. **Reservations:** Recommended. **Métro:** Cité or Pont-Neuf.

$ Prices: Appetizers 62F–90F ($11.50–$16.65); main courses 85F–118F ($15.75–$21.85); three-course fixed-price lunch or dinner 185F ($34.25); menu gastronomique 285F ($52.75). No credit cards.

Open: Lunch Mon–Fri 12:10–2pm, dinner Mon–Fri 7–10pm.

This restaurant is located in the old section of Ile de la Cité near Notre-Dame, just around the corner from the old Pont Neuf. You'll dine with a sophisticated crowd of young Parisians who know that they can expect a good meal at reasonable prices. In warm weather the sidewalk tables overlooking the Palais de Justice are the most popular.

Main dishes include deviled steak, spring lamb chops, a Norman-style veal chop with cooked apples, and a soufflé of scallops with muscadet. For dessert, try the fruit tart of the day, a sorbet, or iced melon (in summer only).

INEXPENSIVE

CHEZ PAUL, 15 place Dauphine, 1er. Tel. 43-54-21-48.

Cuisine: FRENCH. **Reservations:** Required. **Métro:** Pont-Neuf.

$ Prices: Appetizers 40F–88F ($7.40–$16.30), main courses 96F–152F ($17.75–$28.10). MC, V.

Open: Lunch Wed–Sun noon–2:30pm, dinner 7:30–10:15pm. **Closed:** Aug.

 This address used to be given out to first-time visitors by in-the-know Parisians who wanted to tell them about that out-of-the-way bistro where no foreigner ever sets foot. But Chez Paul, on this historic square on the Ile de la Cité, is too good a secret to keep. Nevertheless, food expert Waverly Root once wrote of Chez Paul's "resistance to degeneration," and so it remains an unexpected setting for fine food: The effect inside is much like a cold-water flat. The main-dish specialty is escalope papillotte. For dessert, try baba à la confiture flambé au rhum.

LESCURE, 7 rue de Mondovi, 1er. Tel. 42-60-18-91.
Cuisine: FRENCH. **Reservations:** Not accepted. **Métro:** Concorde.

$ Prices: Appetizers 25F–45F ($4.65–$8.35); main courses 35F–85F ($6.50–$15.75); four-course fixed-price menu 98F ($18.15). MC, V.

Open: Lunch Mon–Fri noon–2:15pm, dinner Mon–Fri 7–10:15pm. **Closed:** Two weeks in Aug.

Lescure is a small, inexpensive restaurant in the high-priced place de la Concorde district. Right off rue de Rivoli, the restaurant has been serving good food since 1919. In fair weather, a few sidewalk tables are placed outside; inside, the decor is rustic with an exposed kitchen. Simple, hearty cooking is the rule. You might begin with a pâté en croûte. Main-course house specialties include confit de canard and salmon in a green sauce. My favorite dessert is one of the chef's fruit tarts.

LA MOISANDERIE, 52 rue de Richelieu, 1er. Tel. 42-96-92-93.
Cuisine: FRENCH. **Reservations:** Recommended. **Métro:** Louvre.

$ Prices: Appetizers 63F–78F ($11.65–$14.45); main dishes 105F–140F ($19.45–$25.90); fixed price menus 108F–172F ($20–$31.85). AE, DC, MC, V.

Open: Lunch Mon–Sat noon–3pm, dinner Mon–Thurs 7–9:30pm and Fri–Sat 7–11:30pm.

This conveniently located bistro, though relatively unknown, has good reasonably priced food. Although La Moisanderie is small, with tables just big enough for sparrows, everything goes smoothly. It has a homey, rustic French decor: wood paneling covered with 16th-century tapestries, a brick fireplace, a basket of crusty bread, and a counter of mouth-watering homemade pastries.

To begin, you are offered eight different hors d'oeuvres, a soup, or marinated herring. Next comes a meat or fowl course—perhaps stuffed chicken, pork with mushrooms, grilled liver, or a veal cutlet in a cream sauce with mushrooms. Fancier dishes include steak with cognac and orange duck. For dessert, help yourself from a large glass bowl of fresh fruit salad, unless you prefer a wedge of green-apple tart. It gets crowded, so go early.

5. 2ND & 9TH ARRONDISSEMENTS

MODERATE

CHEZ GEORGES, 1 rue du Mail, 2e. Tel. 42-60-07-11.
Cuisine: FRENCH. **Reservations:** Required. **Métro:** Sentier.

$ Prices: Appetizers 60F–120F ($11.10–$22.20), main dishes 125F–220F ($23.15–$40.70). AE, MC, V.

Open: Lunch Mon–Sat 12:30–2pm, dinner Mon–Sat 7:30–10pm.

This bistro is something of a local landmark. At lunch it's heavily patronized by members of the Bourse (the stock exchange), which is about a block away. The owner serves what he calls *"la cuisine typiquement bourgeoise,"* or "food from our grandmère in the provinces." Waiters bring around bowls of appetizers, such as celery remoulade, to get you started. Then you can follow with such favorites as pot-au-feu (beef simmered with vegetables), a classic cassoulet, or beef braised in red wine. Beaujolais goes great with this hearty food.

BUDGET

LE DROUOT, 103 rue Richelieu, 2e. Tel. 42-96-68-23.

Cuisine: FRENCH. **Reservations:** Not accepted, except for groups of 20 or more. **Métro:** Richelieu-Drouot.

$ Prices: Appetizers 18F–35F ($3.35–$6.50), main courses 48F–70F ($8.90–$12.95). MC, V.

Open: Lunch daily 11:45am–3pm, dinner daily 6:30–10pm.

 One of the best budget restaurants in the 2nd arrondissement, Le Drouot is usually packed with economy-minded Parisians who know where to go for well-prepared, filling food. Similar to the tradition of the famous *bouillons* at the turn of the century, a breadman comes around to see that your plate is full. For an appetizer, you might select ham from the Ardennes or perhaps artichoke bottoms in vinaigrette. Among the main courses offered, I'd recommend pepper steak with french fries or the filet of turbot in hollandaise sauce. Chocolate mousse is the favored dessert.

LE GRAND ZINC, 5 Faubourg Montmarte, 9e. Tel. 47-70-88-64.

Cuisine: FRENCH. **Reservations:** Not required. **Métro:** rue Montmartre.

$ Prices: Appetizers 28F–55F ($5.20–$10.20); main courses 85F–130F ($15.75–$24.05); fixed price menu 85F–125F ($15.75–$23.15). AE, DC, MC, V.

Open: Lunch Mon–Sat noon–3pm, dinner Mon–Sat 7pm–1am.

 Le Grand Zinc may be in an unfashionable quarter, but Paris of the 1880s survives here, as exemplified by the spirit lamps hanging inside. You make your way into the restaurant past baskets of seafood in which you can inspect the *belons*, or brown-fleshed oysters, from Brittany, a traditional favorite and available all year round. The atmosphere is bustling in the tradition of a brasserie.

Specialties include steak au poivre, magret de canard with grilled peppers, côte de boeuf (prepared only for two diners), confit de canard (duck) prepared in the style of Toulouse and served with ratatouille, and a grilled filet of turbot with beurre blanc (white butter sauce).

HARD ROCK CAFE, 14 bd. Montmartre, 9e. Tel. 42-46-10-00.

Cuisine: AMERICAN. **Reservations:** Recommended. **Métro:** rue Montmartre.

$ Prices: Appetizers 15F–38F ($2.80–$7); sandwiches, salads, and platters 42F–100F ($7.80–$18.50). MC, V.

Open: Daily noon–2am.

Parisian Americaphiles soak up the ambience and nostalgia of the recent past at this newly established French branch of what might be the most successful chain of restaurants to ever hit the post-Eisenhower era. Like its counterparts, which now stretch from London to Reykjavik, the Hard Rock Café offers one of Paris's largest collections of rock 'n' roll memorabilia as well as musical selections from 35 years of rock 'n' roll classics. These are pumped out at reasonable levels during lunchtime, and at slightly less reasonable levels every evening, much to the delight of the crowd, which appreciates both the music and the juicy steaks, hamburgers, veggie burgers, salads, and heaping platters of informal, French-inspired food. As you dine, scan the high-ceilinged room for such venerated objects as the stage tuxedo worn by Buddy Holly, Jim Morrison's leather jacket, Jimi Hendrix's psychedelic vest, or the black-and-gold bustier sported by Madonna during one of her concerts in Paris.

6. 10TH ARRONDISSEMENT

MODERATE

BRASSERIE FLO, 7 cour Petites-Ecuries, 10e. Tel. 47-70-13-59.
   Cuisine: FRENCH. **Reservations:** Recommended. **Métro:** Château-d'Eau or Strasbourg–St-Denis.
$ Prices: Appetizers 40F–108F ($7.40–$20); main courses 74F–167F ($13.70–$30.90). AE, DC, MC, V.
   Open: Lunch daily noon–3pm; dinner daily 7pm–1:30am.
Brasserie Flo is a remembrance of things past. You walk through an area of passageways, stumbling over garbage littering the streets, then come upon this sepia world of turn-of-the-century Paris: old mahogany, leather banquettes, and brass-studded chairs. Some of the choicest people come here (it's the principal rival of the more celebrated Lipp in St-Germain-des-Prés—and it isn't even expensive.

The thing to order, of course, is "la formidable choûcroute" (sauerkraut), but don't expect just a heap of sauerkraut: The mound is surrounded by ham, bacon, and sausages. It's bountiful in the best tradition of Alsace. The onion soup is always good, as is guinea hen with lentils. Look for the plats du jour, ranging from roast pigeon to fricassée of veal with sorrel.

JULIEN, 16 rue du Faubourg St-Denis, 10e. Tel. 47-70-12-06.
   Cuisine: FRENCH. **Reservations:** Required. **Métro:** Strasbourg–St-Denis.
$ Prices: Appetizers 75F–180F ($13.90–$33.30); main courses 135F–320F ($25–$59.20); fixed price menu 149F ($27.55). AE, DC, MC, V.
   Open: Lunch daily noon–2:45pm, dinner daily 7pm–1:30am.
   Closed: July.
Julien offers an opportunity to dine in one of the most sumptuous belle époque interiors in Paris. Located in an area not far from Les Halles, it began life at the turn of the century as an elegant place but declined after World War II, becoming a cheap restaurant; however, the decor remained, albeit grimy and unappreciated. From a dingy working-class eating place, it has now been restored to its former elegance, the dirt cleaned off, and the magnificence of the fin-de-siècle dining area brought back to life. Marble and glass gleam in the mirrored, high-ceilinged room, with 15-foot-high murals, peacock-

shaped coat hooks, twisted rococo pillars, and paintings of oda-
lisques.

The food served here is *cuisine bourgeoise,* but without the heavy
sauce once used. Excellently prepared dishes include soups such as
Billi-By (a creamy mussel soup as good as that served at Maxim's),
soupe au pistou, and vichyssoise. Among the main courses are grilled
lobster with whisky, fresh salmon with sorrel, and chateaubriand
béarnaise. The wine list is good and reasonably priced.

7. 5TH & 6TH ARRONDISSEMENTS

VERY EXPENSIVE

**JACQUES CAGNA, 14 rue des Grands-Augustins, 6e. Tel.
43-26-49-39.**
   Cuisine: FRENCH. **Reservations:** Required. **Métro:** St-
Michel.
$ Prices: Appetizers 170F–330F ($31.45–$61.05); main courses
220F–400F ($40.70–$74); fixed-price lunch 270F ($49.95). AE,
DC, MC, V.
   Open: Lunch Mon–Sat noon–2pm, dinner Mon–Sat 7:30–
10:30pm. **Closed:** Aug.

Both the clientele and the food are considered among the most
sophisticated and/or grandest in Paris. The establishment is
located in a 17th-century town house decorated with massive
timbers and a delectable color scheme of pinkish beige, plus a series
of 17th-century Dutch paintings. The main dining room lies one
flight above street level.

A specialty is the Aberdeen Angus beef, aged for a full three
weeks, which chef Cagna imbues with a shallot-flavored sauce rich
with herbs and seasonings. You might begin with a salad of Brittany
lobster mixed with duck liver and artichoke bottoms, or else a
feuilleté of crayfish with mussels in a sherry-flavored morel sauce.
Other specialties include tender sweetbreads braised in essence of
giant shrimp, pungent leg of baby lamb with tarragon, and perhaps
Breton pigeon with honey and sauterne. Desserts are overwhelmingly
tempting.

**LA TOUR D'ARGENT, 15–17 quai de la Tournelle, 5e. Tel.
43-54-23-31.**
   Cuisine: FRENCH. **Reservations:** Required. **Métro:**
Maubert-Mutualité or Pont-Marie.
$ Prices: Appetizers 200F–645F ($37–$119.35); main courses
285F–620F ($52.75–$114.70); fixed price lunch 400F ($74). AE,
DC, MC, V.
   Open: Lunch Tues–Sun noon–2pm, dinner Tues–Sun 8–10pm.

La Tour d'Argent is a national institution. The view over the
Seine and the apse of Notre-Dame from this penthouse
restaurant is superb.

La Tour d'Argent traces its history back to 1582, when a
restaurant of some sort stood on this ground. The fame of the
establishment was spread during its ownership by Frederic Delair,
who bought the fabled wine cellar of Café Anglais. He was the one

who started the practice of issuing certificates to diners ordering the house specialty: pressed duckling (caneton). The birds, incidentally, are numbered.

Under the sharp eye of its current owner, Claude Terrail, the cooking is superb, and the service impeccable. Dresden china adorns each table. Although a quarter of the menu is taken up with various ways you can order duck, I assure you that the kitchen *does* know how to prepare other dishes. Especially recommendable are quenelles de brochet homard Lagardère and noisettes de Tournelles. To begin your meal, I recommend potage Claudius Burdel, made with egg yolks, fresh cream, chicken broth, sorrel, and butter, whipped together.

EXPENSIVE

CLOSERIE DES LILAS (Pleasure Garden of the Lilacs), 171 bd. Montparnasse, 6e. Tel. 43-26-70-50.

Cuisine: FRENCH. **Reservations:** Required. **Métro:** Port-Royal or Vavin.

$ Prices: Restaurant, appetizers 75F–235F ($13.90–$43.50); main courses 105F–320F ($19.45–$59.20). Brasserie, appetizers 55F–120F ($10.20–$22.20); main courses 120F–230F ($22.20–$42.55). AE, DC, V.

Open: Restaurant, lunch daily 12:30–2:30pm, dinner daily 7:30pm–12:30am. Brasserie, daily noon–1am.

The famous people who have sat in the Closerie watching the falling leaves blow along the streets of Montparnasse are almost countless: Gertrude Stein, Ingrès, Henry James, Châteaubriand, Apollinaire, Lenin and Trotsky at the chess board, and Whistler, who would expound the "gentle art" of making enemies.

To get a seat in what is called the "bateau" section of the restaurant is difficult. However, you may enjoy waiting for a seat at the bar and ordering the best champagne julep in the world. In the bateau, you can order such dishes as poached haddock, beef with a salad, or even steak tartare. In the chic restaurant inside the Closerie, the cooking is classic. Try the escargots façon Closerie for openers. Of the main-course selections, the rognons de veau à la moutarde (veal kidneys with mustard) and ribs of veal in a cider sauce are highly recommended.

MODERATE

AUBERGE DES DEUX SIGNES, 46 rue Galande, 5e. Tel. 43-25-46-56.

Cuisine: FRENCH. **Reservations:** Required for dinner. **Métro:** Maubert-Mutualité.

$ Prices: Appetizers 70F–200F ($12.95–$37); main courses 130F–220F ($24.05–$40.70); fixed price lunch 150F ($27.75); fixed price dinner 230F ($42.55). DC, MC, V.

Open: Lunch daily 12:30–2pm, dinner daily 7:30–10:30pm.

This restaurant was once the chapel of St-Blaise. Auvergne-born Georges Dhulster has this place well under control, and many visitors prefer to come here in the evening to enjoy the view of floodlit Nôtre-Dame (without having to pay the prices charged by Tour d'Argent) and the Church of St-Julien-le-Pauvre. Try to get a table upstairs with a view of the garden, but be prepared for a wait.

The cuisine of the old province of Auvergne is given a *moderne* twist here: Fresh ingredients go into dishes, and menu selections are found on old record discs. Try the Cantal veal medallions or goose confit with flap mushrooms.

INEXPENSIVE

LE BISTRO DE LA GARE, 59 bd. du Montparnasse, 6e. Tel. 45-48-38-01.

Cuisine: FRENCH. **Reservations:** Not accepted. **Métro:** Montparnasse-Bienvenue.

$ Prices: Appetizers 22F–80F ($4.05–$14.80); main courses 62F–105F ($11.45–$19.45); two-course fixed-price menu 78.90F ($14.60). MC, V.

Open: Daily Mon–Fri 11:30am–1am.

In addition to offering low-cost, well-prepared meals, this unusual establishment has an art nouveau decor that is classified as a national treasure by the government. The crowds who elbow into this place wait for an empty table at the standup bar, where an employee offers a free glass of kir to anyone obliged to wait for more than a few minutes. Menu items are straightforward but flavorful, including several kinds of grilled steak, duck, and terrines. A wide assortment of desserts is offered as well as house wine sold in carafes. You'll find other members of this popular chain at strategic locations throughout Paris.

LA CABANE D'AUVERGNE, 44 rue Grégoire-de-Tours, 6e. Tel. 43-25-14-75.

Cuisine: FRENCH. **Reservations:** Recommended. **Métro:** Odéon.

$ Prices: Appetizers 25F–60F ($4.65–$11.10), main courses 69F–90F ($12.75–$16.65).

Open: Lunch Tues–Sat noon–2pm, dinner Mon–Sat 7:30–11pm.

This self-proclaimed "rabbit hutch" is like a rustic tavern from the Auvergne, an ancient province of France (now divided into départements), which was known as a fertile land of copious and rich cookery. Under beamed ceilings, you are served typical regional meals on bare plank tables with provincial stools. It often becomes very crowded, so show up early if you want a seat.

The kitchen specializes in terrines. One is made from marcassin (young boar), another from fricandeau (larded veal loin), yet another from caneton (duckling). Main courses are generous and well cooked. Traditional Auvernat specialties include potée Auvernat (a stewpot simmering with pork, white beans, turnips, and cabbage leaves). Also prominent is a tasty, filling cassoulet. You'll find it an effort to order dessert.

LA CAFETIERE, 21 rue Mazarine, 6e. Tel. 46-33-76-90.

Cuisine: FRENCH. **Reservations:** Recommended. **Métro:** Odéon.

$ Prices: Appetizers 60F–70F ($11.10–$12.95), main courses 100F–138F ($18.50–$25.55). MC, V.

Open: Lunch daily 12:15–2:30pm, dinner daily 7:15–11pm.

In the heart of the Odéon district is this tiny neighborhood bistro that serves good food at reasonable prices. Dining is on two levels, and the restaurant serves both lunch and dinner daily, including Sunday, when many other nearby bistros are closed. A coffee-pot theme informs the decor, and the service is always laudable. Founder and owner Louis Diet, a former merchant seaman, sees to it that his kitchen turns out tenderloin of beef in mustard sauce, rack of lamb, salt pork with lentils, and a delectable pot-au-feu.

AUX CHARPENTIERS, 10 rue Mabillon, 6e. Tel. 43-26-30-05.

Cuisine: FRENCH. **Reservations:** Required. **Métro:** Mabillon.

$ Prices: Appetizers 32F–70F ($5.90–$12.95), main courses 80F–113F ($14.80–$20.90). AE, DC, MC, V.

Open: Lunch Mon–Sat noon–3pm, dinner Mon–Sat 7:30–11:30pm.

 Aux Charpentiers was once the rendezvous of the master carpenters, whose guild was next door. Nowadays it's where the young men of St-Germain-des-Prés take their dates for inexpensive meals in a pleasant atmosphere. Although not especially imaginative, the food is well cooked in the best tradition of cuisine bourgeoise. Appetizers include a rillette of sardines. Especially recommended as a main course is the roast duck with olives. Each day of the week a different plat du jour is offered, with time-tested French home-cooking: petit salé aux lentilles, pot-au-feu, and boeuf à la mode are among the main dishes on the menu. The chef suggests platters of fresh fish daily. There is a large choice of Bordeaux wines direct from the château, including Château Gaussens.

CREMERIE-RESTAURANT POLIDOR, 41 rue Monsieur-le-Prince, 6e. Tel. 43-26-95-34.

Cuisine: FRENCH. **Reservations:** Not accepted. **Métro:** Odéon.

$ Prices: Appetizers 15F–62F ($2.80–$11.45), main courses 40F–75F ($7.40–$13.90). No credit cards.

Open: Lunch daily noon–2:30pm; dinner Mon–Sat 7pm–1am, Sun 7–11pm.

Crèmerie Polidor is the most characteristic bistro in the Odéon area, serving the *cuisine familiale*. It still uses the word *crèmerie* in its title, an appellation dating back to the early part of this century when it specialized in frosted cream desserts, but its origins date back as far as 1845.

In time it became one of the Left Bank's oldest and most established literary bistros. In fact, it was Andre Gide's favorite, and Hemingway, Valéry, Artaud, Charles Boyer, and Kerouac have dined here as well.

The atmosphere is one of lace curtains, polished brass hat racks, and drawers in the back where repeat customers lock up their cloth napkins. It is frequented largely by students and artists, who always seem to head for the rear. Overworked but smiling waitresses serve such dishes as pumpkin soup, snails from Burgundy, rib of beef with onions, rabbit with mustard sauce, and veal in white sauce, followed by such desserts as a raspberry or lemon tart. The menu changes daily.

MOISSONNIER, 28 rue des Fosses St-Bernard, 5e. Tel. 43-29-87-65.

Cuisine: FRENCH. **Reservations:** Required for dinner. **Métro:** Jussieu or Cardinal-Lemoine.

$ Prices: Appetizers 50F–90F ($9.25–$16.65), main courses 95F–145F ($17.60–$26.85). V.

Open: Lunch Tues–Sun noon–2:30pm, dinner Tues–Sat 7–10pm. **Closed:** Aug.

Come here for real French country cooking, the kind many discriminating palates visit Paris just to sample. Big portions of solid old-fashioned food are served here, beginning with *saladiers*, large glass salad bowls filled with a selection of charcuterie. You might also select some excellent terrines, perhaps of Lyonnais sausages. The specialties, from Burgundy and Lyon, include such main dishes as duck with turnips and rack of herb-flavored lamb.

LE PROCOPE, 13 rue de l'Ancienne Comédie, 6e. Tel. 43-28-99-20.

Cuisine: FRENCH. **Reservations:** Recommended. **Métro:** Odéon.

$ Prices: Appetizers 47.50F–122F ($8.80–$22.55), main courses 89.50F–152.50F ($16.55–$28.20). AE, DC, MC, V.

Open: Daily 8am–2am.

Le Procope, originally opened in 1686 by a Sicilian named Francesco Procopio dei Coltelli, is the oldest café in Paris. More of a restaurant than it was originally, it is sumptuously decorated with gilt-framed mirrors, antique portraits of former illustrious clients, crystal chandeliers, banquettes of Bordeaux-colored leather, and marble-top tables.

Former clients have included La Fontaine, Voltaire, Benjamin Franklin, Rousseau, Anatole France, Robespierre, Danton, Marat, Bonaparte (as a youth), Balzac (who drank endless cups of very strong coffee), and Verlaine (who preferred the now illegal absinthe). There are two levels for dining: the spacious upstairs section or the more intimate street-level room. Fresh oysters and shellfish are served from a refrigerated display. A well-chosen selection of classic French dishes is presented, including baby duckling with spices and "green coffee" or "drunken chicken."

8. 7TH ARRONDISSEMENT

VERY EXPENSIVE

LE JULES VERNE, Tour Eiffel, Champ de Mars, 7e. Tel. 45-55-61-44.

Cuisine: FRENCH. **Reservations:** Required. **Métro:** Trocadéro, Ecole-Militaire, or Bir-Hakeim.

$ Prices: Appetizers 185F–320F ($34.25–$59.20); main courses 200F–340F ($37–$62.90); fixed-price lunch 280F ($51.80). AE, DC, MC, V.

Open: Lunch daily noon–2:30pm, dinner daily 7:30–10:30pm.

Today the institution of drinking and dining inside the monument that symbolizes Paris is still alive and well. Many visitors view the elevator ride to the second platform of the Eiffel Tower as one of the highlights of their experience. After the ride, you are ushered into a decor as black as the Parisian night outside, with only strategically placed spotlights set on each of the minimalist tables. The end result seems to bring the twinkling Paris panorama into the restaurant itself.

All of this would be merely a fantasy for ex-aviators and the child in each of us were it not for the exquisite food prepared by a culinary team. The menu changes with the season, but might include a ravioli of sweetbreads with lobster sauce, scallops with sweet-and-sour sauce, duck liver with aged vinegar sauce, filet of turbot with seaweed and a butter flavored with sea urchins, or a cassolette of fresh hot oysters with cucumbers.

EXPENSIVE

L'ARPEGE, 84 rue de Varenne, 7e. Tel. 45-51-20-02.
   Cuisine: FRENCH. **Reservations:** Required. **Métro:** Varenne.
$ Prices: Appetizers 105F–185F ($19.45–$34.25); main courses 165F–320F ($30.55–$59.20); fixed-price lunch 260F ($48.10). AE, DC, MC, V.
   Open: Lunch Mon–Sat 12:30–2pm; dinner Mon–Fri 7:30–10:30pm. **Closed:** July 28–Aug 21.

★ L'Arpège is currently the rage of Paris because of its young chef, Alain Passard. The decor—described by one French food critic as "young, charming, and happy"—is a mere backdrop to what emerges from the kitchen.

The menu is deliberately limited so that chef Passard can give each course his attention. Try, for example, cabbage stuffed with crabmeat or game cock with chicken livers and herb-flavored onions. Sweetbreads are prepared with exotic mushrooms and truffle juice, or you might prefer John Dory with celery juice and asparagus flavored with sage. For dessert, try the chocolate beignets or, strangely, a sugared tomato with a vanilla stuffing. The wine list is something to write home about. The fixed-price lunch has been called a "steal"—that is, if you can get a table. Beverages, even coffee, are extra, but it's a bargain nonetheless.

LE DIVELLEC CUISINE DE LA MER, 107 rue de l'Université, 7e. Tel. 45-51-91-96.
   Cuisine: FRENCH. **Reservations:** Required. **Métro:** Invalides.
$ Prices: Appetizers 180F–320F ($33.30–$59.20); main courses 220F–410F ($40.70–$75.85); fixed-price lunch 280F–380F ($51.80–$70.30). AE, DC, MC, V.
   Open: Lunch Tues–Sat noon–2pm, dinner Tues–Sat 7–11pm. **Closed:** Aug 3–Sept 3.

★ This is one of the great seafood restaurants in all of France. In a long, narrow modern room, you can select some of the most unusual seafood combinations of cuisine moderne. Thanks to Brittany-born chef Jacques le Divellec, dining here is like dining at the captain's table on a private yacht.

Many sophisticated Parisian palates consider the simplest dishes here the best. The more experimental dishes include filet of stingray with truffles, terrine of foie gras studded with crayfish, gratin of codfish, mousseline of shellfish with filet of John Dory, and turbot with noodles tinted with squid ink. Most diners prefer to begin with half a dozen oysters.

MODERATE

L'AUBERGE BASQUE, 51 rue de Verneuil, 7e. Tel. 45-48-51-98.
   Cuisine: FRENCH. **Reservations:** Recommended. **Métro:** rue du Bac.
$ Prices: Appetizers 50F–110F ($9.25–$20.35); main courses 90F–130F ($16.65–$24.05); fixed-price menu 150F ($27.75). MC, V.

Open: Lunch Mon–Sat noon–2:30pm, dinner Mon–Sat 7:30–10:30pm.

Owners Monsieur and Madame Rourre come from the Basque country near the Spanish border, and their excellent meals reflect the rich cookery of that area as well as their daily market selections. Among their satisfied diners are famous sportsmen and French TV stars. You might begin with their Basque pâté, then follow with a pipérade, the famous omelet of the region. They also prepare both magret and confit of canard (duck). Various fresh fish dishes are also served, along with a selection of cheese and fresh fruit tarts. Wines are well chosen.

CHEZ LES ANGES, 54 bd. de Latour-Maubourg, 7e. Tel. 47-05-89-86.
  Cuisine: FRENCH. **Reservations:** Required. **Métro:** Latour-Maubourg.
  $ Prices: Appetizers 68F–185F ($12.60–$34.25); main courses 98F–168F ($18.15–$31.10); fixed-price lunch 350F ($64.75). AE, DC, MC, V.
  Open: Lunch daily noon–2pm, dinner Mon–Sat 7–11pm.

The encyclopedia *Larousse gastronomique* reported that "Burgundy is undoubtedly the region of France where the best food and the best wines are to be had." Whether or not that's true, the "House of Angels" does serve some of the finest Burgundian meals in Paris. The most classic main dish is sauté de boeuf bourguignon, as well as fricassée of veal kidneys. Other main dishes include suprême de barbue (brill) au beurre de poivrons rouges, cassolette of scallops with sea urchins, and tranche épaisse de foie de veau (thickly sliced calves' liver). The goat-cheese selection is varied. Desserts are rich, including a sorbet made with fresh strawberries and Cassis.

INEXPENSIVE

LA PETITE CHAISE, 36–38 rue de Grenelle, 7e. Tel. 42-22-13-35.
  Cuisine: FRENCH. **Reservations:** Required. **Métro:** Sèvres-Babylone.
  $ Prices: Appetizers 55F–65F ($10.20–$12.05); main courses 110F–130F ($20.35–$24.05); fixed-price meal 180F ($33.30). MC, V.
  Open: Lunch daily noon–2:15pm, dinner daily 7–11pm.

⑤ This is one of the oldest restaurants in Paris, dating from 1680. Very Parisian, it invites you into its world of terracotta walls, cramped but attractive tables, wood paneling, and ornate gilt wall sconces. Its special feature is its set meal, which is likely to include such specialties as chicken Pojarski (minced, breaded, and sautéed), noisettes of lamb with green beans, quenelles de brochet (made with pike), trout meunière, escalope de veau normand, and pavé steak with roquefort sauce. The cheese tray, especially the Cantal and Brie, is always respectable, and the desserts are good and rich.

BUDGET

LE JARDIN, 100 rue du Bac, 7e. Tel. 42-22-81-56.
  Cuisine: HEALTH FOOD. **Reservations:** Recommended. **Métro:** rue du Bac.
  $ Prices: Appetizers 42F–56F ($7.75–$10.35); main courses

74F–86F ($13.70–$15.90); fixed-price meal 106F ($19.60). DC, MC.

Open: Lunch Mon–Sat noon–3pm, dinner Mon–Sat 7–10:30pm.

Le Jardin offers health-conscious food so well prepared that some dedicated meat-eaters sometimes arrive for a taste. You'll dine beneath a greenhouse ceiling in a pleasant room filled with sunlight and plants. A fixed-price meal includes generous portions of salad, grain dishes, vegetables au gratin, and a dessert cheese or pastry.

9. 15TH ARRONDISSEMENT

EXPENSIVE

LA GAULOISE, 59 av. de la Motte-Picquet, 15e. Tel. 47-34-11-64.

Cuisine: FRENCH. **Reservations:** Required. **Métro:** La Motte-Picquet–Grenelle.

$ Prices: Appetizers 85F–180F ($15.75–$33.30), main courses 160F–220F ($29.60–$40.70). AE, DC, MC, V.

Open: Lunch Mon–Fri 12:30–2pm, dinner Mon–Fri 7:30–11pm.

Its fire-engine-red canopy evokes a Parisian bistro of the 1930s. Politicians and athletes in particular love its tobacco-tinged walls—in fact, no one wants anything changed around here. Its owner, Jacques Chalvet, goes to the Rungis market outside Paris every morning to seek the freshest of ingredients. From his shopping, he composes his *suggestions du marché,* or market selections, to tempt his hungry diners. Fish and shellfish dishes seem to be the favorites. Try, in particular, the bouillabaisse. In summer you can eat outside, beneath parasols, below the rumbling and roar of an elevated subway that the French call "aerien Métro."

MODERATE

LAJARRIGE, 38 av. de Suffren, 15e. Tel. 43-06-49-40.

Cuisine: FRENCH. **Reservations:** Recommended. **Métro:** Sèvres-Lecourbe.

$ Prices: Appetizers 30F–90F ($5.55–$16.65), main courses 60F–115F ($11.10–$21.30). MC, V.

Open: Lunch daily noon–2:30pm, dinner daily 7–10pm.

Lajarrige is a bright little restaurant that celebrates the cooking of southwest France. Jean-Claude de Lajarrige, longtime restaurateur, presents well-prepared food using the best of ingredients. The menu lists a wealth of good dishes, including a rich foie gras. One of the best specialties is a big cassoulet landais, contrived to let you enjoy the crunchy white beans, the duck confit, and the well-flavored sausages. Another favorite is a duck preparation, magret de canard. This regionally inspired restaurant also has within its premises a food boutique serving conserves, wines, alcohol, and other products. For an apéritif, I'd suggest a fermented brut de pêche (extract of peaches), followed by an appetizer, salade paysanne with chicken livers.

LE WESTERN, in the Hilton Hotel, 18 av. de Suffren, 15e. Tel. 42-73-92-00.

Cuisine: STEAKS. **Reservations:** Required. **Métro:** Bir-Hakeim.

$ Prices: Appetizers 65F–120F ($12.05–$22.20), main courses 120F–190F ($22.20–$35.15). AE, DC, MC, V.

Open: Lunch daily noon–3pm, dinner daily 7–11pm.

American meat and French wine are what it's all about at Hilton's re-creation of the Old West in Paris. The steaks served at this mixture of cattle ranch and French elegance are imported from Kansas, and are as good as anything you'd find in Abilene. Each of the waiters is dressed cowboy-style; the maître d'hôtel is in sheriff's garb.

Contrary to expectations, this has become one of those chic Parisian places where many of the French go to rubberneck at the unusual (for Europe) costumes and decor. You might begin your meal with a crab cocktail, jumbo shrimp, or a Caesar salad, to be followed by one of the array of grilled steaks, or if not that, a roquefort-stuffed chopped sirloin or a saddle chop of salt-marsh lamb with mint jelly.

The portions are large, but if you are still hungry, there is a selection of French cheese and pastries. At trail's end (according to the menu), you might want a steaming cup of outlaw's coffee (made with Kentucky bourbon instead of Irish whiskey).

10. 14TH ARRONDISSEMENT

MODERATE

BOURBONNAIS, 29 rue Delambre, 14e. Tel. 43-20-61-73.
   Cuisine: FRENCH. **Reservations:** Required. **Métro:** Edgar-Quinet or Vavin.
$ Prices: Appetizers 38F–105F ($7.05–$19.45); main courses 98F–210F ($18.15–$38.85). AE, DC, MC, V.
   Open: Lunch Mon–Sat 12:30–2pm, dinner Mon–Sat 7:30–11pm.

Bourbonnaise showcases the talents of Roger Le Meur in the heart of Montparnasse. Don't come here for the decor, because it's rather unappealing, with conspicuously heavy and overly rustic furniture. Instead, come for the food: Monsieur Le Meur is a grand chef, some of his culinary inspiration coming from the oldest of his grandmother's recipes. For example, you might enjoy codfish peasant-style or coq au vin with fresh noodles. Perhaps you'll try his foie gras maison or veal kidneys in a mustard sauce. There is also an array of *petits vins* at very reasonable prices.

LA CAGOUILLE, 10–12 place Constantin-Brancusi, 14e. Tel. 43-22-09-11.
   Cuisine: SEAFOOD. **Reservations:** Required. **Métro:** Montparnasse-Bienvenue.
$ Prices: Appetizers 80F–125F ($14.80–$23.15), main courses 115F–225F ($21.30–$41.65). V.
   Open: Lunch Tues–Sat 12:30–2pm, dinner Tues–Sat 7:30–10:30pm. **Closed:** Aug.

This is the domain of the burly Gérard Allemandou, a native of the cognac district. Here you can sample one of the most splendid selections of cognacs from smaller properties ever amassed in Paris.

But that's not why everyone comes here. It's because you get some of the freshest and most reasonably priced fish in Paris. Fresh from Rungis, the huge red mullet is grilled to perfection. Salmon steak is usually slightly underdone and served without a sauce (a dieter's dream come true). Ungarnished barnacles, grilled snapper, mussels sautéed in cast-iron pans—you get a Neptunian parade of natural and pure fish here. Peppered butter and sea salt are trademarks of the place; a "teardrop" of butter is the adornment for the accompanying perfectly steamed vegetables. The decor is ultraclean and minimalist; the "nonwelcome" is bistro-style, but no one seems to mind.

---

11. 3RD & 4TH ARRONDISSEMENTS

VERY EXPENSIVE

L'AMBROISIE, 9 place des Vosges, 4e. Tel. 42-78-51-45.
Cuisine: FRENCH. **Reservations:** Required. **Métro:** St-Paul-le-Marais.
$ Prices: Appetizers 185F–300F ($34.25–$55.50), main courses 200F–395F ($37–$73.10). V.
Open: Lunch Tues–Sat noon–1:45pm, dinner Tues–Sun 8–10:15pm.

⭐ Bernard Pacaud is one of the most talented chefs in Paris, and his cuisine has drawn world attention. He trained at the prestigious Vivarois before deciding to strike out on his own, first on the Left Bank, now at this ideal location in Le Marais on its square evoking memories of Victor Hugo. Try for a table in the garden.

Pacaud's tables are nearly always filled with satisfied diners, who visit to see where his imagination will take him next. His cooking has a certain simplicity yet is the height of elegance. His favored dishes include a delectable red-pepper mousse (perhaps the finest you are likely to be served in Paris), braised oxtail, wild salmon breaded and pan-fried (and served with a thin potato pancake), and a salad of mâche with a ballotine of duck. For dessert, the chocolate mousse is velvety smooth, or you might try anything in puff pastry.

MODERATE

BOFINGER, 5–7 rue de la Bastille, 4e. Tel. 42-72-87-82.
Cuisine: FRENCH/ALSATIAN. **Reservations:** Recommended. **Métro:** Bastille.
$ Prices: Appetizers 55F–120F ($10.20–$22.20); main courses 120F–200F ($22.20–$37); three-course fixed price menu 170F ($31.45). AE, DC, MC, V.
Open: Lunch daily noon–3pm, dinner daily 7:30pm–1am.
Bofinger was founded in the 1860s, and is the oldest Alsatian brasserie in town—and certainly one of the best. It's actually a dining palace, resplendent with shiny brass. Much restored, it looks better than ever. If you prefer, you can dine on an outdoor terrace, weather permitting.

The fashionable make their way at night through the Marais district, right off the place de la Bastille, to this bustling, popular brasserie. In their floor-length white aprons, the waiters bring dish after dish of satisfying fare at reasonable prices. Choucroûte (sauerkraut) is the preferred dish, accompanied by a vast array of bacon, sausages, and a pork chop. *Tip:* Look for the chef's specials. He features a different one every day, including a superb stew the French call cassoulet.

LA COLOMBE, 4 rue de la Colombe, 4e. Tel. 46-33-37-08.
   Cuisine: FRENCH. **Reservations:** Required. **Métro:** Cité or Hôtel de Ville.
$ Prices: Appetizers 60F–140F ($11.10–$25.90); main courses 95F–140F ($17.60–$25.90); menu gastronomique 280F ($51.80). AE, DC, MC, V.
   Open: Lunch Tues–Sat noon–2:30pm, dinner Mon–Sat 7:30pm–midnight.

La Colombe is on one of the smallest streets in old Paris, on the Ile de la Cité, running into the quai aux Fleurs behind Notre-Dame. The house of La Colombe (the dove), dating from 1275, is an idyllic setting for dining, with more than a dozen doves providing a unique ambience. It's a favorite with tourists who wish to relax in a peaceful, time-tested atmosphere.

The chef, who has presided over the Colombe kitchen for 20 years, creates such delicacies as duck with pears, tournedos with Périgueux sauce, and veal with mushrooms in a fresh cream sauce. Fresh fish is available every day. The desserts are the chef's specialty: cake Colombe, stuffed crêpes with cream, and profiteroles with hot fudge. A copious gastronomical meal is served.

INEXPENSIVE

L'AMBASSADE D'AUVERGNE, 22 rue de Grenier St-Lazare, 3e. Tel. 42-72-31-22.
   Cuisine: FRENCH. **Reservations:** Recommended. **Métro:** Rambuteau.
$ Prices: Appetizers 58F–90F ($10.75–$16.65), main courses 88F–125F ($16.30–$23.15). MC, V.
   Open: Lunch daily noon–2pm, dinner daily 7:30–11pm.

In an obscure district of Paris, this rustic tavern serves the hearty cuisine bourgeoise of Auvergne, the heartland of France. You enter through a busy bar, with heavy oak beams, hanging hams, and ceramic plates. At the entrance is a display of the chef's specialties: jellied meats and fowl, pâtés, plus an assortment of regional cheeses and fresh fruits of the season. Rough wheat bread is stacked in baskets, and rush-seated ladderback chairs are placed at tables covered with bright cloths. Stem glassware, mills to grind your own salt and pepper, and a jug of mustard are on each table.

Specialties include cassoulet with lentils, pot-au-feu, confit de canard, codfish casserole, and stuffed cabbage. Some of these specials are featured on one day of the week only. For a side dish, I recommend aligot, a medley of fresh potatoes, garlic, and Cantal cheese.

CHEZ JO GOLDENBERG, 4 rue des Rosiers, 4e. Tel. 48-87-20-16.
   Cuisine: JEWISH/CENTRAL EUROPEAN. **Reservations:** Recommended. **Métro:** St-Paul.
$ Prices: Appetizers 22F–120F ($4.05–$22.20), main courses 75F–85F ($13.90–$15.75). AE, DC, MC, V.
   Open: Daily noon–1am.

On this "Street of the Rose Bushes" this is the best-known restaurant. Albert Goldenberg, the king of Jewish restaurateurs in Paris, long ago moved to another restaurant in choicer surroundings at 69 av. de

Wagram, 17e. But his brother Joseph has remained at the original establishment, which opened in 1936.

Dining here is on two levels. Look for the collection of samovars and the white fantail pigeon in a wicker cage. Interesting paintings and strolling musicians add to the ambience. The carpe farcie (stuffed carp) is a preferred selection, but the beef goulash is also good. I also like the eggplant moussaka, and pastrami is one of the most popular items. The menu also offers Israeli wines, but Monsieur Goldenberg admits that they're not as good as French wine.

AU GOURMET DE L'ISLE, 42 rue St-Louis-en-l'Ile, 4e. Tel. 43-26-79-27.

Cuisine: FRENCH. **Reservations:** Required. **Métro:** Pont-Marie.

$ Prices: Appetizers 32F–48F ($5.90–$8.90); main courses 65F–80F ($12.05–$14.80); fixed-price menu 130F ($24.05) MC, V.

Open: Lunch Wed–Sun noon–2pm, dinner Wed–Sun 7–10pm.

This restaurant is savored by its loyal habitués. The setting is beautiful: a beamed ceiling, candlelit tables. Many Parisian restaurants approach this in decor, but where other establishments on this popular tourist island fall short (in the food department), this little "Gourmet Island" succeeds.

In the window you'll see a sign, "A.A.A.A.A.," which, roughly translated, stands for the Amiable Association of Amateurs of the Authentic Andouillette. These chitterling sausages are soul food to the French. Popular and tasty, too, is la charbonnée de l'Isle, a savory pork with onions. An excellent appetizer is the stuffed mussels in shallot butter. Your palate will fare as well as your wallet if you order the fixed-price menu.

BUDGET

AQUARIUS, 54 rue Ste-Croix-de-la-Bretonnerie, 4e. Tel. 48-87-48-71.

Cuisine: VEGETARIAN. **Reservations:** Not needed. **Métro:** Hôtel-de-Ville.

$ Prices: Appetizers 18F–28F ($3.35–$5.20); main courses 35F–52F ($6.50–$9.60); fixed-price menu 48F ($8.90). No credit cards.

Open: Mon–Sat noon–9:45pm. **Closed:** Aug.

Aquarius is one of the best-known vegetarian restaurants in Le Marais, which has many health-conscious residents who insist on no smoking. Neither wine nor spirits are sold, but you can enjoy a fruit-flavored beverage. Meals, regardless of what you order, seem to overflow with raw or steamed vegetables. Aquarius is open for lunch, tea, snacks, and dinner.

LA TAVERNE DU SERGENT RECRUTEUR, 41 rue St-Louis-en-l'Ile, 4e. Tel. 43-54-75-42.

Cuisine: FRENCH. **Reservations:** Recommended. **Métro:** Pont-Marie.

$ Prices: All-you-can-eat menu 180F ($33.30). V.

Open: Dinner daily 7pm–2am.

La Taverne du Sergent Recruteur occupies a 17th-century setting on the historic Ile Saint-Louis. But many buildings on this island do that. What makes La Taverne so popular is that it offers an all-you-can-eat meal. You more or less make your own salad with the items placed before you, including black radishes, fennel, celery, cucumbers, green pepper, hard-boiled eggs, and carrots. After that, a huge basket of sausages is brought around, and you can slice as you wish, sampling one or all. The carafe of wine, either red, white, or rosé, is bottomless. Plats du jour, ranging from beef to veal, change daily. You usually select from three different items. Next, a large cheese board makes the rounds, and, if you're still upright, you can select chocolate mousse or ice cream for dessert.

---

12. 18TH & 19TH ARRONDISSEMENTS

EXPENSIVE

BEAUVILLIERS, 52 rue Lamarck, 18e. Tel. 42-54-54-42.
 Cuisine: FRENCH. **Reservations:** Required. **Métro:** Lamarck-Caulaincourt.
$ Prices: Appetizers 105F–215F ($19.45–$39.80); main dishes 185F–285F ($34.25–$52.75); fixed-price lunch 185F ($34.25). V.
 Open: Lunch Tues–Sat noon–2pm, dinner Mon–Sat 7:15–10:30pm.

This Montmartre hideaway is reputedly the favorite Parisian restaurant of master chef Paul Bocuse, who drops in whenever he's visiting from Lyon. The decor is unabashedly romantic, dripping with art nouveau touches that the owners have accumulated since the restaurant was converted from a bakery years ago. Chef Edouard Carlier is the secret behind the success of this restaurant, whose tables are very much in demand.

Amid 19th-century statues, old engravings, and massive bouquets of flowers, you can enjoy subtle transformations of traditional French dishes. Specialties include a flan of mussels with zucchini, duckling en cocotte with a confit of lemons, and a succulent leg of lamb with tarragon. During the summer the restaurant moves outside near a wide stairway leading up to the famous Butte.

COCHON D'OR (Golden Pig), 192 av. Jean-Jaurès, 19e. Tel. 42-45-46-46.
 Cuisine: FRENCH. **Reservations:** Required. **Métro:** Porte-de-Pantin.
$ Prices: Appetizers 52F–190F ($9.60–$35.15); main dishes 76F–275F ($14.05–$50.90); fixed-price meal 270F ($49.95). AE, DC, MC.
 Open: Lunch daily noon–2:30pm; dinner daily 7:30–10:30pm.

The chic come here for some of the best food in the city, even though it means journeying out to the remote Porte-de-Pantin in the 19th arrondissement. The restaurant's history goes back to the turn of the century, when it was created as a bistro for butchers in skullcaps. Nowadays it's run by the Ayral family, who extend personal greetings. You get hefty portions at high prices, but good value nonetheless, considering the quality of the produce and the care that goes into the preparation.

One dish I'd recommend is the charcoal-grilled côte de boeuf with moelle (marrow) sauce, for two. It is usually accompanied by a potato soufflé. Known mainly by gastronomes, an especially satisfying choice is the onglet grillé, one of the best beef cuts I've ever sampled in Paris.

INEXPENSIVE

LE MAQUIS, 69 rue Caulaincourt, 18e. Tel. 42-59-76-07.
Cuisine: FRENCH. **Reservations:** Required. **Métro:** Lamarck-Caulaincourt.
$ Prices: Appetizers 50F–90F ($9.25–$18.65); main courses 100F–150F ($18.50–$27.75); fixed-price lunch 95F ($17.60). V.
Open: Lunch Tues–Sat noon–2pm, dinner Tues–Sat 8–10pm.

Montmartre, for all its local color and atmosphere, has never been a great place for dining—with three or four exceptions. However, if you don't mind leaving the place du Tertre and heading on a 12-minute walk down the Butte, you'll be richly rewarded at this attractive restaurant, which has a tiny terrace open in the fair-weather months. The menu is limited, but select. Among the tasty courses are sauerkraut of fish, rabbit fricassée, stuffed mussels, coq au vin, a filet of sole served with two butters, and pheasant with cabbage. The desserts are often elaborate concoctions.

BUDGET

LE GRAIN DE FOLIE, 24 rue de la Vieuville, 18e. Tel. 42-58-15-57.
Cuisine: VEGETARIAN. **Reservations:** Recommended. **Métro:** Abbesses.
$ Prices: Appetizers 18F–33F ($3.35–$6.10); main courses 45F–85F ($8.35–$15.75); fixed-price menu 70F ($12.95). MC, V.
Open: Lunch Tues–Sun 12:30–2:30pm, dinner daily 7:30–11pm.

Run by a young Frenchwoman, this restaurant has two rooms with inviting ambience. They lie one before the other, halfway up the slope of Montmartre's hill. You can take out or eat in. The fixed-price menu includes a full array of salads, cereal products, vegetable tarts, and vegetable terrines. Desserts include an old-fashioned apple crumble or a fruit salad. Either the house Beaujolais or a frothy glass of vegetable juice might accompany your meal.

LA MAISON ROSE, 2 rue de l'Abreuvoir, 18e. Tel. 42-57-66-75.
Cuisine: FRENCH. **Reservations:** Not required. **Métro:** Blanche or Lamarck-Caulaincourt.
$ Prices: Appetizers 28F–88F ($5.20–$16.30); main courses 48F–132F ($8.90–$24.40); fixed price menus 72F ($13.30) and 105F ($19.45). MC, V.
Open: Winter daily 11:30am–10pm; summer daily 11:30am–midnight.

Painted a rosy shade of pink, this building, classified as a historic monument, once housed the atelier of Utrillo. Legend has it that Utrillo's friends used to lock him in during his periods of greatest emotional upset and financial crisis so that he could produce something to sell. Later, Aznavour sang here. In summer the terrace containing the most desirable tables quickly fills up. Meals might include fish soup, confit or magret de canard (duck), foie gras, blanquette de veau (veal) a l'ancienne, boeuf bourguignon, and paupiettes of sole à la mousseline.

13. 12TH ARRONDISSEMENT

EXPENSIVE

AU TROU GASCON, 40 rue Taine, 12e. Tel. 43-44-34-26.
   Cuisine: FRENCH. **Reservations:** Required. **Métro:** Daumesnil.
$ Prices: Appetizers 88F–168F ($16.30–$31.10); main courses 168F–208F ($31.10–$38.50); fixed-price meals 220F–400F ($40.70–$74). AE, DC, MC, V.
   Open: Lunch Mon–Fri noon–2pm; dinner Mon–Fri 7:30–10pm.
   Closed: Aug.

One of the most acclaimed chefs in Paris today, Alain Dutournier, launched his cooking career in the Gascony region of southwest France. His parents mortgaged their own inn to allow Dutournier to open a turn-of-the-century bistro in an unchic part of the 12th arrondissement. At first he got little business, but word soon spread that this man was a true artist in the kitchen who practiced the real cuisine moderne and not some of its unfortunate derivatives. Today he has opened another restaurant in Paris, but he left his secret recipes with the kitchen staff. The owner's wife, Nicole, is still there to greet you, and the wine steward has distinguished himself for his exciting *cave* containing several little-known wines along with a fabulous collection of Armagnacs. It is estimated that the cellar has some 350 varieties of wine.

Here you get the true cookery of Gascony, and that means cassoulet, wild salmon with smoked bacon, foie gras (offered from November to June), and Gascon ham cooked farmer's style.

14. SPECIALTY DINING

HOTEL DINING

BICE, in the Hôtel Balzac, 6 rue Balzac, 8e. Tel. 45-61-97-22.
   Cuisine: ITALIAN. **Reservations:** Required. **Métro:** George-V.
$ Prices: Appetizers 65F–125F ($12.05–$23.15); main dishes 55F–175F ($10.20–$32.40); fixed-price menus 250F–350F ($46.25–$64.75). AE, DC, MC, V.
   Open: Lunch daily noon–4pm, dinner daily 7pm–midnight.
   Closed: First three weeks of Aug.

This is the exclusive restaurant of one of the most elegant four-star hotels of Paris, lying just off the Champs-Elysées. From around the world the rich and famous flock to this classically refined establishment. It is an offshoot of the restaurant Bice, which opened in Milan in 1936—under the direction of "Mama Bice"—and has since gone international with branches in New York and Los Angeles, among other cities. The well-prepared (and well-received) cuisine features many specialties from Northern Italy, mainly pastas. Try tagliolini with shrimp and ossobuco of veal with risotto alla milanese. Begin with a Caprese salad with mozzarella and tomato or a vegetable carpaccio with a vinaigrette sauce.

DINING WITH A VIEW
EXPENSIVE

BATEAUX-MOUCHES, pont de l'Alma, place de l'Alma, 8e. Tel. 42-25-96-10 for reservations.
  Cuisine: FRENCH. **Reservations:** Required. **Métro:** Alma-Marceau.
$ **Prices:** Fixed-price cruise and lunch 320F ($59.20), fixed-price cruise and dinner 520F ($96.20). AE, DC, MC, V.
  Open: Lunch cruise daily 1–2:45pm, dinner cruise daily 8:30–10:45pm.
Nothing comes close to this combination of sightseeing and dining. For dinner, men are required to wear jackets and ties. During the dinner cruise, live music is featured.

LE CIEL DE PARIS [MAINE-MONTPARNASSE TOWER], 33 av. du Maine, 15e. Tel. 45-38-52-56.
  Cuisine: FRENCH. **Reservations:** Required. **Métro:** Montparnasse-Bienvenue.
$ **Prices:** Fixed-price menu 275F ($50.90). AE, DC, MC, V.
  Open: Lunch daily noon–3pm, dinner daily 7pm–midnight.
Overshadowing the Left Bank quarter of Montparnasse, the tower, completed in 1973, covers an entire block and houses some 80 shops,

---

Ⓕ FROMMER'S COOL FOR KIDS: RESTAURANTS

La Samaritaine *(see p. 115)* Kids will love the sandwiches and fries served at this café with a view of Paris.

La Boutique à Sandwichs *(see p. 125)* If you're in the Champs-Elysées area, drop in for the sandwiches, which come in all shapes and types.

Le Western *(see p. 143)* Kids get a bang out of seeing the servers dressed in western costumes at this unusual steak house.

A la Bonne Crêpe *(see p. 155)* Most children like crêpes, and during a tour of the Latin Quarter, this is a good lunch and early dinner spot.

Le Drug Store *(see p. 155)* This version of an American coffee shop/snack bar is sure to please the younger set.

Self-Rivoli *(see p. 155)* If you're taking your children to the Louvre during the day, break for lunch and head over to this self-serve cafeteria.

Bertillion *(see p. 155)* When they're screaming for ice cream, Bertillion is the place to go.

including Galeries Lafayette, and more than 200 offices. Its floors are serviced by rapid elevators that speed visitors from the lobby to the top floor in less than 40 seconds. The charge for the elevator is 35.50F ($6.60) for adults and 25F ($4.65) for children. From April to October it's open daily from 9:30am to 11pm. Off-season hours are 10am to 10pm. Sightseers go to Montparnasse 56, the covered, glassed-in observation deck on the 56th floor, where a panoramic view of Paris opens from every side. Your ticket includes an audiovisual presentation of the glamour of Paris, expositions of how the tower was built, and highlights of the Paris skyline far above. The Belvedere bar/café, good for lunch, a quick snack, or a drink, is also in the Montparnasse 56 complex.

Le Ciel de Paris is the tallest restaurant in the city, where you can enjoy a full dinner—set menu only—at a reasonable price. When you have finished your meal, you may ask the waiter to give you a ticket for entrance into Montparnasse 56. There is no charge to take the elevator going directly to the restaurant from the lobby.

LE JULES VERNE, Tour Eiffel, Champ-de-Mars, 7e. Tel. 45-55-61-44.
    Cuisine: FRENCH. **Reservations:** Required. **Métro:** Trocadéro, Ecole-Militaire, or Bir-Hakeim.
$ Prices: Appetizers 185F–320F ($34.25–$59.20); fixed-price lunch 280F ($51.80); main courses 200F–340F ($37–$62.90). AE, DC, MC, V.
    Open: Lunch daily noon–2:30pm, dinner daily 7:30–11pm.
This restaurant is reached by taking an elevator ride up to the second level. It's best at night, when you can dine and survey the lights of the "city of lights." For details, see Section 8, above.

TOUR D'ARGENT, 15–17 quai de la Tournelle, 5e. Tel. 43-54-23-31.
    Cuisine: FRENCH. **Reservations:** Required. **Métro:** Maubert-Mutualité or Pont-Marie.
$ Prices: Appetizers 200F–645F ($37–$119.35), main courses 285F–620F ($52.75–$114.70). AE, DC, MC, V.
    Open: Lunch Tues–Sun 12:30–2:30pm, dinner Tues–Sun 8–11:30pm.
This is one of the most spectacular dining views in all of Paris, despite its lethal prices. Nothing equals its view of the illuminated flying buttresses of Notre-Dame at night. For details, see Section 7, above.

FOR BREAKFAST
EXPENSIVE

HOTEL DE CRILLON, 10 place de la Concorde, 8e. Tel. 42-65-24-24.
    Cuisine: FRENCH. **Reservations:** Required far in advance. **Métro:** Concorde
$ Prices: Breakfast from 120F–190F ($22.20–$35.15). AE, DC, MC, V.
    Open: Breakfast daily 7–10:30am.
To experience a luxurious French breakfast, dress the part and head for the Hôtel de Crillon. Along with the international diplomatic and business elite, enjoy your breakfast in style amid the marble and crystal of the Restaurant des Ambassadeurs. The sausages are from England, but the several varieties of cheese are purely French. Fresh

fruit is also served. This is a chic place for power breakfast *à la française*. The 130F ($24.05) breakfast is called *petit déjeuner des affaires* (business breakfast). For 170F ($31.45), you can get an additional light dish, such as tartlet of scrambled eggs studded with smoked salmon. The *buffet des gourmets* is an English-inspired breakfast buffet.

MODERATE

SIR WINSTON CHURCHILL, 5 rue de Presbourg, 16e. Tel. 40-67-17-37.

Cuisine: FRENCH. **Reservations:** Required for lunch or dinner, but not breakfast. **Métro:** Charles-de-Gaulle–Etoile.

$ Prices: English breakfast 100F–150F ($18.50–$27.75), dinner 200F–250F ($37–$46.25). AE, MC, V.

Open: Mon–Sat 9am–2am; breakfast Mon–Sat 9am–noon.

If you like a rib-sticking breakfast as opposed to a café au lait and croissants, go to a corner of "ye olde England in Paris." You can order orange juice, porridge, eggs, bacon, grilled tomato, toast, butter, marmalade, and tea or coffee. You might come back for lunch or even dinner, when the chef prepares such English dishes as roast beef with Yorkshire pudding.

BUDGET

CAFE DE CLUNY, 20 bd. St-Michel, or 102 bd. St-Germain, 5e. Tel. 43-26-68-24.

Cuisine: FRENCH. **Reservations:** Not required. **Métro:** St-Michel.

$ Prices: Continental breakfast 35F ($6.50); café au lait (coffee with milk) 20F ($3.70); plats du jour 48F–62F ($8.90–$11.45). MC, V.

Open: Sun–Thurs 7am–2am, Fri–Sat 24 hrs.

Among the hundreds of Left Bank cafés, this one, located strategically at the intersection of these two famous avenues, overlooks the hub of the Left Bank and the Musée de Cluny. The long open hours will enable you to begin the day here with a morning omelet and come back at night for a brandy. Breakfast is served at any time, day or night. In the afternoon and until closing you can order various grillades and salads, including steak with pommes frites (french fries) and roast loin of pork.

FOR BRUNCH
EXPENSIVE

L'ESPACE, 1 av. Gabriel, 8e. Tel. 42-66-11-70.

Cuisine: FRENCH. **Reservations:** Required. **Métro:** Champs-Elysées.

$ Prices: Breakfast buffet 220F ($40.70), glass of champagne 50F ($9.25). AE, DC, MC, V.

Open: Sun noon–3pm.

Under the ownership of Pierre Cardin, the informal l'Espace presents 70 to 100 delicacies, including cold roasts and ample antipasti. The champagne is extra, but you can order it by the glass. If it's a nice day, ask for a garden table.

HOTEL MERIDIEN, 81 bd. Gouvion-Saint-Cyr, 17e. Tel. 47-58-12-30.

Cuisine: FRENCH. **Reservations:** Recommended. **Métro:** Maillot.

$ Prices: Brunch 285F ($52.75) adults, 145F ($26.85) children under 12. AE, DC, MC, V.

Open: Oct–June Sun 12:30–4pm.

In my opinion, the greatest place for brunch in Paris is "Le Sunday Jazz Brunch," which takes place in the lobby of the Hotel Méridien. Jazz artists entertain while you eat smoked salmon and enjoy excellent roasts and various hot and cold dishes. For details on the Jazz Club Lionel Hampton, see "The Club & Music Scene" in Chapter 9.

LIGHT MEALS & FAST FOOD
MODERATE

CHICAGO PIZZA FACTORY, 5 rue de Berri, 8e. Tel. 45-62-50-23.

Cuisine: AMERICAN. **Reservations:** Accepted only for 10 or more people. **Métro:** Champs-Elysées–Clemenceau.

$ Prices: Appetizers 18F–62F ($3.35–$11.45); main courses 65F–230F ($12.05–$42.55); express menu 80F ($14.80). MC, V.

Open: Daily 11:45–1am.

Sometimes you get a craving for pizza that nothing else will satisfy. If so, head for the Chicago Pizza Factory, right off the Champs-Elysées, in what was once a garage but is now a "Cheers"-style bar. While music or sports broadcasts are aired from the States, you can order deep-dish pizza and other hometown favorites, such as garlic bread, salad, pecan pie, and cheesecake—but no burgers.

CITY ROCK CAFE, 13 rue de Berri, 8e. Tel. 43-59-52-09.

Cuisine: AMERICAN. **Reservations:** Not required. **Métro:** George-V or F.D. Roosevelt.

$ Prices: Appetizers 48F–82F ($8.90–$15.15); main courses 68F–98F ($12.60–$18.15); fixed-price lunch (Mon–Fri) 85F ($15.75); beer 36F–62F ($6.65–$11.45). No credit cards.

Open: Sun–Thurs noon–2am, Fri–Sat noon–4am.

This is where young French people flock to enjoy plenty of good, hot American food. When you walk in you'll be greeted by an Elvis Presley–type pink Cadillac, one of Marilyn Monroe's old dresses hanging on the wall, vintage movie posters, and a nostalgic 1950s atmosphere. Rock 'n' roll is here to stay along with such down-home favorites as cheeseburgers, chili, and banana splits, as well as various Tex-Mex specialties, such as tacos and burritos.

FAUCHON, 26 place de la Madeleine, 8e. Tel. 47-42-60-11.

Cuisine: FRENCH. **Reservations:** Not required. **Métro:** Madeleine.

$ Prices: Lunch from 110F ($20.35). AE, DC, MC, V.

Open: Mon–Sat 9:40am–7pm.

For epicureans this has always been the *haut* grocery store of Paris, a sort of Parisian version of Fortnum and Mason. In fact, it's such a symbol of the Establishment that French Maoists once launched what the press called "a daring caviar and foie gras heist in broad daylight" at this exclusive store.

What many people don't know about Fauchon is that it offers a reasonably priced cafeteria-style lunch. First, place your order at the counter, then pay at the cashier's desk and receive a ticket to give to the clerk behind this counter. The only hitch is that you have to stand at the fast-food counter while you eat. Try the Fauchon's club sandwich and a scoop of ice cream. In the afternoon, Fauchon's cakes and pastries make tea a delight.

BUDGET

A LA BONNE CREPE, 11 rue Grégoire-de-Tours, 6e. Tel. 43-54-60-74.

Cuisine: CREPES. **Reservations:** Not required. **Métro:** Odéon.

$ Prices: Crepes 30F–45F ($5.55–$8.35). No credit cards.

Open: Mon–Sat noon–3pm, 7pm–midnight.

Later at night, when Parisians take over, this typical Left Bank street might not be suitable for children, but during the day and early evening it's just fine. Both main-dish savory crêpes and dessert crêpes filled with luscious delights are served here. Instead of wine, your older child might prefer a glass of Breton cider, which the French children drink. One is enough—it has some alcohol in it.

LE DRUG STORE, 149 bd. St-Germain-des-Prés, 6e. Tel. 42-22-92-50.

Cuisine: FRENCH. **Reservations:** Not required. **Métro:** St-Germain-des-Prés.

$ Prices: Appetizers 32F–82F ($5.90–$15.15), main dishes 60F–125F ($11.10–$23.15). AE, DC, MC, V.

Open: Daily 10am–2am.

This is the most popular of a chain of coffee shop/soda fountain/ snack bar/newsstand/boutiques. When they were opened, these establishments were dismissed by many French as American vulgarisms but they are, in fact, very Parisian today. Le Drug Stores sell everything from mustache cups to hearts of palm. The most popular item to order is a hamburger on a toasted bun. Some of the desserts are smothered in enough whipped cream to make them immoral.

There's another Drug Store at Publicis Champs-Elysées, 133 av. des Champs-Elysées, 8e (tel. 47-23-54-34).

SELF-RIVOLI, 17 rue Bertin-Poirée, 1er. Tel. 42-33-70-78.

Cuisine: FRENCH. **Reservations:** Not accepted. **Métro:** Louvre.

$ Prices: Appetizers 10F–15F ($1.85–$2.75), main courses 24F–38F ($4.45–$7.05). No credit cards.

Open: Lunch only, Mon–Sat 11am–3:30pm.

If it's a cafeteria you have in mind, head for Self-Rivoli, near one of the major department stores—Samaritaine—in Paris. The cafeteria serves one of the least expensive lunches (the only meal offered) in the neighborhood. It caters to businesspeople who work in the area and features good, simply prepared food.

Try one of the fresh salads, hot or cold plats du jour, or a hamburger. Right off rue de Rivoli, this self-service eatery is convenient if you're visiting the Louvre.

ICE CREAM

For some of the best ice cream in Paris, try **Bertillion**, 31 rue St-Louis-en-l'Ile, 4e (tel. 43-54-31-61; Métro: Pont-Marie), which is open Wednesday through Sunday from 10am to 1pm. In business some three dozen years, this store sells some of the most delectable ice-cream flavors ever concocted.

TEAROOMS & PATISSERIES
BUDGET

LADUREE, 16 rue Royale, 8e. Tel. 42-60-21-79.
   Cuisine: FRENCH. **Reservations:** Recommended for lunch.
   Métro: Concorde.
$ Prices: Café au lait 18F ($3.35), tea 26F ($4.80). MC, V.
   Open: Mon–Sat 8:30am–7pm. **Closed:** Aug.

Here, more than at any other salon de thé in Paris, the clientele look important and affluent. In turn-of-the-century grandeur, you can sip tea or coffee at tables barely big enough to hold a napkin. Diners order light lunches or just-baked pastries while talking quietly beneath the ceiling frescos of the main salon. Visit for lunch from noon to 2pm to order from a limited menu of traditional French dishes, such as boeuf bourguignon.

THE TEA CADDY, 14 rue St-Julien-le-Pauvre, 5e. Tel. 43-54-15-56.
   Cuisine: FRENCH. **Reservations:** Not required. **Métro:** St-Michel.
$ Prices: Pot of tea 25F ($4.65), homemade pastries 28F–32F ($5.20–$5.90). No credit cards.
   Open: Thurs–Sat and Mon noon–7pm; Sun 11:30am–7pm.
   Closed: Aug.

This just might be the best spot in Paris for a pot of tea. You'll recognize it by the stained-glass windows set into the oak door of what was probably once a stable. Their "ensemble" of furniture, fabrics, flowers, and darkened paneling would remind tea-lovers of a little corner of London except for a view of Notre-Dame, which rises across the river. Set next to the park of what might be "the most famous lesser-known church of Paris" (St-Julien-le-Pauvre), Tea Caddy is famous for its homemade marmalade, which accompanies the scones; its homemade pastries; and its half-dozen kinds of tea. These include Indian, Chinese, and Russian teas, plus varieties infused with jasmine and mango.

LATE NIGHT/24-HOUR DINING
EXPENSIVE

LA MAISON D'ALSACE, 39 av. des Champs-Elysées, 8e. Tel. 43-59-44-24.
   Cuisine: FRENCH. **Reservations:** Not required. **Métro:** Champs-Elysées.
$ Prices: Appetizers 45F–95F ($8.35–$17.60), main courses 95F–315F ($17.60–$58.30). AE, DC, MC, V.
   Open: 24 hrs.

This is a convenient late-night stopover on the Right Bank for revelers who want to tuck in some food before going back to their hotels. Main courses usually average 95F ($17.60). The higher-priced main dish indicated above is only for the most expensive of shellfish and lobster dishes. You can dine here and spend about 250F ($46.25) per person, wine included.

MODERATE

AU PIED DE COCHON, 6 rue Coquillière, 1er. Tel. 42-36-11-75.

Cuisine: FRENCH. **Reservations:** Recommended for lunch but not accepted for dinner after 8:30pm. **Métro:** Les Halles.

$ Prices: Appetizers 50F–130F ($9.25–$24.05), main courses 84F–160F ($15.55–$29.60). AE, DC, MC, V.

Open: 24 hrs.

The onion soup of Les Halles still lures visitors. Although the great market has moved to Rungis, near Orly Airport, traditions are long in dying. Besides, where in Paris can you be assured of getting a good meal at 3am if not at the famous "Pig's Foot?" The house specialty is the namesake: pig's feet grilled and served with béarnaise sauce, as well as the classic onion soup. Of course, you can sample any of the other tempting fares as well. Try the suckling pig St-Eustache or another well-known specialty, andouillette or chitterling sausage with béarnaise sauce.

Outside on the street, you can buy some of the freshest oysters in town. The attendants will even give you slices of lemons to accompany them, and you can down them right on the spot.

INEXPENSIVE

CAFE LE DEPART, 1 place St-Michel, 5e. Tel. 43-54-24-55.

Cuisine: FRENCH. **Reservations:** Not accepted. **Métro:** St-Michel.

$ Prices: Beer at the bar 9F ($1.65); beer at a table 20F ($3.70); sandwiches 18F ($3.35); burgers 55F ($10.20); grills 58F–62F ($10.75–$11.45). AE, DC, MC, V.

Open: 24 hrs.

One of the most popular cafés on the Left Bank is open 24 hours a day. On the banks of the Seine, within view of both the steeple of the Sainte-Chapelle and the dragon statue of place St-Michel, it is conveniently located for most visitors.

The decor is warmly modern, dominated by shades of brown, and with etched mirrors reflecting the faces of a diversified clientele. House cocktails include a "Saint-Michel"—Polish vodka, grapefruit juice, and cream of banana—costing 48F ($8.90). If you're hungry, select from warm and cold snacks, including sandwiches. The most popular late-night order is a grilled entrecôte with french-fries.

PUB SAINT-GERMAIN-DES-PRÉS, 17 rue de l'Ancienne-Comédie, 6e. Tel. 43-29-38-70.

Cuisine: FRENCH. **Reservations:** Not required. **Métro:** Odéon.

$ Prices: Beer 20F–72F ($3.70–$13.30), meals 105F–125F ($19.45–$23.15). AE, DC, MC, V.

Open: 24 hrs.

For late-night drinking, this is one of the most popular spots on the Left Bank. In the evening, there's both rock and variety band entertainment. The pub is the only one in the country to offer 24 draft beers and 500 international beers. There are nine different rooms and 500 seats, making it the largest pub in France. Leather booths make for a great late-night quiet snack.

LOCAL FAVORITES

RUE DES ROSIERS If the idea of corned beef, pastrami, schmaltz herring, and dill pickles excites you, then strike out for one of the most colorful old neighborhoods in Paris, the rue des Rosiers in the 4th arrondissement (Métro: St-Paul). There is something of the air of a little village about the place. The blue-and-white Star of David is prominently displayed. North African overtones, reflecting the arrival of Jews from Morocco, Tunisia, and especially Algeria, appeared long ago.

John Russell wrote that the rue des Rosiers is "the last sanctuary of certain ways of life; what you see there, in miniature, is Warsaw before the ghetto was razed."

The best time to go is Sunday morning, when many parts of Paris are sleeping. You can actually wander up and down the street, eating as you go—perhaps selecting an apple strudel, a slice of pastrami on Jewish rye bread, even pickled lemons, smoked salmon, and merguez, the typical smoked sausages of Algeria. If you want to have a proper sit-down meal, you'll find many spots.

PICNIC FARE & WHERE TO EAT IT

Paris is full of shops that sell picnic food; some can be found at most *charcuteries* (gourmet food shops), *pâtisseries,* or *boulangeries* (bakeries). Prices are a bit high, but that's just Paris.

For the most elegant picnic makings in town, go to **Fauchon,** 26 place de la Madeleine, 8e (tel. 47-42-60-11; Métro: Madeleine or Fauchon), recommended in "Light Meals & Fast Food," above. Here you'll find a complete charcuterie and a famous pastry shop. It's the best-known food shop in town, said to offer 20,000 kinds of imported fruits, vegetables, and other exotic delicacies, snacks, salads, and canapés—all packed to take out.

Another gourmet supplier is **Chedeville et Bourdon,** 12 rue du Marché Ste-Honoré, 1e (tel. 42-61-11-11; Métro: Pyramides), open Tuesday through Saturday from 8am to 6pm. Pâté and sausages are sold here, as well as baguettes.

These are just two of thousands of shops throughout Paris. You can pick up a variety of pâtés or terrines, which can be consumed cold, as well as quiches and salads (but don't buy anything likely to go bad on a hot day). Many of the salads are made with a vinaigrette dressing, which preserves them better. And don't forget the condiments, such as olives and pickles. Food critic Patricia Wells has called the Parisian charcuterie a "little touch of heaven." She likes to go from shop to shop sampling this and that. That way, she claims, you can make a picnic lunch a "true Parisian feast."

Armed with some sauterne or champagne, or whatever it is you like to drink, you're ready to head for your picnic in the park.

My favorite picnic spot is the **Bois de Boulogne,** but, depending on which part of town you're in, you may find the Right Bank **Jardin des Tuileries** (covered in one of our walking tours in Chapter 7) or the **Parc Monceau** equally enticing. At the **Bois de Boulogne,** you can, if you have a child with you, tie in a visit here with a trip to the Jardin d'Acclimation (read about it in "Cool for Kids," in Chapter 6).

Again, if you have children, you may want to take them to the **Bois de Vincennes** (Métro: Picpus), a big, popular patch of woodland with fine trees, two boating lakes, and a racecourse. This park, a favorite spot for family outings, adjoins the 14th-century Castle of Vincennes, open to visitors.

WHAT TO SEE & DO IN PARIS

The main attraction of Paris is . . . Paris. You'll make that discovery yourself the moment you start sightseeing. For, unless you're taking an organized tour, you are likely to become so enthralled by the vistas you find en route to a particular sight that you run the risk of never getting there.

No single palace, museum, church, or monument is as captivating as any of the hundreds of streets of this city. They work like sirens' songs on a visitor's senses, luring you into hours of aimless rambling when you should be steering resolutely toward some three-star edifice.

I know—it has happened to me more times than I want to remember. And knowing this, I've divided the sightseeing discussion into easy-to-use sections to help you match your interests with all the attractions Paris has to offer.

SUGGESTED ITINERARIES
IF YOU HAVE 1 DAY

The most practical way to see Paris in a day is to take a **guided tour,** since you can't possibly master the city on your own in such a short period of time. Start the day by ordering a café au lait or a café crème and croissants at a sidewalk café. The Cityrama tour, mentioned in "Organized Tours," below, begins at 9:30am. A double-decker bus will take you for a fast two-hour ride through the city, past Notre-Dame and the Eiffel Tower. After the tour, have lunch and go to the **Louvre** for a guided tour, in English, of its most important artworks. If you'd rather explore the museum on your own, follow my two-hour walking tour of the highlights of the Louvre (see Chapter 7). With what's left of the afternoon, stroll along the banks of the **Seine,** ending up at **Notre-Dame** as the sun sets over Paris. If you have an early dinner at a nearby bistro, you may still have the time and energy to attend the Lido or Folies Bergère (see "The Club & Music Scene" in Chapter 9).

IF YOU HAVE 2 DAYS

Start your second day by taking a **Bateaux-Mouches cruise** on the Seine (see "Organized Tours," below), with departures from Pont de l'Alma at place de l'Alma on the Right Bank (Métro: Alma-Marceau). Then go to the **Eiffel Tower** for lunch with a spectacular view (see my recommendation of Jules Verne in "Dining with a View" in Chapter 5).

DID YOU KNOW . . . ?

- The world's oldest "grocery store," Les Halles, moved in 1969—its first relocation in eight centuries.
- Rising 981 feet, the Eiffel Tower was the tallest building in the world in 1889.
- Place Denfert-Rochereau was once called place d'Enfer, or the "Square of Hell"—it was stacked with millions of bones from old charnel houses in 1785.
- On the narrow Seine island Allée des Cygnes stands a smaller version of the Statue of Liberty.
- The place de Charles de Gaulle–Etoile was the world's first organized traffic circle.
- Pont-Neuf (New Bridge) isn't new at all. It is the oldest (1607) and most famous bridge in Paris.
- The Sorbonne began in 1253 as modest lodgings for 16 theology students.
- In 1938 workmen discovered 3,350 22-karat gold coins weighing 1.3 grams each at 51 rue Mouffetard. A note said they belonged to Louis Nivelle, royal counselor to Louis XV, who mysteriously disappeared in 1757.

Next, head for the **Arc de Triomphe,** a perfect place to begin a stroll down the **Champs-Elysées,** the main boulevard of Paris, until you reach the Egyptian obelisk at **place de la Concorde.** This grand promenade, one of the most famous long walks in the world, is included in one of my walking tours (see Chapter 7).

IF YOU HAVE 3 DAYS

Occupy your first and second days as above. Spend your third morning exploring **Sainte Chapelle** and the **Conciergerie.** Have lunch, perhaps on the Ile St-Louis, and then take a walking tour (see Chapter 7). Afterward, spend two or three hours at the **Musée d'Orsay.**

IF YOU HAVE 5 DAYS

On your fourth day, take an organized tour or go on your own to visit **Versailles,** 13 miles south of Paris. After viewing the palace and gardens, head back to the city for an evening stroll through the **Latin Quarter,** perhaps dining in a Left Bank bistro. With a good map, try walking along some of the livelier streets, such as rue de la Hachette and rue Monsieur-le-Prince.

On your fifth day, spend the morning roaming around **Le Marais.** By all means, pay a visit to the **Musée Picasso** and have lunch near the historic **place des Vosges.** Afterward, you might want to head toward **Montmartre** (again, see the walking tour in Chapter 7 for specific sightseeing suggestions). Try to time your visit so you'll be at the **Basilica of Sacré-Coeur** at sunset.

---

1. THE TOP ATTRACTIONS

THE TOP MUSEUMS

There are people—and you might agree with them—who find visiting museums in Paris redundant. Why sacrifice the sunshine to pursue art and culture through dim museum corridors when every Seine-side stroll brings you vistas the masters have painted and every city square is a model of architectural excellence?

If that's your view, stick with it. Of the almost 100 highly worthy Paris museums, only one is a requirement for the world traveler: the Louvre. Some say that the Musée d'Orsay should also be singled out for that honor. But all the rest can be guiltlessly left to people with serious and specific interests, or saved up for that proverbial (and inevitable) rainy day or for your next visit.

Paris museums fit into three categories: city museums, national museums, and those run by private organizations. The municipal and national museums have fairly standard hours. They are often closed on Tuesday and national holidays. Fees vary, but half-price tickets are usually provided to students, children ages three to seven, and extra-large families or groups. If you want to museum-hop in earnest, pick a Sunday, when the majority of the museums let you in for half price.

Whatever time of the year you come, Paris seems to be deeply involved with one or another outstanding exhibition—touted madly from the lampposts by huge and colorful posters. The largest and most comprehensive are showcased at the Grand Palais, between the Seine and the Champs-Elysées on avenue Winston Churchill, built for this purpose for the 1900 Exposition. More modest collections are set out across the street in the Petit Palais. In the halls and museum rooms across the city, there are at least 15 special shows on any given week—a Chagall retrospective, Giacometti sculptures, Art of the Workers' Movement, the public life of Napoléon. . . . Fees charged depend on the exhibit.

I've discussed what I consider the top five museums in Section 1. For information on other Paris museums, see Section 2, "More Attractions," below.

To find out what's showing while you're in town, stop at the **Welcome Office**, 127 av. des Champs-Elysées, 8e (tel. 47-23-61-72; Métro: Charles de Gaulle–Etoile). Here, you can pick up a free copy of the English-language booklet *Paris Weekly Information,* published by the National Tourist Office, open daily from 9am to 8pm in summer, daily from 9am to 6pm in winter.

MUSEE DU LOUVRE, rue de Rivoli, 1er. Tel. 40-20-51-51.

The largest palace in the world, housing a collection of up to 300,000 works of art, the Musée du Louvre is both impressive and exhausting. There's so much to see, so many endless hallways to get lost in that—regardless of how much you may enjoy exploring a museum on your own—here I suggest you start with the guided tour. At least do so until you get the lay of the land. You can always go back to see what you missed. If you're really rushed, take our two-hour walking tour of the Louvre (see Chapter 7).

The entrance to the museum is through I. M. Pei's 71-foot-high glass pyramid in the Louvre's courtyard. First announced in 1983 by President Mitterrand, the modern structure opened in 1990 to acclaim by some, denunciation by others. The pyramid shelters an underground complex of shops and restaurants and, most importantly, increases the gallery space of the Louvre by an astonishing 80%. It also provides garages for all those tour buses that previously created havoc on rue de Rivoli. In addition, automatic ticket machines here help relieve those long, long lines of former days.

The museum buildings are immensely interesting in themselves. French kings have lived on this site by the Seine since the 13th century, but much of the present grand residence was built by Napoléon I and his nephew, Napoléon III. The palace was converted to a museum after the Revolution; the royal arts collections provided the first exhibits. The palace rooms don't function perfectly as skillfully lit museum rooms (for which the Louvre apologizes), but they provide sumptuous settings, which at times even compete with the displays.

Be sure to see at least the highlights of the collection. To the left of

PARIS ATTRACTIONS

the main entrance, at the crest of a graceful flight of stairs, stands the *Winged Victory*, cloak rippling in a wind that blew two centuries before the birth of Christ. In the Department of Greek Antiquities, on the ground floor, stands the supple statue of *Venus de Milo*, the warm marble subtly tinted by sunlight. Upstairs, in the Salle des Etats, covered with bulletproof glass and surrounded by art students, photographers, and awe-struck tourists, hangs the gently chiding portrait *Mona Lisa*.

Among the various museum departments are Egyptian Antiquities, Oriental Antiquities (the world's most complete collection),

Greek and Roman Antiquities, Objets d'Art and Furniture, Paintings, and Sculpture.

There are so many other things to see as well: six more da Vincis (near the *Mona Lisa*), voluptuous Titians, Franz Hals's *The Gypsy,* the enormously lifelike Egyptian *Seated Scribe.* But one can't even start to list the items in this museum. Nor could you see them all if you took three days and brought your lunch. The only blessing is that there is a cut-off point—the collection doesn't go beyond the 19th century.

Tours: 90-minute English tours Mon and Wed–Sat at 11:30am and 3:30pm for 25F ($4.65).

Admission: 30F ($5.55) adults; children under 18 free.

Open: Wed–Mon 9:45am–5pm; Greek section, containing the *Venus de Milo* and the *Winged Victory,* open until 6:30pm; some rooms closed 12:30–2:30pm. **Métro:** Louvre.

MUSEE DE L'ORANGERIE DES TUILERIES, place de la Concorde, 1er. Tel. 42-97-48-16.

After the Louvre, walk to the river's edge, to the place de la Concorde. Often set aside for special exhibits, this museum, a gem among galleries, has an outstanding collection of art and one celebrated display: Claude Monet's exquisite *Nymphéas* (executed between 1890 and 1921), a light-filtered tangle of lily pads and water, paneling the two oval ground-floor rooms, the construction of which was supervised by the artist himself.

The renovated building also shelters the Walter-Guillaume collection, which includes more than 24 Renoirs, including *Young Girl at a Piano.* Cézanne is represented by 14 works, notably *The Red Rock,* and Matisse by 11 paintings. Rousseau's 9 works are highlighted by *The Wedding,* and the dozen paintings by Picasso reach their brilliance in *The Female Bathers.* Other outstanding paintings are by Utrillo (10 works in all), Soutine (22), and Derain (28).

Admission: 25F ($4.65) adults; half price on Sun. Children under 18 free.

Open: Wed–Mon 9:45am–5:15pm. **Métro:** Concorde.

MUSEE D'ORSAY, 1 rue de Bellechasse, 7e. Tel. 40-49-48-14.

⭐ Standing across the Seine from the Louvre, the defunct but handsome neoclassical rail station, the Gare d'Orsay, has been transformed into one of the greatest art museums in the world.

The museum houses thousands of pieces of sculpture and painting in 80 different galleries. It also displays belle époque furniture, photographs, objets d'art, architectural models, even a cinema. A detailed, wide-ranging panorama of international art is presented from the period between 1848 and 1914, from the birth of the Second French Republic to the dawn of World War I. It is a repository of art and civilization of the century just past.

A monument to the Industrial Revolution, the Orsay station, once called "the elephant," is covered by an arching glass roof, flooding the museum with light. The museum displays works ranging from the creations of academic and historic painters such as Ingres to romanticists such as Delacroix, to neorealists such as Courbet and Daumier. In a setting once used by Orson Welles to film a nightmarish scene in *The Trial,* based on a Kafka work, are displayed the impressionists and postimpressionists, including Cézanne, Van Gogh, and the Fauves, along with Matisse, the cubists, expressionists, and the abstract painters. You get the sunny wheatfields by Millet, works from the Barbizon School, the misty landscapes of Corot, and brilliant-hued Gauguins.

But it is mainly the impressionists that keep the crowds lining up. The impressionists, unified in opposition to the dictatorial Académie des Beaux-Arts, chose for their subject matter the world around them, ignoring ecclesiastical or mythological scenes, and insisted on bathing their canvases in light. They painted the Seine, Parisians strolling in the Tuileries, even railway stations such as the Gare St-Lazare (some critics considered Monet's choice of the latter unforgivable vulgarity). The impressionists were the first to paint the most characteristic feature of Parisian life: the sidewalk café, especially in what was then the artists' quarter of Montmartre.

Perhaps the most famous painting displayed from this era is Manet's *The Picnic on the Grass,* which, when it was first exhibited, was decried as *au grand scandale des gens de bien.* Painted in 1863, it depicts a forest setting with a nude woman and two fully clothed men. Two years later, his *Olympia* created another scandal, showing a woman lounging on her bed and wearing nothing but a flower in her hair and high-heeled shoes. Attending her is an African maid. Zola called Manet "a man among eunuchs."

One of Renoir's brightest, most joyous paintings is here—the *Moulin de la Galette,* painted in 1876. Degas is represented by his paintings of racehorses and dancers; his 1876 café scene *Absinthe* remains one of his most reproduced works. Paris-born Claude Monet was fascinated by the changing light effects on Rouen Cathedral, and in a series of five paintings he makes the old landmark live as never before.

One of the most celebrated works is by an American—Whistler's *Arrangement in Gray and Black: Portrait of the Painter's Mother* perhaps better known as *Whistler's Mother.* It is said that this painting heralded the advent of modern art, although many critics denounced it at the time as "Whistler's Dead Mother" because of its funereal overtones. Today the painting has been hailed as a "veritable icon of our consciousness." As far as Whistler was concerned, he claimed he made "Mummy just as nice as possible."

Admission: 30F ($5.55) adults, 15F ($2.80) ages 18–24 and over 60; children 17 and under free.

Open: Tues–Wed and Fri–Sat 10am–6pm, Sun 9am–6pm, Thurs 10:30am–9:45pm. June 20–Sept 20, museum opens at 9am. **Métro:** Solferino. **RER:** Musée d'Orsay.

CENTRE GEORGES POMPIDOU, on the Plateau Beaubourg, east of bd. de Sébastopol, 4e. Tel. 42-77-12-33.

✪ It was Georges Pompidou's dream to create a large cultural center in Paris that would include every form of 20th-century art. As president of France (in 1969), he launched the project for a "temple devoted to art." That center was finally inaugurated in 1977 by yet another French president, Valéry Giscard d'Estaing.

The building housing the center was called "the most avant-garde building in the world" because of its radical exoskeletal design, but Parisians are more likely to refer to it as "the refinery." The colorfully painted pipes and ducts that crisscross the transparent facade are actually the practical housings for the intricate electrical, heating, and telephone systems that service the center. Even the escalators are housed in tubes on the outside of the building. Thus the vast interior has no need for walls, and a grand feeling of open space is created. When walls are needed for exhibits, moving partitions are rolled into place.

All this uniqueness has made the Pompidou Center Paris's favorite sightseeing attraction, surpassing even the Eiffel Tower in the number of tourists who visit.

The **Musée National d'Art Moderne** can be entered on the fourth floor. It offers a large collection of 20th-century art, including French and American masterpieces from the Fauves up to expressionist and abstract works. All the trends of modern art are displayed on two floors in well-lit rooms of varying sizes.

Featured are works by such artists as Ernst (a sculpture, *The Imbecile*), Kandinsky, Vuillard, Bonnard, Utrillo, Chagall, Dufy, Gris, Léger, and Pollock, as well as sketches by Le Corbusier and stained glass by Rouault. Modern sculpture includes works by Calder, Moore, and Epstein. Galeries Contemporaines, on the ground floor, demonstrates the trends in artistic activity today. Special exhibitions and demonstrations are constantly being staged in the Grande Galerie. Guided tours are available.

In addition to the modern art museum, the center contains the largest consulting library in Paris, with more than a million volumes and documents. Its Center of Industrial Design contains exhibits and research facilities in the field of architecture, space planning, publishing, and visual communications. A cinémathèque offers visitors a historical tour of filmmaking. The top-floor restaurant and cafeteria offer a panoramic view of Paris.

Admission: All-day pass 50F ($9) for access to all of the center; Museum of Modern Art only 23F ($4.25); free admission Sun morning.

Open: Mon and Wed–Fri noon–10pm, Sat–Sun 10am–10pm. **Métro:** Rambuteau.

✪ MUSEE PICASSO, 5 rue de Thorigny, 3e. Tel. 42-71-25-21.

When it opened at the beautifully restored Hôtel Salé (salt mansion), the press hailed it as a "museum for Picasso's Picassos." And that's what it is. Almost overnight it became one of the most popular attractions in Paris. The greatest Picasso collection in the world, acquired by the state in payment of inheritance taxes totaling around $50 million, consists of 203 paintings, 158 sculptures, 16 collages, 19 bas-reliefs, 88 ceramics, and more than 1,500 sketches and 1,600 engravings, along with 30 notebooks.

The paintings include a remarkable 1901 self-portrait and such masterpieces as *Le Baiser* (the kiss), painted at Mougins on the Riviera in 1969, and the 1970 *Reclining Nude and the Man with a Guitar*. It's easy to stroll through the handsome museum seeking your own favorite work (mine is a delightfully wicked one, *Young Man with a Lobster*, painted in Paris in 1941). The museum owns several intriguing studies for *Les Demoiselles d'Avignon,* the painting that initiated cubism.

Many of the major masterpieces such as *The Crucifixion* and *Nude in a Red Armchair* should remain on permanent view. However, because the collection is so vast, temporary exhibitions, such as one featuring the studies of the *Minotaur,* are opened to the

⭐ FROMMER'S FAVORITE
PARIS EXPERIENCES

A Stroll Along the Faubourg St-Honoré   In the 1700s it was home to the wealthiest of Parisians, but today it's home to the stores that cater to the wealthy. Even if you don't purchase anything, it's great window-shopping with all the big names: Hermès, Larouche, Courrèges, Cardin, Saint-Laurent.

A Tour of the Rungis Market   Part of every Parisian's daily ritual is food shopping. The wholesale market at Rungis, outside Paris near Orly Airport, is the largest in France, featuring more than a thousand producers and covering some 450 acres. It's not open to the general public, but you can book a guided tour in English from an American, Robert Noah, who operates the Paris en Cuisine school. Tours begin at 5:30am and end at 9am. Contact Mr. Noah at 49 rue de Richelieu, 1er (tel. 41-61-35-23).

A Languid Afternoon of Café Sitting   The Parisian café is an integral part of life. Whether you have one small coffee or the most expensive cognac in the house, nobody will hurry you.

Afternoon Tea at Muscade   Drinking tea in London has its charm, but the Parisian salon de thé is unique. Skip those cucumber-and-watercress sandwiches and get down to the business of rich, luscious desserts, like golden pains au chocolat. Muscade, 36 rue de Monpensier, 1er (tel. 42-97-51-36; Métro: Louvre), is open daily 3:30–7pm.

A Night at the Ballet   Renoir may have hated the building, but a night at the Opéra is still one of the highlights of any trip to Paris. The Opéra, at place de l'Opéra, is now the major center for ballet in Paris, and an evening here takes you back to the Second Empire world of marble and gilt and grand staircases, all sheltered under a controversial ceiling by Chagall. Dress with pomp and circumstance.

A Helicopter View of Paris   Looking at the Parisian skyline from the Eiffel Tower is one thing; flying over it in a helicopter is another. For a price, you can fly over Paris to Versaille and back. Call Héliport de Paris, 4 avenue de la Port de Sèvres, 15e. (tel. 45-57-53-67; Métro: Balard).

A Day at the Races   Paris has eight racing tracks. The most famous (and the classiest) is Longchamp, in the Bois de Boulogne, 16e, the site of the Prix de l'Arc de Triomphe and Grand Prix. If it's a major social event, you'll have to dress up, of course. Take the Métro to Porte d'Auteuil, then a special bus from there to the track. *Paris-Turf,* the racing paper, has details about racing times.

public at the rate of two a year. In addition to Picasso's own art, works by other masters from his private collection are displayed, including the contributions of such world-class artists as Cézanne, Rousseau, Braque, Matisse, Derain, and Miró. Picasso was fascinated with African masks, and many of these are on view as well.

The mansion was constructed in 1656 by Aubert de Fontenay, who collected the dreaded salt tax in Paris.

Admission: 28F ($5.20) adults; 16F ($2.95) children ages 18–25; children under 18 free.

Open: Wed 9:15am–10pm, Thurs–Mon 9:15am–5:15pm.
Métro: St-Paul, Filles-du-Calvaire, or Chemin-Vert.

THE SEINE ISLANDS

The "egg from which Paris was hatched," **Ile de la Cité** lies quietly in the shadow of Notre-Dame. The home of French kings until the 14th century, the island still has a curiously medieval air, with massive gray walls rising up all around you, relieved by tiny patches of parkland.

NOTRE-DAME, 6 place du Parvis Notre-Dame, 4e. Tel. 43-26-07-39.

The Cathedral of Paris and one of civilization's greatest edifices, this is more than a building—it's like a book written in stone and wood and glass. It can be read line by line, the Virgin's Portal alone telling four different picture stories. The doors of Notre-Dame did, in fact, take the place of religious texts during the ages when few of the faithful were literate.

The cathedral replaced two Romanesque churches (Ste-Marie and St-Etienne), which stood on the spot until 1160. Then Bishop Maurice de Sully, following the example of Suger, the abbot of St-Denis, undertook the new structure, and building continued for more than 150 years. The final result was a piece of Gothic perfection, not merely in overall design but in every detail. The rose window above the main portal, for instance, forms a halo 31 feet in diameter around the head of the statue of the Virgin.

More than any other building, Notre-Dame is the history of a nation. Here, the boy-monarch Henry VI of England was crowned king of France in 1422, during the Hundred Years' War when—but for Joan of Arc—France would have become an English dominion. Of course, that is how history is viewed in the English world. A French historian, on the other hand, might point out that the Plantagenets were French, not English, and that England would have become a French/Anjou dominion.

Here, Napoléon took the crown out of the hands of Pope Pius VII, and crowned himself emperor.

Here, General de Gaulle knelt before the altar on August 26, 1944, to give thanks for the liberation of Paris—imperturbably praying while sniper bullets screeched around the choir galleries.

Because of the beauty of its ornaments and of its symbolic meaning of redemption of all evil, Notre-Dame is a joyous church. However, those devils and gargoyles grinning from its ledges add a genuinely macabre touch. You can almost see Victor Hugo's hunchback peering from behind them.

There are many cathedrals larger than Notre-Dame, but the interior has a transcending loftiness that makes it seem immense. The flat-topped twin towers flanking the entrance rise to 225 feet. You can climb the 387 steps, leading to a magnificent view. Incidentally, on national holidays and feast days, you can hear the thunder of the "Bourdon," the 16-ton bell that hangs in the South Tower.

Approached through a garden behind Notre-Dame is the **Le Memorial de la Déportation,** jutting out on the very tip of the Ile de la Cité. Birds chirp nowadays, the Seine flows gently by—but the memories are far from pleasant. It is a memorial to French martyrs of World War II, who were deported to such camps as Auschwitz and Buchenwald. In blood-red are the words, "Forgive, but don't forget." The memorial can be visited daily from 10am to noon and 2 to 7pm. Admission is free.

Admission: Treasury 15F ($2.80) adults, 5F (95¢) children under 18; tower 23F ($4.25) adults, 12F ($2.20) children.

Open: Cathedral daily 8am–7pm, but tourists are asked to refrain from visiting on Sun. Free organ concerts Sun at 5:45pm. Treasury Mon–Sat 10am–6pm, tower Wed–Mon 10am–4:30pm. **Métro:** Cité, Hôtel-de-Ville, or Maubert.

THE CONCIERGERIE, 1 quai de l'Horloge, 1er. Tel. 43-54-30-06.

⭐ The most sinister building in France squats on the north bank of the Ile de la Cité (near the Pont au Change) and forms part of the huge Palais de Justice. Its name is derived from the title concierge (constable), once borne by a high official of the Royal Court. But its reputation stems from the Revolution.

Even on warm days, a chill wind seems to blow around its two bleak towers, and the gray, massive walls feel eternally dank. Here, as nowhere else in Paris, you can see the tall, square shadow of the guillotine.

The Conciergerie was the country's chief prison after the fall of the Bastille. When the Reign of Terror got under way, the Conciergerie turned into a kind of stopover depot en route to the "National Razor."

You forget everything else as you enter those courtyards and passages. There are the splendid remnants of a medieval royal palace in there, complete with refectory and giant kitchen. But the only features that imprint themselves on the mind are the rows of cells and the doghouse hovel in which prisoners—shorn and bound—sat waiting for the dung cart that was to carry them to the blade.

First came the "aristos"—led by Marie Antoinette, the duc d'Orléans, brother of the king, and the notorious Madame du Barry. Then came the moderate liberals known as "Girondins." Then followed the radicals with their leader Danton. At their heels were the ultra-radicals along with their chief, the frozen-faced Robespierre. Finally, as the wheel turned full circle, it was the turn of the relentless public prosecutor Fouquier-Tinville, together with the judges and jury of the Revolutionary Court.

They all had their brief stay in those cells, followed by the even briefer ride to the guillotine. Among the few who stayed there but lived to write about it was America's Thomas Paine, who remembered chatting in English with Danton.

Admission: 24F ($4.45) adults; 12F ($2.20) ages 18–24; free children under 17.

Open: Apr–Sept daily 9:30am–6:30pm; Oct–Mar daily 10am–5pm. **Métro:** Cité, Châtelet, or St-Michel. **RER:** St-Michel.

LA SAINTE-CHAPELLE, Palais de Justice, 4 bd. du Palais, 4e. Tel. 43-54-30-09.

⭐ Within the same building complex as the Conciergerie, but spiritually a thousand miles away, is La Sainte-Chapelle. One of the oldest, most beautiful, and most unusual churches in the world, it was built in 1246 for the express purpose of housing the relics of the Crucifixion, which had been sent from Constantinople at tremendous expense. But the relics were later transferred to Notre-Dame, leaving La Saint-Chapelle an empty showcase, albeit a magnificent one.

Actually, it consists of two separate churches, one humble, the other superb. The lower chapel was for servants, the upper for the gentry—and one glance will tell you the difference. The gentry, in fact, were the royal household, and you can still see the small grated window from which Louis XI could participate in the service without being noticed.

The outstanding feature of the chapel, though, is the stained glass. Fifteen windows flood the interior with colored light—deep blue, ruby red, and dark green—and depict more than a thousand scenes from the Bible.

Admission: 24F ($4.45) adults, 13F ($2.40) ages 18–24; 5F (95¢) ages 7–17; free ages 6 and under.

Open: Apr–Sept daily 9:30am–6pm; Oct–Mar daily 10am–5pm. **Métro:** Cité or St-Michel. **RER:** St-Michel.

ILE ST-LOUIS, 4e.

⭐ As you walk across the little iron footbridge from the rear of Notre-Dame toward the Ile St-Louis, you'll enter a world of tree-shaded quays, aristocratic town houses and courtyards, restaurants, and antique shops. The twin island of the Ile de la Cité is primarily residential, and plaques on the houses' facades make it easy to identify the former residences of the famous who have lived here—such as Marie Curie, who lived at 36 quai de Bethune, near Pont de la Tournelle.

The most exciting mansion is the **Hôtel de Lauzun**, at 17 quai d'Anjou; note that you need special permission to visit. It was the home of the duc de Lauzun, a favorite of Louis XIV, until his secret marriage angered the king and the duc was sent to the Bastille. Baudelaire lived here in the 19th century, squandering his family fortune and penning poetry that would be banned in France until 1949.

Voltaire lived at 2 quai d'Anjou, in the **Hôtel Lambert,** with his mistress, and their quarrels here were legendary. The mansion also housed the Polish royal family for over a century.

Farther along, at no. 9, stands the house where Honoré Daumier, the painter, sculptor, and lithographer, lived between 1846 and 1863. Here he produced hundreds of lithographs satirizing the bourgeoisie and attacking government corruption—his caricature of Louis-Philippe landed him in jail for six months.

Métro: Sully-Morland or Pont-Marie.

THE GRAND PROMENADE & NEARBY ATTRACTIONS

I get a bit tired of repeating "the most in the world," but, of course, the Champs-Elysées is the world's most famous promenade. Extending from the place de la Concorde like a broad, straight arrow to the Arc de Triomphe at the far end, it presents its grandest spectacle at night.

For a complete description of this walk, refer to the walking tour of the Grand Promenade in Chapter 7.

PLACE DE LA CONCORDE, 1er.

Regarded by many as the most beautiful urban square in the world, this immense 85,000-square-yard expanse is so vast that your eye can't take it in at one glance. The center of the oval is swarming with cars, a motorist's nightmare, but the hugeness of the place seems to swallow them up.

In the middle, looking pencil-small, rises a 33-century-old obelisk from Egypt, flanked by cascading fountains. Grouped around the outer edges are eight statues representing eight French cities. Near the statue of Brest was the spot where the guillotine stood during the Revolution. On Sunday morning of January 21, 1793, King Louis XVI lost his royal head there, to be followed by 1,343 other victims, including Marie Antoinette and, subsequently, Danton and Robespierre, the very men who had launched the Terror.

The place de la Concorde borders the Tuileries on the east, and on the west the second great showpiece of Paris, the Champs-Elysées.

Métro: Concorde.

JARDIN DES TUILERIES, place de la Concorde, 1er. Tel. 42-60-38-01.

Stretching along the right bank of the Seine, from the place de la Concorde to the court of the Louvre, this exquisitely formal garden was laid out as a royal pleasure park in 1564, but thrown open to the public by the French Revolution. Filled with statues and fountains and precisely trimmed hedges, it's just a bit too artificial for comfort. The nicest features are the round ponds on which pleasantly disorderly kids sail armadas of model boats.

Métro: Tuileries.

ARC DE TRIOMPHE, place Charles-de-Gaulle–Etoile, 16e. Tel. 43-80-31-31.

This is one of the great Paris symbols, the largest triumphal arch in the world and the centerpiece of the entire Right Bank. It stands as the focus of 12 radiating avenues on the place Charles-de-Gaulle–Etoile, giving it an unequaled position and making it pretty difficult to reach for the uninitiated. The best—in fact, the only—way to get there through the traffic is to use the underground passage leading from the Champs-Elysées.

The arch was begun on Napoléon's orders in 1806 to commemorate the victories of his Grande Armée. But it was not completed for another ten years, when the Grande Armée had long been shattered. Ever since then, the arch has born witness to France's defeats as well as its triumphs.

Twice—in 1871 and 1940—German troops tramped through it in their moments of victory. And twice—in 1919 and 1945—Allied armies staged victory parades through those buttresses.

The arch is 162 feet high and 147 feet wide—a stone fanfare of military glory—and its price. It's ornamented with martial scenes and engraved with the names of the 128 victories of Napoléon and the 600 generals who participated in them.

But underneath burns the Flame of Remembrance that marks the tomb of France's Unknown Soldier. The effect at night is magical—if only that light weren't burning for millions of young men who lost their lives in war.

Admission: 22F ($4.05) adults, 12F ($2.20) ages 18–24; free 17 and under.

Open: Apr–Sept daily 10am–5:30pm; Oct–Mar daily 10am–4:15pm. **Métro:** Charles-de-Gaulle–Etoile.

PALAIS ROYAL, place du Palais-Royal on rue St-Honoré, 1er.

Facing the Louvre, the gardens of the Palais Royal have long been associated with France's most prominent historical figures. The gardens were planted in 1634 for Cardinal Richelieu, who presented them to Louis XIII. As a child, the future Louis XIV played around the fountain, nearly drowning once.

Perhaps its most auspicious event occurred at the long-ago-demolished Café Foy in the Palais Royal, where Camille Desmoulins jumped up on a table and shouted for the mob "to fight to the death," thus marking the first words of the French Revolution. From here an armed mob set off for the Bastille on July 14, 1789.

An 18-year-old lieutenant named Napoléon Bonaparte met his first prostitute in the Palais Royal, and Robespierre and Danton dined here. And during the Directoire, gambling dens flourished.

In time the property became the residence of the ducs d'Orléans. Philippe-Egalité, a cousin of Louis XVI, built his apartments on the grounds, and subsequently rented them to prostitutes. By the 20th century those same apartments were rented by such artists as Colette and Cocteau.

Today it's hard to imagine its former life. From place Colette, you enter the Court of Honor, colonnaded on three sides. The palace is the headquarters of the Councils of State, and the Court of Honor is a parking lot during the day. In the center of the Palais Royal is the Galerie d'Orléans, with two fountains and colonnades. Stroll through the gardens or down the Galerie Montpensier, filled with little shops.

Métro: Louvre.

PLACE VENDOME, 8e.

This is the textbook example of classical French architecture, a pure gem set in the fashionable heart of the Right Bank. The pillared palaces encircling the square include the Ritz Hotel as well as the Ministry of Justice. The center is crowned by a 144-foot-high column, erected to commemorate Napoléon's greatest victory—Austerlitz. The actual column is stone, but the enclosing spiral band of bronze was cast from the 1,200 cannon (a fantastic number) captured by the emperor in the battle. The statue on top of the pillar is, of course, Napoléon, restored there after being pulled down twice: once by Royalist reactionaries, the second time by Communard revolutionaries—an odd combination.

Métro: Opéra.

LA GRANDE ARCHE DE LA DEFENSE, place du parvis de la Défense. Tel. 49-07-26-26.

Designed as the architectural centerpiece of the sprawling and futuristic satellite suburb of La Défense, this massive steel-and-masonry arch rises 35 stories from the pavement. Built with the blessing of President François Mitterand, and ringed with soaring office buildings and a circular avenue (*périphérique*), the design of which imitates that which surrounds the more famous Arc de Triomphe, the deliberately overscaled archway is the latest major landmark to dot the Paris skyline. High enough to shelter the cathedral of Notre-Dame below its heavily trussed canopy, the monument was designed as an extension of the panorama that interconnects the Louvre, the Arc du Carroussel, the Champs-Elysées, the Arc de Triomphe, the avenue de la Grande Armée, and the place du Porte Maillot into one magnificently engineered straight line. An elevator carries visitors to an observation platform, from which visitors get an idea of the carefully conceived geometry of the surrounding street plan.

Admission: 30F ($5.55) adults, 20F ($3.70) 17 and under.

Open: Mon–Fri 9am–5pm, Sat–Sun 10am–7pm. **RER:** La Défense.

AROUND THE EIFFEL TOWER

From the place du Trocadéro, you can step between the two curved wings of the **Palais de Chaillot** and gaze out on a view that is nothing short of breathtaking. At your feet lie the **Jardins du Trocadéro,** centered by fountains. Directly in front, the Pont d'Iéna spans the Seine. Then, on the opposite bank, rises the iron immensity of the **Tour Eiffel.** And beyond, stretching as far as your eye can see, the **Champ de Mars,** once a military parade ground but now a garden landscape with arches and grottoes, lakes and cascades.

TOUR EIFFEL, Champs-de-Mars, 7e. Tel. 45-50-34-56.

Strangely enough, this symbol of Paris wasn't meant to be a permanent structure at all. Erected specifically for the Universal Exhibition of 1889, it was destined to be pulled down a few years later. But by then, wireless telegraphy had appeared on the scene and the 985-foot tower—the tallest on earth—presented a handy signaling station. Radio confirmed its role. During the German advance on Paris in 1914, the powerful beam from the top effectively jammed the enemy's field radios.

You could write a page with nothing but figures about the tower. The plans for it covered 6,000 square yards of paper, it weighs 7,000 tons, and contains 2½ million rivets. But enough of that. Just stand underneath the tower and look straight up. It's like a rocket of steel lacework shooting into the sky. If nothing else, it is a fantastic engineering achievement.

Gustave Eiffel, "the universal engineer," who had previously constructed hundreds of bridges and even the inner structure of the Statue of Liberty, had the overall responsibility for the project of building the tower. Architects and aesthetes hated it. ("That damned lamppost ruins the skyline.") The Parisians loved it. Almost overnight it became a part of local legend. A dozen poems were written about it and at least as many ghastly pieces of music, including an *Eiffel Tower Waltz.* By 1910 its permanence had been confirmed—the "lamppost" was there to stay.

You can visit the tower in three stages. Taking the elevator to the first landing, you'll have a view over the rooftops of Paris. The second landing provides a panoramic view of the city. The third and final stage gives the most spectacular view, allowing you to identify many monuments and buildings.

The tower is well equipped with restaurants—two dining rooms (one deluxe), a snackbar, and a drinking bar at various levels await your decision. On the ground level, the 1899 lift machinery is open to visitors in the eastern and western pillars. On the first level, a ciné-museum showing films on the tower is open when the tower is. Eiffel's office has been re-created on the fourth level, with wax figures of the engineer receiving Thomas Edison.

But it's the view that most people desire, and this extends for 42 miles, theoretically. In practice, weather conditions tend to limit it. Nevertheless, it's fabulous, and the best time for visibility is about an hour before sunset.

Admission: First landing 17F ($3.15), second landing 32F ($5.90), third landing 49F ($9.05).

Open: Sun–Thurs 10am–11pm; Fri–Sat 10am–midnight.

Métro: Trocadéro, Ecole-Militaire, or Bir-Hakeim. **RER:** Champs-de-Mars.

CHAMP-DE-MARS AND ECOLE MILITAIRE, 7e.

Leave some time to explore the Champ-de-Mars, the gardens between the Eiffel Tower and the Military School. Designed in 1170, the gardens are the World's Fair grounds of Paris and the scene of many military parades.

The **Ecole Militaire** was founded in 1751 with the help of one of France's best-known mistresses, Madame de Pompadour. The classical design is by A. J. Gabriel. The school prepared young men for military careers, including Napoléon, who entered in 1784 and graduated a year later as a 16-year-old lieutenant. According to accounts, he wasn't popular with his classmates, many of whom openly made fun of him—one wrote, "All boots, no man." Another French general, Charles de Gaulle, also studied here. You'll need special permission to go inside.

Métro: Trocadéro, Ecole-Militaire, or Bir-Hakeim.

HOTEL DES INVALIDES, place des Invalides, 7e. Tel. 45-55-37-70.

This is not a "hôtel," but a palace and a church combined, which today houses a great museum, dozens of military administration offices, and the **tomb of Napoléon.**

The monumental ensemble was originally built by Louis XIV as a stately home for invalid soldiers (hence the name). There are still a few living there, but most of the enormous space is taken up by the Musée de l'Armée, various army bureaus, and the crypt beneath the dome in the rear that makes it one of Paris's greatest showpieces.

The **Musée de l'Armée** is the finest military museum in the world—outdistancing even Britain's Imperial War Museum in amassed martial relics. Its collection of arms dates back so far it seems to include the first rock thrown by Neolithic man. The museum sets out the war paraphernalia of every age—bronze spearheads and medieval crossbows, intricately engraved armor and doughboy drabs—leading up with a flourish and the recorded strains of "Tipperary" to the bugle that sounded the cease-fire on November 7, 1918, before the general cease-fire on November 11, 1918. The shrinelike aura is distressing. The detail is fascinating.

The west wing, on your right as you enter the courtyard, houses suits of armor, especially in the new so-called Arsenal—arms belonging to the kings and dignitaries of France. The Salle Orientale in the west wing shows arms from the Far East and from Muslim countries of the Middle East, from the 16th to the 19th centuries. Turkish armor (see Bajazet's helmet) and weapons, as well as Chinese and Japanese armor and swords, are on exhibit. Moreover, the west wing houses exhibits from World Wars I and II.

You can gain access to the **Musée des Plans-Reliefs** through the west wing. It is a unique collection in scale model of French towns and monuments.

The east wing, on your left, shows objects dating from the 17th century to 1914. Off the entrance hall in the hushed Salle Turenne (a plaque at the door cues you to proper respect) fly the battleflags of France, including those of Bonaparte's regiments and some shredded remnants of standards from 1940. Opposite, in the Salle Vauban, 18 mounted figures illustrate the showy uniforms of the French cavalry. Go upstairs to view souvenirs of the Napoleonic campaigns, next to the bed in which the great Corsican died, as well as the personal effects from his island exile.

The gloss of the show tends to veil the truth that war is a matter of death and heartbreak. But occasionally it comes through, simply and effectively, as in the display of a silvery cuirass, pierced by a jagged wound the size and shape of a softball—the breastplate of a Carabinier downed by a cannon at Waterloo.

Invalides is a shrine, and, like most shrines, impersonal. Napoléon rests in a sarcophagus of red granite on a pedestal of green granite. Surrounding the tomb are 12 figures of victories. The pavement of the crypt consists of a mosaic of laurel leaves.

It took 19 years for the British to release the body of their most illustrious prisoner, who had originally been buried near his house of banishment. Finally, on December 15, 1840, Napoléon's second funeral took place in Paris. The golden hearse was taken through crowds of mourners who had braved a snowstorm to pay their last respects to the nation's hero.

The same golden dome also covers the tombs of Napoleon's brothers, Joseph and Jerome, his son (who was never crowned), and Marshal Foch, who led the Allied armies to victory in 1918.

Admission: 27F ($5) adults, 14F ($2.60) children 7–18; free children 6 and under. The ticket, valid for two consecutive days, covers admission to the Musée de l'Armée, Napoléon's Tomb, and the Musée des Plans-Reliefs.

Open: Apr–Sept daily 10am–6pm; Oct–Mar daily 10am–5pm.
Métro: Latour-Maubourg, Varenne, or St-Francois-Xavier.

MONTMARTRE

This name has spread chaos and confusion in many an unwary tourist's agenda. So just to make things clear—there are three of them.

The first is boulevard Montmartre, a busy commercial street nowhere near the mountain. The second is the tawdry, expensive, would-be-naughty, and utterly phony amusement belt along bd. de Clichy, culminating at place Pigalle (the "Pig Alley" of World War II GIs). The third—the Montmartre I'm talking about—lies on top, and on the slopes, of the actual *mont.*

The best way to get there is to take the Métro to Anvers, then walk to the nearby rue de Steinkerque, and ride the curious little funicular to the top. It operates daily between 6am and 11pm.

Montmartre used to be the artists' village, glorified by such masters as Utrillo, and painted, sketched, sculpted, and photographed by ten thousand lesser lights. The tourists, building speculators, and nightclub entrepreneurs came and most of the artists went. But a few still linger. And so does some of the village charm that once drew them. Just enough to give you a few delightful hours, and leave you nostalgic for a past you wish you'd known.

The center point, the **place du Tertre,** looks like an almost-real village square, particularly when the local band is blowing and puffing oompah music. All around the square run terrace restaurants with dance floors and colored lights. Gleaming through the trees is the Basilica of Sacré-Coeur.

Behind the church and clinging to the hillside below are steep and crooked little streets that seem—almost—to have survived the relentless march of progress. **Rue des Saules** still has Montmartre's last vineyard, plus a cabaret. **Rue Lepic** still looks—almost—the way Renoir and the melancholy van Gogh and the unfortunate genius Toulouse-Lautrec saw it. This—almost—makes up for the blitz of portraitists and souvenir stores and postcard vendors up on top.

The traditional way to explore Montmartre is on foot. However, since it's at the highest elevation in the city, that is too much for many visitors. Those who prefer can take a miniature train along the steep streets on a 45-minute journey. **Le Petit Train de Montmartre** (for information, contact Promotrain, 38 bd. Flandrin, 16e, tel. 45-04-87-47) carries 72 passengers who can listen to an English commentary as they pass the major landmarks. Boarding is at either place du Tertre (the Church of St. Pierre) or place Blanche (near Moulin Rouge). Trains run March to October from 10am to 7pm and cost 25F ($4.65) for adults, half price for children.

For a more detailed look at Montmartre, refer to the walking tour in Chapter 7.

BASILICA OF SACRÉ-COEUR, place St-Pierre, 18e. Tel. 42-51-17-02.

After the Eiffel Tower, Sacré-Coeur is the most outstanding landmark of Paris. Its five domes and campanile, all gleaming white, make it look like a 12th-century Byzantine church. In fact, the basilica was planned as a votive offering after France's defeat by the Prussians in 1870. Rich and poor alike contributed money to build it. Construction was approved in 1873, but the church wasn't consecrated until 1919.

Like the Eiffel Tower, the design of Sacré-Coeur stirred up controversy. One Parisian called it "a lunatic's confectionary dream." Zola dubbed it "the basilica of the ridiculous." Supporters of Sacré-Coeur included poet Max Jacob and artist Maurice Utrillo. Utrillo never tired of drawing and painting it, and he and Jacob came here regularly to pray.

Try to visit Sacré-Coeur at dusk; from the top steps, there's a spectacular view as the city lights come on. The view from the dome extends 35 miles on a clear day. You can also walk around the inner dome to get a bird's-eye view of the church interior.

Admission: Church, free; dome 15F ($2.80); crypt 10F ($1.85).

Open: Church, daily 7am–11pm; dome and crypt, daily 9am–6pm. **Métro:** Abbesses or Anvers.

LE MARAIS

Very few cities on earth boast an entire district that can be labeled a sight. Paris has several. One of them—Le Marais, or the marshland—is the vaguely defined maze of streets north of the place de la Bastille.

During the 17th century this was a region of aristocratic mansions, which lost their elegance when the fashionable set moved elsewhere. The houses lost status, but they remained standing. Le Marais is becoming increasingly fashionable by today's standards and many artists and craftspeople are moving in. The government is restoring many of the mansions.

You can take the Métro to the **place de la Bastille** to begin a stroll around the district. The actual Bastille, of course, is gone now. But as the history books tell us, the mob attacked this fortress on July 14, 1789, sparking the French Revolution. To commemorate the storming, Bastille Day on July 14 is a major French holiday. Once the prison contained eight towers, housing such illustrious tenants as "The Man in the Iron Mask" and the Marquis de Sade.

Be careful of the speeding cars when you cross the square to look at the Colonne de Juillet. Surprisingly, it honors the victims of the July Revolution of 1830 that marked the fall of Charles X, not the victims of the Bastille.

France honored the bicentennial of the French revolution in 1989 by building the 3,000-seat Opéra Bastille on the south side of the square. The Opéra opened in 1990, with five moving stages. The launching of this cultural center, along with major restoration of the area, has turned the formerly dreary Bastille section into a chic neighborhood, rivaling the Marais, which garnered so much publicity in the 1970s and 1980s.

From the place de la Bastille, head up rue St-Antoine, cutting right on rue des Tournelles, with its statue honoring Beaumarchais (author of *The Barber of Seville*). Take a left again onto the Pas-de-la-Mule, "the footsteps of the mule," which will carry you to the place des Vosges.

See Section 4, "Special-Interest Sightseeing," for information on the Maison de Victor Hugo, also in Le Marais.

PLACE DES VOSGES, 3e.

An enchanted island rather than a city square, this silent, serenely lovely oasis is the oldest square in Paris and—in my opinion—the most entrancing.

Laid out in 1605 by order of Henri IV, it was once called the Palais Royale and was the scene of innumerable cavaliers' duels. The Revolutionary government changed its name but—luckily—left its structure intact. In the middle is a tiny park, and on three sides an encircling arcaded walk, supported by arches and paved with ancient, worn flagstones.

That's all, but the total effect is so harmonious, so delicately balanced between mellow stone and green trees, that it works like a soothing balm on the nerves.

Métro: St-Paul or Chemin-Vert.

MUSÉE CARNAVALET, 23 rue de Sévigné, 3e. Tel. 42-72-21-13.

This museum covers the history of the city to the present time. There are rooms filled with models of the old quarters of Paris—detailed down to the lace on the cap of the baker's girl. You can see the model of the Bastille, of which there is now not a trace. One room is crammed with signposts of the 17th and 18th centuries, designed to let the unlettered know that here at the sign of the tree worked a carpenter, and here where a pig was portrayed you could buy your cold cuts. The striking collection of memorabilia from the French Revolution includes the chessmen with which Louis XVI passed time while imprisoned in the Temple, as well as the boyish diary of the dauphin and some effects of Marie Antoinette.

There is more, such as antique furniture of various periods. The mansion that houses the exhibits, built in 1545, is considered a prime example of Renaissance architecture. The tour continues across the courtyard at the Hôtel le Peletiere de Saint-Fargeau. There, exhibits cover the time of the Revolution up to the present.

Admission: 15F ($2.80) adults, 8.50F ($1.55) ages 7–16; free children 6 and under.

Open: Tues–Sun 10am–5:40pm. **Métro:** St-Paul or Chemin-Vert.

---

2. MORE ATTRACTIONS

QUARTIER LATIN

The Latin Quarter lies on the Left Bank in the 5th arrondissement and consists of the streets winding around the University of Paris, of which the Sorbonne is only a part.

The logical starting point is the place St-Michel, right on the river, decorated by an impressive fountain. This was the scene of some of the most savage fighting during the uprising of the French Resistance in August 1944. Here—as in many, many other spots—you'll see the sombre name tablets, marking the place where a Resistance fighter fell: "Ici est Tombé—le 19 Août 1944. Pour la Libération de Paris."

Running straight south is the main thoroughfare of the quarter, the wide, pulsating boulevard St-Michel (called boul' Mich' by the locals). But we'll turn left and dive into the warren of dogleg alleys adjoining the river—rue de la Huchette, rue de la Harpe, rue St-Severin. Thronged with students; tingling with the spice smells of Arabian, African, and Vietnamese cooking; narrow, twisting, and noisy—the alleys resemble an Asian bazaar more than a European city. This impression is aided by the incredibly garish posters advertising horror movies, belly dancers, and sticky Algerian sweets, the crush of humanity, and the honking of cars bullying a path through the swarming crowds.

We emerge at the Church of St-Severin and are back in Paris again. Dating from the 13th century, this flamboyant Gothic edifice acts like a sanctuary of serenity.

Head down rue St-Jacques and Paris reasserts itself completely. The next crossing is boulevard St-Germain, lined with sophisticated cafés and some of the most avant-garde fashion shops in town.

MUSEE DE CLUNY, 6 place Paul-Painlevé, 5e. Tel. 43-25-62-00.

An enchanting museum, with some of the most beautiful medieval art extant, the Musée de Cluny stands back from the intersection of boulevards St-Michel and St-Germain in a walled courtyard—one of two Gothic private residences of the 15th century left in Paris.

Dark, rough-walled, and evocative, the Cluny is devoted to the church art and castle crafts of the Middle Ages, jewelry (votive crowns of the Visigothic kings and a golden altar from Basel), sculpture, stained glass, and tapestries—among them the world-famous series of *The Lady and the Unicorn* gracefully displayed in a circular room on the second floor. The painstakingly depicted *Life of St. Stephen* hangs in the shadowy chapel, while a third series is concerned with the colorful life at court. The building also includes the remains of an A.D. 200 Roman bathhouse with a well-preserved frigidarium.

Admission: 16F ($2.95) adults, 8F ($1.50) ages 18–24; free 17 and under.

Open: Wed–Mon 9:45am–12:30pm and 2–5:15pm. **Métro:** Cluny–La Sorbonne.

PANTHEON, place du Panthéon, 5e. Tel. 43-54-34-51.

This strangely splendid cross between a Roman temple and a church has at some time been both and is now neither. But it towers impressively on the Left Bank as one of the city's most illustrious landmarks.

Originally the site of a Roman temple, which grew into a medieval abbey, it was constructed as the Church of Ste-Geneviève in the 18th century, finishing up with the capitol-like dome, as well as noble Roman pillars.

Then the Revolutionary government decided to convert it into a purely patriotic shrine for the nation's greats. Under Napoléon it again became a church. Since 1885, however, it has reverted to being a nonreligious temple—a worthy receptacle for those the nation wished to honor.

The interior is stark and bare, with an austere grandeur all its own. It houses the tombs of Rousseau and Voltaire, of Victor Hugo and Emile Zola, of Louis Braille, and of the African Felix Eboué, who rallied his Equatorial colony to the colors of de Gaulle at a time when no other French administrator dared to do so.

Admission: 23F ($4.25) adults; 12F ($2.20) ages 18–24; free 17 and under.

Open: June–Sept daily 10am–noon and 2–6pm; Oct–May daily 10am–noon and 2–4:30pm. **Métro:** St-Michel or Monge.

CHURCH OF ST-SEVERIN, rue des Prêtres, 5e. Tel. 43-25-96-63.

This flamboyant Gothic building, named for the 6th-century recluse St. Severin, lies just a short walk from the Seine. Given to Paris in the 11th century by Henri I, it slowly began to adopt some of the architectural features of Notre-Dame, located across the river.

The present church was built from 1210 to 1230, then reconstructed in 1458. The tower was completed in 1487, the chapels between 1498 and 1520. Hardouin-Mansart designed the Chapel of the Communion in 1673 when he was 27 years old.

Before entering, walk around the church to examine its gargoyles, birds of prey, and reptilian monsters projecting from the top. To the right, facing the church, is the "garden of ossuaries" of the 15th century. Inside, the stained glass is a stunning adornment.

Admission: Free.

Open: Daily 8am–7pm. **Métro:** St-Michel or Maubert-Mutualité.

LES HALLES DISTRICT

The area around the Church of St-Eustace has always had a bad reputation. Centuries ago a Parisian described it as "ideal for assassinations," and it was in front of 11 rue de la Ferronnerie that Henri IV ("Vert Galant") was assassinated by Ravaillac. Nearby is the banking center of Paris, rue des Lombards.

LES FORUM DES HALLES, 1er.

This large complex, much of it underground, contains dozens of shops, several restaurants and movie theaters, and a wax museum. Les Forum des Halles opened in 1979 on the site of the major wholesale fruit, vegetable, and meat market in Paris. The zinc-roofed Second Empire building was torn down after wholesalers moved to the contemporary steel-and-glass structure at Rungis, a suburb near Orly Airport. Replacing the old "umbrellas of iron" is the French version of a modern mall, popular with tourists and residents alike.

Elegantly dressed Parisians drinking cognac with bloody butchers at Les Halles were once a typical early-morning Parisian scene; today, although the old market has moved, it's still a tradition after a night on the town to have a bowl of onion soup at Les Halles, usually at Au Pied de Cochon ("Pig's Foot") or at Au Chien Qui Fume ("Smoking Dog"). Les Halles is one of the few places where you can eat at any hour of the night. Some writers have suggested that eccentric 19th-century poet Gerard de Nerval was the original night-owl here.

Métro: Les Halles. **RER:** Châtelet–Les Halles.

CHURCH OF ST-EUSTACHE, 2 rue du Jour, 1er. Tel. 42-36-31-05.

In my opinion, this mixed Gothic and Renaissance church, completed in 1637, is rivaled only by Notre-Dame. It took nearly a century to build. Many famous Parisians have passed through the doors of St-Eustache. Madame de Pompadour and Richelieu were baptized here, and Molière's funeral was held here in 1673. The church has been known for its organ recitals ever since Liszt played here in 1866. Inside is the black-marble tomb of Jean-Baptiste Colbert, the minister of state under Louis XIV. On top of his tomb is a marble statue of the statesman flanked by statues of *Abundance* by Coysevox and *Fidelity* by J. B. Tuby. There's a side entrance to the church on rue Rambuteau.

Open: Daily 7:30am–7:30pm. **Métro:** Les Halles.

ST-GERMAIN-DES-PRES

This was the postwar home of existentialism, associated with Jean-Paul Sartre, Simone de Beauvoir, Albert Camus, and an intellectual, bohemian crowd who gathered at the Café de Flore, the Brasserie Lipp, and Deux-Magots. Among them, the black-clad poet Juliette Greco was known as "la muse de St-Germain-des-Prés," and to Sartre she was the woman who had "millions of poems in her throat." Her long hair, black slacks, black sweater, and black sandals launched a fashion trend adopted by young women from Paris to California.

In the 1950s new names appeared, like Françoise Sagan, Gore Vidal, and James Baldwin, but by the 1960s the tourists were just as firmly entrenched at the Café de Flore and Deux-Magots. Today St-Germain-des-Prés remains a bohemian and intellectually stimulating street life, full of many interesting bookshops, art galleries, *cave* nightclubs, and bistros and coffeehouses.

ST-GERMAIN-DES-PRES CHURCH, 3 place St-Germain-des-Prés, 6e. Tel. 43-25-41-71.

This church's Romanesque tower, topped by a 19th-century spire, is the most enduring landmark in the village of St-Germain-des-Prés, dating from the 6th century, when Childebert, the son of Clovis, the "creator of France," founded a Benedictine abbey on the site. Unfortunately, the marble columns in the triforium are all that remain from that period. The abbey was a pantheon for Merovingian kings, and their tombs are found in the St-Symphorien Chapel at the entrance to the church. During the restoration of these tombs in 1981, Romanesque paintings were discovered on the triumphal arch of the chapel.

The present building, the work of four centuries, has a Romanesque nave and a Gothic choir with fine capitals. Among the people interested in the church were Descartes and Jean-Casimir, the king of Poland who abdicated his throne.

Across from St-Germain-des-Prés Church is the Deux-Magots, the famous café of the existentialists. As you leave the church, turn right on the rue de l'Abbaye and have a look at the pink 17th-century Palais Abbatial.

Open: Daily 8am–7:30pm. **Métro:** St-Germain-des-Prés.

CHURCH OF ST-SULPICE, rue St-Sulpice, 6e. Tel. 46-33-21-78.

The square on which the church stands has been much celebrated, and it's worth stopping for a moment in this 18th-century square with its fountain by Visconti, portraying four 18th-century bishops: Fenelon, Massillon, Bossues, and Flechier.

Work began on the church in 1646; the facade, "bastardized classic," was completed in 1745. Many architects, including Le Van, worked on the building. Some were summarily fired; others, such as the Florentine Servandoni, were discredited. One of the two towers was never completed.

The main reason to visit St-Sulpice is to see the Delacroix frescoes in the Chapel of the Angels (first on your right as you enter). Seek out his muscular Jacob wrestling with an angel. On the ceiling St. Michael is struggling with the Devil, and yet another mural depicts Heliodorus being driven from the temple. Painted in the final years of his life, the frescoes are a high point in Delacroix's career.

One of the most notable treasures inside the 360-foot-long church is Servandoni's rococo Chapel of the Madonna, with a marble statue of the Virgin, by Pigalle. The church contains one of the world's largest organs, with more than 6,500 pipes, and an 18th-century case depicted by Chalgrin. The Sunday mass concerts—made famous by Charles Widor—draw many visitors.

One of the largest and most prestigious churches in Paris, St-Sulpice was sacked during the Revolution and converted into the Temple of Victory. Camille Desmoulins, the revolutionary who instigated the raid on the Bastille, was married here.

Open: Daily 7:30am–7:30pm. **Métro:** St-Sulpice.

RUE VISCONTI, 6e.

This narrow street was originally designed for pushcarts. Balzac established his printing press in 1825 at no. 17. Balzac's venture ended in bankruptcy—which forced the author back to his writing desk. In the 17th century the French dramatist Racine lived across the street. Such celebrated actresses as Champmesle and Clairon were also in residence. Nearby is the Musée Eugene Delacroix (see below).

MUSEE EUGENE DELACROIX, 6 place de Furstenberg. Tel. 43-54-04-87.

From 1857 through 1863 the great Romantic painter Delacroix had his last studio here, in one of the most bewitching small squares in all Paris. The artist's apartment and rear-garden atelier have been transformed into a museum of his work. This is no poor artist's shabby studio, but the very tasteful creation of a solidly established man. Sketches, lithographs, watercolors, and oils are hung throughout, and a few personal mementos remain, including a lovely mahogany paint box.

Note: To see the work that earned Delacroix his sure niche in art history, go to the Louvre for such passionate paintings as his *Liberty Leading the People on the Barricades,* or to the Church of St-Sulpice, also in St-Germain-des-Prés (Métro: Mabillon), for the famed fresco, *Jacob Wrestling with the Angel,* among others.

Admission: 11F ($2.05).

Open: Wed–Mon 9:45am–5:15pm. **Closed:** Holidays. **Métro:** St-Germain-des-Prés.

MONTPARNASSE

For the "lost generation," life centered around the literary cafés of Montparnasse. Artists, especially American expatriates, frequented the famous brasserie cafés: Le Dôme, La Coupole, La Rotonde, and Le Select. Most were seeking refuge from the tourists that had overrun Montmartre. Picasso, Modigliani, and Man Ray came this way, as did Hemingway and Fitzgerald when he was poor (when he wasn't you'd find him at the Ritz). William Faulkner, Archibald MacLeish, Isadora Duncan, Miró, James Joyce, Ford Madox Ford, even Trotsky—all were here, except Gertrude Stein, who would not frequent the cafés. To see her, you needed an invitation to her salon at 27 rue de Fleurus. She bestowed her favor on Sherwood Anderson, Elliot Paul, and, briefly, Hemingway. When not receiving, she was busy buying the paintings of Cézanne, Renoir, Matisse, and Picasso. One writer said that her salon was engaged in an international conspiracy to promote modern art.

The life of Montparnasse still centers on its cafés and exotic nightclubs, many of them only a shadow of what they used to be. Its heart is at the crossroads of boulevard Raspail and boulevard du Montparnasse, one of the settings of *The Sun Also Rises.*

CEMETERIES

PERE-LACHAISE CEMETERY, 16 rue du Repos, 20e. Tel. 43-70-70-33.

This graveyard, the largest in Paris, contains more illustrious dead than any other place on earth.

A map available at the main entrance will help you find the tombs, and they read like a roll call of international renown. There are Napoléon's marshals Ney and Massena, and the British admiral Sir Sidney Smith who, by holding the fortress of Acre, made the Corsican taste his first defeat.

There are the poets, playwrights, and novelists Beaumarchais, Balzac, Wilde, Colette, La Fontaine, Molière, Apollinaire, and Daudet, the composers Chopin and Rossini, the painter Corot, the singer Piaf, and a legion more. The tomb of rock star Jim Morrison (1971) has been one of the most visited graves.

But the most somber note in Père-Lachaise is a piece of wall called **Mur des Fédéres.** It was among the graves of this cemetery that the last-ditch fighters of the Paris Commune—the world's first anarchist republic—made their final desperate stand against the troops of the regular French government in May 1871. They were overwhelmed, stood up against this wall, and shot in batches. All died except a handful who had hidden in vaults and lived for years in the cemetery like wild animals, venturing into Paris at night to forage for food.

Open: Mar 15–Nov 5 daily 7:30am–6pm; rest of the year daily 8:30am–5:30pm. **Métro:** Père-Lachaise.

MORE MUSEUMS

Below is a listing of the balance of the city's museums. Be sure to refer back to Section 1, "The Top Attractions," for details on where to get information.

MANUFACTURE DES GOBELINS, 42 av. des Gobelins, 13e. Tel. 43-37-12-60.

If you enjoyed seeing the tapestries at the Musée de Cluny (see above), you might also enjoy watching how they are made. Tapestry work is still being done at Les Gobelins in the same way and on looms like those used at the founding of the factory in 1662. You can tour the workshops where weavers sit behind huge screens of thread, patiently thrusting stitch after stitch into work that may take up to three years to complete.

Tours: Given in French Tues–Thurs 2–2:45pm for 22F ($4.05) adults, free for children under 17. **Métro:** Gobelins.

MANUFACTURE NATIONALE DE SEVRES, place de la Manufacture, Sèvres, 7e.

Madame de Pompadour loved Sèvres porcelain. She urged Louis XV to order more of it, thus ensuring its standing among the fashionable people of the 18th century. Two centuries later, it's still chic.

The Sèvres factory has been owned by the state for over two centuries. It was founded originally in Vincennes, and moved to Sèvres, a riverside suburb of Paris, in 1756. It's open on Thursday (closed on holidays and in July and August), and visits are free. The factory's commercial service sells porcelain to the public Mon–Sat (closed holidays).

Next door, the **Musée National de Ceramique de Sèvres** (tel. 45-34-99-05) shelters one of the finest collections of faience and porcelain in the world, some of which belonged to Madame du Barry, Pompadour's hand-picked successor. On view, for example, is the "Pompadour rose" (which the English insisted on calling the "rose du Barry"), a style much in vogue in the 1750s and 1760s. The painter Boucher made some of the designs used by the factory, as did the sculptor Pajou (he did the bas-reliefs for the Opéra at Versailles). The factory pioneered what became known in porcelain as the Louis XVI style—it's all here, plus lots more, including works from Meissen (archrival of Sèvres). Admission is 16F ($2.95) for adults, 8F ($1.50) for seniors and ages 19–25, free for children under 18. It's open Wed–Mon 10am–noon and 1:30–5:15pm.

Métro: Pont-de-Sèvres, then walk across the Seine to the Left Bank.

MUSEE D'ART MODERNE DE LA VILLE DE PARIS, 11–13 av. du Président Wilson, 16e. Tel. 47-23-61-27.

Along the Seine, next door to the Palais de Tokyo, visitors will find a permanent collection of paintings and sculpture as well as temporary exhibitions on contemporary movements and individual artists. On display are works by Chagall, Matisse, Léger, Braque, Picasso, Dufy, Utrillo, Delaunay, Roualt, and Modigliani. See, in particular, Pierre Tal Coat's *Portrait of Gertrude Stein*. The Musée des Enfants has exhibitions and shows for children.

Admission: 28F ($5.20) adults, 14F ($2.60) ages 18–24, free 17 and under.

Open: Tues and Thurs–Sun 10am–5:30pm, Wed 10am–8:30pm. **Métro:** Iéna or Alma–Marceau.

MUSEE MARMOTTAN, 2 rue Louis-Boilly, 16e. Tel. 42-24-07-02.

Time was when nobody but a stray art scholar ever visited the museum on the edge of the Bois de Boulogne. Nowadays it is quite popular. The rescue from obscurity actually occurred on February 5, 1966, when the museum fell heir to more than 130 paintings, watercolors, pastels, and drawings of Claude Monet, the painter considered the father of impressionism. A gift of Monet's son, Michel, an octogenarian safari-lover who died in a car crash, the bequest was valued at $10 million at the time. Of the surprise acquisition, one critic wrote, "Had an old widow in Brooklyn suddenly inherited the fortune of J. P. Morgan, the event would not have been more startling."

The owner of the museum, the Académie des Beaux-Arts, was immediately embarrassed with a lack of space. The Marmottan was just a small town house, adorned with First Empire furniture and objets d'art (although it did own Monet's *Impression: Sunrise*, which named the movement). The house had once been owned by a dilettante, Paul Marmottan, who had donated it, along with his treasures, to the academy. The solution was to go underground.

Now you can trace the evolution of Monet's art, especially his eternal obsession with waterlilies. Presented are about 30-odd pictures of his house at Giverny that so inspired him. Exceptional paintings include his celebrated 1918 *The Willow*, his 1905 *Houses of Parliament*, his undated *African Lilies*, as well as paintings by Monet's masters, Boudin and Delacroix, and by his fellow impressionists (see especially a portrait of the 32-year-old Monet by Renoir). You can also see the extensive collection of miniatures donated by Daniel Waldenstein.

Admission: 25F ($4.65) adults, 10F ($1.85) children ages 12–18, free children 11 and under.

Open: Tues–Sun 10am–5:30pm. **Métro:** La Muette.

MUSEE NATIONAL AUGUSTE RODIN, 77 rue de Varenne, 7e. Tel. 47-05-01-36.

Auguste Rodin, the man credited with freeing French sculpture of classicism, once lived and had his studio in the charming 18th-century mansion Hôtel Biron, across the boulevard from Napoléon's Tomb in the Hôtel des Invalides. Today the house and garden are filled with his works, a soul-satisfying feast for the Rodin enthusiast.

In the cobbled Court of Honor, within the walls as you enter, you'll see *The Thinker* crouched on his pedestal to the right of you; *The Burghers of Calais* grouped off to the left of you; and to the far left, the writhing *Gates of Hell*, atop which *The Thinker* once more meditates. There's a third *Thinker* inside the museum before a second-floor window. In the almost too-packed rooms, men and angels emerge from blocks of marble, hands twisted in supplication, and the nude torso of Balzac rises up from a tree. Wander back from the house through the long wooded garden where more sculptures await you under the trees.

Admission: Tues–Sat 20F ($3.70) adults, 10F ($1.85) ages 18–25, free 17 and under. Half price on Sun.

Open: Apr–Sept Tues–Sun 10am–6pm; Oct–Mar Tues–Sun 10am–5:15pm. **Métro:** Varenne.

MORE CHURCHES

VAL-DE-GRACE, 1 place Alphonse-Laveran, 5e. Tel. 43-29-12-31.

According to an old proverb, to understand the French you must like Camembert cheese, the Pont Neuf, and the dome of Val-de-Grace.

The church was built by Louis XIII in gratitude for being granted an heir—his wife, Anne of Austria, gave birth to the future Sun King after 23 years of childless marriage. In 1645, seven years after his birth, Louis XIV laid the first stone for the church, which replaced a run-down Benedictine monastery. Mansart designed the facade in the Jesuit style. Le Duc designed the dome, and the painter Mignard decorated it with frescoes. Other architects included Le Mercier and Le Muet. In 1793 the church was converted into a military hospital, and in 1850 it became an army medical school.

Admission: Free.

Open: Mon–Sat 9am–noon and 2–5pm. Touring prohibited during services. **Métro:** Port-Royal. **Bus:** 38.

THE BASILICA OF ST-DENIS, 22 bis, rue Gabriel-Peri, St-Denis, 8e. Tel. 42-43-05-10.

The first Gothic building in France that can be dated precisely, St-Denis was named for the first bishop of Paris, who became the patron saint of the French monarchy. In 1429 Joan of Arc surrendered here, and three centuries later Napoléon married Marie-Louise here. This is also considered "the birthplace of the Crusades."

You are conducted through the crypt on a guided tour (in French only). Royal burials began here in the sixth century and continued until the Revolution—it's the burial place of five royal dynasties. François I, Louis XII, Anne of Brittany, Henri II, and Catherine de Médicis are all entombed here. However, the Revolutionaries stormed through, smashing many marble faces and dumping royal remains in a lime-filled ditch in the garden. The royal remains were reburied under the main altar during the 19th century.

In the 12th century Abbot Suger placed an inscription on the bronze doors of St-Denis: "Marvel not at the gold and expense, but at the craftsmanship of the work." The massive facade, with its crenelated parapet on the top similar to the fortifications of a castle, has a rose window. The stained-glass windows, in stunning colors—mauve, purple, blue, and rose—were restored in the 19th century. In the Middle Ages it was believed that Suger had ground up sapphires, emeralds, and rubies to create the rich colors. The sculpture designed for the tombs—some two stories high—spans the country's artistic development from the Middle Ages to the Renaissance.

Admission: 23F ($4.25) adults, 12F ($2.20) for those under 25 and over 60.

Open: Mon–Sat 10am–5:30pm, Sun 2–6:30pm. **Métro:** St-Denis.

ST-ETIENNE-DU-MONT, place Ste-Geneviève, 5e. Tel. 43-54-11-79.

St-Etienne-du-Mont is dedicated to Ste-Geneviève, the patron saint of Paris. Her tomb was destroyed during the Revolution, but the stone on which her coffin rested has now been given a place of honor. Pascal and Racine are also interred here.

The church took more than a century to build, beginning in 1492. The Gothic interior contains a remarkable rood screen across the nave. The carved-wood pulpit is supported by a seminude Samson who clutches a bone in one hand, having slain the lion at his feet. The fourth chapel on the right as you enter contains an impressive example of 16th-century stained glass.

The church replaced a small abbey founded by Clovis and dedicated to Ste-Geneviève. All that remains of the former abbey is the Tower of Clovis, now part of the Lycée Henri IV. It's visible from rue Clovis.

Open: Daily 7:30am–noon and 2:30–7pm. **Closed:** Mon in July–Aug. **Métro:** Cardinal-Lemoine.

ST-GERMAIN L'AUXERROIS, 2 place du Louvre, 1er. Tel. 42-60-13-96.

Once this was the church for the Palace of the Louvre, attended by royalty, courtesans, and artists. The majestic church shares place du Louvre with Perrault's colonnade and has 260 feet of stained glass, including Renaissance rose windows. Around the chancel is an intricate 18th-century grille. The churchwarden's pews are skillfully carved, based on the 17th-century designs by Le Brun. Behind the pews is a 15th-century triptych and a poorly lit Flemish retable. The organ was originally ordered by Louis XVI for Ste-Chapelle.

Built on the site of a primitive chapel, the church contains the foundation stones of its original 11th-century belfry. The crypt contains the tombs of sculptor Coysevox and architect Le Vau.

The darkest day in its history was August 24, 1572. The ringing of its bells unintentionally signaled the St. Bartholomew Massacre, in which many Protestants died.

Open: Daily 8am–7:30pm. **Métro:** Louvre.

PARKS & GARDENS

The most famous garden, the Tuileries, is covered on one of my walking tours of Paris in Chapter 7, and in "The Top Attractions" section, above. In this section, I explore some of the other outstanding gardens and parks of Paris.

JARDIN DU LUXEMBOURG, 6e. Tel. 43-29-12-78.

These classic French gardens, formally laid out and well groomed, are the best on the Left Bank. Even the trees are planted in designs. A large water basin in the center is encircled with urns and statuary on pedestals. The statue of Ste-Geneviève, the patron saint of Paris, has pigtails reaching to her thighs, and another memorial is dedicated to Stendhal.

In the past the gardens were frequented by artists. Watteau came this way, as did Verlaine. Gertrude Stein would cross the gardens to catch the bus to meet Picasso in his studio at Montmartre. In the 1920s the gardens were a feeding ground for poverty-stricken Montparnasse artists. Hemingway told a friend that the Luxembourg Gardens "kept us from starvation." He used to wheel a baby carriage and child through the gardens until the gendarme went across the street for a glass of wine. Then the writer would lure a pigeon with corn, kill it, and hide it under a blanket.

Today the park is a favorite of students from the Sorbonne and of children. On May Day, crowds carrying lilies of the valley throng the park to welcome spring.

The Italianate Luxembourg Palace, overlooking the gardens, was built in 1612 for Marie de Médicis, the much-neglected wife and later widow of the roving Henri IV. She planned to live there with her "witch" friend, Leonora Galigai.

The queen stayed at the palace only briefly before she was exiled by her son, Louis XIII, for plotting to overthrow him. She reportedly died impoverished in Germany. The 21 paintings she commissioned from Rubens, now in the Louvre, were actually intended for her palace.

Admission: Special permission required in advance to visit the palace.

Métro: Odéon. **RER:** Luxembourg.

BOIS DE BOULOGNE, Porte Dauphine, 16e. Tel. 40-67-97-02.

One of the most spectacular parks in Europe, the Bois is often referred to as the main lung of Paris. It would take more than a week to see everything here: lakes, islands, an artificial waterfall, deluxe restaurants, a theater, and two racetracks. You can travel through the park by car or horse-drawn carriage, but many of its hidden pathways are accessible only on foot. Porte Dauphine is the main entrance.

The park, located in western Paris, was once a royal hunting ground. Baron Haussmann designed the park after Emperor Napoléon III made the land public in 1852. In the late 19th century, elegantly attired couples rode along avenue Foch in carriages, but today you're more likely to see middle-class picnickers. (Beware of prostitutes and muggers at night.)

Separating Lac Inférieur from Lac Supérieur is the Carrefour des Cascades (Grand Cascade); you can stroll under this artificial waterfall. The Lower Lake contains two islands connected by a footbridge, accessible by boat from the east bank. There's a café/restaurant on one of them. Restaurants in the Bois are numerous, elegant, and expensive. The Pré-Catelan contains a deluxe restaurant and a Shakespearean theater in a garden, reputedly planted with trees mentioned in the bard's plays.

Longchamp and Auteuil are the park's two racetracks. The annual Grand Prix is run in June at Longchamp, the site of a medieval abbey, and the events attract the most fashionable and best-dressed people of Paris. Directly south of Longchamp is the Grand Cascade.

The 60-acre Bagatelle Park is the site of a small palace built by the comte d'Artois (later Charles X), who won a bet with his sister-in-law, Marie Antoinette, that he could build the palace in three months. Visit the Bagatelle in late May to see one of the finest and best-known rose gardens in Europe.

Métro: Les-Sablons, Porte-Maillot, or Porte Dauphine.

PARC MONCEAU, 8e. Tel. 42-27-39-56.

This park was built in 1778 for the duc d'Orléans, the richest man in Paris at the time. Philippe-Egalité, as he was commonly known, was fond of pleasure and debauchery. No ordinary park would do. Designed by Carmontelle, the park originally included an Egyptian-style obelisk, a medieval dungeon, a thatched alpine farmhouse, a Chinese pagoda, a Roman temple, an enchanted grotto, various chinoiseries, and a waterfall. The park was opened to the public by Napoléon III.

Today all that remains of the fanciful features are a pyramid and an oval naumachie fringed by a colonnade. Newer statuary and monuments were added, one honoring Chopin. Baby carriages are a common sight, and in spring the park blooms with a spectacular display of red tulips and magnolias.

Métro: Monceau or Villiers.

NEARBY ATTRACTIONS

MUSEE NATIONAL DE LA RENAISSANCE, Le Château d'Écouen, Écouen. Tel. 39-90-04-04.

A visit to this museum, just outside Paris on the northern route to Chantilly, can easily be tied in with a visit to St-Denis. Called Le Château d'Ecouen, the castle was constructed between 1538 and 1555 for the high constable, Anne de Montmorency. In 1805 Napoléon used the building as a school for daughters of the Legion d'Honneur.

Valéry Giscard d'Estaing, the former French president, converted the space into a Renaissance museum. Set in a park, the château contains an exceptional collection of tapestries and paintings. Be sure to see the best-known tapestry, the 245-foot-long *David and Bathsheba.*

Admission: 15F ($2.80) Mon–Sat, 8F ($1.50) Sun.

Open: Wed–Mon 9:45am–12:30pm and 2–5:15pm. **Métro:** St-Denis/Porte-de-Paris; then Bus 268C to Ezanville, which stops near the museum.

VINCENNES

CHATEAU DE VINCENNES, av. de Paris, 12e. Tel. 43-28-15-48.

About 5 miles east of Notre-Dame, encircled by the Bois de Vincennes, this château, like Versailles, was originally a hunting lodge. At the south of the town of Vincennes, the castle was built by Louis VII ("The Young") in 1164. Inspired by the Sainte-Chapelle in Paris, Charles V added a chapel in 1379. Louis XIV, however, wasn't especially fond of Vincennes; he, of course, had another home in mind.

The château has been rebuilt several times since, and the present structure is merely a shell of its former self, which was once known as the "Versailles of the Middle Ages." In time the château was to become a porcelain factory, an arsenal under Napoléon, and a supply depot for the Nazis. Now it's being restored by the government. Its most memorable role was that of a prison, whose most famous prisoner was Mirabeau, the revolutionary and statesman.

Admission: 23F ($4.25) for guided tour.

Open: May–Sept, daily 9:30am–7pm; Oct–Apr, daily 10am–5pm. **Métro:** Château-de-Vincennes. **RER:** Vincennes.

ST-GERMAIN-EN-LAYE

Gourmet cooks know that béarnaise sauce was invented here, although it is generally better known for its greater distinctions. Only 13 miles northwest of Paris, St-Germain-en-Laye traditionally drew Parisians escaping the summer heat.

CHATEAU VIEUX, place de la Gare. Tel. 34-51-53-65.

The château, next to the train station, itself has served as a royal getaway since it was built in the 12th century by François I. Louis XIV stayed here at the palace, although he eventually abandoned it for Versailles, and James II died here. Napoléon III ordered that the château—built on a hill on the left bank of the Seine—be turned into a museum tracing the history of France from the cave dwellers until the Carolingian era. And so it is today: the Musée des Antiquités Nationales, with displays of tools, stones, arms, and jewelry used or worn by the early settlers of Gaul.

Sainte-Chapelle, the oldest section of the Château Vieux, is of special interest. Built by St. Louis in the 1230s, this chapel can be visited only with the custodian's permission. At the end of the tour of the château, stroll through **Le Nôtre's gardens,** open daily 7am–9:30pm.

Admission: 15F ($2.80).

Open: Wed–Mon 9:45am–noon and 1:30–5:15pm. **Métro:** A-1 to St-Germain-en-Laye.

MUSEE DEPARTMENTAL DU PRIEURE, 2 bis, rue Maurice Denis. Tel. 39-73-77-87.

This museum, installed in the oldest building in St-Germain-en-Laye, was built in 1678 by the marquise de Montespan, a paramour of Louis XIV. From World War I to World War II it was inhabited by Maurice Denis, a painter who lived here until his death in 1943. Here he befriended a group of artists, known as "Nabis," including Paul Serusier. Nabis masters such as Bonnard and Vuillard are represented in the exhibition, along with members of the Pont-Aven group, including Gauguin and Émile Bernard. Works by other artists, including Toulouse-Lautrec, are also exhibited. You can visit a chapel decorated by Denis, as well as his atelier.

Admission: 20F ($3.70) adults, children under 12 free.

Open: Wed–Sun 10am–5:30pm. **Métro:** A-1 to St-Germain-en-Laye.

WHERE TO STAY & DINE

PAVILLON HENRI IV, 21 rue Thiers, 78100 St-Germain-en-Laye. Tel. 34-51-62-62. Fax 39-73-93-73. 39 rms (all with bath). TV TEL **Métro:** A-1 to St-Germain-en-Laye, then a five-minute walk.

$ Rates: 440F–550F ($81.40–$101.75) single; 1,300F–1,500F ($240.50–$277.50) double. Breakfast 50F ($9.25) extra. AE, DC, MC, V.

In the 1500s Henri IV built the Château Neuf on this terrace as a hideaway for his illegitimate children. The castle was later bequeathed to the comte d'Artois, the brother of Louis XVI, who planned to demolish it until the Revolution aborted his plans.

The château was partly rebuilt in 1836, and today the remains comprise the illustrious Pavillon Henri IV hotel, where Dumas wrote *The Three Musketeers.* Standing at the edge of the belvedere gardens of the old château, it is still elegantly old-fashioned. A corner room has been set aside as a museum, in remembrance of where the Sun King romped with Madame de Montespan. The fortunate visitors who get to spend a night here will find handsomely furnished bedrooms and a good restaurant. You can always order the classic dishes here—carré d'agneau rôti (roast lamb); rognon de veau (veal kidney) dijonnaise; and, of course, pommes soufflés, which were invented here, along with sauce béarnaise, which is just the thing to top your chateaubriand. For a complete meal, expect to spend from 250F ($46.25) at lunch or from 300F ($55.50) at dinner.

3. COOL FOR KIDS

There are fewer special spots for children in Paris than there are, say, in Amsterdam or Copenhagen. But there are some, plus others that will charm both sides of the generation. When you're weary of dragging the kids on your rounds, forcibly inculcating culture, try refreshing the family spirit with a few of these.

MUSEUMS

The only problem for parents in Paris museums is that all the exhibits are identified in French and unless you managed to struggle past that silly aunt's plume in high school or are an expert on the subject under study, you aren't going to distinguish yourself with explanations.

CITE DES SCIENCES ET DE L'INDUSTRIE, La Villette, 30 av. Corentin-Cariou, 19e. Tel. 40-05-70-70.

Perhaps no museum in Paris is more geared to receive and delight children than Cité des Sciences et de l'Industrie. It has entire areas set aside just for them. Of course, many of its exhibits will enthrall both adult and child equally.

Admission: 35F ($6.50); Inventorium 15F ($2.80) extra for children; planetarium 15F ($2.80) extra; Géode 45F ($8.35) extra.

Open: Tues 10am–6pm, Wed noon–9pm, Thurs–Fri 10am–6pm, Sat–Sun and holidays noon–8pm. Show times at Géode, Tues and Thurs at 10am and 6pm, Wed and Fri–Sun at 10am and 9pm. **Métro:** Line 7 to Porte de la Villette station.

MUSEE DE LA MARINE, in the Palais de Chaillot, place du Trocadéro, 16e. Tel. 45-53-31-70.

If your kids have seawater in their veins, take them to the Musée de la Marine, which features a kaleidoscopic collection of models, maps, figureheads, and whole craft, tracing the development of shipping. The most magnificent item on show is the actual "Boat of the Emperor," a gilt-crowned, oar-driven longboat built in 1811 for Napoléon's trip to Antwerp.

Admission: 20F ($3.70) adults, 15F ($2.80) children 17 and under.

Open: Wed–Mon 10am–6pm. **Métro:** Trocadéro.

MUSEE GREVIN, 10 bd. Montmartre, 9e. Tel. 47-70-85-05.

The desire to compare the Musée Grévin to Madame Tussauds of London is almost irresistible. Grévin is the number-one waxworks of Paris, having opened in 1882. From Charlemagne to the mistress-collecting Napoléon III, it shows memorable moments from French history in a series of tableaux.

Depicted are the consecration of Charles VII in 1429 in the Cathedral of Reims (Joan of Arc, dressed in armor and carrying her standard, stands behind the king); Marguerite de Valois, first wife of Henri IV, meeting on a secret stairway with La Molle, who was soon to be decapitated; Catherine de Médicis with the Florentine alchemist Ruggieri; Louis XV and Mozart at the home of the Marquise de Pompadour; and Napoléon on a rock at St. Helena, reviewing his victories and defeats.

Two shows are staged frequently throughout the day. The first, called the "Palais des Mirages," starts off as a sort of Temple of Brahma, and through magically distorting mirrors, changes into an enchanted forest, then a fête at the Alhambra at Granada. A magician is the star of the second show, "Le Cabinet Fantastique"; he entertains children of all ages.

The museum also presents contemporary personalities in the sports world as well as the leaders of many countries. One display presents 50 of the world's greatest film actors.

Admission: 46F ($8.50) adults, 32F ($5.95) children under 14.

Open: Daily 1–7pm; during French school holidays daily 10am–7pm. Ticket office closes at 6pm. **Métro:** Montmartre or Richelieu-Drouot.

MUSEE NATIONAL D'HISTOIRE NATURELLE, 57 rue Cuvier, 5e. Tel. 40-79-30-00.

Among the other museums frequented by the children of Paris is the Musée National d'Histoire Naturelle, in the Jardin des Plantes. Its history dates back to 1635, when it was founded as a scientific research center by Guy de la Brosse, physician to Louis XIII, but that period is a fleeting moment compared to the eons of history covered inside the huge museum complex. In the galleries of Paleontology, Anatomy, Mineralogy, and Botany, your little genius can trace the history and evolution of life on earth, wondering at the massive skeletons of dinosaurs and mastodons, and staring fascinated at the two-headed animal embryos floating forlornly in their pickling jars. Within the museum grounds are tropical hothouses containing thousands of species of unusual plant life along with small animal life in simulated natural habitats.

Admission: 25F ($4.65) adults, 15F ($2.80) ages 18–24, 6F ($1.10) ages 17 and under.

Open: Wed–Mon 10am–5pm. **Métro:** Jussieu or Austerlitz.

PARKS & ZOOS

The large inner-city parks all have playgrounds with tiny merry-go-rounds and gondola-style swings. If you're staying on the Right Bank, take the children for a stroll through the **Tuileries,** where there are donkey rides, ice-cream stands, and a marionette show. At the circular pond, you can rent a toy sailboat. On the Left Bank, equivalent delights exist in the **Luxembourg Gardens.** If you take in the gardens of the **Champ de Mars,** you can combine a donkey ride for the children with a visit to the nearby Eiffel Tower for the entire family.

JARDIN D'ACCLIMATION, on the northern edge of the Bois de Boulogne, 16e. Tel. 40-67-90-82.

The definitive children's park in Paris is the Jardin d'Acclimation. This is the kind of place that satisfies tykes and adults alike—but would be regarded in horror by anyone in his or her teens. The visit starts with a ride from Porte Maillot to the Jardin entrance, through a stretch of wooded park, on a jaunty, green-and-yellow narrow-gauge train. Inside the gate is an easy-to-follow layout map. The park is circular, and if you follow the road in either direction it will take you all the way around and bring you back to the train at the end.

En route you will discover a house of mirrors, an archery range, miniature golf, zoo animals, an American-style bowling alley, a puppet theater (only on Thursday, Saturday, Sunday, and holidays), a playground, a hurdle-racing course, and a whole conglomerate of junior-scale rides, shooting galleries, and waffle stalls. You can trot the kids off on a pony or join them in a boat on a mill-stirred lagoon. Fun to watch (and a superb idea for American cities to copy) is "La Prévention Routière," a miniature roadway operated by the Paris police. The youngsters drive through it in small cars equipped to start and stop and are required by two genuine Parisian gendarmes to obey all street signs and light changes.

Admission: 8F ($1.50) adults, 4F (75¢) children 3–10.
Open: Mon–Sat 10am–6:30pm, Sun 10am–7:30pm. **Métro:** Sablons.

BOIS DE VINCENNES, Jardin des Plantes, 12e. Tel. 43-43-84-95.

There is a modest zoo in the Jardin des Plantes, near the natural history museum. But without a doubt, the best zoo this city has to offer is in the Bois de Vincennes—on the outskirts, but quickly reached by Métro. This modern zoo displays its animals in settings as close as possible to their natural habitats. Here you never get that hunched-up feeling about the shoulders from empathizing with a leopard in a cage too small for stalking. The lion has an entire veldt to himself, and you can view each other comfortably across a deep protective moat. On a cement mountain reminiscent of Disneyland's Matterhorn, lovely Barbary sheep leap from ledge to ledge or pose gracefully for hours watching the penguins in their pools at the mountain's foot. The animals seem happy here and are consequently playful. Keep well back from the bear pools or your drip-dries may be dripping wet.

Admission: 30F ($5.55) adults, 15F ($2.80) ages 4–10.
Open: Mon–Sat 9am–5:30pm, Sun 9am–6pm. **Métro:** Porte Dorée.

PUPPET SHOWS

You can take in a puppet show while visiting the above-mentioned parks—but, once again, all the words are French. Still, they're a great Paris tradition and worth seeing, if only for the joy of sharing a French child's typical experience. The shows are given at the **Tuileries** at 3:15pm on Wednesday, Saturday, and Sunday, all summer long. At the **Luxembourg Gardens,** you'll see puppet productions of sinister plots set in Gothic castles and Asian palaces. Prices vary depending on the extravagance of the production. Some young critics think the best puppet shows are held in the **Champ de Mars.** Performance times in both the Luxembourg Gardens and the Champ de Mars vary with the day of the week and the production being staged. But all are colorfully and enthusiastically produced—and received. You may have to whisper the story line to your monolingual offspring as you go along, but when Red Riding Hood pummels the Wolf over the head with an umbrella, they'll be contorted in glee like the rest of the half-pint audience. That's international kid-talk.

MONTMARTRE

On Sunday afternoon entire French families crowd up to the top of the Butte Montmartre to join in the fiesta atmosphere. Start by taking the Métro to Anvers and walking to the Funiculaire de Montmartre.

The funiculaire is a small, silvery cable car that slides you gently up the steep, grassy hillside to Sacré-Coeur on the hillcrest. Once on top, follow the crowds to the place du Tertre, where a Sergeant Pepper-style band will usually be blasting off-key and where you can have the kids' pictures sketched by local artists.

MUSEE DE CIRE DE LA BUTTE MONTMARTRE, 11 rue Poulbot, 18e. Tel. 46-06-78-92.

Signs lead from the place du Tertre to the Musée de Cire de la Butte Montmartre, a wax museum illustrating the history of Montmartre. All the neighborhood characters—Toulouse-Lautrec, Renoir, Liszt, Chopin—make their somewhat stiff appearances in settings of their time. One of the tableaux represents *Le Bateau Lavoir,* the Montmartre meeting place of painters since 1830. There are guided tours in English if the demand is large enough.

Admission: 25F ($4.65) adults, 15F ($2.80) children.

Open: Easter–Oct, daily 10:30am–noon and 2:30–5:15pm; Nov–Easter, Wed and Sat–Sun 2:30–5pm. **Métro:** Abbesses.

---

4. SPECIAL-INTEREST SIGHTSEEING

FOR THE LITERARY ENTHUSIAST

MAISON DE VICTOR HUGO, 6 place des Vosges. Tel. 42-72-10-16.

The house where Victor Hugo lived and worked from 1832 to 1848 has been turned into a museum devoted to the novelist. You probably know Hugo as a literary giant, but here you'll also see the drawings, carvings, and pieces of furniture he made. The windows of the museum overlook the square.

Admission: 12F ($2.20) adults, 6.50F ($1.20) children 7–17; free for children 6 and under.

Open: Tues–Sun 10am–5:40pm. **Closed:** National holidays. **Métro:** St-Paul, Bastille, or Chemin-Vert.

MAISON DE BALZAC, 47 rue Raynouard, 16e. Tel. 42-24-56-38.

This unpretentious house on the slope of a hill in Passy, a residential district of Paris, was the home—or more accurately, the hideaway—of the great French novelist Honoré de Balzac from 1840 to 1847. The Balzac museum is almost completely unfurnished, but it does contain mementos, documents, manuscripts, and other items associated with the writer. Throughout the house are scattered caricature drawings of Balzac, whose amusing appearance and eccentric dress lent themselves to ridicule. Among the better-known mementos is the famed Limoges coffeepot that Balzac's "screeching owl" kept hot during the long nights while he wrote *La comédie humaine.* Also enshrined here are Balzac's writing desk and chair.

The house contains a library of special interest to scholars, as well as a small courtyard and garden. While the main entrance is on rue Raynouard, the back door leads to rue Berton—a fortunate situation for Balzac, who often had to make hasty retreats from his many creditors.

Admission: 12F ($2.20); 6F ($1.10) Sun. Free for children under 17.

Open: Tues–Sun 10am–5:45pm. **Métro:** Passy or La-Muette.

FOR THE "UNDERGROUND" ENTHUSIAST

CATACOMBS, 1 place Denfert-Rochereau, 14e. Tel. 43-22-47-63.

In the Middle Ages the Catacombs were quarries, but in 1785 city officials decided to use them as a burial ground, since the existing cemeteries were considered a health hazard. First opened to the public in 1810, the Catacombs consist of 1,000 yards of tunnel containing six million skeletons arranged in skull-and-crossbones fashion. In 1830 the prefect of Paris closed the Catacombs to the viewing public as obscene and indecent. Later, in World War II, the Catacombs were the headquarters of the French Underground. Today they are illuminated with overhead electric lights over their entire length.

Admission: 15F ($2.80) adults, 8.50F ($1.55) children 17 and under.

Open: Tues–Sat 2–4pm. **Métro:** Denfert-Rochereau.

THE SEWERS OF PARIS (LES EGOUTS), Pont de l'Alma. Tel. 47-05-10-29.

Some say Baron Haussmann will be remembered mainly for the vast, complicated network of sewers he erected. The *égouts* of the city, as well as telephone and telegraph pneumatic tubes, are constructed around a quartet of principal tunnels, one of them 18 feet wide and 15 feet high. It's like an underground city, with the street names clearly labeled. Further, each branch pipe bears the number of the building to which it is connected (guides are fond of pointing out Maxim's). These underground passages are truly mammoth, containing pipes bringing in drinking water and compressed air as well as telephone and telegraph lines.

That these sewers have remained such a popular attraction is something of a curiosity in itself. They were made famous by Victor Hugo's *Les Misérables.* "All dripping with slime, his soul filled with a strange light," Jean Valjean in his desperate flight through the sewers of Paris is one of the heroes of narrative drama.

A documentary movie on the sewer system is offered, as well as a museum.

Tours: Tours begin on the Left Bank at Pont de l'Alma, where a stairway leads into the hotels of the city. Admission is 22F ($4.05) adults, 7F ($1.30) children for the 1½ hour tour.

Open: May 1–Sept 30, daily 11am–6pm; Oct 1–Apr 30, daily 11am–5pm. **Métro:** Alma-Marceau. **RER:** Pont de l'Alma.

FOR VISITING AMERICANS

Many Left Bank streets hold memories for Americans, and none more so than **rue Monsieur-le-Prince,** 6e, in the Odéon section (Métro: Odéon). During a famous visit in 1959, Martin Luther King, Jr., came to call on Richard Wright, Mississippi-born African-American novelist famous for *Native Son.* King climbed to the third-floor apartment at no. 14, only to find that Wright's opinions on the Civil Rights Movement conflicted with his own. Whistler rented a studio at no. 22, and at no. 49 Longfellow lived for a short time in

1826. Oliver Wendell Holmes, Sr. lived at no. 55. After strolling along this street, you can dine at the former haunt of such figures as Kerouac and Hemingway. See my recommendation of Crèmerie-Restaurant Polidor (41 rue Monsieur-le-Prince, 6e) under "5th & 6th Arrondisssements" in Chapter 5.

HARRY'S NEW YORK BAR, 5 rue Daunou, 2e. Tel. 42-61-71-14.

F. Scott Fitzgerald and Ernest Hemingway drank a lot here, Gloria Swanson talked about her affair with Joseph Kennedy, and even Gertrude Stein showed up. And the place is still going strong. See also "Specialty Bars & Clubs" in Chapter 9.

Métro: Odéon or Pyramides.

LA ROTONDE, 105 bd. Montparnasse, 6e. Tel. 43-26-68-84.

Americans tended to drink on the Right Bank, notably in the Ritz Bar, when they had money. When they didn't, they headed for one of the cafés of Montparnasse, which, according to Hemingway, usually meant La Rotonde.

Métro: Raspail.

DEUX MAGOTS, 170 bd. St-Germain, 6e. Tel. 45-48-55-25.

This long-established watering hole of St-Germain-des-Prés is where Jake Barnes meets Lady Brett in Hemingway's *The Sun Also Rises*.

Métro: St-Germain-des-Prés.

HOTEL ST-GERMAIN-DES-PRES, 36 rue Bonaparte, 6e. Tel. 43-26-00-19.

Another legendary woman of letters, Janet Flanner, correspondent for the *New Yorker*, lived here in the 1920s until she had enough money to stay at the Crillon (see "Paris Accommodations," Chapter 4).

Métro: St-Germain-des-Prés.

HOTEL SELECT, 1 place de la Sorbonne, 5e. Tel. 46-34-14-80.

Right in the heart of the Latin Quarter, this previously recommended hotel once housed news commentator Eric Sevareid for about 60¢ a night when he was a struggling reporter for the *Paris-Herald* in 1937. One of his major accomplishments at the time was getting a rare interview with Gertrude Stein.

Métro: St-Michel.

SHAKESPEARE AND COMPANY, 37 rue de la Bûcherie, 5e. No phone.

The most famous bookstore on the Left Bank was Shakespeare and Company, on rue de l'Odéon, home to the legendary Sylvia Beach, the "mother confessor to the Lost Generation." Hemingway, Fitzgerald, and Gertrude Stein were all frequent patrons. In recent decades, visitors would be likely to find Anaïs Nin, the diarist noted for her description of struggling American artists in 1930s Paris, in the store. At one point she helped her companion, Henry Miller, publish *Tropic of Cancer*, a book so notorious in its day that returning Americans trying to slip a copy through Customs often had it confiscated as pornography. When times were hard, Ms. Nin herself wrote pornography for a dollar a page.

Today the shop is located on rue de la Bûcherie, where expatriates still come to swap books and the latest literary gossip.

Open: Daily 11am–midnight. **Métro:** St-Michel.

5 RUE ST-LOUIS-EN-ILE, Ile St-Louis, 4e.

This was the address of William Aspenwell Bradley, literary agent to the Lost Generation, who drew up the contract for *The Autobiography of Alice B. Toklas* by Gertrude Stein. In addition to Stein, he represented Edith Wharton, author of *House of Mirth* and *The Age of Innocence* (awarded the Pulitzer prize in 1921). Other illustrious clients included Thornton Wilder, who himself won the Pulitzer prize for *The Bridge of San Luis Rey* and *Our Town*. Back from driving ambulances with Hemingway on the Italian front in 1918, John Dos Passos also became one of Bradley's clients. His famous books include *Three Soldiers* (1921), *U.S.A.* (1937), and *Adventures of a Young Man* (1939).

Métro: Pont-Marie.

19 RUE TOURNON, 6e.

This was the home of John Paul Jones, the American revolutionary hero credited with the famous line, "I have not yet begun to fight." After having captured the 50-gun British frigate H.M.S. *Serapis,* he was honored by Louis XVI. Upon meeting Jones, Abigail Adams noted, "I should sooner think of wrapping him up in cotton wool and putting him in my pocket, than sending him to contend with cannon balls." She noted that he seemed aware of "how often the ladies use baths, what color best suits a lady's complexion, what cosmetics are most favorable to the skin." But on July 18, 1792, he died destitute. Even though he'd been penniless, he was honored with a lavish state funeral.

Métro: Odéon.

2 RUE DE L'UNIVERSITE, 7e.

When Benjamin Franklin arrived in Paris in December 1776, he stayed here. In short time, he moved to 52 rue Jacob, 6e (Métro: St-Germain-des-Prés), and later, as minister to the Court at Versailles, he moved into the Hôtel de Valentinois, 62 rue Raynouard, 16e (Métro: Passy), about half a mile from the center of Paris. Beloved by the French, Franklin left Passy on July 11, 1785, at the age of 79.

Métro: Rue-du-Bac or St-Germain.

LE PROCOPE, 13 rue l'Ancienne-Comédie, 6e. Tel. 43-26-99-20.

Dating from 1686, this is the oldest café in Paris and the restaurant of choice for such historical figures as Franklin and Jefferson (see "5th and 6th Arrondissements" in Chapter 5).

Métro: Odéon.

HOTEL DE PONTALBA, 41 rue du Faubourg St-Honoré, 8e.

Did you ever wonder where Lindbergh slept after his solo flight across the Atlantic? He stayed at the American ambassador's residence, the Hôtel de Pontalba, dating from 1720, and once owned by financier Baron Edmond de Rothschild. It's still the American ambassador's residence and not open to the public.

Métro: Concorde or Champs-Elyseés.

5. ORGANIZED TOURS

The most popular way to get acquainted with Paris is on a two-hour double-decker bus tour that takes you past the major attractions. There isn't time to stop at each point of interest, but you'll get a nice view out the numerous large windows. Seats are comfortable, and individual earphones are distributed with a recorded commentary in 10 different languages. Contact **Cityrama,** 4 place des Pyramides, 1er (tel. 42-60-30-14). Tours depart daily between 9:30am and 2:30pm, for 120F ($22.20). **Métro:** Palais Royal.

A separate tour of the nighttime illuminations leaves daily at 10pm in summer and 9pm in winter. The cost is 125F ($23.15).

Bateaux-Mouches cruises on the Seine depart frequently from the Pont de l'Alma on the Right Bank. Boat facilities vary; some include open sun decks, bars, and restaurants. All provide commentaries in six languages, including English. Tours depart daily every 30 minutes from 10am to 11:30pm; in good weather, boats leave every 15 minutes. Dinner cruises depart at 8:30pm; ties and jackets are required for men. Fares are 30F ($5.55) for adults and 15F ($2.80) for children, for a ride lasting about 1½ hours; luncheon cruises cost 300F ($55.50) Monday through Saturday or 500F ($92.50) on Sunday; and a deluxe dinner cruise costs 500F ($92.50). Call 42-25-96-10 for information and reservations. **Métro:** Alma-Marceau.

6. SPECIAL & FREE EVENTS

FREE CONCERTS & OTHER EVENTS

Many cultural events in Paris are free. Concerts, films, and lectures are sponsored by foreign nations, such as the United States and Great Britain. Inquire at the **Centre Culturel Américain,** 261 bd. Raspail, 14e (tel. 43-21-42-20). **Métro:** Raspail. Or try the **Centre Culturel Britannique,** 9–11 rue de Constantine, 7e (tel. 49-55-73-00). **Métro:** Invalides.

For the best free concert in Paris, hear organ music played in one of the old churches. Most concerts are held on Sunday afternoon, and are usually listed in *Pariscope,* the guide to entertainment events.

At the **Institut Neerlandais,** 121 rue de Lille, 7e (tel. 47-05-85-99), free concerts feature jazz, classical, and contemporary music from the Netherlands. **Métro:** Assemblée Nationale.

Free chamber-music concerts are presented at the **American Church,** 65 quai d'Orsay, 7e (tel. 47-05-07-99). **Métro:** Invalides.

STREET ENTERTAINMENT

The spacious forecourt of the **Centre Georges Pompidou,** plateau Beaubourg, is a free "entertainment center" featuring mimes, fire-eaters, would-be circus performers, and sometimes first-rate musicians. **Métro:** Rambuteau or Hôtel-de-Ville.

Classical-music students, often from the Conservatoire National, give free concerts in the corridors of the **Métro.** A hat (or violin case) is passed to collect donations.

If you're in Paris during one of **the major festivals,** you can join in the fun for free. On Summer Solstice (June 21) clowns, fire-eaters, and other performers roam the streets. On July 14 (Bastille Day) the French traditionally drink wine and dance in the streets. There are also fireworks displays, free concerts, and a parade of tanks down the Champs-Elysées.

A DAY AT THE RACES

Paris boasts an army of avid horse-racing fans who disperse whenever possible to any of the city's eight racetracks. Information on any of the races being held in Paris during your visit is available in such newspapers and magazines as *Tierce, Paris-Turf, France-Soir,* or *L'Équipe.* These are sold at kiosks throughout the city.

The premier bastion of the French horseracing world is the **Hippodrome de Longchamp,** Bois de Boulogne (tel. 42-24-13-29). Established in 1855, during the autocratic but pleasure-loving reign of Napoléon III, it carries the most prestige, the greatest number of promising thoroughbreds, and the largest purse in France. The most important racing months at Longchamp are late June (*Le Grand Prix de Paris*) and early October (*Prix de l'Arc de Triomphe*). **Métro:** Auteuil, then one of the shuttle buses that operate on race days.

Another venue for horseracing is the **Hippodrome d'Auteuil,** also in the Bois de Boulogne (tel. 45-27-12-24). Known for its steeplechases and obstacle courses, it sometimes attracts more than 50,000 Parisians at a time who appreciate the park's open-air promenades as much as they do the equestrian events. Established in 1870, the event is scattered over a sprawling 30 acres of parkland, each of which is designed to show to maximum advantage the skill and agility of both horses and riders. **Métro:** Auteuil.

Also popular, a bit rougher, and the most frequented by blue-collar gambling enthusiasts, is the **Hippodrome de Vincennes,** Bois de Vincennes (tel. 47-42-07-70). Less prestigious than either of its competitors, it holds most of its racing events under floodlights during evening hours in midwinter. **Métro:** Château de Vincennes.

CHAPTER 7

STROLLING AROUND PARIS

1. THE GRAND PROMENADE

2. MONTMARTRE

3. THE LATIN QUARTER

4. LES GRANDS BOULEVARDS

5. THE LOUVRE IN 2 HOURS

The best way to discover Paris is on foot, using your own shoe leather. This chapter is organized into a series of walking tours of the major attractions and districts of the City of Light.

Try to spend one day walking the Grand Promenade—the Champs-Elysées —which takes you from the Arc de Triomphe to the Tuileries. The last walking tour, the Louvre, is not, of course, a tour of a district of Paris, but after going through its monumental block, you'll feel as though you have been on one of the major strolls of your life.

WALKING TOUR 1 — The Grand Promenade

Start: Arc de Triomphe.
Finish: Jardin des Tuileries.
Time: 3 leisurely hours; the distance is 2 miles.
Best Time: Sunday morning.
Worst Time: Rush hour.

This is a lengthy walking tour, but it's the most popular walk in Paris. Start at the:

1. **Arc de Triomphe** (see Chapter 6 for details) at place Charles-de-Gaulle–Etoile from which 12 grand avenues radiate. Stand there for a moment (somewhere safe from traffic) and gaze down the long:

2. **Champs-Elysées,** which has been called "the highway of French grandeur." This street has witnessed some of the greatest moments in French history and some of its worst, such as when Hitler's armies paraded down the street in 1940. Louis XIV ordered the construction of the 1.1-mile avenue in 1667. Originally called the Grand-Cour, and designed by Le Nôtre, it was renamed avenue des Champs-Elysées after the Elysian Fields (the home of the virtuous dead) in 1709.

Stroll along this street. On one side it's a chestnut-lined park; on the other, a commercial avenue of sidewalk cafés, automobile showrooms, airline offices, cinemas, lingerie stores, even hamburger joints. The Champs-Elysées has obviously lost the fin-de-siècle elegance described by Proust in *Remembrance of Things Past*. Head down the avenue toward place de la Concorde, staying on the left-hand side. When you reach the:

3. Rue de Berri, turn left to no. 20, site of Thomas Jefferson's residence from 1785 to 1789. Today, the site is a large modern apartment building. Back on the avenue again, continue to Rond-Point des Champs-Elysées. Close to that is a philatelist's delight, the best-known open-air stamp market in Europe, held on Thursday and Sunday.

REFUELING STOP   Make it **4. Fouquet's,** 99 av. des Champs-Elysées (see Chapter 9 for a complete description). Founded in 1901 and still serving coffee and food, this is an institution. Summer sees the flowers come out, and in winter the glass screens will shelter you from the winds. Take plenty of money.

Continue down the avenue until you reach avenue Winston-Churchill on your right (from here there's a good panorama, looking toward the Invalides). Ducking traffic and pausing for a view, cross to the other side of the avenue and go along avenue de Marigny. On your right will be the:

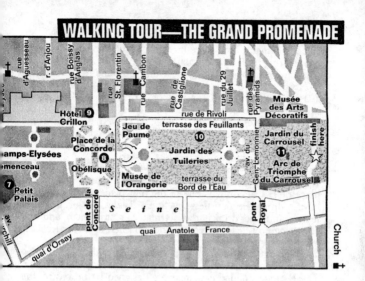

5. Palais de l'Elysée, the "French White House," whose main entrance is along fashionable Faubourg St-Honoré. Napoléon abdicated here. Now occupied by the president of France, it can't be visited without an invitation.

Back at Rond Point and avenue Winston-Churchill, you come to the:

6. Grand Palais, whose galleries stage temporary art exhibitions; read *Pariscope* for details. The Grand Palais was constructed for the World Exhibition of 1900, as was the:

7. Petit Palais (whose entrance is on avenue Winston-Churchill), which now houses the Musée d'Art Moderne de la Ville de Paris (see Chapter 6 for details). Postponing a visit for the moment, continue along this avenue—now the garden-district section— until you come to the landmark:

8. Place de la Concorde, an octagonal traffic hub ordered built in 1757 to honor Louis XV. The statue of the king was torn down in 1792 and the name of the square was changed to place de la Revolution. Floodlit at night, the square is dominated by an Egyptian obelisk from Luxor, considered the oldest human-made object in Paris. It was carved around 1200 B.C. and presented to France in 1829 by the Viceroy of Egypt. During the Reign of Terror, the dreaded guillotine was erected on this spot and claimed the lives of thousands of people.

On each side of the obelisk are two fountains with bronzetailed mermaids and bare-breasted sea nymphs. Gray-beige statues ring the square, honoring the cities of France. To symbolize France's loss of Alsace and Lorraine to Germany in 1871, the statue of Strasbourg was covered with a black drapery that wasn't lifted until the end of World War I. Two of the palaces on place de la Concorde are today the Ministry of the Navy and the deluxe Hôtel Crillon. They were designed in the 1760s by Ange-Jacques Gabriel. For a spectacular sight, look down the Champs-Elysées. The gateway to the Tuileries is flanked by the *Winged Horses* of Coysevox.

REFUELING STOP The **9. Bar of the Hôtel Crillon,** 10 place de la Concorde, is one of the best places in the world to have a drink. Fashion designer Sonia Rykiel has given it new luster, and the drinks, the setting, the ambience, and the atmosphere of "Paree" remain undiminished over the decades.

From place de la Concorde, you can enter the:
10. **Jardin des Tuileries,** as much a part of Paris as the Seine. These statue-studded gardens were designed by Le Nôtre, the gardener to Louis XIV. About 100 years before that, a palace was ordered built here by Catherine de Médicis, which was occupied by Louis XVI after he left Versailles. Napoléon I called it home. Twice attacked by the people of Paris, it was finally burned to the ground in 1871 and never rebuilt. The gardens, however, remain, the trees arranged geometrically in orderly designs. Even the paths are straight, instead of winding as in English gardens. The fountains, though, soften the sense of order and formality.

The neoclassical statuary is often insipid and is occasionally desecrated by rebellious "art critics." Seemingly half of Paris is found in the Tuileries on a warm spring day, listening to the chirping birds and watching the daffodils and red tulips bloom. Fountains bubble, and parents push baby carriages around the grounds where 18th-century revolutionaries killed the king's Swiss guards.

At the end of your walking tour of the Tuileries—2 miles from place Charles-de-Gaulle–Étoile—you'll be at the:
11. **Arc de Triomphe du Carrousel,** at the cour du Carrousel. Pierced with three walkways and supported by marble columns, the monument honors the Grande Armée, celebrating Napoleon's victory at Austerlitz on December 5, 1805. The arch is surmounted by statuary, a chariot, and four bronze horses. At this point, you'll be on the doorstep of the Louvre.

WALKING TOUR 2 — Montmartre

Start: Place Pigalle.
Finish: Place Pigalle.
Time: 5 hours—more if you break for lunch. It's a 3-mile trek.
Best Time: Any day that it isn't raining. Set out by 10am at the latest.
Worst Time: After dark.

The traditional way to explore Montmartre is on foot. It's the highest point in the city, and visitors who find it too much of a climb

WALKING TOUR—MONTMARTRE

Key to map:

1. Bateau-Lavoir (Boat Washhouse)
2. Musée de Cire de la Butte Montmartre
3. La Maison-Rose
4. Le Maquis
5. Place du Calvaire
6. Place du Tertre
7. Church of St-Pierre
8. Sacré-Coeur
9. Musée de Montmartre
10. Cabaret des Assassins
11. Moulin de la Galette
12. Cimetière de Montmartre
13. Moulin Rouge
14. Boulevard de Clichy
15. Place Pigalle

M Métro

✝ Church

---

will want to take the miniature train along the steep streets (45 min.). **Le Petit Train de Montmartre** passes all the major landmarks, taking 72 passengers who can listen to the English commentary. Board at either place du Tertre (the Church of St-Pierre) or place Blanche (near the Moulin Rouge). Trains run daily from 10am to 7pm March through October. For information, contact Promotrain, 38 boulevard Flandrin, 16e (tel. 45-04-87-47).

The simplest way to reach Montmartre is to take the Métro to Anvers, then walk up rue du Steinkerque toward the funicular.

Funiculars run to the precincts of Sacré-Coeur every day from 6am to 11pm.

FROM PLACE PIGALLE TO MONT CENIS Those who prefer to walk can take the Métro to place Pigalle. Turn right after leaving the station and proceed down boulevard de Clichy, turn left at the Cirque Medrano, and begin the climb up rue des Martyrs. Upon reaching rue des Abbesses, turn left onto rue Ravignan, then right, and eventually you'll come to place Emile-Goudeau, a tree-studded square in the middle of rue Ravignan. At no. 13, across from the Timhotel, stood:

1. **Bateau-Lavoir (Boat Washhouse),** called the cradle of cubism. Fire gutted it in 1970, but it has been reconstructed by the city of Paris. Picasso once lived here and, in the winter of 1905–1906, painted one of the world's most famous portraits, *The Third Rose* (Gertrude Stein). Other residents have included Kees van Dongen and Juan Gris. Modigliani had his studio nearby, as did Rousseau and Braque.

   Rue Ravignan ends at place Jean-Baptiste-Clément. Go to the end of the street and cross it onto rue Norvins (which will be on your right). This intersection, one of the most famous street scenes of Montmartre (and painted by Utrillo), is the meeting point of rues Norvins, St-Rustique, and des Saules. Turn left and head down rue Poulbot. At no. 11 you'll come to the:
2. **Musée de Cire de la Butte Montmartre,** the waxworks of Montmartre, with all the neighborhood characters, including Toulouse-Lautrec.

REFUELING STOPS Chances are, you'll be in Montmartre for lunch. Many restaurants, especially those around place du Tertre, are unabashed tourist traps. You'll be asked eight times if you want your portrait sketched in charcoal. However, **3. La Maison-Rose,** 2 rue de l'Abreuvoir (see Chapter 5 for a complete description), is a good bargain. This was once the atelier of Utrillo, and the famous French singer Charles Aznavour used to perform here. The little pink house is about 300 yards from place du Tertre. But if you want better food, then leave the place du Tertre area and take a 12-minute walk down the Butte to **4. Le Maquis,** 69 rue Caulaincourt (see Chapter 5 for details). The food is reasonable, and in sunny weather you can try for a seat on the tiny terrace. The restaurant is open Tuesday through Saturday.

The rue Poulbot crosses the tiny:
5. **Place du Calvaire,** which offers a panoramic view of Paris. On this square (a plaque marks the house) lived artist, painter, and lithographer Maurice Neumont (1868–1930). From here, follow the sounds of an oompah band to:
6. **Place du Tertre,** the old town square of Montmartre. Its cafés are overflowing, its art galleries (in and out of doors) always overcrowded. Some of the artists still wear berets, and the cafés bear such names as La Bohème—you get the point. Everything is so loaded with local color—applied as heavily as on a Seurat canvas—it gets a little redundant.

   Right off the square fronting rue du Mont-Cenis is the:

7. **Church of St-Pierre.** Originally a Benedictine abbey, it has played many roles—Temple of Reason during the Revolution, food depot, clothing store, even a munitions factory. Nowadays it's back to being a church. In 1147 the present church was consecrated; it's one of the oldest in Paris. Two of the columns in the choir stall are the remains of a Roman temple. Note among the sculptured works a nun with the head of a pig, a symbol of sensual vice. At the entrance of the church are three bronze doors sculpted by Gismondi in 1980. The middle door depicts the life of St. Peter. The left door is dedicated to St. Denis, first bishop of Paris, and the right door to the Holy Virgin.

   After visiting St. Peter's, veer left around the huge reservoir of Montmartre and go through the Jardin du Calvaire until you arrive at the terrace of:

8. **Sacré-Coeur,** overlooking Square Willette. After a visit to Sacré-Coeur, walk between the basilica and the Cemetery of St-Pierre, turning left (west) and heading along rue Chevalier-de-la-Barre, taking a right turn onto rue du Mont-Cenis.

FROM MONT CENIS TO PLACE PIGALLE Continue on this street to rue Carot, at which point turn left. At no. 12 is the:

9. **Musée de Montmartre** (tel. 46-06-61-11), with a wide collection of mementos of *vieux Montmartre*. This famous 17th-century house was formerly occupied by Utrillo, Dufy, van Gogh, and Renoir. Suzanne Valadon and her son, Utrillo, also lived here. It's open Tuesday through Sunday from 11am to 6pm. Admission is 20F ($3.70).

   From the museum, turn right heading up rue des Saules past a winery, a reminder of the days when Montmartre was a farming village on the outskirts of Paris. A grape-harvesting festival is held here every October.

   The intersection of rue des Saules and rue St-Vincent is one of the most visited and photographed corners of the Butte. Here, on one corner, sits the famous old:

10. **Cabaret des Assassins,** long ago renamed Au Lapin Agile (see Chapter 9 for details).

    Continue along rue St-Vincent, passing the Cimetière St-Vincent on your right. Utrillo is just one of the many famous artists buried here. Take a left turn onto rue Girardon and climb the stairs. In a minute or two, you'll spot on your right two of the windmills (*moulins*) that used to dot the Butte. One of these:

11. **Moulin de la Galette** (entrance at 1 av. Junot), was immortalized by Renoir.

    Turn right onto rue Lepic and walk past no. 54. In 1886, van Gogh lived here with Guillaumin. Take a right turn onto rue Joseph-de-Maistre, then left again on rue Caulaincourt until you reach the:

12. **Cimetière de Montmartre,** second in fame only to Père-Lachaise, and the resting place of many famous personages. The burial ground (Métro: Clichy) lies west of the Butte, north of boulevard de Clichy. Opened in 1795, the cemetery shelters such composers as Berlioz (d. 1869) and Offenbach (d. 1880). Heinrich Heine, Stendhal, the Goncourt brothers, and poets Alfred de Vigny and Théophile Gautier are buried here. I like to pay my respects at the tomb of Alphonsine Plessis, the heroine of

La Dame aux Camélias, and Madame Recamier, who taught the world how to lounge.

From the cemetery, take avenue Rachel, turn left onto boulevard de Clichy, and go to place Blanche, where an even better-known windmill than the one in Renoir's painting stands, the:

13. **Moulin Rouge,** one of the most talked-about nightclubs in the world. It was immortalized by Toulouse-Lautrec.

From place Blanche, you can begin a descent down:

14. **Boulevard de Clichy,** fighting off the pornographers and hustlers trying to lure you into tawdry sex joints. With some rare exceptions—notably the citadels for the *chansonniers*—boulevard de Clichy is one gigantic tourist trap. Still, as Times Square is to New York, boulevard de Clichy is to Paris: Everyone who comes to Paris invariably winds up here. The boulevard strips and peels its way down to:

15. **Place Pigalle,** center of nudity in Paris. The square is named after a French sculptor, Pigalle, whose closest association with nudity was a depiction of Voltaire in the buff. Place Pigalle, of course, was the notorious "Pig Alley" of World War II. Toulouse-Lautrec had his studio right off Pigalle at 5 avenue Frochot. When she was lonely and hungry, Edith Piaf sang in the alleyways, hoping to earn a few francs for the night.

WALKING TOUR 3 — The Latin Quarter

Start: Place St-Michel.
Finish: The Panthéon.
Time: 3 hours, not counting stops.
Best Time: Any school day, Monday through Friday, from 9am to 4pm.
Worst Time: Sunday morning, when everybody is asleep.

This is the precinct of the Université de Paris (known for its most famous constituent, the Sorbonne), where students meet and fall in love over coffee and croissants. Rabelais named it the *quartier Latin* after the students and the professors who spoke Latin in the classroom and on the streets. The sector teems with belly dancers, exotic restaurants, sidewalk cafés, bookstalls, *caveaux,* and *clochards* and *chiffonniers* (bums and ragpickers).

A good starting point for your tour is:

1. **Place St-Michel** (Métro: Pont St-Michel), where Balzac used to get water from the fountain when he was a youth. This center was the scene of much Resistance fighting in the summer of 1944. The quarter centers around:

2. **Boulevard St-Michel** to the south, which the students call "boul Mich." From place St-Michel, with your back to the Seine, turn left down:

3. **Rue de la Huchette,** the setting of Elliot Paul's *The Last Time I Saw Paris.* Paul first wandered into this typical street "on a soft summer evening, and entirely by chance," in 1923. Although much has changed since his time, some of the buildings are so old that they have to be propped up by timbers. Paul captured

the spirit of the street more evocatively than anyone, writing of "the delivery wagons, makeshift vehicles propelled by pedaling boys, pushcarts of itinerant vendors, knife-grinders, umbrella menders, a herd of milk goats, and the neighborhood pedestrians." The local bordello has closed, however. Branching off from this street to your left is:

4. **Rue du Chat-qui-Pêche** (Street of the Cat Who Fishes), said to be the shortest, narrowest street in the world, containing not one door and only one window. It's usually filled with garbage or lovers—or both.

Now, retrace your steps toward place St-Michel and turn left at the intersection with rue de la Harpe, which leads to rue St-Séverin. At the intersection, take a left to see the:

5. **Church of St-Séverin** (see Chapter 6 for details). After a visit to this flamboyant Gothic church, go back to rue St-Séverin and follow it to rue Galande. Stay on rue Galande until you reach the:

6. **Church of St-Julien-le-Pauvre.** First stand at the gateway and look at the beginning of rue Galande, especially the old houses with the steeples of St-Séverin rising across the way—one of the most characteristic and most painted scenes on the Left Bank. Enter the courtyard and you'll be in medieval Paris. The garden to the left of the entrance offers the best view of Notre-Dame.

Everyone from Rabelais to Thomas Aquinas has passed through the doors of this church. Prior to the 6th century a chapel stood on this spot. The present structure goes back to the Longport monks, who began work on it in 1170 (making it the oldest existing church in Paris). In 1655 it was given to the Hôtel Dieu, and in time it became a small warehouse for salt. In 1889 it was given to the followers of the Melchite Greek rite, a branch of the Byzantine church.

REFUELING STOP At 14 rue St-Julien-le-Pauvre, **7. The Tea Caddy** (tel. 43-54-15-56) is perhaps one of the most charming tea salons in Paris (see Chapter 5 for details). It serves light lunches, salads, omelets, quiches, and, of course, tea.

Return to rue Galande. Turn left at the intersection with rue St-Séverin. Continue on until you reach rue St-Jacques, then turn left and follow it to boulevard St-Germain. Turn right onto this boulevard and follow it until you reach rue de Cluny. Turn left and follow the street to the entrance to the:

8. **Musée de Cluny** (see Chapter 6 for details). Even if you're rushed, take time out to see the *Lady and the Unicorn* tapestry. After your visit to the Cluny Museum, exit onto boulevard St-Michel, but instead of heading right back to place St-Michel, turn left, and walk down to place de la Sorbonne and the:

9. **Sorbonne,** which is what everyone calls the Université de Paris, one of the most famous academic institutions in the world. Founded in the 13th century, it had become the most prestigious university in the West by the 14th century, drawing such professors as Thomas Aquinas, and was subsequently reorganized by Napoléon in 1806.

At first glance from place de la Sorbonne, it seems architecturally undistinguished. In truth, it was rather indiscriminately reconstructed at the turn of the century. The same cannot be said for the:

Church ⛪

10. **Church of the Sorbonne** (Métro: St-Michel), built in 1635 by Le Mercier, which contains the marble tomb of Cardinal Richelieu, a work by Girardon based on a design by Le Brun. At his feet is the remarkable statue *Learning in Tears*.

From the church take rue Victor-Cousin south to the intersection with rue Soufflot. Turn left. At the end of this street lies place du Panthéon and the:

11. **Panthéon** (see Chapter 6). Sitting atop Mont Ste-Genieviève, this nonreligious temple is the final resting place of such distinguished figures as Hugo, Zola, Rousseau, and Voltaire.

WALKING TOUR 4 — Les Grands Boulevards

Start: Place de la Madeleine.
Finish: Place Vendôme.
Time: 2 hours, not counting stops; it's a 2-mile trek.
Best Time: Monday through Friday from 10am to 5pm, when the shops are open.
Worst Time: Rush hours.

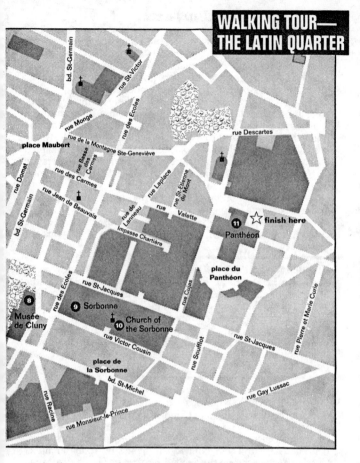

Map labels: bd. St-Germain · rue St-Victor · rue des Ecoles · rue Monge · rue Descartes · rue de la Montagne Ste-Geneviève · **place Maubert** · rue Basse des Carmes · rue des Carmes · rue Domat · bd. St-Germain · rue Jean de Beauvais · rue Laplace · rue St-Etienne du Mont · rue de Lanneau · rue Valette · Impasse Chartière · rue des Ecoles · rue St-Jacques · rue Cujas · ☆ **finish here** · **11** Panthéon · **place du Panthéon** · **8** Musée de Cluny · **9** Sorbonne · **10** Church of the Sorbonne · rue Victor Cousin · **place de la Sorbonne** · bd. St-Michel · rue Soufflot · rue St-Jacques · rue Pierre et Marie Curie · rue St-Jacques · rue Gay Lussac · rue Racine · rue Monsieur-le-Prince

Once there was nothing more fashionable than dining at a restaurant along one of the *grands boulevards*. They became chic in the mid-18th century, reached a pinnacle with the carriage trade, but were later abandoned in favor of the Champs-Elysées. Stretching from the Church of the Madeleine to Baron Haussmann's place de la République, the boulevards are lined with many fine department stores and shops.

The promenade begins at the Madeleine, one of the most imposing Grecian-inspired temples in the world.

1. La Madeleine Church stands right in the heart of the Right Bank on the landmark "place de la Madeleine." Actually, "La Madeleine" is a nickname—the church is dedicated to St. Mary Magdalene. An old, small parish church of the area was torn down, and construction of the new one began in 1764 but was stopped by the French Revolution. During Napoléon's reign, several projects from different architects were drawn up—one of them planned to build "The Temple of Glory," honoring the "Grande Armée." Finally a church was erected on the same place with the same frame as formerly. It opened in 1842. The building resembles a huge Greek temple ringed with a Corinthian colonnade, its columns holding up an encircling frieze (one of the pediments depicts the Last Judgment). Bas-reliefs on the bronze door represent the Ten Commandments, and in niches along the facade are statues of saints. From the portal you have a panoramic vista down rue Royale to the Egyptian obelisk and through place de la Concorde up to the Palace of the Assemblée Nationale. Inside the church, a trio of skylit domes illuminates the central nave, the gilded globe lanterns, and the inlaid marble floors. Have a look at the chapel, left of the door entrance, where you will find the *Baptism of Jesus,* by Rude (who sculpted the famous *Marseillaise* on the Arc de Triomphe. Concerts are staged here at least once a month (tel. 42-65-52-17 for information).

Boulevard de la Madeleine turns into boulevard des Capucines, where, at the:

2. Hôtel Scribe, at no. 14, a plaque honors those pioneers of the cinema, the Lumière brothers, who launched their films on December 28, 1895.

REFUELING STOP If you're ready for a snack, stop at **3. Café de la Paix,** 12 boulevard des Capucines. During the liberation of Paris, the Yanks practically established a beachhead at this world-famous "watering hole" across from American Express, and they've been firmly entrenched ever since. The long parade has included everybody from Harry Truman to the chanteuse Josephine Baker. Teas, breakfasts, and apéritifs are your best choices at what has been called the "factory of *la vie parisienne.*"

The tour now leads to place de l'Opéra, and its:

4. Opéra ✪, which is no longer the musical center of Paris (the opera at the Bastille now has that honor), but it is still a showcase for ballet and concerts. Walk around the entire building to enjoy its magnificence. Inside you'll find memorabilia of such great dancers as Pavlova and Nijinsky. Designed by young architect Charles Garnier during the Second Empire, its facade is adorned with marble and sculptures, including *The Dance* by Carpeaux. (The present version is a copy; the original is in the Louvre.) At one time or another, most of the great, glittering personages of Europe, including Henry James and "the divine Sarah" (Bernhardt), have descended the wide marble steps of the Grand Staircase. The auditorium's dome was decorated by Chagall in 1964.

To walk around the Opéra, take rue Halévy to rue Gluck, which leads into place Diagilev, opening onto boulevard Haussmann. To head back, take rue Scribe, bypassing the offices of American Express on your right, then rue Auber. Then head down rue de la Paix, which intersects with rue Daunou.

REFUELING STOP Ready to rest your feet? **5. Harry's Bar,** 5 rue Daunou (see Chapter 9), has always been the place where Americans, along with a parade of world celebrities, have gone to drink. It is said that the 1920s roared louder here than anywhere else. Eisenhower made it his "second headquarters," and Gershwin worked on *An American in Paris* here. Have a drink and soak up some of the atmosphere.

WALKING TOUR—LES GRANDS BOULEVARDS

0 150 m
0 160 y

N

PARIS

Les Grands
Boulevards

❶ La Madeleine Church
❷ Hôtel Scribe
❸ Café de la Paix
❹ Opéra
❺ Harry's Bar
❻ Place Vendôme

Rue de la Paix honored Napoléon before its name was changed. Dating from 1806, the boulevard today is one of the most gilded shopping streets of the world. Each jewelry store, notably Cartier at no. 11, seems to offer a king's ransom of gems. Continue along rue de la Paix and eventually reach your final stop:

6. Place Vendôme ✪ (Métro: Opéra). Always aristocratic, sometimes royal, place Vendôme enjoyed its golden age during the Second Empire. Dress designers—the great ones, such as Worth—introduced the crinoline there. Louis Napoléon lived here, wooing his future empress at the Hôtel du Rhin. In its halcyon days the waltzes of Strauss echoed across the plaza.

Today banks and offices abound, but the most prestigious tenant on the plaza is the Ritz. Place Vendôme is one of the most harmonious squares in France, evoking the Paris of *le grand siècle*—that is, the age of Louis XIV. Originally planned by Mansart to honor Louis XIV, the square contained a statue of the Sun King until the Revolution, when it was replaced briefly by

Liberty. Today it's dominated by a column crowned by Napoléon, erected to celebrate his victory at Austerlitz. It was made of bronze melted from captured Russian and Austrian cannons. After Napoléon's downfall the statue was replaced by one of Henri IV, everybody's favorite king and every woman's favorite man. Later Napoléon surmounted it once again, this time in uniform and without the pose of a Caesar.

The Communards of 1871, who detested royalty and the false promises of emperors, pulled down the statue. They were allegedly led by the artist Courbet, who was jailed and fined the cost of restoring the statue. He couldn't pay it, of course, and was forced into exile in Switzerland. Eventually, the statue of Napoléon, wrapped in a Roman toga, won out. The plaza is one of the best known in Paris. It has attracted such tenants as Chopin, who lived at no. 12 until his death in 1849.

But who was Vendôme, you ask? He was the son (delicate writers refer to him as "the natural son") of the roving Henri IV and his best-known mistress, Gabrielle d'Estrées.

WALKING TOUR 5 —— The Louvre in 2 Hours

Start: Louvre Pyramid.
Finish: Apollo Gallery.
Metro Station: Louvre.
Best Time: 9:45am, when it opens.
Worst Times: Noon to 2pm, when some rooms close for lunch; after 3pm any day; and on Tuesday, when it's closed.

You might think it's impossible to visit the Louvre in just two hours, but some visitors don't have any more time. To do this tour, wear a pair of comfortable shoes and be prepared to walk quickly.

The Louvre started with only 12 paintings, but now it has 400,000 works of art—too many to display. The Louvre divides its art into six or seven major categories. Its greatest collections are paintings and classical sculpture, so a first-time, two-hour viewer may want to concentrate on these and save the others for another day.

Enter through the dramatic new Pyramid. Begin at the:
1. **Galerie Daru** for a brief look at the Greek and Roman antiquities, passing the Escalier Daru to enter the:
2. **Salle du Parthénon.** You will now be in the southwest corner of the old palace. The frieze on the rear wall is an original fragment from one of the world's most famous buildings, the Parthenon, originally built by the Athenians between 447 and 438 B.C. In Room 9 stands the:
3. **Venus de Milo,** one of the three great "ladies of the Louvre." Dating from the 2nd century B.C., she is a masterpiece of Hellenistic design in all her serene beauty. The statue was discovered in 1820 in a cave on the Greek island of Melos.
   Head now to Room 14, the:
4. **Salle des Caryatides (Caryatid Gallery),** with replicas of 4th-century B.C. and Hellenistic works. Once the great hall of the old palace (built for Henri II), it now houses masterpieces of

WALKING TOUR — THE LOUVRE IN 2 HOURS

FIRST FLOOR

GROUND FLOOR

PARIS

The Louvre

1. Galerie Daru
2. Salle du Parthénon
3. Venus de Milo
4. Salle des Caryatides (Caryatid Gallery)
5. Nike of Samothrace
6. Salle Carré
7. Grande Galerie
8. Salle des Etats
9. Galerie d'Apollon

sculpture. Look especially for *Diana of Versailles,* a copy of a work from the 4th-century B.C., and the *Venus of Arles.* See also *Hermes Fastening his Sandal.* Return to the Escalier Daru. On this landing towers the:

5. **Nike of Samothrace,** or *Winged Victory,* the second major attraction of the Louvre. The headless *Winged Victory* (dating from between 300 and 200 B.C.) spreading her wings at the top of the main staircase is the world's most famous farewell to arms.

Take the monumental staircase to the first floor. There, go through the Salles Percier et Fontaine and the Salle Duchâtel to enter the:

6. **Salon Carré,** where the wedding feast of Marie-Louise and Napoléon took place in 1819. The paintings section is arranged in chronological order and divided into schools. Now go along the corridors of the:

7. **Grande Galerie,** a room the size of three football fields. In the eastern section of the gallery is a stunning display of the works of 17th- and 18th-century French artists. The Italian masterpieces hang at the western end. There, you'll see works by such masters as Cimabue and Giotto.

To the right, adjoining the Grande Galerie (just follow the crowds), is the:

8. **Salle des Etats** ✪, containing great masterpieces of Italian art, including the most famous of all, *La Gioconda* (1506), or *Mona Lisa* as she's known. Once stolen, this is the world's most famous painting, and it's under glass.

The salle also contains four other great works by da Vinci: *Virgin of the Rocks, Virgin and Child with St. Anne, St. John the Baptist,* and *La Belle Ferronnière.* See Veronese's *Marriage at Cana,* which incorporates 130 portraits in one painting, plus works by Titian, including *Man with a Glove.*

If you can tear yourself from the enigmatic smile of *La Gioconda,* wander back to the Grande Galerie. Continue along the corridors until you reach the western sector, where you'll be dazzled by one Italian masterpiece after another—too many, frankly, to even comprehend in such a short visit. Study five or six that especially appeal to you.

Return to the Salon Carré. Before leaving the Louvre, wander into the adjoining:

9. **Galerie d'Apollon** for a look at the crown jewels of France. Built during the reign of Henri IV, the gallery is a *grand siècle* backdrop for a stunning display of jewels, including the 137-carat Regent diamond, which was purchased from England by the duke of Orléans in 1717, and the 105-carat Côte-de-Bretagne ruby.

CHAPTER 8

SAVVY SHOPPING

1. THE SHOPPING SCENE

2. SHOPPING A TO Z

Should you buy anything in Paris? Are there any good buys? Is there any item here that you can't find back home?

Yes, there are items unique to France that are not easily found in America, and there is also the joy of bringing "something back from Paris," a reminder of your stay— memories of strolling along one of the chic boulevards of Paris, browsing in the smart boutiques, and finally, purchasing a scarf or handbag.

1. THE SHOPPING SCENE

BEST BUYS

Perfumes in Paris are almost always cheaper than in the States. That means all the famous brands—Guerlain, Chanel, Schiaparelli, Jean Patou. Cosmetics bearing French names, such as Dior and Lancôme, also cost less. Gloves, too, are a fine value.

Paris, with the possible exception of London, is stocked with more antiques and "curios" than any city of Europe. Of course, many visitors come to Paris just to shop for fashion. From Chanel to Yves St. Laurent, from Nina Ricci to Sonia Rykiel, the city literally overflows with fashion boutiques ranging from haute couture to daringly modern dress. Likewise, going hand in glove, fashion accessories in Paris are among the finest and best designed in the world. If you don't believe me, then ask Louis Vuitton or perhaps Celine. French lingerie may be every woman's dream. The top lingerie designers sell in Paris. Galeries Lafayette and Printemps have large sections.

AIRPORT TAX-FREE BOUTIQUES

You are better off buying certain products in the airport. In the duty-free shops at Orly and Charles de Gaulle airports, you will get a minimum discount of 20% on all items, and up to 50% on liquor, cigarettes, and watches. Among the items on sale are crystal, cutlery, chocolates, luggage, wine, whiskey, pipes and lighters, lingerie, silk scarves, perfume, knitwear, jewelry, cameras and equipment, cheeses, and antiques.

The drawbacks of airport shopping are that the selections are limited, and of course, you must carry your purchase with you onto the plane.

BUSINESS HOURS, TAXES & CUSTOMS

BUSINESS HOURS Shops are *usually* open Tuesday through Saturday from 9am to 7pm, but the hours can vary greatly. Small shops sometimes take a two-hour lunch break. The flea market and some other street markets are open on Saturday, Sunday, and Monday. That intriguing sign on shop doors reading *Entree Libre* means you may browse at will. *Soldes* means "sale." *Soldes Exceptionelles* means they're pushing it a bit.

TAX REFUNDS If you've been in the country less than six months, you are entitled to a refund on the value-added tax (VAT) on purchases made in France to take home—under certain conditions. These export discounts range from 20% to 30%, but it depends on the item purchased, of course. The *détaxe*, or refund, is allowed on purchases of goods costing more than 1,200F ($222) in a single store, but it's not automatic. For United Kingdom residents and Common Market citizens, the figure is almost 2,400F ($444). Food, wine, and tobacco don't count, and the refund is only granted on purchases you carry with you out of the country, not on merchandise you have shipped back home.

Here's what you must do:

Show the clerk your passport to prove you're eligible for the refund. You will then be given an export sales document in triplicate (two pink sheets and a green one), which you must sign. You'll also be given an envelope addressed to the store. Go early to your departure point, as there are sometimes queues waiting at the booth marked "Detaxé" at French Customs. If you're traveling by train, go to the detaxé area in the station before boarding. You can't get your refund documents processed on the train. The refund booths are outside the passport checkpoints, so you must take care of that business before you proceed with the passport check.

Only the person who signed the documents at the store can present them for the refund. Give the three sheets to the Customs official, who will countersign and hand you back the green copy. Save this in case problems arise about the refund. Give the official the envelope addressed to the store (be sure to put a stamp on the envelope). One of the processed pink copies will be mailed to the store for you. Usually you will be reimbursed by check in convertible French francs sent by mail to your home; sometimes the payment is made to a credit-card account. In some cases, you may get your refund immediately, paid at an airport bank window. If you don't receive your tax refund in four months, write to the store, giving the date of purchase and the location where the sheets were given to Customs officials. Include a photocopy of your green refund sheet.

U.S. CUSTOMS You're allowed to bring back into the United States overseas purchases with a retail value of $400, providing you have been out of the country at least 48 hours and you must have claimed no similar exemptions within 30 days. After your duty-free $400 is exceeded, a tax of 10% is levied on the next $1,000 worth of items purchased abroad.

You pay no duty on antiques or art, if such items are 100 years old or more, even if they cost $4 million or more. In addition, you're allowed to send one gift a day to family or friends back home, providing its value does not exceed $50. Perfumes costing more than $5, liquor, cigarettes, and cigars can't be sent duty-free.

SHIPPING IT HOME There are restrictions on what merchandise can be shipped. Customs regulations change, so when in doubt it's best to check before you buy so that your purchase doesn't show up on a "prohibited" list.

If you buy something at a Parisian department store or an upscale boutique, ask the clerk about reliable shippers. Most major hotel desks in Paris also maintain up-to-date lists of shipping companies. Many shoppers even talk to their local shipping companies before they go. Remember, however, that there is always some degree of risk involved in shipping goods.

Check with the shipper in Paris to make sure you understand the arrangement that you've made, and ask about insurance. Don't forget to ask about duties and clearance fees in your home country, what kind of packing will be used, and whether there will be any warehouse penalties if you can't pick up the item right away.

2. SHOPPING A TO Z

ANTIQUES

LA COUR AUX ANTIQUAIRES, 54 rue du Faubourg St-Honoré, 8e. Tel. 42-66-58-77.
Near the Elysée Palace is an elegant Right Bank arcade frequented by the most discerning Parisians and international designers. At some 18 shops you can peruse the offerings, including antiques, paintings, and objets d'art (usually from the 16th to the 20th century). The complex also prints a catalogue. **Open:** Mon 2–7pm, Tues–Sat 10:30am–7pm. **Métro:** place de la Concorde.

LE LOUVRE DES ANTIQUAIRES, 2 place du Palais-Royal, 1er. Tel. 42-97-27-00.
The largest antique center in Europe attracts collectors, browsers, and those interested in everything from Russian icons to 19th-century furniture to art deco. The center stands across from a giant parking lot beside the Louvre. Housing some 240 dealers, the showrooms are spread across 2½ acres of well-lit modern salons. The building, a former department store, was erected in 1852, according to Napoléon's plans for the rue de Rivoli. Down an enormous flight of skylit stairs, past a café and reception area, you enter the inner sanctum where you find the dealers operating. **Open:** Tues–Sun 11am–7pm. **Métro:** Louvre.

THE VILLAGE SUISSE, 78 av. de Suffren, 15e, and 54 av. de la Motte-Picquet, 15e. Tel. 43-06-69-90.
This is a vast Left Bank complex of 200 antiques shops and boutiques. Parisian interior decorators frequent the gallery for their wealthy clients, looking for oil paintings, silver, copper, pewter, or antique furniture from all major periods and styles. Bargain hunters should look elsewhere. **Métro:** La Motte-Picquet–Grenelle.

ART

CARNAVALETTE, 2 rue des Francs-Bourgeois, 3e. Tel. 42-72-91-02.
Carnavalette is just off place des Vosges in the Marais. It sells unusual, one-of-a-kind engravings, plus a large collection of satirical 19th-century magazines and newspapers. **Métro:** St-Paul.

GALERIE DOCUMENTS, 53 rue de Seine, 6e. Tel. 43-54-50-68.

Galerie Documents contains one of the most original collections of old posters (1870–1930) in Paris. Many are inexpensive, although you could easily pay dearly for an original. The store will mail your poster home. **Métro:** Odéon.

GALERIE 27, 27 rue de Seine, 6e. Tel. 43-54-78-54.

Galerie 27 sells lithographs by some of the most famous artists of the early 20th century, including Picasso. The inventory ranges from art posters selling for 50F ($9.25) each to original paintings by Chagall, Miró, Picasso, and Léger. **Métro:** St-Germain-des-Prés.

MAEGHT EDITEUR & ADRIEN MAEGHT GALLERY, 42 rue du Bac, 7e. Tel. 45-48-31-01.

This gallery has an interesting collection of posters and pictorial books by important artists, such as Matisse. Exhibits include modern sculpture and engravings by established and unknown artists. **Métro:** rue-du-Bac.

ART NOUVEAU & ART DECO ACCESSORIES

SCHMOCK BROC, 15 rue Racine, 6e. Tel. 46-33-79-98.

Mlle Clément Nadine, one of the city's leading collectors of the increasingly fashionable art nouveau and art deco accessories, runs this specialty shop. Her boutique is on the Left Bank near the Théâtre de l'Odéon. The glorious, more flamboyant world of yesterday comes alive here, as you explore the collection of jewelry, lighting fixtures, whatever the owner herself has discovered on her frequent shopping expeditions. **Open:** Tues–Sat 9:30am–6pm. **Métro:** Odéon.

BATH FIXTURES

RAYMOND, 100 rue du Faubourg St-Honoré, 8e. Tel. 42-66-69-49.

Near the Elysée Palace is one of the principal outlets for Porcelaine de Paris in the city. And if you're shopping for what might be the most elegant bathroom fixtures in the world, including basins and faucets fashioned from hand-painted porcelain, they have it here. They'll mail your purchases anywhere in the world. **Open:** Tues–Fri 9:30am–6:30pm, Sat 9:30am–12:30pm and 2–6:30pm. **Closed:** Aug. **Métro:** Concorde or Champs-Élysées–Clemenceau.

BOOKS

THE ABBEY BOOKSHOP, 29 rue de la Parchemin, 5e. Tel. 46-33-16-24.

An offshoot of the Abbey Bookshop of Toronto, this Left Bank shop specializes in works of Canadian writers. Browse through new and used books while sipping complimentary tea or coffee. The shop also specializes in high-quality hardcovers dealing with history, politics, literature, and philosophy. **Métro:** St-Michel.

BRENTANO'S, 37 av. de l'Opéra, 2e. Tel. 42-61-52-50.

Brentano's is one of the leading English-language bookstores in Paris, offering guides, maps, novels, and nonfiction. **Métro:** Opéra.

W.H. SMITH & SON, 248 rue de Rivoli, 1er. Tel. 42-60-37-97.

Books, magazines, and newspapers published in the English-speaking world are widely available. You can get the *Times* of London, of course, and the *New York Times* is available every Monday. You'll find many American magazines, too. There's a fine selection of maps if you plan to do much touring. Across from the Tuileries, W. H. Smith also has excellent reference books, language books, and a special children's section. **Open:** Mon–Sat 9:30am–7:30pm. **Métro:** Concorde.

CHAMPAGNE

MAISON DU CHAMPAGNE, 48 rue des Belles Feuilles, 16e. Tel. 47-27-58-23.
All Paris lines up outside to buy its holiday bubbly. In addition to more than 90 labels of champagne, the shop has rare and fine burgundies and Bordeaux dating back to the turn of the century, as well as cognacs and armagnacs from the 19th century, plus Eau de Vie. Owner-connoisseur Charles Delmare will guide you in your selection. **Open:** Tues–Sat 10am–1pm and 3–8pm. **Métro:** Victor-Hugo or Dauphine.

CHINA, SILVER, GLASSWARE & CRYSTAL

BACCARAT, 30 bis, rue de Paradis, 10e. Tel. 47-70-64-30.
Purveyor to kings and presidents of France since 1764, Baccarat produces world-renowned full-lead crystal requested by and created for perfectionists. A visit here is worth the time, even for visitors not intending to purchase. There is a museum of the company's most historic models on premises. **Open:** Mon–Fri 9am–6pm, Sat 10am–noon and 2–5pm. **Métro:** Château d'Eau, Poissonière, or Gare de l'Est.

GALERIE D'AMON, 28 rue St-Sulpice, 6e. Tel. 43-26-96-60.
Just off the Luxembourg Gardens and the Church of St-Sulpice, the Amon Gallery has a permanent exhibition of glasswork, with a wide range of items from France and abroad. Madeleine and Jean-Pierre Maffre display items in blown glass, blown engraved glass, molded glass, and paperweights by top artisans. **Open:** Tues–Sat 11am–7pm. **Métro:** Odéon.

AU GRAND SIECLE, 31 rue La Boétie, 8e. Tel. 45-63-25-96.
Au Grand Siècle is a small, elegant shop filled to the brim with antique and reproduction furniture, silver, and crystal, especially Daum, Baccarat, and Swarovski. There is a splendid collection of lamps and small gifts. Lladró porcelain is also sold here. No low-price merchandise is offered, but it is a memorable shopping experience. **Open:** Summer Mon–Fri 9:30am–6:30pm; off season Mon noon–6:30pm, Tues–Sat 9:30am–6:30pm. **Métro:** Miromesnil.

LALIQUE, 11 rue Royale, 8e. Tel. 42-65-33-70.
Directed today by the granddaughter of the original founder, René Lalique, a silversmith who launched the shop during the belle époque, Lalique is known around the world for its glass sculpture and decorative lead crystal. The shop sells a wide range of merchandise at

prices slightly lower than the celestial prices charged abroad. **Open:** Mon–Sat 9:30am–noon and 2–6:30pm, Tues–Fri 9:30am–6:30pm. **Métro:** Concorde.

LIMOGES-UNIC, 12 and 58 rue de Paradis, 10e. Tel. 47-70-54-49.

There's a wide stock of Limoges china such as Ceralane, Haviland, and Bernardaud, as well as Villeroy & Boch, Hermès, Dior, Lanvin, Lalique, Daum, St. Louis, and Sèvres crystal, Christofle & Ercuis silverware, and many other items for table decoration. **Open:** Mon–Sat 10am–6:30pm. **Métro:** Gare de l'Est or Poissonnière.

CHOCOLATE

DALLOYAU, 99–101 rue du Faubourg St-Honoré, 8e. Tel. 43-59-18-10.

When it was established in 1802, the newly rich bourgeoisie of Paris rushed to its doorstep to enjoy the luscious chocolate suddenly flooding the market from France's colonial plantations. Today, still very much in business, the shop can ship its chocolates, elegantly packaged, anywhere you specify. In addition to a variety of chocolates in a bewildering array of sweetnesses, it sells pastries, petits-fours, and cakes. The shop is located near some of the most fashionable clothing stores in Europe, provoking endless calorie-induced guilt from the appearance-conscious women browsing through the shops nearby. **Open:** Daily 9am–9pm. **Métro:** Champs-Elysées–Clemenceau.

LA MAISON DU CHOCOLAT, 225 rue du Faubourg St-Honoré, 8e. Tel. 42-27-39-44.

Racks and racks of chocolates are priced individually or by the kilo. Each is made from a blend of as many as six different kinds of South American and African chocolate, and flavorings include just about everything imaginable. Chocolate pastries are also sold. Everything here is made in the super-modern facilities in the establishment's cellars before being sent up on an old-fashioned dumbwaiter. **Open:** Mon–Sat 9:30am–7pm. **Closed:** Aug. **Métro:** Ternes.

CRAFTS

BOUTIQUE DU MUSÉE DES ARTS DECORATIFS, 107 rue de Rivoli, 1er. Tel. 42-61-04-02.

This boutique connected with the Musée des Arts Decoratifs offers a variety of handsome household goods, some of them exact copies of items displayed in the museum. Craftspeople have copied faïence, molded crystal, art nouveau jewelry, porcelain boxes, scarves, and other items of fine workmanship and great beauty. There is no charge for admission, and you can find interesting items in low to expensive price ranges. **Open:** Daily 10:30am–6:30pm. **Métro:** Palais-Royal or Tuileries.

LE PRINTEMPS, 64 bd. Haussmann, 9e. Tel. 42-82-50-00.

In addition to its other merchandise, Le Printemps (see "Department Stores," below) offers one of the largest selections of handcrafts in Paris. **Métro:** Havre-Caumartin.

TROUSSELIER, 73 bd. Haussmann, 8e. Tel. 42-66-97-95.

Trousselier is a century old. At first you'll think it's simply a florists shop, with some artfully displayed sprays. But look again or touch—

and you'll see that every flower is artificial, shaped in silk and hand-painted by people who pursue this famous French craft in the workshops in the rear. And what exquisite work! Everything is lifelike in the extreme. One cluster will bear a bud, a full-blown flower, and then one just past its prime and fading at the edges. The prices reflect the high quality. **Open:** Mon 2–6pm, Tues–Sat 10am–6pm. **Métro:** Havre-Caumartin.

DEPARTMENT STORES

GALERIES LAFAYETTE, 40 bd. Haussmann, 9e. Tel. 42-82-34-56.

⭐ A landmark in the Parisian fashion world and a beautiful example of the city's belle époque architecture, Galeries Lafayette is one of the leading department stores of the world. A special entrance marked "Welcome" brings you to English-speaking hosts available to assist you with your shopping needs. The department store includes the Galfa Club men's store, Lafayette Sports, and the main store, featuring the latest in international fashion designs, unusual gifts, perfumes, and quality housewares. Finish your shopping day with an exceptional view of Paris on the Galeries Lafayette rooftop terrace. **Open:** Mon–Sat 9:30am–6:45pm. **Métro:** Chaussée d'Antin or Opéra. **RER:** Auber.

LE PRINTEMPS, 64 bd. Haussmann, 9e. Tel. 42-82-50-00.

The city's largest department store actually consists of three stores connected by bridges on the second and third floors. Go to Brummell for clothing for men, both sports and dress. Printemps de la Maison is mainly for records and books, furniture, and housewares, while Printemps de la Mode sells clothes for women, young people, and children. The ground floor is mainly for perfume, cosmetics, gifts, and Paris handcrafts. The perfumery at Printemps is one of the largest in Paris, maybe the largest.

Interpreters stationed at the Welcome Service in the basement will help you claim your discounts, find departments, and make purchases. International customers are also invited to one of the store's fashion shows held under the historic 1923 glass dome every Tuesday at 10:15am throughout the year, every Tuesday and Friday at 10:15am from March through October. **Open:** Mon–Sat 9:30am–6:30pm. **Métro:** Havre-Caumartin.

LA SAMARITAINE, 19 rue de la Monnaie, 1er. Tel. 40-41-20-20.

A much more economical and family-oriented department store is La Samaritaine. It has a little bit of everything—and some good clothing buys. A restaurant on the premises serves meals Monday through Saturday from 11:30am to 3pm. **Open:** Mon, Wed, and Fri–Sat 9:30am–7pm; Tues and Thurs 9:30am–8:30pm. **Métro:** Pont-Neuf.

DISCOUNT SHOPPING

Paris no longer caters to just the well-heeled in its boutiques. Many formerly high-priced items are often on sale at tabs cut from 20% to 40% of their original price when displayed in a store along the Champs-Elysées. Several shops have opened that offer leftover merchandise from some of the better-known fashion houses. Of course, the famous labels have been cut out, but it's still the same clothing.

Discount houses tend to be crowded, often bustling, and a bit rushed. At each of the following stores, however, at least one of the employees speaks English.

ANNA LOWE, 35 av. Matignon, 8e. Tel. 43-59-96-61.

This is considered the premier boutique in Paris for the discriminating woman who wishes to purchase high-quality clothing—but at discount prices. The boutique lies only half a block from rue du Faubourg St-Honoré, where haute couture is much more expensively priced. All items sold by Anna Lowe (a former model herself) have the designer's label still attached, including Chanel, Valentino, Givenchy, and Guy Laroche. Prices are often half the normal selling price of a garment. The merchandise does not contain factory rejects or seconds. Some of the clothing is models' samples. Alterations are done for a nominal price, often within two or three days. **Open:** Tues–Sat 9:30am–6pm. **Métro:** Concorde.

AU FIL DE LAURE, 7 rue Sedillot, 7e. Tel. 47-05-46-31.

Originally established by a woman named Laura in the early 1980s, this is one of Paris's most famous boutiques for secondhand dresses. Many have been worn only once or twice. Dresses, sold *with the tickets and labels intact,* are arranged by countries or designer rather than by size. There are about 1,400 dresses in stock, many formal, designed by such luminaries as Saint-Laurent, Ungaro, Lanvin, Nina Ricci, and Scherrer. Don't expect it to be terribly well organized, but with an open imagination, a stylish woman with flexible tastes can have a lot of fun. **Métro:** Ecole-Militaire.

MENDES (SAINT-LAURENT), 65 rue Montmartre, 2e. Tel. 42-36-83-32.

Mendès (Saint-Laurent) is where many of the fashion-conscious, but also budget-conscious, women of Paris come to buy ready-to-wear lines of Saint-Laurent called "sportswear." Sometimes discounts on "last season's" clothing average as much as 50%. There are no dressing rooms, no alterations, and no exchanges or refunds, but that doesn't prevent a battalion of determined women from buying clothes from the winter collection at reduced prices after the middle of January. Clothes from the summer collection become available after mid-July. All of the activity takes place on two floors of a building at the edge of the garment district. **Open:** Mon–Thur 9:30am–5:30pm, Fri–Sat 9:30am–4:30pm. **Métro:** Les Halles.

MOUTON A CINQ PATTES, 8 rue St-Placide, 6e. Tel. 45-48-86-26.

Located in the Montparnasse area, Mouton à Cinq Pattes has another outlet in the St-Germain neighborhood at 19 rue Grégoire-de-Tours, 6e (tel. 43-29-73-56), both offering heavily discounted creations of several well-known women's designers, usually with their labels removed.

A few storefronts away from the first of these, you'll find a similar system for men's clothing, with comparable discounts. It's under the same management and called **Annexe,** 48 rue St-Placide, 6e (tel. 45-48-86-26). The management also maintains a branch for children, **Le Mouton à Cinq Pattes pour Enfants** at 10 rue St-Placide (tel. 45-48-86-26). Here, designer garments, *sans etiquettes,* for toddlers and pre-teenagers are sold in imaginative combinations at discounted prices.

The rock-bottom cheapest of the stores in this mini-chain is the **Mouton à Cinq Pattes** at 18 rue St-Placide, 6e (tel. 45-44-83-25), where even the goods on sale are on sale. These garments might have been somewhat "picked over," but you'll find clothes priced low, a price almost certain to whisk them off the racks within one week.

Open: Mon 2–7pm, Tues–Sat 10am–7pm (same store hours for all). **Métro:** (for the all stores mentioned above): Mabillon or Odéon.

FASHION

FOR CHILDREN

BASTIEN-BASTIENNE, 87 rue de Ranelagh, 16e. Tel. 45-27-09-09.
This store sells exclusively children's clothes for boys and girls ages 1 day to 14 years. Tennis clothes, tennis shoes (by the famous French-based children's manufacturer Chipie), and formal wear are on sale here. **Métro:** Ranelagh.

BONPOINT, 15 rue Royale, 8e. Tel. 47-42-52-63.
Located near Maxim's, Bonpoint is part of a well-known haute couture chain for children. Clothing is well tailored—and very expensive. The shop sells clothes for boys and girls ages 1 day to 16 years. Its strongest inventories are in formal dresses, confirmation dresses, and the long and elegant baptism robes, embroidered in France and edged in lace. **Métro:** Concorde.

FOR WOMEN

CELINE, 24 rue François 1er, 8e. Tel. 47-20-22-83.
This is one of the best choices for ultraconservative, well-made clothes that Parisian women say almost never wear out. There's also a selection of elegant shoes and handbags. **Open:** Mon–Fri 9:30am–6:30pm. **Métro:** F.D. Roosevelt.

CHANEL, 31 rue Cambon, 1er. Tel. 42-86-28-00.
The spirit of Chanel lives on, and her shop across from the Ritz is more than ever in business with haute couture, a landmark design showcase of classical French fashion. Prices, of course, are celestial. The shop also sells accessories, perfumes, cosmetic lines, and watches. **Open:** Mon–Sat 10am–7pm. **Métro:** Concorde or Tuileries.

CHANEL, 42 av. Montaigne, 8e. Tel. 47-23-74-12.
For Chanel's ready-to-wear, which is more reasonably priced but still very expensive, try this shop. It is said that every woman—at least those who can afford it—should own a "basic Chanel," and that it will never go out of style. Accessories are also sold here. **Open:** Mon–Sat 9:30am–6:30pm. **Métro:** F.D. Roosevelt.

CHRISTIAN DIOR, 26–32 av. Montaigne, 8e. Tel. 40-73-54-44.
World-famous for its custom-made haute couture, Christian Dior has a wide selection of both women's and men's ready-to-wear, sportswear, and accessories, including separate salons for shoes and leather goods, furs, children's clothing, and a variety of gift items, genuine and costume jewelry, lighters, and pens, among other offerings. **Open:** Mon–Sat 10am–6pm. **Métro:** F.D. Roosevelt.

HERMES, 24 rue du Faubourg St-Honoré, 8e. Tel. 44-17-47-17.
Hermès is a legend, of course. The shop is especially noted for its scarves, made of silk squares that are printed with antique motifs.

Three well-known Hermès fragrances, two for women and one for men, make excellent gift choices.

The gloves sold here are without peer, especially those for men in reindeer hide, doeskin, or supple kid. The leather-goods store at Hermès is the best known in Europe. The craftspeople working on the premises turn out the Hermès handbag, an institution that needs no sales pitch on these pages. **Open:** Mon–Sat 10am–6:30pm. **Métro:** Concorde.

JOSEPHINE FISSE, 5 rue Clément-Marot, 8e. Tel. 47-23-45-27.

Near the corner of the avenue Montaigne is a super-chic, super-expensive boutique that carries the latest fashions of six of the most fashionable designers in France and Italy, including Sonia Rykiel. It is designed in a high-tech format. **Open:** Mon–Sat 10am–7pm. **Métro:** F.D. Roosevelt.

LANVIN, 22 rue du Faubourg St-Honoré, 8e. Tel. 47-63-80-21.

Lanvin specializes in women's fashions and accessories. On the second floor, Lanvin's marvelous haute couture dresses are presented in the house's salon. On the first floor, chic and contemporary *prêt-à-porter* (ready-to-wear) day and evening dresses and ensembles are to be found together with beautiful Lanvin shawls. **Open:** Tues–Fri 9:30am–6:30pm. **Métro:** Concorde.

AUX MUSES D'EUROPE, 64 rue de Seine, 6e. Tel. 43-26-89-63.

Aux Muses d'Europe offers antique lace dresses of rare beauty, as well as contemporary clothing (1900 to 1950) and accessories. With items collected from all over France by the mother-daughter team of Marguerite and Katia Belleville, the shop has appeared in nationwide television broadcasts in Japan and frequently welcomes actresses who need to dress in period costume. The shop is not large, but the clothing accessories, costume jewelry, bags, and gloves (1940 to 1950) are displayed on racks that reach the ceiling. Ask to see the lace-trimmed baby dresses as well. **Open:** Mon 2–7pm, Tues–Sat 11am–7pm. **Métro:** Odéon or St-Germain-des-Prés.

PIERRE CARDIN COUTURE, 27 av. Marigny, 8e. Tel. 42-66-92-25.

Pierre Cardin boutiques seem to pop up on every corner. The ready-to-wear styles for women range from conservative to ultra-modern. All the clothing, no matter what style, is extremely well made. The most expensive and original Cardin designs are displayed at Pierre Cardin Couture, 14 place François-1er, 8e (tel. 45-63-29-13). **Métro:** Champs-Elysées–Clemenceau.

SARA SHELBURNE, 10 rue du Cygne, 1er. Tel. 42-33-74-40.

Now that Les Halles is going through a rebirth, the produce market having long moved elsewhere, a growing number of fashionable boutiques have taken over, opening on the sidestreets. And Sara Shelburne is what happens when a law graduate switches to couture. This is a luxurious ready-made boutique for women, with colorful dresses, separates, hostess gowns, coats, knits, and sexy evening wear.

An interesting detail: Sara designs and makes most of her fabrics: machine-washable combed-wool knits and Egyptian cottons for daytime; dyed-to-match silks, velvets, and lace for evening. She will make garments to your measurements for the same price as ready-to-wear within two days. In addition to her one-of-a-kind wedding-dress department that attracts people from all over the world, Sara Shelburne has added a collection of handmade shoes coordinated with the colors of her clothes, in suede, leather, or covered in the same silk as a dress. **Open:** Mon–Sat 10am–7pm. **Métro:** Les Halles or Etienne Marcel.

FOR MEN

ALAIN FIGARET, 21 rue de la Paix, 2e. Tel. 42-65-04-99.
Alain Figaret has one of Paris's best selections of men's shirts. Although there is a broad range of fabrics, each shirt has the same classic appeal. The store prides itself on selling cotton (never silk) shirts and all-silk (never synthetic) neckties. They also sell men's underwear and elegant pajamas. **Métro:** Opéra.

CERRUTI, 1881, 27 rue Royale, 8e. Tel. 42-65-66-72.
Cerruti, just down the street from Maxim's, is my favorite store for men's designer clothing. The clothes are beautiful but expensive. The store is named after a Milanese couturier who established the first branch, as the name implies, in 1881. It specializes in well-styled and lightweight men's clothing, closely fitted, in the Italian style, to men of medium builds. Much of the apparel is designed for warm-weather climates. **Métro:** Concorde.

LANVIN, 15 rue du Faubourg St-Honoré, 8e. Tel. 42-65-14-40.
This shop, one of the most elegant in Paris, is just one of many Lanvin boutiques throughout the city. Specializing in "the latest" conservative but stylish fashion, Lanvin also sells a handsome collection of shirts and ties and will custom-make shirts and suits. **Métro:** Concorde.

PIERRE CARDIN BOUTIQUE HOMMES, 59 rue du Faubourg St-Honoré, 8e. Tel. 42-66-92-25.
Pierre Cardin carries a large assortment of sophisticated men's clothing and some of the finest accessories available, including an unusual selection of men's shoes. As you'd expect, everything is expensive. **Métro:** Champs-Elysées–Clemenceau.

FOOD

FAUCHON, place de la Madeleine, 8e. Tel. 47-42-60-11.
At the place de la Madeleine stands one of the most popular sights in the city—not the church, but Fauchon, a vast shop crammed with gastronomical goodies. Never have I seen faces so rapt—not even before the Mona Lisa—as those of Parisians gazing at the Fauchon window display. Plump chickens coated in a glazing of sliced almonds, a thigh of lamb opening out like a cornucopia, filled with bright, fresh vegetables made to look like fruits. It's the French version of the Garden of Eden.

English-speaking hosts will assist you, if needed. In the fruit-and-vegetable department you'll find such items as rare mushrooms and fraises des bois (wild strawberries). The pastry and confectionary store features different types of pastry, candies, and a self-service stand-up bar. The candies, incidentally, are divine, including glazed tropical fruits, whisky truffles, stuffed dates, and chocolate-dipped ginger. After seeing the self-service bar, you'll probably decide to stay for lunch. Go first to the display case, make your decision, then tell the cashier what you want. She'll give you a check for each item, which you in turn surrender to the serving woman. You may order an omelet, a shrimp salad, or even a club sandwich. A cup of ice cream makes a soothing dessert. Also on the premises are a cocktail department, a gifts department, a selection of porcelain and table settings, and an impressive collection of very drinkable wines. **Open:** Mon–Sat 9:40am–7pm. A "Mini-Fauchon," selling mainly food products, is open Mon–Sat 7–9pm. **Métro:** Madeleine.

HATS

E. MOTSCH, 42 av. George-V, 8e. Tel. 47-23-79-22.
One of the most distinguished outlets for classic handmade hats for both men and women is E. Motsch, right off the Champs-Elysées. This sedate corner store, in business since 1887, offers almost every type of headgear, ranging from berets to Scottish tam-o'-shanters. The section for women contains some of the most stylish, if conservative, hats in Paris. **Open:** Mon–Sat 9:30am–1pm and 2–6:30pm. **Métro:** George-V.

JEWELRY

VAN CLEEF & ARPELS, 22 place Vendôme, 1er. Tel. 42-61-58-58.
This is the headquarters of a store that was established around the turn of the century. A premier jewelry store of world renown (and numerous branches), its motto is, "There is nothing a man in love can refuse to the woman who makes him happy." This exclusive shop is known for its special settings and also carries a range of deluxe watches. **Open:** Mon–Fri 9:30am–1pm and 2:30–6pm. **Métro:** Opéra or Tuileries.

LEATHER GOODS

GUCCI, 2 rue du Faubourg St-Honoré, 8e. Tel. 42-96-83-27.
This is one of the world's largest showcases for this fabled Italian designer, with his trademark red-and-green trim in leather goods. Gucci makes fine shoes and handbags, as well as other items, including wallets, gloves, and clothing. This outlet has an excellent selection of scarves and two-piece ensembles. Its sweaters are especially outstanding. **Open:** Mon–Sat 9:30am–6:30pm. **Métro:** Concorde.

LINGERIE & BATHING SUITS

CADOLLE, 14 rue Cambon, 1er. Tel. 42-60-94-94.
All of Paris nostalgically remembers the founding mother of this store, Hermine Cadolle, as the person who in 1889 invented the brassiere. Today the store is managed by Hermine's great-great- and great-great-great-granddaughters, Alice and Poupie Cadolle. This is the place to go for a made-to-order or a ready-to-wear fit. For custom-made fit, it is best to make an appointment long in advance, preferably before leaving for France or at least as soon as you arrive.

Custom-made whalebone corsets are still available, and the night-gowns range from the demure to the scandalous. There is also a fashionable collection of bathing suits. This is the home of Cadolle's fine perfume, Le No. 9. **Open:** Mon–Sat 9:30am–1pm and 2–6:30pm. **Métro:** Concorde or Madeleine.

MALLS

FORUM DES HALLES, 1–7 rue Pierre-Lescot, 1er. Tel. 42-96-68-74.

Once the great old vegetable markets, Les Halles is now a vast crater in the middle of Paris, selling, among other things, clothing, accessories, food, and gifts. **Métro:** Etienne-Marcel.

MONTPARNASSE SHOPPING CENTRE, between rue de l'Arrivée and 22 rue de Départ, 14e. Tel. 45-38-52-87.

Boutiques in this shopping center offer men's and women's fashions, jewelry, perfume, cosmetics, gifts, shoes, art, wool, records, glasses, and children's wear. Shoppers will also find a branch of Galeries Lafayette, restaurants, a travel agent, and even a swimming pool inside. **Métro:** Montparnasse-Bienvenue.

PALAIS DES CONGRES DE PARIS BOUTIQUES, 2 place de la Porte-Maillot, 17e. Tel. 40-68-26-24.

Palais des Congrès de Paris Boutiques, located inside the convention building, offers art, fine food, fashion, jewelry, toys, books, records, and children's wear. You'll also find a Japanese department store and hairdresser. **Métro:** Porte-Maillot.

MARKETS

MARCHE AUX PUCES, av. de la Porte de Clignancourt.

A landmark, the Flea Market is both adored and abused. Even if you don't purchase one item (an unlikely possibility), it's an experience to be savored. This is a complex of 2,500 to 3,000 open stalls and shops on the fringe of Paris, selling everything from antiques to junk, from new to second-hand clothing. Occupying a vast triangular area, it is spread over half a mile and is almost impossible to cover entirely in just one visit.

The first clues showing you're there will be the stalls of cheap clothing along avenue de la Porte de Clignancourt. As you proceed, various streets will tempt you. Some of these streets are narrow, lined with little shops that start pulling out their offerings around 9am and start bringing them in around 6pm. Monday is the traditional day for bargain seekers, as there is smaller attendance at the market and a greater desire on the part of the merchants to sell.

Naturally, you are supposed to bargain. Nobody pays the first price quoted. Many don't even pay the second or third price. Of course, a little basic French helps too. The sound of an English-speaking voice is known to drive the price up right away. In addition to the permanent stalls, there are "dropcloth" peddlers as well. They spread out their wares on canvas or sheets (and are predictably viewed with scorn by the permanently installed vendors).

The big question everybody asks is, "Do you get any real bargains at the Flea Market?" Or, conversely, "Will you get fleeced?" Actually, it's all comparative. Obviously, the best buys have been skimmed by dealers (who often have a prearrangement to have items held for them). It's true, the same merchandise in the provinces of France will sell for less. But from the point of view of the visitor who has only a few days to spend in Paris—and only half a day for shopping—the Flea Market is worth the experience. **Open:** Sat–Mon 9am–6pm. **Métro:** Porte de Clignancourt. From there, turn left and cross bd. Ney, then walk north on av. de la Porte de Clignancourt. **Bus:** 56.

MARCHE AUX TIMBRES, off the Champs-Elysées.

The Marché aux Timbres draws the avid stamp collectors. Nearly two dozen stalls are set up on a permanent basis under shady trees on the eastern edge of the Rond Point. The variety of stamps is almost unlimited—some common, some quite rare. **Open:** Generally Thurs and Sat–Sun 10am–7pm. **Métro:** Champs-Elysées-Clemenceau.

MARCHE AUX FLEURS, place Louis-Lepine, Ile de la Cité, 4e.

⭐ Artists love to paint the Flower Market; photographers love to click away. But for the most part, travelers go there to refresh their souls, enjoying a feast of fragrance. The stalls are ablaze with color, each a showcase of flowers, usually from the French Riviera (those that escaped a fate of being hauled to the perfume factories of Grasse). The Flower Market is along the Seine, behind the Tribunal de Commerce. **Open:** Daily 8am–4pm. **Métro:** Cité.

MARCHE AUX OISEAUX, place Louis-Lepine, Ile de la Cité, 4e.

The Bird Market comes alive with feathered creatures. Even if you don't plan to buy a rare parrot, you'll want to go for a look. From the Louvre to the Hôtel de Ville, you can visit the small stalls with vendors along the Seine. **Open:** Sun 9am–7pm. **Métro:** Cité.

PERFUME

FREDDY OF PARIS, 10 rue Auber, 9e. Tel. 47-42-63-41.

Freddy, near the American Express office and the Opéra, offers discounts of up to 40% on all name-brand perfumes, creams, novelties, gifts, handbags, scarves, ties, and costume jewelry. **Open:** Mon–Fri 9am–6:30pm. **Métro:** Opéra. **RER:** Auber.

MICHEL SWISS, 16 rue de la Paix, 2e. Tel. 42-61-61-11.

The outside of Michel Swiss looks like many of the ultra-chic facades near the place Vendôme. But once you get inside (there's no storefront window), you'll see the major brands of luxury perfumes, makeups, leather bags, pens, neckties, fashion accessories, and gifts. All items are discounted by 25%, plus an additional tax discount for non–EC residents amounting to 18.6% to 22% depending on the product. The store is two flights above ground level, and is reached by a small elevator. Avoid the crowds who pile in here at lunchtime. **Open:** Mon–Sat 9am–6:30pm. **Métro:** Opéra.

PARFUMERIE FRAGONARD, 9 rue Scribe, 9e. Tel. 47-42-93-40.

In a Napoléon III town house, near the Paris Opéra, this perfume house contains a more edited version of the museum of perfume in Grasse (established in 1782 on the French Riviera). This Parisian shop is an outlet for the scent factories in Eze and Grasse. The aluminum containers in which it sells its scents are said to keep the perfume fresh for up to 10 years. **Métro:** Opéra.

SOUVENIRS & GIFTS

EIFFEL SHOPPING, 9 av. de Suffren, 7e. Tel. 45-66-55-30.

Have a free glass of cognac while you browse through the designer collection (Dior, Saint-Laurent, Lanvin, Cartier, Chanel, to name just a few) of handbags, ties, scarves, watches, sunglasses, jewelry, perfumes, Lalique crystal, and much more. This tax-free shopping center, only one block from the Eiffel Tower, offers top-quality merchandise at discount prices, and all the salespeople are bilingual. **Open:** Mon–Sat 9:15am–8pm, Sun 11am–8pm. **Métro:** Bir-Hakeim.

STATIONERY

CASSEGRAIN, 422 rue St-Honoré, 8e. Tel. 42-60-20-08.

Cassegrain opened right after World War I, and it's been attracting letter writers ever since. It is considered by many the premier stationery shop in the city. Beautifully engraved stationery, most often in traditional patterns, is offered, although businesspeople can also get their business cards engraved to order. Several other items for the desk—many suitable for gifts—are for sale as well.

Cassegrain also has a shop at 81 rue des Saints-Pères, 6e (tel. 42-22-04-76; Métro: Sèvres-Babylone).

Open: Both stores Mon–Fri 9:30am–6:30pm, Sat 9:30am–1pm. **Métro:** Concorde.

TABLEWARE & BED LINEN

AU BAIN MARIE, 10 rue Boissy d'Anglas, 8e. Tel. 42-66-59-74.

Between Hermès at Faubourg St-Honoré and the Hôtel Crillon is one of Paris's best choices for new and antique table and bedroom linen, some of it painstakingly embroidered. The two floors of merchandise include virtually everything that might touch a dining table, including tableware of many different styles, inspired by many different eras. There's also a collection of books relating to food and wine, and a good selection of bathroom towels. **Open:** Mon–Sat 10am–7pm. **Métro:** Concorde.

TOYS & KIDS' STUFF

AU NAIN BLEU, 406 rue St-Honoré, 8e. Tel. 42-60-39-01.

Any child you love is expecting a present from Paris, and at the "Blue Dwarf" you'll be bedazzled by the choice. Browse through this paradise of playthings that has been in business for a century and a half. It's a world of toy soldiers, stuffed animals, games, model airplanes, technical toys, model cars, even a "Flower Drum Kit." Puppets come in all shapes, sizes, and costumes. **Open:** Mon–Sat 9am–6:15pm. **Métro:** Concorde.

LE MONDE EN MARCHE, 34 rue Dauphine, 6e. Tel. 43-26-66-53.

A large assortment of creative playthings for children is offered at reasonable prices, including music boxes and little tin animals. **Open:** Tues–Sun 10:30am–7:30pm. **Métro:** Odéon.

RIGODON, 13 rue Racine, 6e. Tel. 43-29-98-66.

On a street branching off from place de l'Odéon is a puppet-and-doll world for every child, even for those who are children only at heart—but they're dolls to look at, not to play with. Hanging from the ceiling is one of the most varied collections of puppets in Paris. They come in all characters, sizes, and prices, and include everything from angels to witches on broomsticks to bat women with feather wings. Rigodon also makes porcelain dolls. The painting on the faces and the costumes are unique for each model, be it a queen with all her power or the amazon of the hunt. There are marionettes (with strings) from French artisans. **Open:** Tues–Sat 9:30am–6:30pm. **Métro:** Odéon.

PARIS NIGHTS

With five national theaters, including a new opera house and 55 theaters of lesser renown, Paris is both the hub of French culture and host to all the best on the international circuit. Whatever the season, the choice is fantastic: top pop stars, French classics, chamber concerts, lavish music-hall spectaculars. In one cavernous hall, an American singer might be belting out a standard to a packed crowd of Parisians, while in a shabby Left Bank lane, a young playwright anxiously watches his first work performed on the same small stage that launched Ionesco or Beckett.

Contemporary Paris has less nudity than London, less vice than Hamburg, and less drunkenness than San Francisco. Nevertheless, the quantity and the variety of Paris's nocturnal pleasures still beat those of any metropolis on earth. Nowhere else will you find such a huge and mixed array of clubs, bars, discos, cabarets, jazz dives, music halls, and honky-tonks, ranging—in the subtlest of gradations—from the corniest tourist traps to the most sophisticated connoisseurs' fare.

And to leave out cafés from any description of Paris would be like writing about London without mentioning a pub.

1. THE CAFES OF PARIS

Contrary to general belief, the coffeehouse is not a French invention. It began in 17th-century Vienna and flourished in London long before taking root in France. But when the Parisians adopted it, they infused it with such Gallic flair and local flavor that it became an accepted symbol of their inimitable brand of joie de vivre.

It's almost impossible to venture a guess at the number of cafés in Paris. A single block in the central arrondissements may house three or four. They thin out a little in the farther suburbs, but still remain far more numerous than, for instance, hamburger stands in the United States. And somehow each gets its quota of customers.

It's nearly as difficult to define their precise function. They aren't restaurants, although the larger ones may serve complete and excellent meals. They aren't bars, although they offer an infinite variety of alcoholic potions. And they aren't coffee shops in the Anglo-American meaning, because they'll serve you a bottle of champagne just as readily as an iced chocolate.

Parisians use them as combination club-tavern-snackbars, almost as extensions of their living rooms. They are spots where you can read your newspaper or meet a friend, do your homework or write your memoirs, nibble at a hard-boiled egg or drink yourself into oblivion. At cafés you meet your dates to go on to a show or to stay and talk. Above all, cafés are for people-watching.

Perhaps their single common denominator is the way they let you sit. Regardless of whether you have one small coffee or the most expensive cognac in the house, nobody badgers, pressures, or hurries you. If you wish to sit there until the place closes, *eh bien,* that's your affair. For the café is one of the few truly democratic institutions—a solitary soda buys you the same view and sedentary pleasure as an oyster dinner.

All cafés sport an outdoor portion. Some, merely a few tables on the pavement; others, immense terraces, glassed in and heated in winter. Both categories, however, fulfill the same purpose: They offer a vantage point from which to view the passing parade.

Coffee, of course, is the chief potion. It comes black in a small cup, unless you specifically order it *au lait* (with milk). Tea (*thé,* pronounced "tay") is also fairly popular, but not on the same level of quality.

The famous apéritifs, French versions of the before-dinner drink, are the aniseed-flavored, mild-tasting Pernod, Ricard, and Pastis, all mixed with ice and water. There are also St. Raphael and Byrrh, tasting rather like port wine, and the slightly less sweet Dubonnet.

If you prefer beer, I advise you to pay a bit more for the imported German, Dutch, or Danish brands, incomparably better than the local brew. If you insist on the French variety, at least order it *à pression* (draft), which is superior. A great local favorite as an apéritif is the Italian Campari, drunk with soda and ice, very bitter and refreshing. Try it at least once.

In the teetotal bracket, you get a vast variety of fruit drinks, as well as Coca-Cola and the specifically French syrups, like Grenadine. They're about on the same level as the stuff you get at home. But French chocolate drinks—either hot or iced—are absolutely superb and on a par with the finest Dutch brands. They're made from ground chocolate, not a chemical compound.

Cafés keep delightfully flexible hours, depending on the season, the traffic, and the part of town they're in. Nearly all of them stay open till one in the morning, some till two, a few all night.

Now just a few words on café etiquette. You don't pay when you get your order—only when you intend to leave. Payment indicates that you've had all you want. *Service compris* means the tip is included in your bill, so it isn't really necessary to tip extra; still, feel free to leave an extra franc or so if service has been attentive.

You'll hear the locals call the "garçon," but as a foreigner it would be more polite to use "monsieur." *All* waitresses, on the other hand, are addressed as "mademoiselle," regardless of age and marital status.

In the smaller establishments, you may have to share your table. In that case, even if you haven't exchanged one word with them, you bid your table companions good-bye with a perfunctory *messieurs et dames,* on leaving.

BRASSERIE LIPP, 151 bd. St-Germain, 6e. Tel. 45-48-53-91.

On the day of Paris's liberation in 1944, former owner Roger Cazes (now deceased) spotted Hemingway, the first man to drop in for a drink. But famous men—then and now—customarily drop into the Lipp for its beer, wine, and conversation. Food is secondary, of course, yet quite good, providing you can get a seat (an hour and a half waiting time is customary if you're not a "friend of the management"). The specialty is sauerkraut garni. You can perch on a banquette, admiring your face reflected—along with that of, say, Françoise Sagan—in the "hall of mirrors." The Lipp was opened in 1870–71, following the Franco-Prussian War, when its founder, Monsieur Lipp, fled German-occupied territory for Paris. It's been a Parisian tradition ever since. Even if you don't drop inside for a drink, you can sit at a sidewalk café table, enjoying a cognac and people-watching. **Open:** Daily 8am–2am. **Closed:** Eight days for Christmas and mid-July to mid-Aug. **Prices:** Plats du jour 95F–150F ($17.60–$27.75). **Métro:** St-Germain-des-Prés.

FOUQUET'S, 99 av. des Champs-Elysées, 8e. Tel. 47-23-70-60.

Fouquet's has been collecting anecdotes and a patina since it was founded at the turn of the century. A celebrity favorite, it has attracted Chaplin, Chevalier, Dietrich, Mistinguett, even Churchill and Roosevelt. The premier café on the Champs-Elysées, it sits behind a barricade of potted flowers at the edge of the sidewalk. You can select a table outdoors in the sunshine or retreat to the glassed-in elegance of the leather banquettes and the rattan furniture of the street-level grill room. There, you can order meals; most visitors, however, simply stop in for a glass of wine or a sandwich. The café and grill room are open all year long. On the upper level, the restaurant and private banqueting rooms are closed Saturday, Sunday, and from mid-July to late August. **Open:** Mon–Fri 8am–midnight. **Prices:** Meals from 250F ($46.25); glass of wine 45F ($8.35); sandwich 68F ($12.60). **Métro:** George-V.

CAFE DE FLORE, 172 bd. St-Germain, 6e. Tel. 45-48-55-26.

Sartre, the granddaddy of existentialism, often came here during the war and was a key figure in the Resistance. Wearing a leather jacket and beret, he sat at his table and wrote his trilogy, *Les Chemins de la Liberté* (The Roads to Freedom). In *A Memoir in the Form of a Novel (Two Sisters)*, Gore Vidal introduces his two main characters with "I first saw them at the Café de Flore in the summer of 1948. They were seated side by side at the center of the first row of sidewalk tables, quite outshining Sartre and de Beauvoir, who were holding court nearby." Camus, Picasso, and Apollinaire also frequented the Flore. The café is still going strong, although the famous folks have moved on. **Open:** Daily 7am–1:30am. **Closed:** July. **Prices:** Espresso 20F ($3.70), glass of beer 35F ($6.50). **Métro:** St-Germain-des-Prés.

DEUX MAGOTS, 170 bd. St-Germain, 6e. Tel. 45-48-55-25.

This legendary café is still the hangout for the sophisticated residents of St-Germain-des-Prés and a tourist favorite in summer. Visitors, in fact, virtually monopolize the limited number of sidewalk tables. Waiters rush about, seemingly oblivious to your needs. Off-season, it's not a lonesome café, as the regulars quickly learn who's who.

The Deux Magots was once a gathering place of the intellectual elite, including Sartre, Simone de Beauvoir, and Jean Giraudoux.

Inside are two large Asian statues that give the café its name. The crystal chandeliers are too brightly lit, but the regulars seem used to the glare. After all, some of them even read newspapers there. **Open:** Daily 7:30am–1:30am. **Prices:** Espresso 20F ($3.70), beer 26F–40F ($4.80–$7.40). **Métro:** St-Germain-des-Prés.

CAFE DE LA PAIX, place de l'Opéra, 8e. Tel. 40-07-30-10.

This hub of the tourist world virtually commands the place de l'Opéra, and the legend goes that if you sit there long enough, you'll see someone you know passing by. Huge, grandiose, and frighteningly fashionable, it harbors not only Parisians, but, at some time or another, every visiting American, a tradition that dates from the end of World War I. Once Emile Zola and Oscar Wilde sat on the terrace; later, Hemingway and F. Scott Fitzgerald frequented it. **Open:** Daily 10am–1:30am. **Prices** (including service): Whiskey 42F–53F ($7.75–$9.80), café espresso 17F ($3.15). **Métro:** Opéra.

LA COUPOLE, 102 bd. du Montparnasse, 14e. Tel. 43-20-14-20.

Once a leading center of Parisian artist life, La Coupole is now a bastion of traditionalism in Montparnasse in the grand Paris brasserie style. This big, attractive café has, however, grown more fashionable with the years, attracting fewer locals—such as Sartre and de Beauvoir in the old days—and rarely a struggling artist. But some of the city's most interesting foreigners show up. In days of yore patrons included Josephine Baker, Henry Miller, Dali, Calder, Hemingway, Dos Passos, Fitzgerald, and Picasso. Today you might see Belmondo with Catherine Deneuve.

The sweeping outdoor terrace is among the finest to be found in Paris. At one of its sidewalk tables, you can sit and watch the passing scene, ordering a coffee or a cognac VSOP. The food is quite good, despite the fact that the dining room resembles a railway station. Try, for example, such main dishes as sole meunière, curry d'agneau (lamb), or cassoulet. The fresh oysters and shellfish are especially popular. A petit dejeuner is served on a buffet from 7:30 to 10:30am. **Open:** Daily noon–2am. **Prices:** Breakfast buffet 75F ($13.90); coffee 20F ($3.70); complete meal from 280F ($51.80). **Métro:** Vavin.

LA ROTONDE, 105 bd. du Montparnasse, 6e. Tel. 43-26-68-84.

Once patronized by Hemingway, the original Rotonde faded into history but it still is a memory, drawn from the pages of *The Sun Also Rises*. Papa wrote, "No matter what café in Montparnasse you ask a taxi driver to bring you to from the right bank of the river, they always take you to the Rotonde." Lavishly upgraded, the reincarnation of La Rotonde has an art deco paneled elegance, sharing the once-hallowed site with a motion-picture theater. If you stand at the bar, prices are lower. **Open:** Sun–Thurs 7:30am–2am, Fri–Sat 7:30am–3am. **Prices:** Full meals from 200F ($37), glass of wine 21F ($3.90). **Métro:** Vavin.

LE SELECT, 99 bd. du Montparnasse, 6e. Tel. 45-48-38-24.

Le Select may be down the social ladder from the other glittering cafés of Montparnasse, but I find it the liveliest and friendliest. It opened in 1923, and really hasn't changed all that much. At one time it was the favorite hangout of Cocteau. They have 40 different whiskies and 20 different cocktails, some rather exotic. **Open:**

Sun–Thurs 8am–2am, Fri–Sat 8am–3:30am. **Prices:** Coffee 15F ($2.80), hard drinks from 52F ($9.60). **Métro:** Vavin.

LE DOME, 108 bd. du Montparnasse, 14e. Tel. 43-35-25-81.

After an unsuccessful attempt as a drugstore, Le Dome, the most famous of the Montparnasse cafés, is back in business but elegantly modernized in an art deco format. All that remains of Le Dome of times past are recollections of the café in its heyday. The memories of Hemingway linger here, and some of the most celebrated names in the world of art sat on the terrace in the years between 1920 and 1925.

Many guests come here for only a coffee, but you can also order a full meal. Fresh oysters are sold right on the sidewalk. At a table, you might select such specialties as pot-au-feu or turbot with fresh morels, perhaps bourride provençale, served only for two persons. **Open:** Tues–Sun 10am–2am. **Prices:** Coffee 14F ($2.60), full meal from 450F ($83.25). **Métro:** Vavin.

LE MANDARIN, 148 bis, bd. St-Germain, 6e. Tel. 46-33-98-35.

This elegantly decorated corner café is thronged with young people of the Left Bank or visitors soaking up the atmosphere of St-Germain-des-Prés. At the brass bar you can order fine wines, certainly a coffee. Decorated with lace-covered hanging lamps, brass trim, and lots of exposed wood, the establishment serves good food, including crêpes or onion soup. **Open:** Daily 8am–2am. **Prices:** Coffee 14F–18F ($2.60–$3.35), crêpes 22F–48F ($4.05–$8.90). **Métro:** Odéon or Mabillon.

CAFE DE CLUNY, 20 bd. St-Michel or 102 bd. St-Germain, 5e. Tel. 43-26-68-24.

Placed strategically at the intersection of two famous avenues, Café de Cluny overlooks the hub of the Left Bank and the Musée de Cluny. This large, bustling oasis is one of the main meeting places for visiting and locals alike. The café also serves meals. For example, a plate of sauerkraut garni costs 56F ($10.35). **Open:** Daily 7am–2am. **Prices:** Local beer 20F ($3.70), coffee 11F ($2.05). **Métro:** St-Michel.

2. THE PERFORMING ARTS

The only limitation to your enjoyment of French theater is language. Those of you with modest French can still delight in a lively, sparkling Molière at the Comédie-Française. But those with no French at all might prefer an evening that is longer on melody and shorter on speech.

Announcements of shows, concerts, even the opera programs are plastered all around town on kiosks. A better way to find out what's playing is to consult *Pariscope, Une semaine de Paris,* a weekly entertainment guide that includes a section of arts, with full listings of theaters, concerts, and more.

Ticket agents are dotted all over Paris but clustered thickest near the Right Bank hotels. Avoid them if possible, because you'll get the least expensive tickets at the theater box offices. Remember to tip the usher who shows you to your seat. This holds true in movie houses as well as theaters. Performances start later in Paris than in London or New York—anywhere from 8 to 9:30pm—and Parisians tend to dine after the theater. You don't have to follow suit, since many of the modest, less expensive restaurants close as early as 9pm.

DISCOUNT TICKETS

Several agencies sell tickets for cultural events and plays at discounts of up to 50%.

One outlet for discount tickets is the **Kiosque Théâtre** at 15 place de la Madeleine, 8e (no phone; Métro: Madeleine), offering leftover tickets for about half price on the day of the performance. Tickets for evening performances are sold Tues–Fri 12:30–8pm, Sat 2–8pm. If you'd like to attend a matinee, buy your ticket on Sat 12:30–2pm or Sun 12:30–4pm.

For 20% to 40% discounts on tickets for festivals, concerts, and theater performances, try **Alpha FNAC: Spectacles,** 136 rue de Rennes, 6e (tel. 42-71-58-26; Métro: Montparnasse-Bienvenue). Other locations are **Forum des Halles,** 1–7 rue Pierre Lescot, 1er (tel. 42-61-81-18; Métro: Châtelet–Les-Halles), and 26 av. de Wagram, 8e (tel. 47-66-52-50; Métro: Charles-de-Gaulle–Etoile). To get the discounts you must purchase a *carte alpha* for 50F ($9.25), good for one year. These agencies are open Tues–Sat 10am–7pm.

THEATER

COMEDIE-FRANCAISE, 2 rue de Richelieu, 1er. Tel. 42-96-10-24.
If you've a taste for fine theater, don't let the language barrier scare you off—spend at least one night of your Paris stay at the Comédie-

---

THE MAJOR CONCERT & PERFORMANCE HALLS

Comédie-Française, 2 rue de Richelieu, 1er (tel. 42-96-10-24). French and contemporary theater. Métro: Palais-Royal.

Opéra-Comique, place Boildieu, 2e (tel. 42-96-12-20). Light-opera productions. Métro: Richelieu-Drouot.

L'Opéra Paris Garnier, place de l'Opéra, 9e (tel. 40-17-35-35). Ballet and musical performances. Métro: Opéra.

Radio France Auditorium, 116 av. President-Kennedy, 16e (tel. 42-30-15-16). The best orchestra concerts in Paris. Métro: Passy.

Salle Pleyel, 252 rue du Faubourg St-Honoré, 8e (tel. 45-61-06-30). Home of the Orchestre de Paris. Métro: Ternes.

Théâtre des Champs-Elysées, 15 av. Montaigne, 8e (tel. 47-20-30-88). Operas, concerts, and ballets. Métro: Alma-Marceau.

Théâtre Musical de Paris, 1 place du Châtelet, 1er (tel. 40-28-28-40). Opera and ballet. Métro: Châtelet.

Théâtre National de Chaillot, place du Trocadéro, 16e (tel. 47-27-81-15). One of the largest concert halls in Paris. Métro: Trocadéro.

Française. Nowhere else will you see the French classics—Molière, Racine—so beautifully staged in the original language. A national theater, it was established to keep the classics in the cultural mainstream and to promote the most important contemporary authors. **Prices:** Tickets 50F–155F ($9.25–$28.70). **Closed:** Aug 1–Sept 15. **Métro:** Palais-Royal.

OPERA

L'OPERA BASTILLE, place de la Bastille, 120 rue de Lyon, 4e. Tel. 40-01-17-89.

✪ The controversial building was designed by Canadian architect Carlos Ott, with curtains created by Issey Miyake, the Japanese fashion designer. The giant showplace was inaugurated in July 1989, and on March 17, 1990, the curtain rose on Hector Berlioz's opera *Les Troyens*. The main hall is the largest of any opera house in France, with 2,700 seats. The building also contains three additional concert halls, including an intimate room with only 250 seats. Both operas and symphony concerts are presented here.

Several concerts are presented free, in honor of certain French holidays. Write ahead for tickets to the Opéra de Paris Bastille, 120 rue de Lyon, 75012 Paris. **Prices:** Tickets 45F–525F ($8.35–$97.15). **Métro:** Bastille.

OPERA-COMIQUE, place Boildieu, 2e. Tel. 42-96-12-20.

For light-opera productions, try the Opéra-Comique. If possible, make arrangements two weeks before the performance. **Open:** Box office Mon–Sat 11am–7pm. **Closed:** July–Aug. **Prices:** 45F–435F ($8.35–$80.50). **Métro:** Richelieu-Drouot.

THEATRE MUSICAL DE PARIS, 1 place du Châtelet, 1er. Tel. 40-28-28-40.

The Théâtre Musical de Paris, presenting less expensive opera and ballet performances than l'Opéra or l'Opéra Bastille, is known for its good acoustics. **Prices:** Opera 90F–400F ($16.65–$74); concerts, 80F–285F ($14.80–$52.75); ballets, 80F–185F ($1.50–$34.25). **Closed:** July 15–Sept 15. **Métro:** Châtelet.

BALLET

L'OPERA PARIS GARNIER, place de l'Opéra, 9e. Tel. 40-17-35-35.

✪ L'Opéra is the premier stage for ballet and musical productions. Because of the competition from the Opéra at the Bastille, the original opera has made great efforts to present more up-to-date works, including choreography by Jerome Robbins, Twyla Tharp, Agnes de Mille, and Georges Balanchine. This architectural wonder was designed as a contest entry by a young architect in the heyday of Empire. The facade is adorned with marble and sculpture, including *The Dance* by Carpeaux. The great musical performers of the world, including Sarah Bernhardt, have appeared here. **Prices:** Tickets 35F–650F ($6.50–$120.25). **Métro:** Odéon.

MAJOR CONCERT HALLS & ALL-PURPOSE AUDITORIUMS

The concertgoing public is kept busy year-round in Paris, with daily offerings taking up full newspaper columns. Organ recitals are featured in the churches (the largest organ is in Saint-Sulpice); jazz shatters the peace of the city's modern art museum.

RADIO FRANCE AUDITORIUM, 116 av. President-Kennedy, 16e. Tel. 42-30-15-16.

The best orchestra in France belongs to Radio France, and top-flight concerts with guest conductors are presented in the Radio France Auditorium. **Prices:** Tickets for Orchestra National 120F ($22.20), for the Orchestre Philharmonique 80F ($14.80). **Métro:** Passy.

SALLE PLEYEL, 252 rue du Faubourg St-Honoré, 8e. Tel. 45-61-06-30.

Host to the Orchestre de Paris, the Salle Pleyel, a few blocks northeast of the Arc de Triomphe, has a season running from September to Easter. **Prices:** Tickets 80F–250F ($14.80–$46.25). **Métro:** Ternes.

THEATRE DES CHAMPS-ELYSEES, 15 av. Montaigne, 8e. Tel. 47-20-30-88.

Opera, ballet, and concerts are performed at the Théâtre des Champs-Elysées, with both national and international orchestras. Open: Box office Mon–Sat 11am–7pm. **Closed:** July–Aug. **Prices:** Tickets 40F–600F ($7.40–$111). **Métro:** Alma-Marceau.

THEATRE NATIONAL DE CHAILLOT, place du Trocadéro, 16e. Tel. 47-27-81-15.

One of the largest concert halls is the Théâtre National de Chaillot, with programs announced on big showboards out front. **Prices:** Tickets 40F–400F ($7.40–$74). **Métro:** Trocadéro.

3. THE CLUB & MUSIC SCENE

Paris today is still a nirvana for night owls, even though some of its once-unique attractions have become common. The fame of Parisian nights was established in those distant days of innocence when Anglo-Americans still gasped at the sight of a bare bosom in a chorus line, and free love was something you only whispered about in polite transatlantic circles.

Some of the best and most genuinely Parisian attractions are the so-called *boîtes* in which chansonniers sing ballads and ditties intended only for local consumption. A few performers, like Edith Piaf and Juliette Greco, graduated to international fame from these places. But the lyrics that delight the patrons there are so slangy, so topically witty, so heavily laced with verbal innuendos and double-entendres that they're incomprehensible to foreigners. Your French wouldn't just have to be good, but Pigalle-perfect.

Luckily, there are hundreds of other establishments where lingual ignorance is of no consequence. Sometimes it can even be an advantage, because the verses perpetrated by, say, a French rock group are every ounce as inane as their Stateside brethren's.

Many of the Right Bank—but few of the Left Bank—hostelries are lavishly sprinkled with mademoiselles whose job it is to push a man's tab up to astronomical heights. They're incomparably skillful at it, and you could be in for a staggering bill including champagne, cigarettes, candy, teddy bear, and what-have-you. Under their gentle touch, an evening that might have cost you the equivalent of $15 can rapidly mount up to $200 and more—much more. Don't be afraid to respond with a firmly polite no to an unsolicited approach. The reaction is usually a regretful Gallic shrug, and she'll rarely try again. That way you'll retain control of your night's expenditure.

The other general rule to remember is that the Right Bank, by and large, is plusher, slicker, and more expensive than the Left, which contains more of the avant-garde entertainment, the younger clientele, and a minimum of professional "companions."

Before starting the round of establishments, let me repeat that this is a town for genuine night owls. Few spots get swinging before 11pm and most acquire their full heads of steam around midnight—or later. Since the Métro stops running at 1am, be prepared to use taxis and to sleep-in the next morning.

BOITES & MUSIC HALLS

The *chansonniers* (literally "song writers") provide bombastic musical satire of the day's events. This combination of parody and burlesque is a time-honored Gallic amusement and a Parisian institution. The wit and ridicule these performers shower upon prostitutes and presidents alike make for an extravagant revue. Songs are often created on the spot, depending for their inspiration on "the disaster of the day." The best boîtes of the chansonniers are on the tawdry boulevard de Clichy.

AU LAPIN AGILE, 22 rue des Saules, 18e. Tel. 46-06-85-87.

⭐ Picasso and Utrillo once patronized this little cottage near the top of Montmartre, formerly known as the Café des Assassins. It has been painted by artists, known and unknown, including Utrillo. For many decades it has been the heartbeat of French folk music, featuring folk songs, sing-alongs, and poetry readings. You'll sit at carved wooden tables in a low, dimly lit room with walls covered with bohemian memorabilia.

Songs include old French folk tunes, love ballads, army songs, sea chanteys, and music-hall ditties. You're encouraged to sing along, even if it's only the "oui, oui, oui—non, non, non" refrain of "Les Chevaliers de la Table Ronde." You can always hum along with "Larilette" and "Madelon." The best sing-alongs are on weeknights after tourist season ends. **Open:** Tues–Sun 9:15pm–2am. **Admission:** 110F ($20.35), including first drink. **Prices:** Drinks 30F ($5.55). **Métro:** Lamarck.

AU CAVEAU DE LA BOLEE, 25 rue de l'Hirondelle, 6e. Tel. 43-54-62-20.

You descend into the catacombs of the early-14th-century Abbey of Saint-André, once a famous literary café, drawing such personages as Verlaine and Oscar Wilde, who downed (or drowned in) glass after glass of absinthe here. The French songs are good and bawdy and just what the young students, who form a large part of the audience, like. Occasionally the audience sings along.

A fixed-price dinner is served Monday through Saturday at 9pm and is followed by a cabaret show. However, you won't understand the jokes and references made in the show unless your French is extremely good. The cabaret starts at 10:30pm and if you've already had dinner, you can order just a drink. On Sunday, a jazz show begins at 10pm. In lieu of an entrance price, you can order either dinner or a drink, or both.

You'll find this establishment, which seats only 24, on a tiny street leading into the western edge of the place St-Michel. The beginning of the street is down a short flight of steps under a giant archway beneath one of the square's grandiose buildings. **Admission:** Fixed price dinner 260F ($48.10), drinks 100F ($18.50). **Métro:** St-Michel.

CAVEAU DES OUBLIETTES, 11 rue St-Julien-le-Pauvre, 5e. Tel. 43-54-94-97.

It's hard to say which is more interesting in this place—the program or the environment. Located in the Latin Quarter and just across the river from Notre-Dame, this nightspot is housed in a genuine 12th-century prison—complete with dungeons, spine-crawling passages, and scattered skulls. The word *oubliette* means a dungeon with a trap door at the top as its only opening, but some victims were pushed through portholes into the Seine to drown. The caveau is beneath the subterranean vaults that communicated many centuries ago with the fortress prison of the Petit Châtelet.

Performers in medieval costumes sing French folk songs and tavern choruses—sentimental, comic, and bawdy—to exclusively tourist audiences. It's rather artificial and stagey, but with charm. There's nothing artificial, however, about the adjoining museum, which displays a working guillotine, chastity belts, and instruments of torture. **Open:** Mon–Sat 9pm–2am. **Admission** (including first drink): 120F–190F ($22.20–$35.15). **Métro:** St-Michel.

THEATRE DES DEUX ANES, 100 bd. de Clichy, 18e. Tel. 46-06-10-26.

If you speak colloquial French, you'll enjoy this revue of song and satire, down the street from the Moulin Rouge. A sign, LEAVE YOUR CHEWING GUM AT THE DOOR, sets the tone. **Open:** Performances Tues–Sun 9pm; box office Tues–Sun 11am–7pm. **Prices:** Tickets 175F–180F ($32.40–$33.30). **Métro:** Blanche.

MUSIC HALLS

That old music-hall format of sing a little, dance a little, juggle a few balls, and sprinkle generously with jokes, is very much alive and doing well in Paris today. The combination, slickly carried off, adds up to a top value in entertainment for the visitor.

OLYMPIA, 28 bd. des Capucines, 9e. Tel. 47-42-82-45.

The first-rank city music hall offering packed programs of professional talent and international stars is the Olympia, the cavernous hall where the likes of Charles Aznavour make frequent appearances. On one occasion the late Yves Montand appeared, but you had to reserve a seat four months in advance. A typical lineup would include an English rock duo singing its latest record hit, a showy group of Italian acrobats, a well-known French crooner, a talented dance troupe, a triple-jointed American juggling act/comedy team (doing much of their work in English), plus the featured "Big Name," all laced together neatly by a witty emcee and backed by an onstage band. **Open:** Shows presented Tues–Sun at 8:30pm, Saturday matinees at 2:30 or 5pm. **Prices:** Tickets 55F–420F ($10.20–$77.70). **Métro:** Opéra.

NIGHTCLUBS/CABARET

Leading off is an array without which no Paris roll call would be complete. While decidedly expensive, they give you your money's worth by providing some of the most lavishly spectacular floor shows to be seen anywhere.

FOLIES BERGERE, 32 rue Richer, 9e. Tel. 42-46-77-11.

According to legend, the first GI to reach Paris at the Liberation in 1944 asked for directions to the Folies Bergère. His son and grandson do the same today. Even the old man comes back for a second look.

A roving-eyed Frenchman would have to be in his second century to remember when the Folies began. Apparently, it's here to stay, like Sacré-Coeur and the Eiffel Tower. The affection of Parisians for it has long turned into indifference (but just try to get a seat on a July night). Some, however, recall it with sentimentality. Take, for example, the night the "toast of Paris," Josephine Baker, descended the celebrated staircase, tossing bananas into the audience.

Opened in 1886, since the turn of the century the Folies Bergère has stood as the symbol of unadorned female anatomy. Fresh off the boat, Victorians and Edwardians—starved for a glimpse of even an ankle—flocked to the Folies to get a look at much more. Yet the Folies also dresses its women (at least 1,600 costumes at the last revue I saw) in those fabulous showgirl outfits you associate with Hollywood musicals of the 1930s. Open: Revue Tues–Sun 9:30pm, box office daily 10am–10pm. **Admission:** 100F–385F ($18.50–$71.25), with seats ranging from the galerie to a loge in the orchestra or balcony. A scale model at the box office shows locations of the various seats. **Métro:** rue Montmartre or Cadet.

LIDO CABARET NORMANDIE, 116 bis, av. des Champs-Elysées, 8e. Tel. 45-63-11-61.

In a panoramic room with 1,200 seats, having excellent visibility, this palatial nightspot puts on an avalanche of glamour and talent, combined with enough showmanship to make the late Mr. Barnum look like an amateur. The permanent attraction is the Bluebell Girls, a fabulous precision ensemble of long-legged international beauties. The rest of the program changes. Go at least once in a lifetime. **Admission:** Dinner dance at 8:30pm 615F–750F ($113.80–$138.75), including half a bottle of champagne. La Revue at 10:15pm or 12:30am 430F ($79.55) minimum, including half a bottle of wine. Service and taxes included. **Métro:** George-V.

MOULIN-ROUGE, place Blanche, Montmartre, 18e. Tel. 46-06-00-19.

Toulouse-Lautrec, who put this establishment on the map about a century ago, probably wouldn't recognize it today. The windmill is still there and so is the cancan. But the rest has become a super-slick, gimmick-loaded variety show with the accent heavy on the undraped female form. You'll see underwater ballets in an immense glass tank, a magnificent cascade, young women in swings and on trick stairs, all interspersed with animal acts, comic jugglers, and song trios. These are just a smattering of the acts usually found on the daily bill of fare. This multicolored candy-floss stuff is expertly staged, but any connection with the old Moulin-Rouge is purely coincidental. Open: Nightly, dinner 8pm, revue 10pm. **Prices:** dinner and revue 615F–750F ($113.80–$138.75); revue only 430F ($79.55), including champagne. No minimum if you sit at the bar (where the view is not as good). Drinks around 210F ($38.85). **Métro:** Place Blanche.

LE PARADIS LATIN, 28 rue Cardinal-Lemoine, 5e. Tel. 43-25-28-28.

The building was Gustave Eiffel's only venture into theater architecture, using the same metallic skeleton format he used for the Eiffel Tower. That theater takes credit for formalizing the introduction of vaudeville and musical theater to Paris. This monument's darkest days came in 1903, when the premises became a warehouse. In the 1970s, it was transformed, glossier than ever, into one of the most successful cabarets in Paris. The patter of the master of ceremonies is in both French and English. The revue ends at midnight. **Open:** Wed–Mon, dinner revue 8pm; revue only 10pm. **Admission:** Dinner revue 625F ($115.65); revue only 430F ($79.55), including a half bottle of champagne. **Métro:** Jussieu or Cardinal-Lemoine.

MILLIARDAIRE, 68 rue Pierre-Charron, 8e. Tel. 42-23-25-17.

The stylish, elegant Milliardaire is just off the Champs-Elysées, reached through a backyard that is not nearly as plush as the interior. The program includes comics, jugglers, and first-rate dance interludes. The place maintains a popular and discreet piano bar open every night after the last show 1:30am–dawn. In the piano bar, drinks cost 130F ($24.05) each. Open: Two different shows staged nightly at 10pm and midnight. During July and August no shows are presented on Sunday, and in August only one show is presented (at 11pm). **Prices:** Show and two drinks 320F ($59.20); show and half bottle of champagne, 400F ($74). **Métro:** F.D. Roosevelt.

CRAZY HORSE SALOON, 12 av. George-V, 8e. Tel. 47-23-32-32.

Texans in ten-gallon hats are fond of "Le Crazy," which is considered by many to be the leading nude dancing joint in the world. Alain Bernardin parodies the American West in the decor, but only purists claim that Cheyenne was never like this.

Two dozen performers do their acts entirely nude. Sandwiched between the more sultry scenes are three international variety acts. **Open:** Daily, first show (less than two hours) 9pm, second show 11:30pm. **Prices:** Drinks 390F–510F ($72.15–$94.35), including the cover charge and two drinks; third drink from 55F ($10.20). **Métro:** George-V.

VILLA D'ESTE, 4 rue Arsène-Houssaye, 8e. Tel. 42-56-14-65.

When Amalia Rodrigues, Portugal's leading fadista and an international star, is in Paris, she's likely to appear at this supper club. Its owners book top talent from Europe and America. A short stroll from the Champs-Elysées, the Villa d'Este has been around for a long time, and the quality of its offerings remains high. The place is a *diner-dansant* club more than pure cabaret. The fixed-price menus include wine that grows increasingly better as the price rises. It's also possible to attend and order only a drink. The doors open at 8pm, with an orchestra playing from 9pm. A comedy/cabaret/magic act lasts until around midnight, with dancing until 2am. The place is closed in August. Reservations are necessary. Every Sunday afternoon a tea dance with a live orchestra is presented 3–7pm. **Prices:** Fixed-price menus 335F–670F ($62–$123.95); drinks 150F ($27.75) each; tea-dance admission 100F ($18.50), including first drink. **Métro:** Charles-de-Gaulle–Etoile.

JAZZ & ROCK

You can probably listen and dance to more jazz in Paris than in any U.S. city, with the possible exception of San Francisco. The great jazz revival that long ago swept America is still going full swing in Paris, with Dixieland or Chicago rhythms being pounded out in dozens of jazz cellars, mostly called *caveaux*.

This is one city where you don't have to worry about being a self-conscious dancer. The locals, even young people, are not particularly good. The best dancers on any floor are usually American. And although Parisians take to rock with enthusiasm, their skill does not match their zest.

The majority of the jazz/rock establishments are crowded into the Left Bank near the Seine between rue Bonaparte and rue St-Jacques, which makes things easy for syncopation-seekers.

LE BILBOQUET, 13 rue St-Benoît, 6e. Tel. 45-48-81-84.

This restaurant, jazz club, and piano bar offers some of the best music in Paris. In the heart of St-Germain-des-Prés, the site was famous during the heyday of existentialism. The film *Paris Blues* was shot here. Jazz is played on the upper level in Le Bilboquet restaurant. The wood-paneled room has a copper ceiling, a sunken bar with brass trim, and a Victorian candelabrum. Tables are on a raised tier and elevated balcony. The menu is limited but classic French, specializing in carré d'agneau, fish, and beef. Appetizers include smoked salmon and terrines. **Open:** Le Bilboquet, nightly 8pm–2:45am, live music presented 10:45pm–2:45am. Club St. Germain disco (downstairs), Mon–Sat 11:30pm–dawn. **Admission:** One drink requirement 65F–95F ($12.05–$17.60). Clients can walk from one club to the other, but they have to buy a new drink each time they change venues. **Prices:** Dinner at Le Bilboquet 250F–300F ($46.25–$55.50); admission (without dinner) 130F ($24.05), including first drink.

TROIS MAILLETZ, 58 rue Galande, 5e. Tel. 43-54-42-94.

This medieval cellar once housed the masons who built Notre-Dame, many of whom carved their initials into the walls. Today it attracts jazz aficionados from all over the world. It's one of the few places in the district where students don't predominate. Musical celebrities appearing here have included Memphis Slim, Bill Coleman, and Nina Simone. Traditional French meals, such as salmon tartare and grills, are served in a restaurant adjacent to the piano bar during its entire opening time. Reservations are recommended on weekends. The restaurant and piano bar are on the main level, and the jazz is in the cellar. **Open:** Wed–Sun 10:30pm–"whenever"; piano bar, daily 5pm–5am. **Admission:** Cellar, 65F ($12.05); restaurant and piano bar, free. **Prices:** Meals from 200F ($37), drinks 50F ($9.25). **Métro:** Maubert-Mutualité.

CAVEAU DE LA HUCHETTE, 5 rue de la Huchette, 5e. Tel. 43-26-65-05.

This celebrated jazz cave draws a young crowd, mostly students, who dance to the music of well-known jazz combos. This caveau is reached by a winding staircase. In prejazz days, it was frequented by Robespierre and Marat. **Open:** Sun–Fri 9:30pm–3am, Sat and holidays 9:30pm–4am. **Admission:** Sun–Thurs 50F ($9.25); Fri 60F ($11.10); Sat 65F ($12.05). Women students 45F ($8.35). **Prices:** Drinks 18F ($3.35). **Métro:** St-Michel.

SLOW CLUB, 130 rue de Rivoli, 1er. Tel. 42-33-84-30.
One of the most famous jazz cellars in Europe, the Slow Club features the well-known French jazz band of Claude Lutter, who played for 10 years with the late Sidney Bechet. **Open:** Tues–Thurs 10pm–3am; Fri–Sat and holidays 10pm–4am. **Admission:** Tues–Thurs 55F ($10.20), Fri–Sat and holidays 65F ($12.05). **Prices:** Drinks 17F ($3.15). **Métro:** Châtelet.

NEW MORNING, 7–9 rue des Petites-Ecuries, 10e. Tel. 45-23-51-41.
New Morning was named for Bob Dylan's 1969 album. The premises were once occupied by a daily newspaper and designed in 1981 to become a jazz club. The high-ceilinged loft allows jazz-maniacs to dance, talk, flirt, and drink elbow-to-elbow at the stand-up bar. The appropriate dress code is jeans or whatever, and concerts and musical soirées might include a range of practically everything except disco. The only rule here seems to be that there are few rules. It might be open at 9:30pm or closed just any night, but when it's in business, closing (except on salsa nights) is at 1:30 or 2am. If Stan Getz or Dizzy Gillespie can be booked on a Sunday, the place is open on Sunday. A phone call will let you know what's going on on the night of your visit. No food is served. **Admission:** 100F–150F ($18.50–$27.75). **Métro:** Château d'Eau.

JAZZ CLUB LIONEL HAMPTON, in the Hotel Méridien, 81 bd. Gouvion-St-Cyr, 17e. Tel. 40-68-30-42.
This club prides itself on such guest stars as Lionel Hampton (after whom it was named), Fats Domino, and Nita Whitheker. **Open:** Daily 10:30pm–2am. **Admission** (including the first drink): 135F ($25). **Métro:** Porte Maillot.

DANCE HALLS & DISCOS

Although Paris is supposedly the birthplace of the discothèque, nobody here seems to know anymore what, precisely, constitutes one. Originally the discos were small, intimate dives where patrons danced to records—hence the term. Now, however, the tag is applied to anything from playground-size ballrooms with full orchestras to tiny bars with taped tunes—where they don't let you dance at all.

The entire region opposite and around the church of St-Germain-des-Prés is so honeycombed with dance dives of one sort or another, and they are so ephemeral (some have the life spans of sickly butterflies), that it's almost impossible to keep track of their coming and closing. What's hopping at the time of writing might be a hardware store by the time you get there. But chances are there'll be two new joints in the same block.

The samples below are a few of the hundreds of spots where people go chiefly to dance—as distinct from others where the main attraction is the music.

LE PALACE, 8 rue du Faubourg-Montmartre, 9e. Tel. 47-70-75-02.

One of the leading nightclubs of Paris, La Palace re-creates 1940s Hollywood glamour. It's designed in the spirit and allure of a Roman or Greek amphitheater, with four different bars scattered over three different levels. Music is recorded, and there's plenty of room to dance. Management does not allow sneakers or jeans with holes pierced in indiscreet places. **Open:** Daily 11pm–dawn. **Admission:** 130F ($24.05), including first drink. **Métro:** Montmartre.

LA COUPOLE, 102 bd. Montparnasse, 14e. Tel. 43-20-14-21.

La Coupole is reviewed separately as a historical landmark café. One of the big Montparnasse cafés and a former stronghold of bohemia, it is a throwback to the days when locals waltzed and tangoed to the strains of a live orchestra. If you caught *Last Tango in Paris* on the late show, it would help as a prelude to a visit here. In addition to its upstairs café, La Coupole has a large basement ballroom reserved for dancing. **Open:** Fri 9pm–3am, Sat 3–7pm and 9pm–3am, Sun 3–7pm. **Admission:** Café, free. Ballroom, Sat matinee 60F ($11.10); Sunday matinee 80F ($14.80); Fri–Sat nights 90F ($16.65). **Métro:** Vavin.

CLUB ZED, 2 rue des Anglais, 5e. Tel. 43-54-93-78.

One of the most frequented after-dark haunts in Paris offers . . . well, you name it. Just show up and be surprised by, say, samba music straight out of Rio, nostalgic tunes from the 1960s, a jazz beat, and le rock on Sunday afternoon or Wednesday night. **Open:** Wed–Thurs 10:30pm–3:30am, Fri 10:30pm–4:30pm, Sun 4–8pm. **Closed:** Aug. **Admission:** First drink 50F–100F ($9.25–$18.50). **Métro:** Maubert-Mutualité.

LE BALAJO, 9 rue de Lappe, 11e. Tel. 47-00-07-87.

Remember the "little sparrow," Edith Piaf? This famous French chanteuse is still dearly remembered by the people of Paris, even the young ones who never saw her live but still listen to her recorded music. Le Balajo is the club—practically a national shrine—where Piaf used to appear frequently during her tortured lifetime. The place is still popular, drawing a medley of the young and the "Oh, to be young again" crowd. After performances at l'Opéra Bastille are over, you can continue the night here, listening to reggae, salsa, and rap. **Open:** Thurs–Mon 10pm–5am. **Admission** (including first drink): 100F ($18.50). **Métro:** Bastille.

L'ESCALE, 15 rue Monsieur-le-Prince, 6e. Tel. 43-25-55-22.

One of the true charmers of St-Germain-des-Prés, it's not exactly cheap, but worth every cent in terms of atmosphere and artistry. The bar is semidark and very intimate. The Mexican mural on the wall is almost invisible in the dim light. This is the oldest salsa and Latin music nightclub of Paris, set in a 17th-century building. Musicians play Latin American songs, not the diluted stuff you usually hear, but the really melancholy and wild gaucho airs, with the smoldering fire that is their special idiom. The club also has a *cave* where you can dance to a Latin combo. **Open:** Daily 10:30pm–3 or 4am. **Admission:** First drink, which you can nurse as long as you like, 90F ($16.65). **Métro:** Odéon.

RIVERSIDE CLUB, 7 rue Grégoire-de-Tours, 6e. Tel. 43-54-46-33.

There is usually a line at the door to this typical Left Bank cellar disco with an interesting, international crowd. Some dance *comme des foux* (like lunatics) to the music, which ranges from reggae to punk. **Open:** Daily 11pm–6 or 7am. **Admission** (including first drink): Sun–Thurs 75F ($13.90); Fri–Sat 85F ($15.75). **Prices:** Drinks 35F ($6.50). **Métro:** St-Michel or Odéon.

4. THE BAR SCENE

WINE BARS

Many Parisians now prefer to patronize wine bars instead of the traditional café or bistro. The food is often better, and the ambience more inviting. Wine bars come in a wide range of styles, from old traditional places to modern gathering centers.

WILLI'S WINE BAR, 13 rue des Petits-Champs, 1er. Tel. 42-96-37-86.

Journalists and stockbrokers alike are attracted to this popular wine bar in the center of the financial district, close to the Bourse. Surprisingly, it is run by two Englishmen, Mark Williamson and Tim Johnston. They offer about 250 different kinds of wine, and each week about a dozen "specials" are featured.

Very crowded at lunchtime, it often settles down to a lower decibel level in the evening, when you can better admire the 16th-century beams and the warm, friendly ambience. A blackboard menu lists the daily specials, which are likely to include brochette of lamb flavored with cumin or lyonnaise sausage in a truffled vinaigrette with pistachios, and a spectacular dessert, the chocolate terrine. You can enjoy wines by the glass. **Open:** Mon–Sat noon–2:30pm and 7–11pm. **Prices:** Fixed price menu 150F ($27.75), wine by the glass 20F ($3.70). **Métro:** Bourse or Louvre.

AU SAUVIGNON, 80 rue des Saints-Pères, 7e. Tel. 45-48-49-02.

Perhaps the best-known wine bar in Paris, Au Sauvignon is minuscule, although it overflows onto a covered terrace. Still, it has a very chic reputation. The owner is from Auvergne, and when he's not polishing his zinc countertop or preparing a plate of charcuterie, he will sell you wines by the glass. Beaujolais is the cheapest, and Puligny Montrachet the most expensive. Auvergne specialties, including goat cheese and terrines, are served if you'd like to have a snack with your wine. The fresh Poilane bread is ideal with the Auvergne ham, the country pâté, or the Crottin de Chavignol goat cheese. The place has a decor of old ceramic tiles and frescoes done by Left Bank artists. **Open:** Mon–Sat 9:30am–10:30pm. **Closed:** Major religious holidays; three weeks in Aug. **Prices:** Glass of wine 16F–36F ($2.95–$6.65); all wines cost an additional 2F (35¢) if consumed at a table. **Métro:** Sèvres-Babylone.

BLUE FOX BAR, 25 rue Royale (Cité Berryer), 8e. Tel. 42-65-10-72.

The Blue Fox adjoins Moulin du Village (see Chapter 5, "Paris Dining"). A large selection of wines by the glass is sold, along with *charcuterie*, salads, cheeses, and *plats du jour*. It's an unpretentious place, but frequented by some of the chicest people of Paris. It's on two levels, with lace curtains and a lot of country-style wood. At lunch it tends to be overcrowded, as it fills quickly with the people who staff the shops around the place de la Madeleine and along rue Royale. The entrance is on a little alleyway around the corner from Maxim's. **Open:** Mon–Fri noon–10pm. **Prices:** Glass of wine 20F–75F ($3.70–$13.90); plats du jour 70F–100F ($12.95–$18.50). **Métro:** Concorde or Madeleine.

MA BOURGOGNE, 19 place des Vosges, 4e. Tel. 42-78-44-64.

This fine brasserie with a good selection of wines sits in an area that has had a facelift and is lit up both day and night. You can come here to sit and contemplate this dreamy square, following in the footsteps of Victor Hugo. Under the arcades you can enjoy coffee or a glass of Beaujolais. Monsieur Aimé, the owner, selects all the wines himself. There are rattan sidewalk tables for summer sitting and a cozy room within with a beamed ceiling. Madame Aimé offers a wide choice of country dishes. Customers come from all over the city to eat her famous steak tartare. **Open:** Daily 8am–1am. **Closed:** Feb. **Prices:** Coffee 11F ($2.05); glass of wine from 18F ($3.35); meals 185F ($34.25). **Métro:** St-Paul or Bastille.

LA TARTINE, 24 rue de Rivoli, 4e. Tel. 42-72-76-85.

Resembling a movie set, this is Old Paris. Inset mirrors, decorative brass details, a zinc bar, and frosted globe chandeliers frame the door. At any moment you expect to see Tito, Trotsky, or Lenin walk in the door (each was a former patron). At least 50 wines are offered at reasonable prices, and all categories of wine are served by the glass. A plate of charcuterie will cost from 38F ($7.05), or you can order sandwiches. At least seven kinds of Beaujolais are offered, along with a large selection of Bordeaux. The light wine Sancerre is more favored than ever. With your wine, why not taste some young goat cheese from the Loire Valley? **Open:** Thurs–Mon 8am–10pm, Wed noon–10pm. **Closed:** Two weeks in Aug. **Prices:** Glass of wine from 8F–15.50F ($1.50–$28.70); sandwiches from 15F ($2.80). **Métro:** St-Paul.

BARS & PUBS

These are Anglo-American imports to France and—with few notable exceptions—strike an alien chord. They're about equally divided between those trying to imitate Stateside cocktail bars and those pretending to be British pubs. Some go to amazing lengths in the process.

Bar-hopping is fashionable with Paris's smart set, as distinct from café-sitting, which is practiced by the entire populace. Bar prices, therefore, are generally a fraction higher, a biggish fraction if the place boasts a well-known bartender.

LE BAR, 10 rue de l'Odéon, 6e. Tel. 43-26-66-83.

Le Bar is the actual name of this small and intimate hangout right off the place de l'Odéon on the Left Bank. This place is permanently thronged with swarms of noisy, friendly, amorous, and argumentative university students and is an ideal spot to make contact with them—if that's what you desire. Plastered with posters, both antique and pop, it reverberates to the strains of an overworked jukebox. **Open:** Daily 5:30pm–2am. **Prices:** Drinks from 36F ($6.65). **Metro:** Odéon.

PUB SAINT-GERMAIN-DES-PRES, 17 rue de l'Ancienne-Comédie, 6e. Tel. 43-29-38-70.

This is the only pub in the country to offer 24 draft beers and 450 international beers. Leather niches render drinking discreet. The decor consists of gilded mirrors on the walls, hanging gas lamps, and a stuffed parrot in a gilded cage. Leather-cushioned handrails are also provided for some mysterious purpose—guidance perhaps? You'll need it. There are nine different rooms and 500 seats, which makes the pub the largest in France. The atmosphere is quiet, relaxed, and rather posh, and it's open day and night. Genuine Whitbread beer is sold, and Pimm's No. 1 is featured. You can also order snacks or complete meals here. In the evening, there is band entertainment, both rock and variety. **Open:** Daily 10:30am–4am. **Prices:** Drinks from 19F ($3.50), menus from 130F ($24.05). **Métro:** Odéon.

RENAULT, 53 av. des Champs-Elysées, 8e. Tel. 42-25-28-17.

If you like to combine your hamburgers with shopping for a Renault, you'll be at the right place if you drop in at the Renault. At first you'll think you've come to an automobile showroom . . . and you have. But proceed to the rear, where a bar of "horseless carriages" is waiting. Here you can order either a set menu, an à la carte meal, or just a drink. **Open:** Daily 11am–1:30am. **Prices:** Set menu 110F ($20.35); à la carte meal 200F ($37); whiskey from 40F ($7.40) at the bar. **Métro:** F.D. Roosevelt.

SIR WINSTON CHURCHILL, 5 rue de Presbourg, 16e. Tel. 45-00-75-35.

On a fashionable Right Bank street is the most authentic-looking pub in Paris. It uses English advertising posters and serves real ale and imported British tea—along with roast beef and Yorkshire pudding. All the elements of Edwardian decor are here: cut-glass mirrors, plush banquettes, highly polished dark wood. At night a pair of enthusiastic musicians play guitar and piano. **Open:** Daily 9am–2am. **Prices:** Complete meal 220F–250F ($40.70–$46.25); whiskey 40F ($7.40). **Métro:** Charles-de-Gaulle–Etoile.

GRAND HOTEL BARS

If you want to re-create the elegance of the salons of 18th-century France, try one of the bars of the grand hotels of Paris. Dress up, talk softly, and be prepared to spend a lot for a drink. You're not paying for the drink but for an ambience unmatched in most other places.

GEORGE V BAR, 31 av. George-V, 8e. Tel. 47-23-54-00.

This is a divinely elegant combination of modern and classical design. All of it is arranged in an attractively symmetrical format of black accents over beige and maroon marble in a design that looks almost like a stage set. Most prominent is the massive crystal lighting fixture, the edges of which pleasingly correspond to the dimensions of the rectangular room. Of course, if there's someone you're trying to avoid, you can always sit among the upholstered couches and Regency antiques of the nearby salon. **Open:** Daily 11am–2am. **Prices:** Mixed drinks from 75F ($13.90). **Métro:** George-V.

HOTEL DE CRILLON, 10 place de la Concorde, 8e. Tel. 42-65-24-24.

This world-famous watering hole inside this world-famous hotel used to attract some of the most eminent members of the Lost

Generation, including Hemingway and Scott and Zelda Fitzgerald. Do you recall that Hemingway's fictional heroine, Brett Ashley, broke her promise to rendezvous there with Jake Barnes in *The Sun Also Rises?* Over the years it has also attracted most of the Kennedys, along with Noël Coward and practically every upper-level staff member of the American Embassy. Today's patrons might be Tom Cruise, Madonna, or perhaps Debra Winger. Classified as a historic monument, the hotel was recently refurbished under the watchful eye of fashion designer Sonia Rykiel. The decor of the bar no longer basks in its 1950s glow, but has undergone a covering of wood paneling. **Open:** Daily noon–2am. **Prices:** Drinks from 75F ($13.90). **Métro:** Concorde.

BAR ANGLAIS, in the Hôtel Plaza Athenée, 25 av. Montaigne, 8e. Tel. 47-23-78-33.

On your way through this deluxe citadel, you'll pass a chattering telex machine, which carries recent quotes from the world's leading stock exchanges, in case you want to check on your investment portfolio. In the rarefied atmosphere of this elegant bar, it seems appropriate to do so. As its name would imply, the bar, in the lower level of the hotel, has a decor that is vintage Anglo-Saxon, although the service is definitely French and the drinks are international. **Open:** Daily 10am–1am. **Prices:** Drinks from 85F ($15.75). **Métro:** Alma-Marceau.

HOTEL BRISTOL BAR, 112 rue du Faubourg St-Honoré, 8e. Tel. 42-66-91-45.

Looking over a central courtyard covered with latticework and dotted with greenery, you can sit in wicker chairs between pink marble columns and thick Asian rugs. Some distance away (one thing about the Bristol is that it has plenty of space), a raised platform has a better view of the Regency-style bar. Specialties are usually mixed by the chief barman, Michel Le Regent, who has developed such prize-winning combinations as a "crazy horse cocktail" (strawberries, bananas, scotch, and champagne), a nanny's cocktail (lemon and pineapple juice, blue curaçao, banana liqueur, and vodka), or a Pluton (orange juice, pineapple juice, Pernod, vodka, and strawberries). A pianist adds to the pleasure nightly between 7:30pm and midnight. **Open:** Daily 11am–1:30am. **Prices:** Drinks from 80F ($14.80). **Métro:** Miromesnil.

5. SPECIALTY BARS & CLUBS

GAY PARIS

Gay life is mostly centered around Les Halles and Le Marais, with the greatest concentration of gay clubs, restaurants, bars, and shops located between the Hôtel-de-Ville and Rambuteau Métro stops. Gay discos come and go so fast that even a magazine devoted somewhat to their pursuit, *Gay Pied,* has a hard time keeping up. That magazine is sold at many news kiosks, as is *Lesbia,* a monthly national lesbian magazine.

LE BOY, 6 rue Caumartin, 9e. Tel. 47-42-68-05.

For some time now, this has been the leading gay club of Paris, lying near the Opéra. A half-moon seating and standing area surrounds a large dance floor. Mirrors and lights show off the all-male clients, most of whom are in their late 20s. **Open:** Daily 10pm–4am. **Admission:** Sun–Thurs free, Fri–Sat 55F ($10.20). **Prices:** Beer 32F ($5.90). **Métro:** Opéra.

LA CHAMPMESLE, 4 rue Chabanais, 2e. Tel. 42-96-85-20.

With dim lighting, background music, and comfortable banquettes, La Champmesle offers a cozy meeting place for women. It is, in fact, the leading women's bar of Paris. The club is contained within a 300-year-old building, decorated with exposed stone and heavy ceiling beams, with "retro"-style furnishings evocative of the 1950s. Every Thursday night one of the premier lesbian events of Paris is a cabaret held here beginning at 10pm. The entrance price and drinks cost the same on Thursday as any other time. Josy is the charming entrepreneur who established this place some 15 years ago. **Open:** Daily 6pm–2am. **Admission:** 35F ($6.50), including first drink. **Prices:** Drinks 50F ($9.25). **Métro:** Opéra.

MADAME ARTHUR, 75 bis, rue des Martyrs, 18e. Tel. 42-54-40-21.

Madame Arthur is one of the leading female-impersonator cabarets of Europe. This place Pigalle showplace, drawing both straights and gays, is directed by Madame Arthur, who is no lady. The joke is, this place has been around so long it welcomed the invading armies of Julius Caesar—and it's still going strong. You can visit just to drink, or you can dine from a fixed-price menu, the very expensive one offering caviar. Reservations are a good idea. **Open:** Daily, show 10:30pm–12:30am. **Admission:** 280F ($51.80) including first drink. **Prices:** Drinks 95F ($17.60); fixed-price menu 280F–695F ($51.80–$128.60). **Métro:** Abbesses.

LE NEW MONOCLE, 60 bd. Edgar-Quinet, 14e. Tel. 43-20-81-12.

Located in the center of Montparnasse, Le New Monocle has been a traditional lesbian hangout since the days of Gertrude and Alice. It is a *disco féminin* and does not admit any men. Inside is a bar (all drinks cost the same), plus a dance floor ringed with seats and banquettes, and comfortably battered 1950s-inspired accessories. **Open:** Mon–Sat 11pm–dawn. **Closed:** Aug. **Admission:** Free. **Prices:** Drinks 85F ($15.75). **Métro:** Edgar-Quinet.

LE BAR CENTRAL, 33 rue Vieille-du-Temple, 4e. Tel. 42-78-11-42.

Le Bar Central is one of the leading bars for men in the Hôtel-de-Ville area. In fact, it is probably the most famous gay men's bar in Paris today. The club has established a small hotel upstairs with a few facilities and only seven bedrooms. Singles are 320F ($59.20) daily and doubles are 410F ($75.85), including breakfast. Both the bar and its little hotel are within a 300-year-old building in the heart of Le Marais. The hotel caters especially to gay men, less frequently to lesbians. **Open:** Daily 4pm–2am. **Admission:** Free. **Prices:** Beer 15F ($2.80). **Métro:** Hôtel-de-Ville.

LE PIANO ZINC, 49 rue des Blancs-Manteaux, 4e. Tel. 42-74-32-42.

This ever-popular place with no cover charge is unusual. Founded by a German-born Francophile named Jurgen about 10 years ago, it is both a piano bar and a cabaret, filled with singing patrons who belt out old French *chansons* with humor and gusto. It defines itself as a gay bar, "but you can happily bring your grandmère, as some of our clients do," management assures us. The place is contained on three different floors of a building, with the cabaret presented in the basement nightly at 10pm for no charge. **Open:** Daily 6pm–2am. **Prices:** Mixed drinks 42F ($7.75), beer 20F ($3.70). **Métro:** Rambateau.

LITERARY HAUNTS

HARRY'S NEW YORK BAR, 5 rue Daunou, 5e. Tel. 42-61-71-14.

⊛ "*Sank roo doe Noo,*" as the ads tell you to instruct your cab driver, is the most famous bar in Europe—quite possibly in the world. Opened on Thanksgiving Day in 1911, it's sacred to Hemingway disciples as the spot where Ernest did most of his Parisian imbibing. To others it's hallowed as the site where white lady and sidecar cocktails were invented in 1919 and 1931, respectively. Also, it is the birthplace of the Bloody Mary and French '75, as well as headquarters of the International Bar Flies (IBF).

The upstairs bar is excessively hearty and masculine, but it gets smoother down below under the influence of an excellent pianist performing from 10pm to 2am. The bars are always crammed with Anglo-Americans and their Gallic admirers. The downstairs room has been redecorated and fitted with its own wet bar. **Open:** Daily 10:30am–4:30am. **Closed:** Christmas. **Prices:** Dry martini 42F ($7.75), whiskey from 50F ($9.25). **Métro:** Opéra or Pyramides.

ROSEBUD, 11 bis, rue Delambre, 14e. Tel. 43-35-38-54.

The name is taken from Orson Welles' greatest film, *Citizen Kane*. Rosebud is just around the corner from the famous cafés of Montparnasse. It once attracted such devotees as the late Jean-Paul Sartre and Simone de Beauvoir, Eugene Ionesco, and Marguerite Duras. Drop in at night for a glass of wine or perhaps something to eat, maybe a hamburger or chile con carne. **Open:** Daily 7pm–2am. **Prices:** Light meals from 150F ($27.75), drinks 55F–62F ($10.20–$11.45). **Métro:** Vavin.

LA CLOSERIE DES LILAS, 171 bd. du Montparnasse, 6e. Tel. 43-26-70-50.

Hemingway, Picasso, Gershwin, and Modigliani all loved the Closerie, and it has once again become one of the hottest bars in Paris. Look for the brass nameplate of your favorite Lost Generation artist along the banquettes or at the well-oiled bar. **Open:** Daily 11am–2am. **Prices:** Scotch and soda 55F ($10.20), beer 32F ($5.90). **Métro:** Port-Royal.

HISTORIC TAVERNS

AU FRANC PINOT, 1 quai de Bourbon, 4e. Tel. 43-29-46-98.

At the foot of Pont Marie, this is the oldest wine bistro in Paris. Its double tier of vaulted cellars dates from the early 17th century. The establishment was renovated in 1980 by the owners, who added an inventory of about two dozen wines that are sold by the glass. These you can consume while standing at the large wooden bar (which is crowned by a large metal rooster), or seated on one of the bentwood chairs in the warm glow of the stained-glass windows.

If you descend into one of the deepest cellars of Paris, you will find a cozily intimate restaurant offering such specialties as lamb with crayfish in a tarragon cream sauce, or terrine of foie gras with fresh duckling from Landes, and a small selection of other classic French dishes. The last glass of red Sancerre, Beaujolais, or riesling is consumed at the bar at 11:30pm, but you can go as early as 6pm for food. It is closed every Sunday and Monday. **Open:** Tues–Sat 6–11:30pm. **Prices:** Set menu 210F ($38.85); à la carte dinners average 300F ($55.50). **Métro:** Pont-Marie.

TAVERNE HENRI-IV, 13 place du Pont-Neuf, 1er. Tel. 43-54-27-90.

Quite different from my other recommendations, this is called both a *taverne* and *bistro à vin*. The location couldn't be more magnificent—in a 17th-century building at the Pont Neuf, on the Ile de la Cité. The host, Monsieur Cointepas, does his own bottling, or at least some of it. His prize wines are listed on a blackboard menu. You might order a special Beaujolais or perhaps a glass of Chinon, the latter "tasting more of the earth"; all drinks are cheaper at the bar. Snacks include wild-boar pâté, and as the owner puts it, the price depends on what you spread on your slice of bread. Eight farmer's lunches are offered. **Open:** Mon–Sat 11:30am–9:30pm. **Closed:** Aug. **Prices** (including service): Glass of wine 20F–30F ($3.70–$5.55); snacks 20F–25F ($3.70–$4.65); farmer's lunch 58F ($10.75). **Métro:** Pont-Neuf.

EASY EXCURSIONS FROM PARIS

1. VERSAILLES
2. FONTAINEBLEAU
3. EURO DISNEY

Paris—the city that grew from an island—is itself the center of a curious landlocked island known as the Ile de France.

Shaped roughly like a saucer, it lies encircled by a thin ribbon of rivers: the Epte, Aisne, Marne, and Yonne. Fringing these rivers are mighty forests with famous names—Rambouillet, St-Germain, Compiègne, and Fontainebleau. These forests are said to be responsible for Paris's clear, gentle air, and the unusual length of its spring and fall. This may be a debatable point, but there's no argument that they provide the capital with a chain of excursion spots, all within easy reach.

The forests were once the possessions of kings and the ruling aristocracy, and they're still sprinkled with the magnificent châteaux, or palaces, of their former masters. Together with ancient hamlets, glorious cathedrals, and little country inns, they turn the Ile de France into a traveler's paradise. On a more modern note, Euro Disney draws visitors from all over the world. Because of Paris's comparatively small size, it's almost at your doorstep.

The difficult question is where to go. What I'm offering in this chapter is merely a handful of the dozens of possibilities for one-day jaunts.

---

1. VERSAILLES

13 miles SW of Paris, 44 miles NE of Chartres

GETTING THERE By Train Take the RER line (C5), which leaves every 15 minutes from Paris, to Versailles–Rive Gauche. Turn right when you exit. Eurailpass holders travel free.

By Métro Get off at Pont de Sèvres and transfer to Bus 171. The trip takes 15 minutes. To get there from Paris, it's cheaper to pay with three Métro tickets from a *carnet* packet. You'll be let off near the gates of the palace.

By Car Take the N10 highway. Park on place d'Armes in front of the palace.

ESSENTIALS The town is dominated by the palace. Three main avenues radiate from place d'Armes in front of the palace. The **tourist office** is at 7 rue des Reservoirs (tel. 39-50-36-22).

The kings of France built a glittering private world for themselves, far from the grime and noise and bustle of Paris: the **Château de Versailles** ✪, place d'Armes (tel. 30-84-74-00). Seeing all of the palace's rooms would take up an entire morning and leave you pretty exhausted, so you should probably skip some of them and save energy for the park, which is the ultimate in French landscaping—every tree, shrub, flower, and hedge disciplined into a frozen ballet pattern and blended with soaring fountains, sparkling little lakes, grandiose stairways, and hundreds of marble statues. More like a colossal stage setting than a park—even the view of the blue horizon seems embroidered on—it's a Garden of Eden for puppet people, a place where you expect the birds to sing coloratura soprano.

Inside, the **Grand Apartments,** the **Royal Chapel,** and the **Hall of Mirrors** (where the Treaty of Versailles was signed) can be visited without a guide Tuesday through Sunday between 9:45am and 5pm (closed holidays). Admission is 30F ($5.55) for adults and 15F ($2.80) for children 5 to 14. Other sections of the château may be visited only at specific hours or on special days. Some of the sections are temporarily closed as they undergo restoration.

Try to save time to visit the **Grand Trianon,** which is a good walk across the park. In pink-and-white marble, it was designed by Hardouin-Mansart for Louis XIV in 1687. The Trianon is mostly furnished with Empire pieces. You can also visit the **Petit Trianon,** built by Gabriel in 1768. This was the favorite residence of Marie Antoinette, who could escape the rigors of court here. Once it was a retreat for Louis XV and his mistress, Madame du Barry. The Grand Trianon is open Tuesday through Sunday from 9:45am to noon and 2 to 5pm. Entrance costs 15F ($2.80). The Petit Trianon is open the same days from 2 to 5pm; admission is 10F ($1.85). A combination ticket to both Trianons is 18F ($3.35).

On Sunday, reduced rates are available to all visitors: 15F ($2.80) for the château, 8F ($1.50) for the Grand Trianon, 5F (95¢) for the Petit Trianon. The same reduced rates are offered Tuesday through Saturday to people ages 18 through 25 and over 60. For more information, call 39-50-58-32.

EVENING SPECTACLES The tourist office in Versailles (see above) offers a program of evening fireworks and illuminated fountains on several occasions throughout the summer. These spectacles are announced a full season in advance. Dates usually fall on Saturday night, although schedules change from year to year. Spectators sit on bleachers clustered at the boulevard de la Reine entrance to the Basin of Neptune. The most desirable frontal view seats cost 160F ($29.60); seats with a side view go for 80F ($14.80); and standing room on the promenoir sells for 50F ($9.25), free for children under 10. Gates admitting you to the Grande Fête de Nuit de Versailles open one and a half hours before showtime.

Tickets can be purchased in advance at the tourist office in Versailles, or in Paris at Agence Perrossier, 6 place de la Madeleine, 8e (tel. 42-60-58-31), and Agence des Théâtres, 78 av. des Champs-Elysées, 8e (tel. 43-59-24-60). If you've just arrived in Versailles from Paris, you can always take your chances and purchase tickets an hour ahead of showtime at boulevard de la Reine. The show lasts for one and a half hours.

From the beginning of May until the end of September, a less elaborate spectacle is staged each Sunday. Called Grandes Eaux

1. Versailles
2. Fontainebleau
3. Euro Disney

Musicales, it is a display of fountains in the park. Classical music is also played.

WHERE TO DINE

LES TROIS MARCHES, Hotel Trianon Palace, 1 bd. de la Reine. Tel. 30-84-38-00.
Cuisine: FRENCH. **Reservations:** Required.

$ Prices: Appetizers 175F–240F ($32.40–$44.40); main courses 185F–355F ($34.25–$65.70); fixed price lunch 280F ($51.80). AE, DC, MC, V.

Open: Lunch daily noon–2pm, dinner daily 7:30–10pm.

For lunch, you can dine in regal style at the Trianon Palace Hotel. Set in a five-acre garden, the hotel became world famous in 1919 when it was the headquarters for the signers of the Treaty of Versailles. It still retains its Old World splendor, its dining room decorated with crystal chandeliers and fluted columns. The chef, Gérard Vié, is, it is conceded, the most talented and creative chef feeding visitors to Versailles these days. He attracts a discerning clientele who don't mind paying the high prices. The cuisine moderne is subtle, often daringly inventive and conceived, the service smooth. Specialties are likely to include roast pigeon in a garlic-and-cream sauce (bound with the animal's own blood), a celery terrine with duck liver, and veal with sea urchins, along with ravioli stuffed with lobster, truffles, and spinach.

LE RESCATORE, 27 av. St-Cloud. Tel. 39-50-23-60.

Cuisine: SEAFOOD. **Reservations:** Required.

$ Prices: Appetizers 120F–160F ($22.20–$29.60); main courses 145F–200F ($26.85–$37); fixed-price lunch 225F ($41.65). AE, MC, V.

Open: Lunch Mon–Fri 12:30–2pm; dinner Mon–Sat 7:30–10pm.

The decor is classic and conservative, within a pink-hued, high-ceilinged room, the tall French doors of which overlook ornate wrought-iron balconies and the busy avenue in the center of town below. The chef de cuisine, Jacques Bagot, creates an illusion of living near the sea with his cassoulet of fish, his perfectly prepared turbot sweetened with mild garlic, and his pot-au-feu of seafood. Occasionally he offers a selection of grilled exotic fish.

LE POTAGER DU ROY, 1 rue du Maréchal Joffre. Tel. 39-50-35-34.

Cuisine: FRENCH. **Reservations:** Required.

$ Prices: Appetizers 95F–145F ($17.60–$26.85); main courses 105F–170F ($19.45–$31.45); fixed-price menu 170F ($31.45). MC, V.

Open: Lunch Tues–Sat noon–2pm, dinner Tues–Sat 7:30–10pm.

Philippe Le Tourneur used to work for another Versailles chef, Gérard Vié, before setting up his own attractive restaurant on a busy streetcorner in a commercial part of town. Set behind a maroon facade, in a modern decor of several warmly decorated rooms, he offers a set menu or comparably priced à la carte meals. You might begin with a lamb terrine with raisins and pistachio nuts, then follow with calf's head in a ravigote sauce or steamed filet of sole with summer vegetables. You might also try roast lamb en papillote.

---

2. FONTAINEBLEAU

37 miles S of Paris, 46 miles NE of Orléans

GETTING THERE By Train Trains to Fontainebleau depart from the Gare de Lyon in Paris and take from 35 minutes to an hour. Fontainebleau station is just outside the town in Avon, a suburb of

VERSAILLES

0 [scale] 700 m / 770 y

Carriage Museum ④
Cathédrale St-Louis ⑫
Château ⑥
Grand Trianon ③
Hamlet (Hameau) ①
Lambinet Museum ⑦
Library ⑪

Notre-Dame ⑧
Petit Trianon ②
Royal Stables ⑨
Tourist
  Information ⑤
Town Hall (Hôtel
  de Ville) ⑩

⊕ PARIS
• Versailles

Paris; the town bus makes the 2-mile trip to the château every 10 to 15 minutes on weekdays (every 30 minutes on Sunday).

ESSENTIALS Dominated by its château, the town is surrounded by the dense **Forêt de Fontainebleau**. The main squares are place du Général-de-Gaulle and place d'Armes. The **Office de Tourisme** is at 31 place Napoléon-Bonaparte (tel. 64-22-25-68).

Napoléon called the **Palace of Fontainebleau** ✪ the house of the centuries. Much of French history has taken place within its walls, perhaps no moment more memorable than when Napoléon I stood on the horseshoe-shaped stairway and bade a loving farewell to his army before his departure to Elba and exile. That scene has been the subject of countless paintings, including Vernet's *Les Adieux* of the emperor.

Napoléon's affection for Fontainebleau was understandable. He was following the pattern of a grand parade of French kings in the pre-Versailles days who used Fontainebleau as a resort and hunted in its magnificent forests. François I tried to turn the hunting lodge into a royal palace in the Italian Renaissance style—he brought artists, including Benvenuto Cellini, to work for him.

Under the patronage of François I, the School of Fontainebleau, led by painters Rosso Fiorentino and Primaticcio, grew in prestige. The artists adorned the 210-foot-long **Gallery of François I**. Stucco-framed panels depict such scenes as *The Rape of Europa;* the *Nymph of Fontainebleau;* and the monarch holding a pomegranate, a symbol of unity. The salamander, the symbol of the Chevalier King, is everywhere.

Sometimes called the Gallery of Henri II, the **Ballroom** is in the mannerist style, with the interlaced initials *H&D* in the decoration. This was a reference to Henri's mistress, Diane de Poitiers. You can also see the initials *H&C*, symbolizing Henri and his wife, Catherine de Médicis. At one end of the room is a monumental fireplace supported by two bronze satyrs, made in 1966 (the originals were melted down in the Revolution). At the other side is the balcony of the musicians, with sculptured garlands. The ceiling contains octagonal coffering adorned with rosettes. Above the wainscoting is a series of frescoes, painted between 1550 and 1558, which depict such mythological subjects as *The Feast of Bacchus*.

An architectural curiosity is the richly and elegantly adorned **Louis XV Staircase.** The ceiling above it was originally decorated by Primaticcio for the bedroom of the duchesse d'Etampes, but when an architect was designing the stairway, he simply ripped out her floor and used the bedroom ceiling to cover the stairway. Of the Italian frescoes that were preserved, one depicts the Queen of the Amazons climbing into Alexander's bed.

When Louis XIV ascended to the throne, Fontainebleau was virtually neglected because of his preoccupation with Versailles. However, he wasn't opposed to using the palace for house guests—specifically such unwanted ones as Queen Christina, who had abdicated the throne of Sweden. Apparently thinking she still had "divine right," she ordered one of the most brutal royal murders on record—that of her companion Monaldeschi, who had ceased to please her.

Louis XV and, later, Marie Antoinette also took an interest in Fontainebleau.

The château found renewed glory—and shame—under Napoléon I. You can walk around much of the palace on your own, but most of the **Napoléonic Rooms** are accessible by guided tour only. His throne room and bedroom (look for his symbol, a bee) are equally impressive. You can also see where the emperor signed his abdication—the document exhibited is a copy. The furnishings in Empress Joséphine's apartments and the grand apartments of Napoléon evoke the imperial heyday.

After your long trek through the palace, visit the **gardens** and, especially, the carp pond; the gardens, however, are only a prelude to the Forest of Fontainebleau.

The apartments (tel. 64-22-27-40) are open Wednesday through Monday from 9:30am to 12:30pm and 2 to 5pm. Entrance to the Grands Apartments is 25F ($4.65); to the Petits Apartments, 14F ($2.60).

WHERE TO STAY & DINE

LE BEAUHARNAIS, in the Hôtel de l'Aigle Noir, 27 place Napoléon-Bonaparte. Tel. 64-22-32-65.
  Cuisine: FRENCH. **Reservations:** Required.
$ **Prices:** Appetizers 95F–160F ($17.60–$25.60); main courses 140F–165F ($25.90–$30.55); fixed-price meals 250F–330F ($46.25–$61.05). AE, DC, MC, V.
  Open: Lunch daily noon–2pm, dinner daily 7:30–9:30pm.
One of the leading restaurants is Le Beauharnais at the Hôtel de l'Aigle Noir. Although it's been completely renovated, it has retained its old charm. Opposite the château, the building was once the home of the Cardinal de Retz. It dates from the 16th century, but was converted into a hotel in 1720. The restaurant, the most beautiful in town, was installed in a former courtyard. The interior is filled with Empire furniture and potted palms. Specialties include roast duckling

FONTAINEBLEAU

0 — 200 m / 220 y

N

rue Guérin · r. de la Faisanderie · rue Victor Hugo · rue de la Paroisse · rue des Bois · rue Saint-Honoré · rue Grande · rue A. Briand

bd. J.F. Kennedy · bd. André Maginot · rue de Fleury · rue de France · rue Saint-Merri · rue Royale

bd. de Constance

rue Saint-Honoré · rue Saint-Merri · rue de l'Arbre Sec

rue de Ferrare · rue Dénecourt

place Dénecourt

rue Grande · r. du Parc · rue du Château · rue d'Avon

place d'Armes · place Bois-d'Hiver

Pavillon de Sully · Les Cascades

place du Gen. de Gaulle

❷ ❾ ❸ ❺ ❺ ❿ ⓫ ❻ ❼ ❹

cour de la Fontaine · Le Tibre · Parterre · Le Romulus

bd. Magenta · Etang des Carpes · av. de Maintenon

❶ · ⓬ Jardin Anglais

route de Cascades

N6

cour do l'Obélisque · bd. du Maréchal Juin · cour de Maintenon

N152 Orléans · N7 Nemours · N6 Moret & Sens →

★ PARIS

● Fontainebleau

Cour du Cheval-Blanc ❸
Cour du Offices ⓫
Cour Ovale ❻
Galerie de Diane ❿
Jardin Anglais ⓬
Jardin Diane ❷
Louis XV Staircase ❹
Musée Bibliothèque ❶
Napoleon's Apartment ❺

Porte du Baptistère ❽
Salle de Bal ❼
Throne Room ❾

---

in the style of Rouen, sweetbreads with foie gras served pot-au-feu, and grilled pigeon with pistachio nuts. There is a changing array of other dishes, depending on seasonal produce.

The hotel has 57 bedrooms and 6 suites, all with private baths and such modern conveniences as color TVs, radios, minibars, direct-dial phones, double windows, and electric heating. Each is individually decorated, often with antiques and pleasantly tasteful colors. Singles or doubles range in price from 1,000F ($185), suites from 1,300F ($240.50).

LE DAUPHIN, 24–26 Grande-Rue. Tel. 74-22-27-04.
Cuisine: FRENCH. **Reservations:** Recommended.

$ Prices: Appetizers 24F–74F ($4.45–$13.70); main courses 52F–100F ($9.60–$18.50); fixed-price meal 80F ($14.80) Mon–Sat, 155F ($28.70) Sun. MC, V.
Open: Lunch Thurs–Tues noon–2pm, dinner Thurs–Mon 7–9:30pm. **Closed:** Feb; one week in Sept.

Le Dauphin offers one of the best and most inexpensive meals in town. Located in the inner city, it is near the tourist office and a short walk from the château. The decor is that of a country tavern, with walls upholstered in flowery fabrics. Specialties include endive in Roquefort dressing, steak au poivre flambé in cognac, and confit de canard (duck) from Landes with flap mushrooms. Dessert could be a tarte tatin or a pear sorbet.

---

3. EURO DISNEY

20 miles E of Paris

GETTING THERE By Train The resort is linked to the RER commuter express rail network (Line A), with a stop at the entrance. Board the RER at inner-city Paris stops, which include Invalides, Nation, or Châtelet–Les Halles, descending at Marne-la-Vallée/Chessy, a 45-minute ride from the place Charles-de-Gaulle–Etoile in the center of Paris. The round-trip fare is 62F ($11.50). Trains run every 10 to 20 minutes, depending on the time of day.

By Bus Each of the hotels within the resort is connected by shuttlebus to and from Orly Airport (departing every 45 minutes daily between 9am and 7pm) and Roissy–Charles de Gaulle (departing every 30 minutes daily between 8am and 8pm). One-way transport to the park from either airport costs 65F ($12). Within the park, a free shuttlebus interconnects the various hotels with the theme park, stopping every 6 to 15 minutes, depending on the time of year. They begin their runs an hour before the opening of the park, and stop an hour after its closing.

By Car Take the A-4 highway east. Exit where it's marked "Park Euro Disney."

Guest parking at any of the thousands of parking spaces costs between 30F ($5.55) and 50F ($9.25), depending on the size of the vehicle. An interconnected series of moving sidewalks speeds up pedestrian transit from the parking areas to the entrance of the theme park.

ESSENTIALS Information All of the hotels recommended below offer information about the theme park, but for specific details, contact the **Euro Disney Guest Relations** office, located within City Hall on Main Street, U.S.A. (tel. 64-74-30-00 for French-language or 49-41-49-10 for English-language information).

Fast Facts Coin-operated lockers can be rented for 10F ($1.85) per use, and larger bags can also be stored for 10F ($1.85) per day. Children's **strollers** and **wheelchairs** can be rented for 30F ($5.55) per day, with a 20F ($3.70) deposit. **Babysitting** for up to 45 children (ages 3 to 14) is available every evening between 5pm and midnight. The price is 40F ($7.40) per hour, with a required minimum of 120F ($22.20). Meals, from a nearby diner, cost extra.

After evoking some of the most enthusiastic and most controversial reactions in recent French history, in 1992 **Euro Disney** ✪ opened the doors to one of the most lavish theme parks in the world. Set on a 5,000-acre site (about one-fifth the size of Paris) in the suburb of Marne-la-Vallée, the park incorporates the elements of its Disney predecessors—but with a European flair.

The Euro Disney resort is conceived as a total vacation destination, clustering together five different "lands" of entertainment, six massive and well-designed hotels, a campground, and dozens of restaurants, shows, and shops. Visitors from virtually every country in Europe stroll amid an abundance of flowerbeds, trees, reflecting ponds, fountains, and a very large artificial lake flanked with hotels (see below). An army of smiling employees and Disney characters (many of whom are multilingual) including Buffalo Bill, Mickey and Minnie Mouse, and Caribbean pirate Jean Laffitte are on hand to greet and delight the thousands of children in attendance.

Of the attractions, Main Street, U.S.A., is replete with horse-drawn carriages, and street-corner barbershop quartets. From there steam-powered railway cars embark from the "Main Street Station" for a trip through a Grand Canyon Diorama to Frontierland, with its paddlewheel steamers reminiscent of the Mississippi Valley of Mark Twain's era, "The Critter Corral at the Cottonwood Creek Ranch" petting zoo, and "The Lucky Nugget Saloon," straight from the gold-rush era. There, visitors find an array of cancan shows (ironically originating from the cabarets of turn-of-the-century Paris).

The resort's steam trains chug past Adventureland—with its swashbuckling pirates of the 18th century, the treehouse of the Swiss family Robinson, and reenacted legends from the *Arabian Nights*—to Fantasyland. There lies the symbol of the theme park, the Sleeping Beauty Castle ("Le Château de la Belle au Bois Dormant"), the soaring pinnacles and turrets of which are an idealized (and spectacular) interpretation of the châteaux of France. Parading within its shadow are time-tested but European versions of Snow White and the Seven Dwarfs, Peter Pan, Dumbo the Flying Elephant, Alice in Wonderland's Mad Tea Party, and Sir Lancelot's magic carrousel.

Visions of the future are exhibited at Discoveryland, whose tributes to human invention and imagination are drawn from the works of da Vinci, Jules Verne, H. G. Wells, the modern masters of science fiction, and the *Star Wars* series.

In addition to the theme park, Disney maintains an entertainment center, **Le Festival Disney,** the layout of which might remind visitors of a mall in California. Illuminated inside by a spectacular gridwork of lights suspended 60 feet above the ground, the complex contains dance clubs, shops, restaurants (one of which offers a dinner spectacle, "Buffalo Bill's Wild West Show" (see below), bars, a French government tourist office, post office, babysitting service, and a marina.

Admission: Admission for one day costs 225F ($41.60) for adults (ages 12 and over), and 150F ($27.75) for children ages 3 to 11. Admission for two days costs 425F ($78.63) for adults and 285F ($52.72) for children.

Open: June 21–Aug 31, daily 9am–11pm; Sept 1–June 20, daily 9am–9pm.

Tours: Guided tours can be arranged for 45F ($8.35) for adults and 35F ($6.50) for children ages 3 to 11. Lasting 3½ hours and incorporating 20 or more people, the tours offer one of the best opportunities for a complete visit. Note that whether you participate in a guided tour or not, you may still be required to wait in line.

WHERE TO STAY

The resort contains six hotels, each of which evokes a different theme and shares a common reservations service. For information within

North America, call 407/W-DISNEY (934-7639). For reservations within France, contact the Central Reservations Office, Euro Disney S.C.A., B.P. 105, F-77777 Marne-la-Vallée Cedex 4. Tel. 49-41-49-10.

EXPENSIVE

DISNEYLAND HOTEL, Euro Disney Resort, B.P. 105, F-77777 Marne-la-Vallée Cedex 4. Tel. 60-45-65-00. Fax 60-45-65-33. 479 rms, 21 suites. A/C MINIBAR TV TEL
$ **Rates:** 1,300F–1,950F ($240.50–$360.80) for 1 to 4 persons; suites from 3,000F ($555). Continental breakfast 65F ($12) extra. AE, DC, MC, V.

Considered the flagship hotel of the resort and positioned at the entrance to the park, the hotel resembles a massive Victorian seaside hotel, with red-tile turrets and jutting balconies, which some observers liken to the town hall of a major European city. Bedrooms are plushly and conservatively furnished, and contain private safes. On the "Castle Club" floor, free newspapers, all-day beverages, and access to a well-equipped private lounge are provided.

Dining/Entertainment Three restaurants (the California Grill is recommended separately), two bars.

Facilities: Health club with indoor/outdoor pool, whirlpool, sauna, private dining and banqueting rooms.

Services: Room service, laundry, babysitting.

HOTEL NEW YORK, Euro Disney Resort, B.P. 105, F-77777 Marne-la-Vallée Cedex 4. Tel. 60-45-73-00. Fax 60-45-73-33. 539 rms, 36 suites. A/C TEL TV MINIBAR
$ **Rates:** 1,100F–1,600F ($203.50–$296) for 1 to 4 persons. Continental breakfast 60F ($11.10) extra. AE, DC, MC, V.

Inspired by the Big Apple at its best, this hotel was designed around a nine-story central "skyscraper" flanked by the Gramercy Park Wing and the Brownstones Wing. (The exteriors of both of these wings evoke the row houses of their respective Manhattan neighborhoods.) Set at the edge of Lake Buena Vista, the hotel incorporates an ornamental pool that, in winter, is transformed into a lookalike version of the skating rink at Rockefeller Center. Bedrooms are comfortably appointed with art deco accessories and New York–inspired memorabilia.

Dining/Entertainment: A diner, two cocktail and wine bars.

Services: Room service, laundry, babysitting.

Facilities: Indoor/outdoor pool, two outdoor tennis courts, health club.

MODERATE

NEWPORT BAY CLUB, Euro Disney Resort, B.P. 105, F-77777 Marne-la-Vallée Cedex 4. Tel. 60-45-55-00. Fax 49-30-71-00. 1,083 rms, 15 suites. A/C TV TEL MINIBAR
$ **Rates:** 750F–1,100F ($138.80–$203.50) for 1 to 4 persons. Continental breakfast 60F ($11.10) extra. AE, DC, MC, V.

This hotel is designed with a central cupola, jutting balconies, and a fresh color scheme of blue and cream, inspired by a harborfront New England hotel. The hotel is ringed with verdant lawns and a large front porch with comfortable rocking chairs. Each of the nautically inspired bedrooms contains closed-circuit TV movies. The upscale Yacht Club and the less formal Cape Cod restaurants are the dining choices. Facilities include a lakeside promenade, croquet, a glassed-in pool pavilion, an outdoor pool, and a health club with sun beds and a sauna.

SEQUOIA LODGE, Euro Disney Resort, B.P. 105, F-77777 Marne-la-Vallée Cedex 4. Tel. 60-45-51-00. Fax 60-45-51-33. 997 rms, 14 suites. A/C TV TEL MINIBAR
$ Rates: 750F–1,100F ($138.80–$203.50) for 1 to 4 persons. Continental breakfast 60F ($11.10) extra. AE, DC, MC, V.

Built of gray stone and roughly textured planking, and capped with a gently sloping green copper roof, this hotel evokes a rough-hewn but comfortable lodge in a remote section of the Rocky Mountains. Located at the edge of the resort's largest lake, the hotel consists of a large central building with five additional chalets (each containing 100 bedrooms) nearby. Rooms are comfortably rustic—a departure from the glossiness of other sections of the resort. By the light of an open fireplace, the Hunter's Grill serves juicy portions of spit-roasted meats carved directly onto your plate. Less formal is the Beaver Creek Tavern. Facilities include a business center with computer and secretarial services, plus an indoor pool and health club.

INEXPENSIVE

HOTEL CHEYENNE AND HOTEL SANTA FE, Euro Disney Resort, B.P. 105, F-77777 Marne-la-Vallée Cedex 4. Tel. 60-45-62-00 (Cheyenne) or 60-45-78-00 (Santa Fe). Fax 60-45-62-33 (Cheyenne) or 60-45-62-33 (Santa Fe). 2,000 rms. TV TEL
$ Rates: 550F–750F ($101.80–$138.80) for 1 to 4 persons. Continental breakfast 45F ($8.30) extra. AE, DC, MC, V.

These both qualify as the two most cost-conscious hotels at the resort. Both lie adjacent to a re-creation of Texas's Rio Grande River and evoke different aspects of the Old West. The Cheyenne houses visitors within 14 two-story buildings scattered along "Desperado Street." Each building is a re-creation of a clapboard-sided outpost from the gold-rush era. Towering above them is a giant drive-in movie screen painted with a likeness of Clint Eastwood. Nearby, a volcano erupts regularly. Its companion hotel, the Santa Fe, sports a desert theme, and houses four different "nature trails" winding among 42 adobe-style pueblos.

Tex-Mex specialties are offered at La Cantina (Hotel Santa Fe), while barbecue and smokehouse specialties are served at the Chuck-wagon Café (Hotel Cheyenne). Two-fisted drinks are the order of the day at the Cheyenne's Red Garter Saloon and at the Santa Fe's Apache Bar. Children's play areas include a log fort, a corral, a teepee village, a covered wagon, the Totem Pole playground, and the Pow Wow video arcade.

WHERE TO DINE

There are, within the resort, at least 45 different restaurants and snack bars, each trying to please millions of French palates. Here follow a few recommendations.

THE CALIFORNIA GRILL, Disneyland Hotel. Tel. 60-45-65-00.
Cuisine: CALIFORNIAN. **Reservations:** Recommended.
$ Prices: Appetizers 60F–160F ($11.10–$29.60); main courses 140F–230F ($25.90–$42.60). AE, DC, MC, V.

Open: Lunch daily noon–3pm, dinner daily 6:30–10pm.

Dedicated to the new and lighter recipes that have placed the Golden State on the world's culinary map, this airy and elegant restaurant features specialties from a mesquite grill and a wood-burning oven. Specialties include a salad of arugula with hickory-smoked duck, beetroot, and ginger oil; veal sweetbreads roasted with rosemary and served with peppered lemon aïoli; smoked salmon with chive-baked ricotta cheese and grilled baby leeks; lobster stew with grilled leeks, rice cakes, and lemongrass broth; veal chops baked under a black olive crust with creamed polenta and tomato-basil marmalade; and a vegetarian specialty consisting of grilled vegetables and tofu. The wine cellar is heavily stocked with California vintages.

KEY WEST SEAFOOD, Le Festival Disney Building. Tel. 49-32-40-15.

Cuisine: SEAFOOD. **Reservations:** Recommended.

$ Prices: Appetizers 50F–95F ($9.30–$17.60); main courses 130F–190F ($24.10–$35.20). AE, DC, MC, V.

Open: Lunch daily 11:30am–3:30pm, dinner daily 6–11pm.

Evocative of a seafood restaurant in the Florida Keys, the restaurant regales European diners with exposed timbers, a raffish hint of salt spray, and one of the most amply stocked oyster bars anywhere. Drinks include an American version of French kir, made with loganberry juice and sparkling wine, as well as spice-laden Bloody Marys. Your meal might consist of a sand digger's bucket brimming with steamed mussels, crabs served either steamed or fried with garlic, two different versions of chowder, and heaping platters of shrimp, oysters, and clams.

THE YACHT CLUB, Newport Bay Club Hotel. Tel. 64-74-30-00.

Cuisine: AMERICAN. **Reservations:** Recommended.

$ Prices: Appetizers 65F–115F ($12–$21.30); main courses 135F–160F ($25–$29.60). AE, DC, MC, V.

Open: Lunch daily noon–3pm; dinner daily 6–10pm.

Decorated like the dining room of a rustically elegant yacht club on the New England coast, this restaurant serves such dishes as crab cakes with mustard chive sauce, platters of raw oysters with little neck clams, roasted salmon with polenta and wild mushrooms, double-cut veal chops with lemon, thyme, and sautéed mushrooms, and at least two succulent versions of seafood chowder. The house specialty, served to a minimum of two diners, is a New England lobster clambake, served steaming from a bed of hot seaweed. Desserts might include a maple-syrup mousse with toasted walnut poundcake, or an apple-and-cranberry crumble with applejack custard.

NIGHTLIFE

HURRICANE'S DISCO, Disney Festival Building. Tel. 60-45-70-00.

Skilled at entertaining adults as well as children, Disney offers electronic music, multicolored lights, an amply stocked bar, and a surprisingly understated dance floor to adults who want to get away from their offspring for a while. **Admission:** 120F ($22.20), including first drink. **Open:** Daily 9pm–2am.

APPENDIX

A. BASIC PHRASES & VOCABULARY

ENGLISH	FRENCH	PRONUNCIATION
Hello	**Bonjour**	bohn-*joor*
How are you?	**Comment allez-vous?**	*koh*-mawhn-*ta*-lay-voo
Very well	**Très bien**	tray *byanh*
Thank you	**Merci**	mayr-*see*
Goodbye	**Au revoir**	*aw* ruh-*vwhar*
Please	**S'il vous plaît**	sill voo *play*
Yes	**Oui**	wee
No	**Non**	nawh
Excuse me	**Pardon**	par-*dawh*
Give me	**Donnez-moi**	*duh*-nay mwah
Where is it . . . ?	**Où est . . . ?**	oo-ay
the station	**la gare**	la-*gar*
a hotel	**un hôtel**	uh-*no*-tel
a restaurant	**un restaurant**	uh-*res*-tow-rawh
the toilet	**le lavabo**	luh-*lah*-vah-bo
To the right	**A droite**	a-drwaht
To the left	**A gauche**	a-gohsh
Straight ahead	**Tout droit**	too-drwah
I would like . . .	**Je voudrais . . .**	juh voo-*dray*
to eat	**manger**	mowhn-*jay*
a room	**une chambre**	ewn *shawm*-bruh
for one night	**pour une nuit**	poor ew *nwee*
How much is it?	**Combien ça coute?**	kawm-*byanh* sah koot
The check	**L'addition**	la-dee-*syohnh*
When?	**Quand?**	kawhn
Yesterday	**Hier**	yair
Today	**Aujourd'hui**	oh-joor-*dwee*
Tomorrow	**Demain**	duh-manh
Breakfast	**Le petit déjeuner**	luh-puh-*tee*-day-juh-*nay*
Lunch	**Déjeuner**	day-juh-*nay*
Dinner	**Dîner**	dee-nay

NUMBERS

1 **un** (uhnh)	10 **dix** (deess)	17 **dix-sept** (dee-*set*)
2 **deux** (duh)	11 **onze** (ohnze)	18 **dix-huit** (deez-*weet*)
3 **trois** (trwa)	12 **douze** (dooze)	19 **dix-neuf** (deez-*nuff*)
4 **quatre** (kahtr)	13 **treize** (trezz)	20 **vingt** (vanh)
5 **cinq** (sank)	14 **quatroze** (ka-*torze*)	30 **trente** (trawnt)
6 **six** (seess)	15 **quinze** (kanze)	
7 **sept** (set)	16 **seize** (sezz)	
8 **huit** (weet)		
9 **neuf** (nuff)		

40 **quarante** (ka-*rawnt*)	70 **soixante-dix** (swa-zawnt-*deess*)	90 **quatre-vingt-dix** (kahtr-vanh-*deess*)
50 **cinquante** (san-*kawnt*)	80 **quatre-vingts** (kahtr-*vanh*)	100 **cent** (sawnh)
60 **soixante** (swa-*zawnt*)		

B. MENU SAVVY

A la "In the manner of" or "accompanied with"

A l'ancienne Old-fashioned, "in the style of grandmother"

Alsacien/a l'Alsacienne Alsace-style (usually with sauerkraut, foie gras, or sausage)

Aiguillettes Long thin slivers, usually of duck

Aïoli Garlic-laced mayonnaise

Amuse-gueule A pre-appetizer

Andouillette Chitterling or tripe sausage

Apéritif Pre-dinner libation said to "awaken" the appetite

A point Medium rare

Assiette du pêcheur Mixed seafood plate

Baguette The famous long loaf of French bread

Ballottine Deboned, stuffed, and rolled poultry

Basquais/à la Basquaise Basque-style, usually with tomatoes, red peppers, and ham

Béarnaise Sauce made with egg yolks, shallots, white wine, vinegar, butter, and tarragon

Béchamel Buttery white flour sauce flavored with onion and herbs

Beurre blanc "White butter" sauce with white wine, butter, and shallots

Bigarade Bitter orange sauce, often served with duck

Blanc de volaille Breast of hen

Blanquette Stewed meat with white sauce, enriched with cream and eggs

Boeuf à la môde Marinated beef braised with red wine and served with vegetables

Boeuf en Daube Beef stew with red wine

Bordelais/à la Bordelaise Bordeaux-style; usually accompanied with a wine-laced brown sauce flavored with shallots, tarragon, and bone marrow

Boudin noir Blood sausage

Bouillabaisse Mediterranean fish soup, made with tomatoes, garlic, saffron, and olive oil

Bourguignon/à la Bourguignonne Burgundy-style, usually with red wine, mushrooms, bacon, and onions

Bourride Mediterranean fish soup with aïoli, served over slices of bread

Breton/à la Bretonne Brittany-style, often with white beans

Brunoise Tiny cut-up vegetables

Canard à la presse Duck killed by suffocation, then pressed to extract the blood and juices, which are simmered with cognac and red wine

Canard sauvage Wild duck

Carbonnade Beef stew, originally from Flanders, often cooked with beer

Carré d'agneau Crown roast or loin of lamb

Cassolette Dish served in a small casserole

Cassoulet Toulousien specialty of white beans cooked with preserved goose or duck, pig's trotters, sausages, carrots, and onions

Céleri rémoulade Shredded celery root with a tangy mayonnaise

Cépes à la bordelaise Large, meaty wild boletus mushrooms cooked with oil, shallots, and herbs

Choucroute garni Alsatian sauerkraut garnished with pork products and boiled potatoes

Cochon de lait Roast suckling pig

Confit Meat (usually duck or goose) cooked and preserved in its own fat

Coq au vin Chicken stewed with mushrooms and red wine

Côte d'agneau Lamb chop

Côte de boeuf Rib steak

Court bouillon A broth with white wine, herbs, carrots, and soup greens in which poultry, fish, or meat is cooked

Crème brûlée Thick custard dessert with a caramelized topping

Crème chantilly Sugared whipped cream

Crème fraîche Sour heavy cream

Crème pâtissière Custard filling for cakes

Croque-monsieur Toasted sandwich containing cheese and ham; if prepared with a fried egg on top, it's called a *croque-madame*

Darne A slice of fish steak, usually salmon

Daurade Prized sea bream (similar to porgy)

Desmoiselles de Cherbourg Small Norman lobsters in court bouillon

Diable Devilled and peppery

Digestif Any after-dinner liqueur (e.g., Armagnac) that is presumed to aid the digestive processes

Dijonnais/à la Dijonnaise Denotes the presence in a dish of mustard, usually Dijon

Duxelles Chopped shallots and mushrooms sautéed and mixed with rich cream

Eau-de-vie "Water of life"—brandy distilled from fruit or herbs; usually has a very high alcohol percentage and is usually consumed at the end of a meal

Ecrevisse Freshwater crayfish

Escabèche Provençale dish of small fish (often sardines) browned in olive oil, marinated, and served cold

Escargot de Bourgogne Land snail prepared with garlic, parsley, and butter

Estoficado Purée of dried codfish, tomatoes, olive oil, onions, and herbs; a specialty of Nice

Faisan Pheasant

Farci Stuffed

Feu de bois, au Cooked over a wood fire

Fraise des bois Wild strawberry

Française, à la Garnish of peas with lettuce, pearl onions, and herbs

Fricassée Braised meat or poultry stew; any medley of meat, even fish, that is stewed or sautéed

Friture Fried food

Fromage blanc White cheese (like cottage cheese)

Fumet Fish-based stock

Galantine Classic dish of cooked meat or fowl, served cold in jelly aspic

Galette Flat round cake or pastry; in Brittany, a crêpe of buckwheat flour

Garni Garnished

Gâteau Cake

Gelee Jelly or aspic

Gibelotte Rabbit fricassée in wine sauce

Gigot Haunch (or leg) of an animal, almost always that of lamb or mutton

Glaces Ice in general; ice cream in particular

Glaçons Ice cubes

Gratin Brown crust that forms on top of a dish when it's oven-browned; a dish that is covered with bread crumbs and melted cheese

Grenouilles Frogs' legs

Grillé Grilled

Herbes de Provence A medley of rosemary, summer savory, bay leaf, and thyme

Hollandaise Yellow sauce of egg yolk, butter, and lemon juice whipped into a smooth blend

Homard à l'Armoricaine Lobster browned and simmered with shallots, cognac, white wine, and onions

Hors d'oeuvres Appetizers

Huile d'olive Olive oil

Ile Flottante "Floating Island," a rich dessert of a kirsch-soaked biscuit dressed with maraschino cherries and whipped cream

Jambon de Bayonne Salt-cured ham from the Basque region

Jardinière Garnish of freshly cooked vegetables

Julienne Cut into thin strips

Jus Juice; "au jus" means, with natural, unthickened gravy

Landais/à la landaise Landes-style—a garnish of goose fat, pine nuts, and garlic

Langouste Clawless spiny lobster or rock lobster

Langoustine Clawed crustacean (in Britain, a prawn)

Lardons Cubes of bacon, often served with soups and salads

Léger/légère Light in texture, flavor, and calories

Legume Vegetable

Limande Lemon sole

Lotte Monkfish or angler fish

Lou magret Breast of fattened duck

Loup de mer Wolf-fish, a Mediterranean sea bass

Lyonnais/à la Lyonnaise White wine sauce with shredded and sautéed onions

Macédoine Medley of diced vegetables or fruits

Marchand de vins Wine-merchant; it also implies a rich sauce made from shallots and red wine

Marmite A thick soup made from beef and vegetables, simmered for hours on a low fire; the pot in which the soup is cooked. A *marmite des pêcheurs* refers to a fish soup, or stew, prepared in a marmite

Ménagère, à la "Housewife style"—accompanied with potatoes, onions, and carrots

Meunière, à la "In the style of the miller's wife"—rolled in flour and sautéed in butter

Meurette A red wine sauce, often served with poached eggs and freshwater fish; any wine sauce

Mignonette A substance (usually beef) cut into small cubes

Millefeuille A napoleon

Mirepoix Minced onions, ham, and carrots sautéed in butter and flavored with herbs

Mornay Béchamel sauce flavored with cheese

Moules à la marinière Mussels in herb-flavored white wine with shallots

Nage, à la An aromatic court bouillon used for poaching

Nantua Pink sauce made of white wine, crayfish, and tomatoes

Navarin Mutton prepared with potatoes and turnips

Normande Sauce of eggs, cream, and mushrooms, Norman-style; meat or fish flavored with Calvados

Oeufs à la neige "Eggs in snow"—beaten egg whites poached in milk and served with a vanilla-flavored custard

Omelette Norvegienne Baked Alaska à la française

Pain Bread

Palourde Clamlike mollusk, most often stuffed

Pamplemousse Grapefruit

Panaché Any mixture

Papillote, en Cooked in parchment paper

Parfait Layered ice-cream dessert

Parisienne, à la With leeks and potatoes

Parmentier A dish with potatoes

Pâté Minced meat that is spiced and baked in a mold and served either hot or cold; sometimes made from fish or vegetables

Pâté feuilletée Puff pastry

Paysanne Chicken or meat braised and garnished with vegetables

Périgourdine, à la Sauce usually made with foie gras and truffles

Pipérade Classic Basque dish of scrambled eggs with onions, tomatoes, peppers, and ham

Piquante Tangy sauce made with shallots, vinegar, herbs, small pickles, and white wine

Pistou Sauce of garlic, fresh basil, and olive oil, from Provence

Plat du jour The daily special

Poêlé Panfried

Poisson Fish—*de mer* is from the ocean; *de lac* from the lake; *de rivière* from the river

Poivrade Peppery brown sauce made with wine and vinegar

Pomme Apple

Pommes de terre Potato; *pommes de terre* is frequently shorted to *pommes*, as in *pommes frites* (french fries)

Porc Pork; *porc salé* is salt pork

Pot-au-feu "Pot on the fire"—meat stew cooked in an earthenware pot

Poulet, Poularde Chicken—*poulet fermier* is free-range; *poussin* is a chick

Pré salé Seaside meadow whose grasses are said to be especially beneficial for the pasturing of lambs or sheep; flesh from lambs raised in these meadows is especially succulent

Pressé Pressed or squeezed, as in fresh orange juice

Prix fixe A set meal with a fixed price

Profiteroles Small cream puffs of chou pastry with a filling of whipped cream or custard

Provençal/à la Provençale In the style of Provence, most often with garlic, tomatoes, onion

Purée Mashed or forced through a sieve

Quenelles Rolls of pounded and baked fish, often pike, usually served warm; can also be made from chicken or veal

Ragoût Stew, usually made from beef

Rascasse A scorpion fish in Mediterranean bouillabaisse

Ratatouille A Mediterranean medley of peppers, tomato, eggplant, garlic, and onions

Ravigote Sauce made with vinegar, lemon sauce, white wine, shallot butter, and herbs

Rémoulade Cold mayonnaise flavored with mustard

Rillettes Minced pork spread popular in Tours

Ris de veau Veal sweetbreads

Rognons Kidneys, usually veal

Rosé Meat or poultry cooked rare

Rôti Roasted

Rouennaise (canard à la . . .) Duck stuffed with its liver in a blood-thickened sauce

Rouille Olive-oil based mayonnaise, with peppers, garlic, and fish broth, served with bouillabaisse in Provence

Roulade Meat or fish roll, most often stuffed

Sabayon Egg custard flavored with Marsala wine

Saignant/saignante "Bleeding"—referring to anything cooked rare, especially roast beef

Salade lyonnaise Green salad flavored with cubed bacon and soft-boiled eggs

Salade niçoise Made with tomatoes, green beans, tuna, black olives, potatoes, artichokes, and capers

Salade verte Green salad

Sandre Pickerel; a perch-like river fish

Saucisse French pork sausage

Sole cardinal Poached filet of sole with a crayfish-flavored cream sauce

Sommelier Wine steward

Sorbet Sherbet, usually flavored with fresh fruit

Soubise A béchamel sauce with onion

Soufflé A "blown up" fluffy baked egg dish flavored with almost anything, from cheese to Grand Marnier

Steak au poivre Pepper steak, covered with fresh peppercorns, with a cognac flambé

Suprême White sauce made with heavy cream

Table d'hôte A fixed-price, preselected meal, usually offering a limited (if any) choice of the specific dishes that comprise it

Tartare Any preparation of cold chopped raw meat flavored with piquant sauces and spices (including capers and onions)

Tartare (sauce) Cold mayonnaise spiced with herbs, vinegar, and mustard

Tarte tatin Caramelized upside-down apple pie

Tartine Open-faced sandwich, or bread slathered with jam and butter

Terrine Potted meat in a crock

Timbale Fish or meat dishes cooked in a casserole

Tournedos Rossini Beef filet sautéed in butter with pan juices, served with a foie gras garnish

Tripes à la môde de Caen Beef tripe cooked in Calvados with carrots, leeks, onions, herbs, and spices

Truite au bleu Fish that is gutted moments before being plunged into a mixture of boiling vinegar and water, which turns the flesh blue

Vacherin Ice cream in a meringue shell; a rich cheese from eastern France

Velouté Classic velvety sauce, thickened with a roux of flour and butter

Véronique, à la Garnished with peeled white grapes; usually applies to filet of sole

Vichy With glazed carrots

Vichyssoise Cold creamy potato-and-leek soup

Vinaigrette Oil-and-vinegar dressing flavored with herbs and perhaps a hint of mustard

Vol-au-vent Puff pastry shell

Xérès, vinaigre de Sherry-flavored vinegar

Zeste Citrus peel without its white pith, twisted and used to flavor drinks, such as vermouth

INDEX

GENERAL INFORMATION

SIGHTS & ATTRACTIONS

NOTE: An asterisk (*) indicates an Author's Favorite

ACCOMMODATIONS

PARIS

EXCURSION AREAS

KEY TO ABBREVIATIONS: B = Budget; E = Expensive; I = Inexpensive; M = Moderately priced; VE = Very Expensive; $ = Exceptional Value for the Money; * = an Author's Favorite.

RESTAURANTS

PARIS

ALSATIAN/SWISS/FRENCH
Bofinger, 4e (*M*), 145–6
La Boutique à Sandwichs, 8e (*I$*), 125

AMERICAN
Chicago Pizza Factory, 8e (*M*), 154
City Rock Café, 8e (*M*), 154
Hard Rock Café, 9e (*B*), 134–5
Joe Allen, 1er (*M*), 131

BREAKFAST
Café de Cluny, 5e (*B*), 153
Hôtel de Crillon, 8e (*E*), 152–3
Sir Winston Churchill, 16e (*M*), 153

BRUNCH
L'Espace, 8e (*E*), 153
Hôtel Méridien, 17e (*E*), 153–4

CREPES
A la Bonne Crêpe, 6e (*B*), 155

DINING WITH A VIEW
Bateaux-Mouches, 8e (*E*), 151
Le Ciel de Paris (Maine-Montparnasse Tower) 15e (*E*), 151–2
Le Jules Verne, 7e (*VE*), 152
La Tour d'Argent, 5e (*VE*), 152

FRENCH
Alain Senderens' Lucas-Carton, 8e (*VE**), 115–17
L'Ambassade d'Auvergne, 8e (*I*), 146
L'Ambroise, 4e (*VE*), 145
Androuët, 8e (*M*), 121–2
L'Arpège, 7e (*E**), 141
L'Assiette au Boeuf, 8e (*I$*), 124–5
L'Auberge Basque, 7e (*M*), 141–2
Auberge des Deux Signes, 5e (*M*), 137–8
Bateaux-Mouches, 8e (*E*), 151
Beauvilliers, 18e (*E*), 148
Brasserie Flo, 10e (*M*), 135
Bourbonnais, 14e (*M*), 144
La Cabane d'Auvergne, 6e (*I*), 138
La Cafetière, 6e (*I*), 138–9
La Cagouille, 14e (*M*), 144–5
Carre des Feuillants, 1er (*E**), 130–1
Au Charpentiers, 6e (*I$*), 139
Chez Andre, 8e (*M*), 122–3
Chez Edgard, 8e (*M*), 123
Chez Georges, 2e (*M*), 133–4

Chez les Anges, 7e (*M*), 142
Chez Paul, 1er (*I$*), 133
La Colombe, 4e (*M*), 146
Closerie des Lilas, 6e (*E*), 137
Cochon d'Or, 19e (*E*), 148–9
Crèmerie-Restaurant Polidor, 6e (*I$*), 139
Le Diveilec, 7e (*E**), 149
Le Drouot, 2e (*B$*), 134
Le Drug Store, 6e (*B*), 155
Escargot-Montorgueil, 1er (*M*), 131
L'Espace, 8e (*M$*), 123, 153
L'Etoile Verte, 17e (*I$*), 129
Fauchon, 8e (*M*), 154–5, 158
Faugeron, 16e (*VE*), 125
La Fermette Marbeuf 1990, 8e (*M*), 123–4
La Gauloise, 15e (*E*), 143
Au Gourmet de l'Isle, 4e (*I$*), 147
Le Grain de Folie, 18e (*B*), 149
La Grande Cascade, 16e (*E*), 126–7
Le Grand Véfour, 1er (*VE**), 129–30
Le Grand Zinc, 9e (*B$*), 134
Guy Savoy, 17e (*E**), 128
Hôtel de Crillon, 8e (*E*), 152–3
Jacques Cagna, 6e (*VE*), 136
Jamin, 16e (*VE*), 125–6
Le Jardin, 7e (*B*), 142–3
Le Jules Verne, 7e (*VE*), 140–1, 152
Julien, 10e (*M*), 135–6
Ladurée, 8e (*B*), 156
Lajarrige, 15e (*M*), 143
Lasserre, 8e (*VE**), 117–20
Le Départ, Café, 5e (*I*), 157
Lescure, 1er (*I$*), 132
La Maison d'Alsace, 8e (*E*), 156
La Maison Rose, 18e (*B*), 149–50
Le Maquis, 18e (*I*), 149
Maxim's, 8e (*VE*), 120
Méridien, Hôtel, 17e (*E*), 153–4
Michel Rostang, 17e (*E**), 128–9
Minim's, 8e (*VE*), 127
La Moisanderie, 1er (*I$*), 133
Moissonier, 6e (*I*), 139–40
Moulin du Village, 8e (*M$*), 124
La Petit Bedon, 16e (*M*), 127–8
La Petite Chaise, 7e (*I$*), 142
Au Petit Montmorency, 8e (*E*), 121
Au Pied de Cochon, 1er (*M*), 156–7
Pharamond, 1er (*M*), 132
Le Procope, 6e (*I*), 140
Pub Saint-Germain-des-Prés, 6e (*I*), 157

KEY TO ABBREVIATIONS: *B* = Budget; *E* = Expensive; *I* = Inexpensive; *M* =Moderately priced; *VE* = Very Expensive; *$* = Exceptional Value for the Money; * = an Author's Favorite.

EXCURSION AREAS

Now Save Money On All Your Travels by Joining
FROMMER'S ® TRAVEL BOOK CLUB
The World's Best Travel Guides at Membership Prices

FROMMER'S TRAVEL BOOK CLUB is your ticket to successful travel! Open up a world of travel information and simplify your travel planning when you join ranks with thousands of value-conscious travelers who are members of the FROMMER'S TRAVEL BOOK CLUB. Join today and you'll be entitled to all the privileges that come from belonging to the club that offers you travel guides for less to more than 100 destinations worldwide. Annual membership is only $25 (U.S.) $35 (Canada and all foreign).

The Advantages of Membership

1. Your choice of three free FROMMER'S TRAVEL GUIDES (you can pick two from our FROMMER'S COUNTRY and REGIONAL GUIDES and one from our FROMMER'S CITY GUIDES).
2. Your own subscription to **TRIPS AND TRAVEL** quarterly newsletter.
3. You're entitled to a **30% discount** on your order of any additional books offered by FROMMER'S TRAVEL BOOK CLUB.
4. You're offered (at a small additional fee) our **Domestic Trip Routing Kits.**

Our quarterly newsletter **TRIPS AND TRAVEL** offers practical information on the best buys in travel, the "hottest" vacation spots, the latest travel trends, world class events and much, much more.

Our **Domestic Trip Routing Kits** are available for any North American destination. We'll send you a detailed map highlighting the best route to take to your destination--you can request direct or scenic routes.

Here's all you have to do to join:
Send in your membership fee of $25 ($35 Canada and foreign) with your name and address on the form below along with your selections as part of your membership package to FROMMER'S TRAVEL BOOK CLUB, P.O. Box 473, Mt. Morris, IL 61054-0473. Remember to select 2 FROMMER'S COUNTRY and REGIONAL GUIDES and 1 FROMMER'S CITY GUIDE on the pages following.

If you would like to order additional books, please select the books you would like and send a check for the total amount (please add sales tax in the states noted below), plus $2 per book for shipping and handling ($3 per book for all foreign orders) to:

FROMMER'S TRAVEL BOOK CLUB
P.O. Box 473
Mt. Morris, IL 61054-0473
1-815-734-1104

[ ] YES. I want to take advantage of this opportunity to join FROMMER'S TRAVEL BOOK CLUB.
[ ] My check is enclosed. Dollar amount enclosed_____*

Name_____

Address_____

City_____ State_____ Zip_____

To ensure that all orders are processed efficiently, please apply sales tax in the following areas: CA, CT, FL, IL, NJ, NY, TN, WA and CAN.

*With membership, shipping and handling will be paid by FROMMER'S TRAVEL BOOK CLUB for the three free books you select as part of your membership. Please add $2 per book for shipping and handling for any additional books purchased ($3 per book for all foreign orders).

Allow 4-6 weeks for delivery. Prices of books, membership fee, and publication dates are subject to change without notice.

FROMMER GUIDES

	Retail Price	Code		Retail Price	Code
Alaska 1990–91	$14.95	C001	Jamaica/Barbados 1993–94	$15.00	C105
Arizona 1993–94	$18.00	C101	Japan 1992–93	$19.00	C020
Australia 1992–93	$18.00	C002	Morocco 1992–93	$18.00	C021
Austria/Hungary 1991–92	$14.95	C003	Nepal 1992–93	$18.00	C038
Belgium/Holland/ Luxembourg 1993–94	$18.00	C106	New England 1992	$17.00	C023
Bermuda/Bahamas 1992–93	$17.00	C005	New Mexico 1991–92	$13.95	C024
Brazil 1991–92	$14.95	C006	New York State 1992–93	$19.00	C025
California 1992	$18.00	C007	Northwest 1991–92	$16.95	C026
Canada 1992–93	$18.00	C009	Portugal 1992–93	$16.00	C027
Caribbean 1993	$18.00	C102	Puerto Rico 1993–94	$15.00	C103
The Carolinas/Georgia 1992–93	$17.00	C034	Puerto Vallarta/ Manzanillo/Guadalajara 1992–93	$14.00	C028
Colorado 1993–94	$16.00	C100	Scandinavia 1991–92	$18.95	C029
Cruises 1993–94	$19.00	C107	Scotland 1992–93	$16.00	C040
DE/MD/PA & NJ Shore 1992–93	$19.00	C012	Skiing Europe 1989–90	$14.95	C030
Egypt 1990–91	$14.95	C013	South Pacific 1992–93	$20.00	C031
England 1993	$18.00	C109	Switzerland/Liechtenstein 1992–93	$19.00	C032
Florida 1993	$18.00	C104	Thailand 1992–93	$20.00	C033
France 1992–93	$20.00	C017	USA 1991–92	$16.95	C035
Germany 1993	$19.00	C108	Virgin Islands 1992–93	$13.00	C036
Italy 1992	$19.00	C019	Virginia 1992–93	$14.00	C037
			Yucatán 1992–93	$18.00	C110

FROMMER $-A-DAY GUIDES

	Retail Price	Code		Retail Price	Code
Australia on $45 a Day 1993–94	$18.00	D102	Israel on $45 a Day 1993–94	$18.00	D101
Costa Rica/Guatemala/ Belize on $35 a Day 1991–92	$15.95	D004	Mexico on $50 a Day 1993	$19.00	D105
Eastern Europe on $25 a Day 1991–92	$16.95	D005	New York on $70 a Day 1992–93	$16.00	D016
England on $60 a Day 1993	$18.00	D107	New Zealand on $45 a Day 1993–94	$18.00	D103
Europe on $45 a Day 1993	$19.00	D106	Scotland/Wales on $50 a Day 1992–93	$18.00	D019
Greece on $45 a Day 1993–94	$19.00	D100	South America on $40 a Day 1991–92	$15.95	D020
Hawaii on $75 a Day 1993	$19.00	D104	Spain on $50 a Day 1991–92	$15.95	D021
India on $40 a Day 1992–93	$20.00	D010	Turkey on $40 a Day 1992	$22.00	D023
Ireland on $40 a Day 1992–93	$17.00	D011	Washington, D.C. on $40 a Day 1992	$17.00	D024

FROMMER CITY $-A-DAY GUIDES

	Retail Price	Code		Retail Price	Code
Berlin on $40 a Day 1992–93	$12.00	D002	Madrid on $50 a Day 1992–93	$13.00	D014
Copenhagen on $50 a Day 1992–93	$12.00	D003	Paris on $45 a Day 1992–93	$12.00	D018
London on $45 a Day 1992–93	$12.00	D013	Stockholm on $50 a Day 1992–93	$13.00	D022

FROMMER TOURING GUIDES

Amsterdam	$10.95	T001	New York	$10.95	T008
Australia	$10.95	T002	Paris	$ 8.95	T009
Barcelona	$14.00	T015	Rome	$10.95	T010
Brazil	$10.95	T003	Scotland	$ 9.95	T011
Egypt	$ 8.95	T004	Sicily	$14.95	T017
Florence	$ 8.95	T005	Thailand	$12.95	T012
Hong Kong/Singapore/ Macau	$10.95	T006	Tokyo	$15.00	T016
Kenya	$13.95	T018	Turkey	$10.95	T013
London	$12.95	T007	Venice	$ 8.95	T014

FROMMER'S FAMILY GUIDES

California with Kids	$16.95	F001	San Francisco with Kids	$17.00	F004
Los Angeles with Kids	$17.00	F002	Washington, D.C. with Kids	$17.00	F005
New York City with Kids	$18.00	F003			

FROMMER CITY GUIDES

Amsterdam/Holland 1991–92	$ 8.95	S001	Miami 1991–92	$ 8.95	S021
Athens 1991–92	$ 8.95	S002	Minneapolis/St. Paul 1991–92	$ 8.95	S022
Atlanta 1991–92	$ 8.95	S003	Montréal/Québec City 1991–92	$ 8.95	S023
Atlantic City/Cape May 1991–92	$ 8.95	S004	New Orleans 1993–94	$13.00	S103
Bangkok 1992–93	$13.00	S005	New York 1992	$12.00	S025
Barcelona/Majorca/ Minorca/Ibiza 1992	$12.00	S006	Orlando 1993	$13.00	S101
Belgium 1989–90	$ 5.95	S007	Paris 1993–94	$13.00	S109
Berlin 1991–92	$10.00	S008	Philadelphia 1991–92	$ 8.95	S028
Boston 1991–92	$ 8.95	S009	Rio 1991–92	$ 8.95	S029
Cancún/Cozumel/Yucatán 1991–92	$ 8.95	S010	Rome 1991–92	$ 8.95	S030
Chicago 1991–92	$ 9.95	S011	Salt Lake City 1991–92	$ 8.95	S031
Denver/Boulder/Colorado Springs 1990–91	$ 7.95	S012	San Diego 1993–94	$13.00	S107
Dublin/Ireland 1991–92	$ 8.95	S013	San Francisco 1993	$13.00	S104
Hawaii 1992	$12.00	S014	Santa Fe/Taos/ Albuquerque 1993–94	$13.00	S108
Hong Kong 1992–93	$12.00	S015	Seattle/Portland 1992–93	$12.00	S035
Honolulu/Oahu 1993	$13.00	S106	St. Louis/Kansas City 1991–92	$ 9.95	S036
Las Vegas 1991–92	$ 8.95	S016	Sydney 1991–92	$ 8.95	S037
Lisbon/Madrid/Costa del Sol 1991–92	$ 8.95	S017	Tampa/St. Petersburg 1993–94	$13.00	S105
London 1993	$13.00	S100	Tokyo 1992–93	$13.00	S039
Los Angeles 1991–92	$ 8.95	S019	Toronto 1991–92	$ 8.95	S040
Mexico City/Acapulco 1991–92	$ 8.95	S020	Vancouver/Victoria 1990–91	$ 7.95	S041
			Washington, D.C. 1993	$13.00	S102

Other Titles Available at Membership Prices—
SPECIAL EDITIONS

	Retail Price	Code		Retail Price	Code
Bed & Breakfast North America	$14.95	P002	Marilyn Wood's Wonderful Weekends (within 250-mile radius of New York City)	$11.95	P017
Caribbean Hideaways	$16.00	P005			
Honeymoon Destinations	$14.95	P006			
			New World of Travel 1991 by Arthur Frommer	$16.95	P018
			Where to Stay USA	$13.95	P015

GAULT MILLAU'S "BEST OF" GUIDES

	Retail Price	Code		Retail Price	Code
Chicago	$15.95	G002	New England	$15.95	G010
Florida	$17.00	G003	New Orleans	$16.95	G011
France	$16.95	G004	New York	$16.95	G012
Germany	$18.00	G018	Paris	$16.95	G013
Hawaii	$16.95	G006	San Francisco	$16.95	G014
Hong Kong	$16.95	G007	Thailand	$17.95	G019
London	$16.95	G009	Toronto	$17.00	G020
Los Angeles	$16.95	G005	Washington, D.C.	$16.95	G017

THE REAL GUIDES

	Retail Price	Code		Retail Price	Code
Amsterdam	$13.00	R100	Morocco	$14.00	R111
Barcelona	$13.00	R101	Nepal	$14.00	R018
Berlin	$11.95	R002	New York	$13.00	R019
Brazil	$13.95	R003	Able to Travel (avail April '93)	$20.00	R112
California & the West Coast	$17.00	R102	Paris	$13.00	R020
Canada	$15.00	R103	Peru	$12.95	R021
Czechoslovakia	$14.00	R104	Poland	$13.95	R022
Egypt	$19.00	R105	Portugal	$15.00	R023
Florida	$14.00	R006	Prague	$15.00	R113
France	$18.00	R106	San Francisco & the Bay Area	$11.95	R024
Germany	$18.00	R107	Scandinavia	$14.95	R025
Greece	$18.00	R108	Spain	$16.00	R026
Guatemala/Belize	$14.00	R109	Thailand	$17.00	R114
Holland/Belgium/ Luxembourg	$16.00	R031	Tunisia	$17.00	R115
Hong Kong/Macau	$11.95	R011	Turkey	$13.95	R116
Hungary	$12.95	R012	U.S.A.	$18.00	R117
Ireland	$17.00	R110	Venice	$11.95	R028
Italy	$13.95	R014	Women Travel	$12.95	R029
Kenya	$12.95	R015	Yugoslavia	$12.95	R030
Mexico	$11.95	R016			